RECHARTING THE HISTORY OF ECONOMIC THOUGHT

RECHARTING THE HISTORY OF ECONOMIC THOUGHT

EDITED BY

KEVIN DEANE AND

ELISA VAN WAEYENBERGE

BLOOMSBURY ACADEMIC
LONDON • NEW YORK • OXFORD • NEW DELHI • SYDNEY

BLOOMSBURY ACADEMIC
Bloomsbury Publishing Plc
50 Bedford Square, London, WC1B 3DP, UK
1385 Broadway, New York, NY 10018, USA
29 Earlsfort Terrace, Dublin 2, Ireland

BLOOMSBURY, BLOOMSBURY ACADEMIC and the Diana logo
are trademarks of Bloomsbury Publishing Plc

First published 2020 by RED GLOBE PRESS
Reprinted by Bloomsbury Academic

A catalogue record for this book is available from the British Library.

A catalog record for this book is available from the Library of Congress.

ISBN: PB: 978-1-1376-0524-5
ePDF: 978-1-1376-0525-2

BRIEF CONTENTS

TABLE OF CONTENTS

ACKNOWLEDGEMENTS

We would like to thank all our contributors for their excellent submissions. This was very much a collective effort – thanks for your patience and enthusiasm!

We are grateful for the support for our original idea shown by Kirsty Reade who commissioned the book. Verity Rimmer and Jon Finch provided further support and encouragement to help us finalise everything and Christina Laskaridis' excellent research assistance helped to push it over that final hurdle.

Kevin would like to thank Bruce Caldwell, the HOPE Centre, Duke University, and all participants at the 2014 Duke Summer Institute on the History of Economics, Mark and Lynda Cooper for encouraging and facilitating the submission of the initial idea for this book to Red Globe Press, and all the students at the University of Northampton who took the History of Economic Thought module (ECN2011) and helped this teaching approach take shape in the classroom.

Finally, thanks also go to Kingston University for funding an initial workshop in which the book, teaching approach, and ideas for various chapters were discussed.

All royalties from this book will be donated to the Reteaching Economics network.

Publisher's Acknowledgements

The publisher would like to thank the American Economic Association for their permission to reproduce Figure 2.1: 'Three Cognitive Systems', which is taken from Kahneman (2003).

Reference

Kahneman, D. (2003). Maps of Bounded Rationality: Psychology for Behavioral Economics. *The American Economic Review, 93*, 1449–1475.

CONTRIBUTORS

Shawky Arif is Senior Lecturer in International Development at the University of Northampton and a member of Reteaching Economics. Shawky teaches Introduction to Key Economic Thinkers, History of Economic Thought, Political Economy of Development, and Development Economics. His research interests focus on Neoliberalism, democracy, and Imperialism, with a focus on the region of the Middle East and North Africa.

Hannah Bargawi is a Senior Lecturer in Economics at the School of Oriental and African Studies (SOAS), University of London. She convenes courses in Feminist Economics and Development Economics for undergraduate and postgraduate students. Hannah's research spans macroeconomic policies and employment as well as gender and labour market issues, such as the links between paid and unpaid work. Her research is focused on East Africa and the Middle East as well as Europe. Hannah has been involved in numerous research and consultancy projects for international agencies such as the Asian Development Bank, the International Labour Organisation, UNDP and UN Women. Recent research on macroeconomic policies and gender in Europe has been published by Routledge as a co-edited volume entitled *Economics and Austerity in Europe: Gendered Impacts and Sustainable Alternatives.*

Bruno Bonizzi is Senior Lecturer in Finance at Hertfordshire Business School. He was previously at the University of Winchester, where he taught History of Economic Thought. He researches and has published on financial integration and financial crisis, with specific attention to emerging economies and institutional investors.

Chakib Bourayou is a PhD student in Development Economics, and a Graduate Teaching Assistant in Macroeconomics and Quantitative Methods at SOAS, University of London, UK. His PhD thesis explores how business cycles affect the development of regions and industries by focusing on learning and innovation systems and processes. The thesis draws upon structural and evolutionary economics, and takes the UK as a case study.

Kevin Deane is Lecturer in Global Public Health at Queen Mary University of London. He is a member of Reteaching Economics, and the co-coordinator of the Teaching Political Economy Working Group for the International Initiative for the Promotion of Political Economy (IIPPE). His research interests focus on the political economy of health and development, primarily with an application to the HIV epidemic in Eastern and Southern Africa.

Ourania Dimakou is Lecturer in Economics at SOAS, University of London. She teaches macroeconomics to undergraduate and postgraduate students, as well as economic policy and econometrics courses. Her research interests include macroeconomic theory and its critiques, central banking theories and the role of international financial institutions for macroeconomic theory and policy. She has authored a few articles on these topics and has also co-authored the book *Macroeconomics: A Critical Companion* (with Ben Fine, 2016).

Ben Groom is Professor of Environment and Development Economics at the Department of Geography and Environment, London School of Economics and Political Science. He is also an associate of the Grantham Research Institute on Environment and Climate Change. His research has focused on the welfare analysis of public policies that have long-term welfare effects. In particular, he has worked on the determinants of the social discount rate (SDR) and empirical measures of intergenerational and intragenerational fairness. Current projects include research on the impact of different positions on intergenerational fairness on climate change policy; devising new measures of economic performance that internalise and reflect aversion to income inequality; empirical measures of inequality aversion over environmental quality; and the causes of deforestation and biodiversity loss and the effectiveness of preventative policies. His work in these areas covers both developed and developing countries, including Indonesia, Bolivia, and Ethiopia. Ben's work has fed into advice for international organisations such as the World Bank, the OECD, the Asian Development Bank, and the WWF. He has also advised governments in the UK, the USA, Norway, France, China, and Pakistan, on various aspects of environmental policy.

Peter T. Hughes is Lecturer in Economics at Leeds University Business School. His research interests include the economics of trust, theories of money, and the history of economic thought.

Rob Calvert Jump is a research fellow at the University of Greenwich, based in the Institute of Political Economy, Governance, Finance, and Accountability. He is a member of Reteaching Economics and an associate editor at the *Review of Social Economy* and the *Review of Evolutionary Political Economy.* Most of Rob's research is on macroeconomics and public policy. He is particularly interested in the sources of economic instability, including financial cycles, self-fulfilling expectations and hysteresis, and institutional changes that might mitigate their effects. He takes New and Post-Keynesian approaches to these problems, and has also published on the stability of general equilibrium and wage posting models.

Annina Kaltenbrunner is Associate Professor in the Economics of Globalisation and the International Economy at Leeds University Business School. Her research focuses on financial processes and relations in emerging capitalist economies. She has published on financial integration, currency internationalisation, financialisation, and macroeconomic policy, among others, in the *Cambridge Journal of Economics, Development & Change, Environment and Planning A, The Journal of Post Keynesian Economics*, and *New Political Economy.* She has participated in several large externally funded projects and is currently collaborating with the Brazilian Central Bank on currency regionalisation and regional payment systems.

Ewa Karwowski is Senior Lecturer in Economics at Hertfordshire Business School, University of Hertfordshire, and Senior Research Associate at the University of Johannesburg. She has worked as an economist for the South African Treasury and as policy adviser for international organisations such as the ILO and OECD. Her research interests include firm finance, financialisation, and development.

Jo Michell is Associate Professor in Economics at UWE Bristol. He has a PhD and MSc in Economics from SOAS, University of London. His current research interests include macroeconomics, money and banking, income distribution, and Brexit. He teaches modules on Banking and Finance and History of Economic Thought. He has published on macroeconomics and finance in journals such as the *Cambridge Journal of Economics* and *Metroeconomica*. He is currently working on the ESRC-funded Rebuilding Macroeconomics project, 'Managing Supercycles: Globalisation and Institutional Change'. He has done consultancy work for the United Nations Conference on Trade and Development (UNCTAD), the International Labour Organisation (ILO), and the Federation for European Progressive Studies (FEPS). He co-edited the *Handbook of Critical Issues in Finance* with Jan Toporowski (2012). He was involved in two large European Commission-funded research projects, AUGUR and FESSUD. He blogs regularly and has written articles for a number of publications including the *Guardian* and *Jacobin*. He is currently Secretary of the Post-Keynesian Economics Society and was a founder of Reteaching Economics.

Satoshi Miyamura is a Senior Lecturer in the Economy of Japan at the Department of Economics, SOAS, University of London. His research interests are in the political economy of development in India and Japan, the economics of labour and institutions. He is a co-editor of *Class Dynamics of Development* (2017). His recent publications include: 'Rethinking Labour Market Institutions in Indian Industry: Forms, Functions and Socio-historical Contexts', *Journal of Peasant Studies*, 43(6) (2016); and 'Diverse Trajectories of Industrial Restructuring and Labour Organising in India' and (with Liam Campling, Jonathan Pattenden, and Benjamin Selwyn) 'Class Dynamics of Development: A Methodological Note', *Third World Quarterly*, 37(10) (2016).

Susan Newman is Associate Professor of Economics at the University of the West of England where she takes an integrated approach to teaching and research in the field of Global Political Economy. She has published in the areas of financialisation and the organisation of production, agro-food supply chains and industrial policy with a focus on the Global South.

Marco Veronese Passarella is Lecturer of Macroeconomics and History of Economic Thought, based in the Economics Division of the Leeds University Business School. He is mainly interested in theories of value and distribution, macroeconomic modelling, monetary economics, and history of economic thought. He has authored many articles in economics journals, including the *Cambridge Journal of Economics*, the *Journal of Economic Behavior & Organization*, the *Review of Political Economy*, *Metroeconomica*, the *Review of Keynesian Economics*, the *European Journal of Economics and Economic Policies*, and the *Italian Economic Journal*. In addition, he has authored several chapters in collective volumes, reviews, and books. He is a member of the Reteaching Economics group.

Jeff Powell is Senior Lecturer in Economics at the University of Greenwich. He is a founding member of Reteaching Economics, and a member of the Greenwich Political Economy Research Centre. Jeff teaches macroeconomics, monetary economics, history of economic thought, and economic history; his research interests relate to these and all things finance and development.

Mary Robertson is Head of Economic Policy at the UK Labour Party. Before starting work at the Labour Party in 2016, Mary was a Lecturer in International Business at the University of Greenwich and a Postdoctoral Research Fellow in the Economics Division of Leeds University Business School. She has a PhD in Economics from SOAS, University of London.

Marta Talevi is a PhD candidate in Environmental Economics at the Department of Geography and Environment, London School of Economics. Her research focuses on environmental protection, development, and sustainable energy transition. Her recent works include research on clean cookstoves, public lights and electricity access in refugee settlements in Sub-Saharan Africa, preferences for traditional and non-traditional cooking technologies in rural India, and the uptake of residential solar PV in developed countries.

Elisa Van Waeyenberge is a Senior Lecturer in Development Economics and Head of the Economics Department (job-share) at SOAS, University of London. Her research interests include alternative macroeconomic policies in developing countries, the role of international financial institutions across policy and scholarly realms, as well as the financing of infrastructure and public service provision. She has authored several articles on these topics as well as edited books with colleagues, including *The Political Economy of Development: The World Bank, Neoliberalism and Development Research*, together with Kate Bayliss and Ben Fine. She enjoys teaching macroeconomics from a historical perspective as well as drawing the attention of students to different research methods in economics and political economy.

A TIMELINE OF THE KEY ECONOMISTS COVERED IN THIS BOOK

Last name	First name	Birth	Death	Key works
Smith	Adam	1723	1790	1759 The Theory of Moral Sentiments, or, An essay towards an analysis of the principles by which men naturally judge concerning the conduct and character, first of their neighbors, and afterwards of themselves
				1776 An Inquiry into the Nature and Causes of the Wealth of Nations
Ricardo	David	1772	1823	1810 The High Price of Bullion, A Proof of the Depreciation of Bank Notes
				1817 On the Principles of Political Economy and Taxation
Mill	John Stuart	1806	1873	1844 Essays on Some Unsettled Questions of Political Economy
				1848 Principles of Political Economy
Marx	Karl	1818	1883	1859 A Contribution to the Critique of Political Economy
				1848 The Communist Manifesto with F. Engels
				1867 Capital, volume I
Walras	Léon	1834	1910	1874 Éléments d'économie politique pure, ou théorie de la richesse sociale
Jevons	William Stanley	1835	1882	1871 The Theory of Political Economy. Reprint. Edited by R. D. Collison Black
				1875 Money and the Mechanism of Exchange
Menger	Carl	1840	1921	1871 Principles of Economics
				1888 The Theory of Capital
				1892 On the Origins of Money
Marshall	Alfred	1842	1924	1890 Principles of economics
Veblen	Thorstein	1857	1929	1899 The Theory of the Leisure Class
				1898 Why is Economics Not an Evolutionary Science? Q. J. Econ. 12
Luxemburg	Rosa	1871	1919	1951 The Accumulation of Capital
				2011 The Complete Works of Rosa Luxemburg
Pigou	Arthur Cecil	1877	1959	1912 Wealth and Welfare
				1914 Unemployment. New York: Holt.
				1932 The Economics of Welfare. 4th ed
				1933 The Theory of Unemployment
Keynes	John Maynard	1883	1946	1919 The Economic Consequences of the Peace
				1921 Treatise on Probability
				1923 A Tract on Monetary Reform,
				1930 Treatise on Money
				1936 General Theory

Last name	First name	Birth	Death	Key works
Schumpeter	Joseph	1883	1950	1934 The Theory of Economic Development: An Inquiry Into Profits, Capital, Credit, Interest, and the Business Cycle 1939 Business cycles 1994 Capitalism, socialism and democracy
Hoteling	Harold	1895	1973	1931 The economics of exhaustible resources. Journal of Political Economy 39: 137–75. 1932 'Edgeworth's Taxation Paradox and the Nature of Supply and Demand Functions', Journal of Political Economy 1947 The economics of public recreation, The Prewitt Report
Sraffa	Piero	1898	1983	1960 Production of Commodities by Means of Commodities
Hayek	Friedrich	1899	1992	1929 Monetary Theory and the Trade Cycle 1931 Prices and Production 1944 The Road to Serfdom 1960 The Constitution of Liberty
Kalecki	Michal	1899	1970	1938 Kalecki, M. The Determinants of Distribution of Income, Econometrica 1939 Kalecki, M. (1939) Essays in the Theory of Economic Fluctuations 1943 Kalecki, M. (1943). Political Aspects of Full Employment. The Political Quarterly, Vol. 4 1954 Theory of Economic Dynamics: An Essay on Cyclical and Long-Run Changes in Capitalist Economy in Collected Works of Michal Kalecki (1990) edited by Jerzy Ostatynski
Harrod	Roy	1900	1978	1931 'The Law of Decreasing Costs', The Economic Journal 1936 The Trade Cycle: An essay 1939 'An Essay in Dynamic Theory', The Economic Journal 1948 Towards a Dynamic Economics: Some recent developments of economic theory and their application to policy
Prebisch	Raúl	1901	1985	1950 Theoretical and Practical Problems of Economic Growth 1950 The economic development of Latin America and its principal problems
Rosenstein Rodan	Paul	1902	1985	1943 Problems of Industrialisation of Eastern and South-eastern Europe, Economic Journal, vol. 53 1944 'The International Development of Economically Backward Areas', International Affairs v 20 1961 'Notes on the theory of the "big push"', in Ellis, H.S. and Wallich, H. C. (eds.)

Last name	First name	Birth	Death	Key works
Robinson	Joan	1903	1983	1933 The economics of imperfect competition 1956 The Accumulation of Capital 1962 Essays in the Theory of Economic Growth
Kaldor	Nicholas	1908	1986	1940 'A Model of the Trade Cycle', 1940, Economic Journal 1954 The Relation of Economic Growth and Cyclical Fluctuations. The Economic Journal 64 1955 Alternative Theories of Distribution, The Review of Economic Studies, Vol 23 1957 A model of economic growth. The Economic Journal, 67 1966 Causes of the Slow Rate of Growth of the United Kingdom
Baran	Paul Alexander	1909	1964	1957 The Political Economy of Growth 1965 Monopoly Capital
Coase	Ronald	1910	2013	1937 The Nature of the Firm, Economica, Volume 4, Issue 16 1960 The Problem of Social Cost. In: Gopalakrishnan C. (eds) Classic Papers in Natural Resource Economics
Friedman	Milton	1912	2006	1953 Essays in Positive Economics 1956 'The Quantity Theory of Money: A restatement', in Friedman, editor, Studies in Quantity Theory 1963 A Monetary History of the United States, 1867–1960, with Anna J. Schwartz 1968 'The Role of Monetary Policy (Presidential Address)', 1968, AER
Domar	Evsey	1914	1997	1944 The Burden of the Debt and the National Income, American Economic Review 1948 The Problem of Capital Accumulation, American Economic Review 1957 Essays in the Theory of Economic Growth
Lewis	Arthur	1915	1990	1954 'Economic Development with Unlimited Supplies of Labor', 1954, Manchester School 1955 The Theory of Economic Growth 1965 Politics in West Africa
Minsky		1919	1996	1982 Can 'It' Happen Again? 1986 Stabilising an Unstable Economy
North	Douglas	1920	2015	1989 Institutions and Economic Growth: An Historical Approach. World Development 1991 Institutions. The Journal of Economic Perspectives, 5
Arrow	Kenneth	1921	2017	1951 Social Choice and Individual Values (1st ed.)

Last name	First name	Birth	Death	Key works
				1954 (with Gerard Debreu). 'Existence of a Competitive Equilibrium for a Competitive Economy.' Econometrica 22, no. 3: 265–290.
				1962 'The Economic Implications of Learning by Doing.' Review of Economic Studies 29 (June):
Debreu	Gerard	1921	2004	1954 (with K Arrow). 'Existence of a Competitive Equilibrium for a Competitive Economy.' Econometrica 22, no. 3: 265–290.
				1959 The theory of value: an axiomatic analysis of economic equilibrium
				1981 Mathematical Economics: Twenty Papers of Gerard Debreu. Edited by W. Hildenbrand
Solow	Robert	1924	n/a	1956 'A Contribution to the Theory of Economic Growth.' Quarterly Journal of Economics 70
				1957 'Technical Change and the Aggregate Production Function.' Review of Economics and Statistics 39
				1958 (with Robert Dorfman and Paul Samuelson). Linear Programming and Economic Analysis
				1963 Capital Theory and the Rate of Return
Bergmann	Barbara	1927	2015	1971 The Effect on White Incomes of Discrimination in Employment. Journal of Political Economy
				1980 with Eliasson, Gunnar; Orcutt, Guy H (1980). Micro simulation – models, methods, and applications
				1986 The Economic Emergence of Women
				1993 Bergmann, Barbara R; Folbre, Nancy; Agarwal, Bina; Floro, Maria (1993). Women's work in the world economy
Frank	Andre Gunder	1929	2005	1967 Capitalism and Underdevelopment in Latin America
				1975 On Capitalist Underdevelopment
				1978 Dependent Accumulation and Underdevelopment
Becker	Gary	1930	2014	1975 Human Capital. New York: Columbia University Press.
				1976 The Economic Approach to Human Behavior
				1981 Treatise on the Family
Nelson	Ricard	1930	n/a	1982 An Evolutionary Theory of Economic Change with S Winter
				2002 'Evolutionary Theorizing in Economics', Journal of Economic Perspectives, 16 with S Winter
				2004 An evolutionary theory of economic change

Last name	First name	Birth	Death	Key works
Ostrom	Elinor	1933	2012	1990 Governing the Commons: The Evolution of Institutions for Collective Action 1997 'A Behavioral Approach to the Rational Choice Theory of Collective Action.' The American Political Science Review Vol. 92
Kahneman	Daniel	1934	n/a	1979 with Tversky, A., Prospect Theory: An Analysis of Decision under Risk. Econometrica 47 2003 Maps of Bounded Rationality: Psychology for Behavioral Economics. Am. Econ. Rev. 93
Chick	Victoria	1936	n/a	1977 The Theory of Monetary Policy 1983 Macroeconomics After Keynes
Lucas	Robert	1937	n/a	1967 'Econometric Policy Evaluation: A critique', 1976, CROCH 1984 'Optimal Growth with Many Consumers' JET with N. L. Stokey 1988 'On the Mechanics of Economic Development', 1988, JME 1990 'Why Doesn't Capital Flow from Rich to Poor Countries?', 1990, AER
Bhaduri	Amit	1940	n/a	1993 Unconventional Economic Essays
Fine	Ben	1948	n/a	1975 Marx's 'Capital' 1980 Economic Theory and Ideology 2009 From Political Economy to Economics, with D Milonakis 2009 From Economic Imperialism to Freakonomics with D Milonakis
Dow	Sheila	1949	n/a	2002 Economic Methodology: An Inquiry
Romer	Paul	1955	n/a	1986 Increasing Returns and Long-Run Growth. Journal of Political Economy 94 1990 Endogenous Technological Change. Journal of Political Economy 98
Chang	Ha-Joon	1963	n/a	2002 Kicking Away the Ladder: Development Strategy in Historical Perspective 2010 23 Things They Don't Tell You About Capitalism 2014 Economics: The User's Guide

LIST OF TABLES

LIST OF FIGURES

LIST OF BOXES

1 INTRODUCTION

Kevin Deane and Elisa Van Waeyenberge

Background

The 2007/08 financial crisis marked an important moment in the recent history of economics. The dominant Neoclassical school that had successfully purged academia of rivals over the preceding decades was increasingly called into question by policymakers, academics, students, the general public and even the Queen of the United Kingdom! Neoclassical economics was accused of failing to predict the crisis and had little to say about why the crisis occurred or how its fallout could be remedied. The dramatic exposure of its limitations opened up a (perhaps temporary) space for the (re)consideration of alternative economic approaches and revitalised demands for the introduction of pluralist teaching into higher education economics curricula from academics and students alike. Yet, whilst a vibrant student movement developed from the Post-Crash Economics Society in Manchester and a small number of economics departments in the UK engaged in curriculum reform, overall the pace of change has been slow.

Those calling for the introduction of pluralist teaching in economics face numerous challenges. Chief amongst these is that mainstream economics departments remain strongly resistant to change, often displaying little interest in transforming the discipline so that it provides tools to engage meaningfully with actual existing economies. Indeed, despite the turmoil in the global economy, the majority of undergraduate economics curricula and, in particular, core courses of microeconomics and macroeconomics, have barely changed. Students continue to be presented with a particular version of economics (what we refer to as Neoclassical economics) with little acknowledgement that there are other approaches that contest some of its main tenets. These alternative approaches seek to accommodate better core features of contemporary capitalism, including, for instance, but not exhaustively, finance, internationalisation of production and trade, income and wealth distribution, etc.

Mainstream economists remain opposed to the introduction of pluralist teaching, often arguing that economics is a technocratic field within which students should focus on specific mathematical concepts and tools (despite their rejection by many policymakers in the messy world of the real economy) and that the introduction of alternative perspectives is best left to the postgraduate level. Occasionally they advocate for the inclusion of optional courses, including on the History of Economic Thought (HET) (the latter itself marginalised in many economics curricula) as a way to accommodate discontent. A course on the HET can then be offered as an add-on, with little implication for the substantive content of the rest of the curriculum. As such, the challenges that the HET could pose for mainstream economics through the critical light it could cast on its methods and scope remains carefully warded off.

Beyond resistance to pluralism within mainstream economics departments, other factors such as the capture of elite economics journals by the mainstream provide institutional disincentives for the introduction of pluralist economics research and teaching. Moreover, when opportunities to introduce pluralism into the classroom arise, academics face further challenges. These include pressures on time and the lack of pluralist teaching resources, including core texts suitable for undergraduate teaching. This book, then, is a response to this challenge and seeks to contribute to academic teaching materials in support of pluralist teaching.

Whilst the notion of pluralism in economics can take many forms, the approach embedded in this book is that students should be exposed to a range of different economic perspectives which are grounded in different assumptions about the world. It is our contention that the economics curriculum should not be dominated by one school of thought. Through exposure to a broader spectrum of sometimes conflicting propositions, students are encouraged to evaluate the strengths, weaknesses and relevance of different theoretical propositions. Evidence from a small number of studies reports positive feedback from students when pluralism is introduced into the curriculum (Deane et al., 2019; Harvey, 2011). Furthermore, the student movement that has given rise to Rethinking Economics, a student organisation campaigning for greater pluralism in economics curricula, suggests that there is strong appetite for change in economics teaching.

Origins of the book

Recharting the History of Economic Thought originates in the redesign by one of the editors of a course on the HET. Having started a new role at the University of Northampton in 2013, Kevin Deane was asked to teach a new HET course that sat alongside a primarily standard mainstream economics curriculum. Following a failed initial attempt at teaching the course in the conventional (chronological) way, discussions with co-editor Elisa Van Waeyenberge led to a complete overhaul of the course. Instead of material being presented chronologically, the new teaching approach followed a thematic approach. An important economic question, such as, for instance, 'Are we all rational optimising agents?' or 'What is the role of the state in economy?', provided the starting point for each lecture which then proceeded to engage with the question following a set of steps. First, what answers does Neoclassical economics provide? Second, what are the critiques of this approach? And, third, how have other schools across the HET sought to answer the question?

This approach uses the HET as a vehicle through which pluralist teaching can be introduced into a mainstream curriculum without the need for broader curriculum review. It has the benefit of covering the 'canonical' economists and ideas, but now through the critical lens of the HET. Embedded in this approach is an explicit rejection of the cumulative view of the development of economic thought, in which theory is viewed as building on and improving past iterations (whilst throwing out ideas that were invalid or disproven) in a process of theoretical refinement (Kurz, 2006). Rather, the approach subscribes to a competitive view of the HET which seeks to 'confront students with the idea that there are different approaches to economics, and providing them with some notion of the conceptual foundations of such approaches' (Roncaglia, 2014, p. 7). The new approach was well received by students who had never previously been exposed to economic theories that went beyond their standard microeconomics and macroeconomics textbooks.

This book formalises the teaching approach developed by Kevin Deane, which was trialled at a UK university over a period of five years (2013–2018). It presents a set of chapters organised thematically which discuss a set of perspectives, including of Neoclassical economics, that can be brought to bear on the topic. Whilst to some extent the historical context in which different ideas arose is lost, we opted for this trade-off to support pluralist teaching. The main aims of the book are then as follows:

- To provide an overview of the different ways in which economic issues and ideas can be thought about, drawing from the HET.
- To create a resource that will enhance the relevance of HET courses, especially those taught in mainstream environments.
- To develop critical thinking skills of economics students.

This book complements other recent work that compares and contrasts different schools of thought, such as Chang's *Economics: A User's Guide*, the *Introductory Pluralist Economics Textbook* by Rethinking Economics, and the Exploring Economics website (https://www.exploring-economics.org/en/). Our focus is on the exploration of different perspectives on specific economic questions through the HET, rather than a focus on the critique of Neoclassical economics. The latter can be found in greater detail in Keen's *Debunking Economics* (2001) and Myatt and Hill's *Economics Anti-Textbook* (2011).

Considerations

Writing and editing this book encountered two main challenges. The first was to clarify what we understand by Neoclassical economics, a term which we use interchangeably with mainstream economics. A main concern is not to present a 'straw man' when criticising Neoclassical economics by way of the HET. This is to an extent easier for topics that are more closely aligned with microeconomics, where undergraduate textbooks are uniform and have coalesced around an approach that focuses on optimising choices by different economic actors, specifically the individual and the firm. This contrasts with macroeconomics textbooks which draw more heavily on concepts from other economists, such as Keynes, although their original scope and meaning have often disappeared in a mainstream approach organised around optimisation and the individual economic agent.

To resolve this conundrum, we opted for a general definition of Neoclassical economics which refers to those contributions to the discipline that reconstruct the economy on the basis of optimisation by independent individual economic agents. Agents can be households, individuals, firms, governments, etc., and their optimising behaviour is argued to be an expression of their rationality. These optimisation exercises are subject to a number of constraints and differences emerge within mainstream or Neoclassical economics as to how these constraints are specified. The agents are also endowed with a set of features, which again may differ depending on which school of mainstream economics you consider (a clear distinction in mainstream economics relates to the availability of perfect as compared to imperfect information, or agents being characterised by bounded or unlimited rationality). Equally, differences within mainstream economics exist regarding the description of the economic environment within which economic agents optimise. Is exchange characterised by imperfect competitive markets instead of perfect competition or is production subject to increasing rather than constant returns to scale. The way in which these questions are resolved divides Neoclassical economics into different schools of thought.

The underlying methodological principle characterising all mainstream or Neoclassical economics, however, is that economic outcomes are understood to emerge as a result of optimisation exercises (under whichever constraints) of individual agents (with whatever characteristics). This core methodological tenet of Neoclassical economics is referred to as *methodological individualism*. At its heart it implies that there are no structural features in the economy that produce systemic relations or effects that should be taken into account when trying to understand economic outcomes (and the behaviour of agents within the economic system). It also implies that relations between agents or their interdependencies do not need to be taken into account as we try to move from the analysis of the unit (micro) to the analysis of the whole (macro). And, finally, with economic outcomes understood as the result of (possibly boundedly) rational behaviour of agents, these outcomes are not affected by context or historical trajectories. For Neoclassical economics, context and history are incidental to optimisation efforts and not fundamental to our understanding of economic phenomena.

This characterisation of Neoclassical economics focuses on its distinct methodological features and implies a broad landscape of mainstream economics that, nevertheless, includes some strong divides between those that align themselves more to paradigms in support of perfect working markets (often referred to as more Classical schools of thought) and those that seek to theorise the imperfections of the market (often referred to as more of a Keynesian inclination, even if this is somewhat of a misnomer as will transpire across the various chapters of this book). Traditional definitions of Neoclassical economics tend to imply the inclusion of the former, while often placing the latter contributions outside of its realm. An example is provided by a popular definition of Neoclassical economics as offered by (Weintraub, 2002), for whom Neoclassical economics is characterised by three core fundamental assumptions about the world:

1. People have rational preferences among outcomes.
2. Individuals maximise utility and firms maximise profits.
3. People act independently on the basis of full and relevant information.

Such a characterisation would imply that contributions drawing on, for instance, imperfections in information are not considered as part of Neoclassical or mainstream economics. As clarified above, we diverge from this characterisation and opt for a more fundamental (and hence broader) definition, that identifies what is mainstream or Neoclassical economics on the basis of its first principles of theorising which we distinguish as methodological individualism and rationality.

Neoclassical or mainstream economics is then characterised by a deductive logic, where the deductive logic proceeds from an initial axiom which is taken to be true (like, for instance, optimisation) to more concrete propositions (such as how resources are distributed in the economy). The idea is that logic prevails over evidence and evidence is consulted, in the pure deductive tradition, to falsify an original (axiomatic) proposition. Rather than taking empirical observations as the starting point, propositions regarding the workings of the economy are derived via reasoning or logic (which is often formalised by way of mathematics). This contrasts with an inductive logic which takes observations as point of departure and seeks to derive more general and theoretical propositions from the evidence (rather than from an initial a priori proposition or axiom).[1]

Mainstream economics' deductive logic combines with particular ontological assumptions. These are assumptions regarding the way in which the world is organised and, for mainstream economics, these are best captured through the concept of 'atomism' 'Atomism' as an ontological position implies that the world in itself is understood to be constituted of a set of elements that are randomly ordered, meaning that their relation to one another is incidental and that recognising these relations is not necessary for the different elements that constitute the world to acquire meaning. This contrasts with an ontological position that argues that the world is ordered in particular ways and that we need to recognise its internal relations (or structural features) to make sense of it. It is often also proposed that, for Neoclassical economics, the world is a 'closed system', which means that it obeys law-like regularities which themselves derive from the adoption of the principles of rationality and optimisation. These regularities are assumed to hold across time and space, making the theory universal and ahistorical. Another way to capture these features is to refer to the 'ergodic' nature of the assumptions of Neoclassical economics. This contrasts with the proposition of the world as an 'open' system, where a certain degree of regularity or 'closure' is possible but, because of the interplay between human agency and structures, these regularities are partial and not necessarily predictable nor universal. The world as an 'open' system lacks 'event regularities'.[2]

These broad set of observations seek to capture the essence of what we refer to as the Neoclassical (or mainstream) school in economics. It contrasts with other approaches, often grouped together under the umbrella of 'heterodox' economics, that recognise systemic features and historical trajectories when accounting for economic outcomes.[3] In short, as summed up by Brown and Spencer (2014, p. 945), heterodox economics, while encompassing distinct theoretical traditions, including those drawing on Marx, Keynes, the Old-Institutionalists like Veblen, or with specific interest in issues of gender, recognises 'the importance of social structure and relations and incorporates them into the analysis of how the economy works'. The aim of the book is then to emphasise that economics has not always been monopolised by the Neoclassical tradition and that alternatives from the HET can offer important ways forward as we seek to move beyond the fundamental failures of Neoclassical economics.

A second challenge we faced while putting together the contributions to the book relates to the selection both of topics and of economists or schools of thought for each topic. In terms of the selection of topics, this was in part guided by the original redesign of the HET course. When the new approach was piloted, the students were initially asked to suggest topics. These were amended as the teaching approach grew, and so the topics selected here emerge from various conversations with and feedback from students. The original list of topics was refined for the purpose of the book. This entailed including a number of topics that reflect central methodological and conceptual issues in Neoclassical economics to enable students to think critically about what is typically taught in standard microeconomic and macroeconomic courses. Therefore, we address the role of maths in economics, rationality, consumption, production, equilibrium, income distribution, value, the role of money, and the role of the state. To these we added topics that are particularly pertinent to current global issues, such as economic crises, economic growth and development, the environment, and gender. The latter two have not traditionally been addressed within the HET. Of course, there are many other topics that could be included and we hope that this textbook encourages colleagues to develop the approach to whatever economic questions they see fit.

With respect to decisions on which economists (or schools of thought) to include, we predominantly drew from the core 'canon' of HET material, and selected economists who had something specific to say about each question. In general, alongside the Neoclassical School, many chapters include the perspectives of Classical Political Economy, Keynes, and Marx as three important alternative schools of thought. This ensures that this redesign remains applicable to HET courses (though of course these chapters could be useful across almost all economics courses in standard economics curricula). We provide a list of key economists on pp. xix–xxiii, along with a list of their key works that have been referred to across the different chapters.

Book structure

The book is structured broadly in two parts. A first part, consisting of Chapters 2 and 3, addresses two preliminary concerns which we consider to be central to the standard Neoclassical framework as it appears in undergraduate textbooks. This is followed, in the second part, by chapters on specific topics. Each chapter tends to start off with an account of the neoclassical approach to a given question. This is then followed by a discussion of a range of alternative economic perspectives from the HET. The rest of this section briefly summarises the contribution of each chapter.

Chapter 2 (*Are We All Rational, Optimising Agents?*) addresses the notion of rationality and how economists understand behaviour. The rational, optimising agent that dominates neoclassical economics is first contrasted with the behavioural approach, which puts forward the notion that agents act in a 'boundedly' rational way and that behaviour is shaped by a range of other factors such as intuition, habit and custom. The chapter goes on to discuss the self-interested individual that appears in Smith's work across the *Theory of Moral Sentiments* and *The Wealth of Nations*, emphasising the nuanced, socially embedded notion of self-interest. Questions of agency are addressed with respect to the importance of structure and historical specificity of the social/economic system in shaping patterns of consumption and production, and thus behaviour, in the work of Marx, Veblen, before finishing with a discussion of how Keynes understood economic behaviour as shaped by uncertainty about the future, privileging systemic dynamics in the macroeconomy over the isolated optimising behaviour of atomised individuals.

Chapter 3 (*What Is the Role of Mathematics in Economics?)* addresses a second key issue, which is the role and importance of mathematics in economics. This is particularly pertinent given the focus on econometrics and mathematical skills within most standard undergraduate curricula, though as the chapter emphasises, mathematics has not always been at the core of the economics discipline. The chapter traces the mathematisation of economics from the marginalist revolution in the 1870s to the formalist revolution and the 'proof' (in the mathematical sense) of the existence of general equilibrium by Arrow and Debreu in the 1950s, to the further consolidation of the mathematical approach. This is contrasted with the work of Smith, Ricardo, Marx, and Keynes, in which mathematics does not play a central role, with economic theorising based on inductive, historical, and philosophical approaches, rather than the deductive method of neoclassical economics.

In Chapters 4 (*How Are Things Produced*?) and 5 (*How and Why Are Things Consumed?)* focus on the two main forces of supply and demand that are central to the Neoclassical framework. In Chapter 4, the Neoclassical production function and the decision-making process of the firm, which underpins supply, is contrasted with competence and contract-based theories of the firm. These approaches arguably draw on Smith's analysis of the production process in which the example of the pin factory is used as the basis, highlighting the role of the division of labour in expanding productivity and economic growth. Similarly, the sphere of production is central to Marx's theory of exploitation within the capitalist system and capitalist dynamics, such as the concentration of capital, more generally. Chapter 5 starts with a description of the neoclassical theory of consumption, in which individuals, under a certain set of assumptions and for a given budget constraint, make consumption decisions that maximise their utility. Following some critical reflections on the assumptions and implications of the neoclassical approach to our understanding of consumption, these critiques are developed to show how consumption can be understood alternatively through the lens of behavioural economics, on the one hand, and Veblen's *Theory of the Leisure Class*, on the other. For Veblen, consumption habits are shaped by cultural refractions of economic inequalities, mediated by perceptions of status and image. The systemic forces that shape consumption are further explored in Marx's commodity fetishism, and more recent theoretical developments such as the System of Provisions approach in which consumption is shaped by culturally endowed norms that emerge out of the material circumstances and chain of activities through which a particular good is provided, thus bridging the gap between production and consumption.

Chapter 6 (*Do Economies Reach Equilibrium?*) traces the development of equilibrium theory from Marshall and Walras to contemporary neoclassical theory, and focuses on how the forces of demand and supply are coordinated in the market. For other economists, equilibrium is not a key organising concept. For Marx, where the notion of a concept similar to equilibrium can be identified, it is arguably not a state that an economy is likely to reach, and for Keynes, when equilibrium is reached is it neither static nor stable. Both approaches present versions of the business cycle which emphasise fluctuations around, but not necessarily toward, an equilibrium point. Ultimately, the chapter questions the role of equilibrium as a theoretical tool in alternative approaches, which are at odds with Neoclassical economics in which general and partial equilibrium models inform analysis.

The distributional consequences of competing theoretical views are discussed in Chapter 7 (*How Is Income Distributed?*). The chapter critically discusses the neoclassical view, rooted in the Marginalist perspective that income distribution is determined by relative contributions to production of different 'factors of production'. Following this line of argument, wages are the marginal product of labour, and thus workers are paid what they 'deserve'. This view is contrasted with the Classical approach, which provided (incomplete) explanations through the functional distribution of income and an early version of the labour theory of value. The labour theory of value was developed further by Marx to demonstrate that far from workers earning what they deserve, capitalist exploitation ensured that workers received less than the value they create, with capitalists accumulating the surplus value. Post-Keynesian approaches point to social and political factors, as well as the market power of firms, as determining the share of profits and wages within the economy. In conclusion, the chapter wonders whether marginalist theories provide convincing explanations for current distributional realties in a world characterised by increasing inequality.

Chapter 8 (*What Is the Role of Money in Economics?*) examines issues regarding the role of money in the economy, linking to key themes pursued subsequently in Chapter 10 (on crisis). The chapter poses questions such as what is money?, where does it come from?, why do we need it and what are its functions? In the Neoclassical view, the role of money is primarily related to its ability to act as a medium of exchange to make trading easier. Following this line of argument, the introduction of money has no substantive implication for the analysis and the monetary economy functions just like the barter economy, with money merely acting as a veil. However, contrasting views of money promoted by Keynes and Schumpeter focus on the role that money plays as credit in an economy that operates over historical time. For Schumpeter, money is needed to facilitate the production process, where inputs need to be purchased before the product can be sold. For Keynes, money is furthermore the ultimate liquid asset that allows entrepreneurs to postpone committing to a particular physical investment when faced with significant uncertainty. The role of money sits at the heart of the way in which the capitalist system operates and any attempt to theorise it needs to recognise its central role. The capitalist economy is indeed a *monetary* production economy.

Chapter 9 moves onto the problem of value in economics (*How Are Goods and Services Valued in Economics?*). The chapter contrasts the ordinal approach to value, in which the value of a good or service depends on the subjective view of individuals with a given set of preferences, to the labour theory of value first proposed by Smith and later developed by Ricardo and Marx. The classical conception of value reflects the human labour expended in the production process, an objective measure of value as opposed to a subjective measure. A final strand of thinking relates value to the energy required to produce it. As with other chapters, the exploration of the question of value allows other theoretical distinctions to be considered, such as the level of analysis (micro, meso, macro) and the economic sphere that is the focus of each theoretical approach (exchange, production, ecosystem).

The rest of the book addresses more applied questions that compare how different issues, rather than basic conceptual issues common to most theoretical approaches, are understood. Chapter 10 (*What Causes Economic Crises? And What Can We Do about Them?*), looks more closely at the phenomenon of economic crisis – clearly stimulated by debates concerning the 2007/08 financial crisis. The chapter contrasts the Neoclassical approach, which, in general, views crisis as an outcome of government intervention in markets that otherwise left alone would allocate resources in the most efficient manner (i.e. crises are exogenous), with Keynesian and Marxian approaches for which crisis is inherent to the capitalist system – or an endogenous feature of the economic system. The chapter synthesises the many strands of thinking that have developed from these perspectives to present three key views on crises: crises of realisation, crises of profitability, and crises of financial instability. These different views also have implications for what should be done about crises, with policy recommendations ranging from allowing 'bad' institutions to fail, correcting market failures, and more radical attempts to pursue government interventions to stabilise markets and/or other roles for the public sector.

Chapter 11 (*How Do Economies Grow?*) compares competing views on economic growth. The chapter first sets the scene by discussing how the issue of time is addressed (or not) in economics, as this has important consequences for how growth as a process of change is understood. Mainstream approaches, such as 'old' and 'new' Neoclassical growth theories are contrasted with Classical, Post-Keynesian and Schumpeterian approaches. These alternative approaches shed light on some of the limitations of mainstream theories, with the chapter attributing the main divergences between theories to how time is addressed, the role that equilibrium plays, the role of demand, and how the process of growth is understood.

A closely related but nevertheless distinct question concerning how development is understood is the focus of Chapter 12 (*How Do Countries Develop?*). The chapter traces changes over time in the mainstream approach to development, from the principles of the Washington Consensus, which emphasised the allocative efficiency of the market, through the Post-Washington consensus, which engaged with the notion of market failure, to the New Structural Economics of Lin that forwards the case for a narrow set of industrial policies to stimulate development. These are contrasted with accounts of the process of development that focus attention on structural change within the economy, and specifically the process of industrialisation which is seen as a necessary (but not sufficient condition) for enhancing living standards. However, in light of the challenges that many developing countries face, alternative schools of thought have emphasised the barriers to development. The Structuralists of Latin America view the economic system as tilted against developing countries, with the core capitalist economies impeding the development of countries in the periphery. The core–periphery analogy also appears in the work of the Dependency School which further deepens the analysis of the role of unequal and extractive relationships in shaping patterns of uneven development.

Chapter 13 (*How Does Economics Address Gender?*) addresses a topic quite alien to the HET, which is how economics engages with the issue of gender. To ensure that the chapter is not presented in an overly abstract manner, and also to reflect the piecemeal approach to gender by economics, general themes are illustrated through an application to the prominent topic of work. Neoclassical economics primarily addresses gender issues in the language of rational choice, with gendered differences in labour market participation explained through differences in the choices made by men and women. The work of Becker, incorporating human capital theory, illustrates how the gendered division labour is the outcome of utility-maximising decisions made by the household as a unified unit. After some critical reflections on the Neoclassical approach, the chapter surveys a range of other perspectives, such as the Old Institutional economics and more recent developments. These emphasise the role of patriarchy, power, gendered norms, and the gendered nature of institutions such as the labour market that produce and reproduce gender inequalities.

Chapter 14 (*How Does Economics Address the Environment?*) addresses an issue of great contemporary importance that has also received little attention in the HET, though, in contrast to gender, the environment and natural resource use have long been of interest to economists. The chapter covers a range of applications of marginalist and Neoclassical theory to issues of welfare in the face of (environmental) externalities, economic growth and the optimal extraction of resources, and climate change. These are contrasted with the school of ecological economics, which addresses key planetary boundaries and incorporates an 'economy–society–environment' nexus that emphasises that economic activity occurs within a specific environmental context, and is subject to a range of biophysical limits. The chapter also emphasises differences in the interdisciplinary nature and methodological approaches between Neoclassical and ecological economics.

The penultimate chapter (*What Is the Role of the State in Economics?*) covers a final important consideration concerning the role of the state in the economy. The chapter commences with a description of the Neoclassical approach to the state, in which the state is primarily needed to correct cases of market failure. As noted above, in the absence of market failures, state intervention is viewed to lead to sub-optimal market outcomes. This view is contrasted first with the Classical Economics of Smith and Mill, who, whilst subscribing to some extent to the notion that the state does not know better than the self-interested individual, do note that there is a range of roles for the state. These include providing and upholding the conditions for the market to function, but also extend to circumstances where individuals may not always be able to act freely in their own self-interest. The interventionist stance of Keynes, in which the state needs to correct an economy that will not automatically adjust to optimal and stable equilibria is then further contrasted with the Marxist view, in which the state is theorised as a tool of oppression that reflects the interest of the dominant (capitalist) class.

The final chapter (*Can Economics Explain Everything and Solve All Our Problems?*) reflects on the explanatory power of economics and on the power of economics to solve what Keynes termed 'the economic problem'. The chapter is motivated by the expansion of economics beyond its own borders, with the Neoclassical framework of rational choice invading other social sciences, a form of Economics Imperialism, and claiming to be able to explain almost anything. These strong claims are contrasted with similar views emanating from the Marxian literature, though from a different perspective, in which the economic system (capitalism) shapes the world around it in its own image. The base–superstructure analogy is presented to illustrate this. Subsequently, the question of whether economics can solve the economic problem is explored through the lens of Keynes's work and the degrowth perspective. For Keynes, increasing productivity can solve the economic problem once and for all, leading to improved living standards and shorter working weeks as the human species becomes able to produce all the things it need to survive with increasing ease. However, in opposition to this view, the quest for continued economic expansion is seen by some as the primary cause for long-term environmental degradation, and that a programme of degrowth is needed to reorient the economy and to avoid irreversible environmental damage.

References

Brown, A., & Spencer, D. (2014). Understanding the global financial crisis: Sociology, political economy and heterodox economics. *Sociology, 48*(5), 938–953.

Deane, K., van Waeyenberge, E., & Maxwell, R. (2019). Recharting the history of economic thought: Approaches to and student experiences of the introduction of pluralist teaching in an undergraduate economics curriculum. *International Journal of Pluralism in Economics Education, 10*(2), 137–154.

Dow, S. (2002). *Economic methodology: An Inquiry*. Oxford: Oxford University Press.

Fischer, L., Hasell, J., Christopher Proctor, J., Uwakwe, D., Ward Perkins, Z., & Watson, C. (2018). *Rethinking economics. An introduction to pluralist economics*. London: Routledge.

Harvey, J. T. (2011). Student attitudes toward economic pluralism: Survey-based evidence. *International Journal of Pluralism and Economics Education, 2*(3), 270–290. https://doi.org/10.1504/ijpee.2011.044271.

Hill, R., & Myatt, T. (2011). *The economics anti-textbook*. London: Zed Books.

Keen, S. (2001). *Debunking economics*. New York: Zed Books.

Kurz, H. D. (2006). Whither the history of economic thought? Going nowhere rather slowly? *The European Journal of the History of Economic Thought, 13*(4), 463–488. https://doi.org/10.1080/09672560601063929.

Lawson, T. (2004). Modern economics: The problem and a solution. In E. Fullbrook (Ed.), *A guide to what's wrong with economics*. London: Anthem Press.

Roncaglia, A. (2014). Should the history of economic thought be included in undergraduate curricula? *Economic Thought, 3*(1), 1–9.

Weintraub, E. R. (2002). Neoclassical economics. *The concise encyclopedia of economics:*. Library of economics and liberty, https://www.econlib.org/library/Enc1/NeoclassicalEconomics.html.

2 ARE WE ALL RATIONAL, OPTIMISING AGENTS?

Satoshi Miyamura

The author acknowledges helpful inputs from the editors and Jonathan Pattenden who gave useful comments on earlier drafts.

Introduction

This chapter focuses on a particular methodological aspect in the history of economic thought, namely how the actions and behaviour of individual economic agents are conceptualised. As discussed in more detail in this chapter, Neoclassical economics is founded on a particular type of methodological individualism (see Box 2.1), which includes the assumption that individuals are rational in their decision-making (see Box 2.2). The behaviour of decision-makers in society, whether they are consumers, firms, or other, are modelled as optimising particular objective functions, allegedly leading to socially optimal outcomes. Whilst this Neoclassical conception of individual agents' behaviour is challenged also by some of today's mainstream economists, it nevertheless constitutes the foundation for what has been described as an 'increasingly pluralistic mainstream economics' (Santos, 2011, p. 705), and continues to be one of the central organising principles in most, if not all, microeconomics textbooks.

This chapter commences with a discussion of the notion of rationality embedded in Neoclassical economics. It then contrasts the Neoclassical economics approach to the Classical political economy of Smith and Marx, as well as Veblen and Keynes. Each offers alternative understandings of motives and behaviour of economic agents but in very different ways. This has implications for how one conceives the role of human agency in economic and social change. The chapter closes with a guide to further reading and suggestions for discussion topics.

The method of Neoclassical economics

For the purpose of the discussion in this chapter about how economics conceives of human behaviour and its role in the economy and society, two central methodological features of Neoclassical economics can be highlighted. The first is Neoclassical economics' framing of economic models as choice problems by individual decision-makers. This is most explicit in microeconomics, where the behaviour of individual

Box 2.1: Methodological individualism

Many social science and political economic theories adopt individualist methods of various types, placing emphasis on the interests and motives of individuals in understanding economic and social order, including some of the authors discussed in this chapter, as well as others such as David Hume (Infantino, 2014). Indeed, the term 'methodological individualism' is defined and used in various ways (Hodgson, 2007). However, methodological individualism adopted in Neoclassical economics is a specific type in which the explanations of economic and social phenomena are reduced to behavioural models of individuals. In its narrow definition, methodological individualism is a method in which 'the ultimate unit of analysis is always the individual' (Brennan and Tullock, 1982, p. 225; see also Chapter 6).

In practice, many mainstream economists recognise the role of interactions between individuals which give rise to social order, institutions, and structure. Branches of theoretical approaches within the mainstream, including game theory and New Institutional economics, have emerged in an attempt to legitimise social interactions and institutions, but are still grounded in behaviours of individuals. Also, methodological individualism has penetrated social sciences beyond Neoclassical economics.

Box 2.2: Rationality

As Hodgson (2012, p. 94) notes, rationality is a 'slippery' concept as it has multiple and overlapping meanings. Rationality can in everyday parlance simply mean that individuals make reasoned decisions. Developing this thinking, rationality can also be seen as individuals doing 'the best they can' in a given situation or set of circumstances (Hodgson, 2012, p. 95). However, whilst these forms of rationality may describe behaviour and even elements of Neoclassical theory, they fail to unpack the decision-making processes in more depth and fail to address a number of questions such as how 'the best' is identified, or the way in which decisions are made. In Neoclassical economics, the notion of rationality has a specific and technical element, with 'strictly' rational decisions needing to conform to a set of mathematical conditions and assumptions (see Chapters 4, 5, and 6).

economic actors (or agents) is characterised in the form of constrained optimisation. But the requirement to be consistent within the Neoclassical economic framework has also made macroeconomics conform to its 'microfoundation' so that consumption, savings, demand, unemployment, prices and wages for the economy as whole is also explained on the basis of atomised individual agents' behaviour. This method in Neoclassical economics whereby the whole is explained in terms of its individual parts (members) is called 'methodological individualism' (Milonakis and Fine, 2008, p. 98; see Box 2.1).

In standard microeconomic textbooks, economic agents typically refer to the consumer and the firm. Consumers are modelled to maximise their 'utility' subject to budget constraints, while firms are conceived as maximising profits subject to technological capabilities. The same logical principle, however, has also been extended to model the behaviour of institutions such as trade unions, as well as non-economic actors, such as policymakers, nations, and others, giving rise to what Fine terms 'economics imperialism' (see Chapters 5 and 16). The agents are also often assumed to be independent from one another in 'Robinson Crusoe' fashion, as often referred to in standard microeconomic textbooks. This contrasts with Marx, Veblen, and Keynes who, in their different ways, conceived the workings of the economic system not to be reducible to atomised individual decision-making and highlight how the relations between agents are core determinants of economic outcomes (see below).

The second methodological feature of Neoclassical economics is the assumption that economic agents are 'instrumentally rational'. As with individualist methodology (see Box 2.1), rationality is conceptualised in a variety of different ways in social sciences and political economy. The choice-theoretic framework in Neoclassical economics is associated with 'instrumental rationality', defined 'as the choice of actions which best satisfy a person's objective' (Hargreaves-Heap et al., 1992, p. 4). This implies that individuals can compare the satisfaction or 'utility' gained from different set or 'bundles' of objectives, e.g. baskets of goods purchased by a consumer (see Chapter 5); a portfolio of assets and securities invested by an investor; or even political parties and candidates voted in an election.

The rational choice models have also come under scrutiny from within mainstream economics, including by Behavioural economists, for whom human decision-making is context-dependent and often shaped by intuitive judgements rather than expected utility based on computation of probabilities. Another extension of the choice theoretical framework in Neoclassical economics has focused on interactions between individuals. Game theory provides a method to model how instrumentally rational individuals act in a situation in which the actions of one affect the welfare of another. Sometimes the agents' interests are in conflict with each other. In other scenarios, agents collude as they enhance their payoffs through cooperation. Typically most games will contain a combination of both. As agents try to predict the reaction of other 'players' in response to their own actions, game theory models scenarios in which individuals' choices may seem contrary to their immediate self-interest (see Box 2.3). While game theory provides a framework for economists to describe choices and decision-making when a number of agents interact, it nevertheless 'impose[s] a remarkably sophisticated (unrealistic?) degree of calculating rationality on the analysis of problems involving social interaction' (Hargreaves-Heap et al., 1992, p. 124), and is firmly rooted in the choice theoretic framework of Neoclassical economics.

Finally, the rational choice framework in Neoclassical economics takes for granted that its fundamental logic applies universally across different historical periods and social settings. This is in contrast to Smith, Marx, and Veblen discussed later in this chapter, who, albeit in different ways, postulated that the motives and actions of individuals are socially and historically constructed, and hence endogenous to socio-economic processes and structures.

The game depicted in Table 2.1 is set out to show that for a prisoner the best outcome is to denounce their partner but not be denounced him/herself, thus gaining the payoff of 6, while the other has –1. The second-best outcome is for neither prisoner to denounce each other, with the payoff of 5 each. The third-best is for both to denounce

Box 2.3: Game theory

The modern approach to game theory is attributed to von Neumann and Morgenstern (1944) and was closely associated with the Rand Corporation in the US with its application to the prospects of intercontinental nuclear warfare (Hargreaves-Heap and Varoufakis, 2004, pp. 49–50). More generally, game theory has been applied to various social interactions in which agents understand that the outcome of their actions will be affected by the actions of others (Hargreaves-Heap and Varoufakis, 2004, pp. 1–2). A famous example is the prisoners' dilemma, which depicts a hypothetical situation in which two accomplices are held in separate cells (Kreps, 1991, pp. 37–38). The prisoners are told that they will be held for the maximum amount of time permitted without charges being made if each of the two prisoners does not denounce their colleague. If one of them denounces the other without being denounced, the prisoner who denounced will be released while the other prisoner will receive the maximum sentence permitted by law. If both prisoners denounce each other, both will receive leniency in sentencing. These four possible outcomes are depicted in Table 2.1. The first figure represents the 'payoff' to Prisoner A and the second represents that of Prisoner B.

Table 2.1 The prisoners' dilemma

		Prisoner B	
		Don't denounce	**Denounce prisoner A**
Prisoner A	Don't denounce	5, 5	-1, 6
	Denounce prisoner B	6, -1	0, 0

each other, resulting in the payoff of 0 each. And the worst outcome is to be denounced without denouncing the colleague. In the absence of other considerations or any mechanism for cooperation, the predicted outcome will be for each prisoner to denounce the other, resulting in the 0,0 payoff – this is called the 'dominant strategy' for each.

While there are many variations of games and more complex processes of interaction can be considered, the above illustration demonstrates that game theory is ultimately based on the fundamental assumptions of Neoclassical economics outlined in the text above. Reductionist methodological individualism and instrumental rationality underpin the way in which individual behaviour is understood. In this sense, like the case for Behavioural economics (see next section), the question remains as to whether game theory constitutes a fundamental challenge to Neoclassical economics or whether it, instead, constitutes a technical approach that can be accommodated by it.

Behavioural economics

Traditional Neoclassical economics modelling of human behaviour is based on the assumption that self-interested individuals choose to maximise utility with no cognitive limitations in calculating benefits and costs of alternative choices. Over recent decades, Behavioural economics has challenged these assumptions by applying insights from experimental psychology to highlight behavioural deviations from rational choice models. Most notably, Simon (1979) proposed the notion of 'bounded rationality' to emphasise how decision-making may not always be optimal due to restriction in the ability to process information. This does not necessarily mean that people are irrational or make decisions based on poor reasoning. Rather, Behavioural economics asserts that people tend to act intuitively rather than on the basis of careful computation of expected utility.

Psychologists distinguish between two distinct systems of cognitive processes, in addition to the automatic process of 'perception' (Kahneman, 2012, pp. 20–21):

System 1 operates automatically and quickly, with little or no effort and no sense of voluntary control.

System 2 allocates attention to the effortful mental activities that demand it, including complex computations. The operations of System 2 are often associated with the subjective experience of agency, choice, and concentration.

As outlined in Figure 2.1, Kahneman locates System 1, which is based on intuition, 'between the automatic operations of perception and the deliberate operations of reasoning' (Kahneman, 2003, p. 1452). Like perception, intuitive judgements made through System 1 are fast, automatic, and effortless, in contrast to judgements of System 2, which are slow, deliberately controlled, and effortful. But System 1 goes beyond response to current stimulation and, like System 2, deals with stored conceptual representations. Due to the limited capacity for mental effort, intuition, or

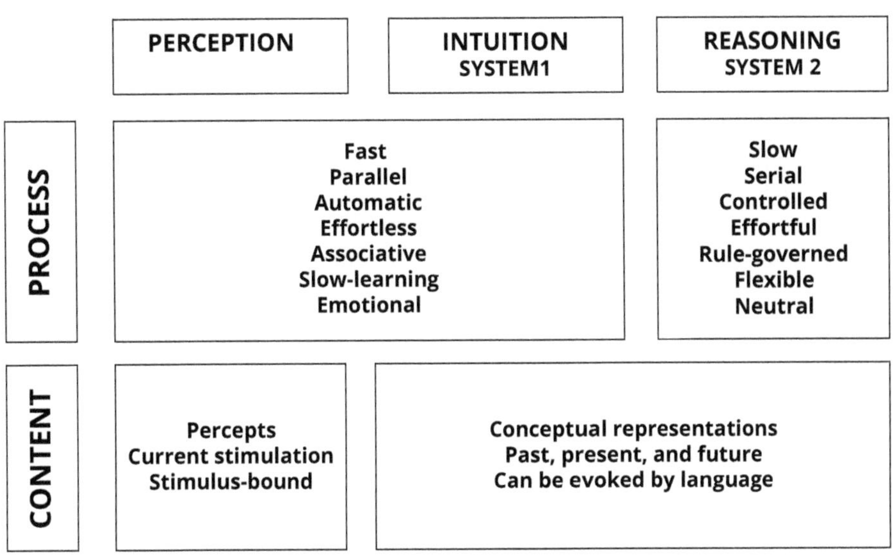

Figure 2.1 Three cognitive systems

Source: (Kahneman, 2003, p. 1451) Copyright American Economic Association; reproduced with permission of the American Economic Review

requiring relatively less effort, System 1 tends to play a large role in people's decision-making. Further, it is argued that Neoclassical economics conflates the two systems of thinking, ascribing individuals the ability to make decisions with the speed of System 1 and the computation power of System 2.

Kahneman and Tversky have presented a series of experimental results that undermined the behavioural assumption of instrumental rationality (Kahneman, 2003, 2012; Kahneman and Tversky, 1979; Tversky and Kahneman, 1981). For example, the following two problems were posed to respondents in experimental settings (Kahneman, 2003, pp. 1455–1456):

> Problem 1:
> Would you accept this gamble?
> 50 percent chance to win $150
> 50 percent chance to win $100
> Problem 2:
> Which would you choose?
> lose $100 with certainty
> or
> 50 percent chance to win $50
> 50 percent chance to lose $200

Despite the expected reward from gambling in the two problems being identical, Kahneman and Tversky found that while most people rejected the gamble in Problem 1, the majority of respondents found the gamble in Problem 2 attractive. Such sudden switch from risk aversion to risk-seeking behaviour cannot be explained by the traditional Neoclassical framework of expected utility function. This observation prompted the authors to propose an alternative theory of risk known as the prospect theory, in which people's *loss* aversion leads to different preferences for risk aversion/seeking behaviour depending on the perceived potential gains or losses. Their work more broadly asserts that people often act intuitively rather than seek 'optimal' decisions by computing probabilities of all possible outcomes.

Although Simon, Kahneman, and Tversky's contributions were seen as a challenge to the fundamental assumptions of Neoclassical economics, the application of Behavioural economics to policy can be seen to ultimately 'retain two fundamental principles of Neoclassical economics—rationality and efficiency' (Santos, 2011, p. 707). The Behavioural economics approach to policy is often described as a 'nudge' – subtle and 'minor changes to context' that induce individuals to make better choices without addressing underlying structural problems (Fine et al., 2016, p. 642). However, even proponents of Behavioural economics recognise that as opposed to the 'nudge' approach to policymaking that derives from Behavioural economics, 'occasionally a good shove advances individual and social welfare considerably' (Loewenstein et al., 2012, p. 24), suggesting that the limitations of this theoretical approach are acknowledged. This raises a question as to whether Behavioural economics can potentially serve as a radical point of departure from Neoclassical economics and the development of alternative frameworks to replace Neoclassical economics, or merely serves to identify instances in which individuals are not behaving in a strictly rational way in order for these deviations to be 'corrected' through interventions designed to nudge them towards optimal decisions.

Smith, morality, and self-interest

Smith is often considered the intellectual founder of today's Neoclassical economics. In particular, Smith is frequently associated with the idea of the 'invisible hand', which ensures that self-interested private individuals' optimising decisions lead to socially optimal outcomes in spite of their intentions. In a frequently quoted passage from *The Wealth of Nations*, Smith (1776, p. 9) wrote:

> As every individual ... endeavours as much as he can both to employ his capital in the support of domestic industry, and so to direct that industry that its produce may be of the greatest value; every individual necessarily labours to render the annual revenue of the society as great as he can. He generally, indeed, neither intends to promote the public interest, nor knows how much he is promoting it. By preferring the support of domestic to that of foreign industry, he intends only his own security; and by directing that industry in such a manner as its produce may be of the greatest value, he intends only his own gain, and he is in this, as in many other cases, led by an invisible hand to promote an end which was no part of his intention. Nor is it always the worse for the society that it was no part of it. By pursuing his own interest he frequently promotes that of the society more effectually than when he really intends to promote it. I have never known much good done by those who affected to trade for the public good. It is an affectation, indeed, not very common among merchants, and very few words need be employed in dissuading them from it.

On the face of it, the above quote appears to imply that individuals following their own self-interest are optimising not only at the individual level, but also for the society as a whole. Similarly, in another famous passage from the same work, Smith (1776, p. 119) argued that:

> It is not from the benevolence of the butcher, the brewer, or the baker that we expect our dinner, but from their regard to their own interest. We address ourselves, not to their humanity but to their self-love.

Despite being frequently cited as a rationale for the market mechanism (although Smith never specified that the 'invisible hand' was the market) and individual self-interest as the sole guiding force for the economy, the above two quotes only reflect part of Smith's thinking, and in particular his discussion of 'the motivation underlying exchange (rather than what makes normal exchanges sustainable, such as trust and confidence in each other)' (Sen, 2010, p. 55). Indeed, Smith's writings deal extensively with various motivations beyond self-interest that shape human behaviour, and in this sense differ significantly from today's mainstream economics.

It is worth noting that Smith (like many other political economists at the time) came from the background of moral philosophy and, as such, viewed human behaviour in a more nuanced way than today's mainstream economists. For example, in his earlier work, the *Theory of Moral Sentiments*, Smith (1759, p. 83) recognised that there are broader institutional rules and practices that govern individuals' norms and actions:

> The regard to those general rules of conduct, is what is properly called a sense of duty, a principle of the greatest consequence in human life, and the only principle by which the bulk of mankind are capable of directing their actions. Many men behave very decently, and through the whole of their lives avoid any considerable degree of blame, who yet, perhaps, never felt the sentiment upon the propriety of which we found our approbation of their conduct, but acted merely from a regard to what they saw were the established rules of behaviour.

Underlying these 'established rules of behaviour' is the role of 'sympathy' to other members of society, which restrains individuals' 'self-love' (Smith, 1759, p. 44):

> he must ... humble the arrogance of his self-love, and bring it down to something which other men can go along with ... In the race for wealth, and honours, and preferments, he may run as hard as he can, and strain every nerve and every muscle, in order to outstrip all his competitors. But if he should justle, or throw down any of them, the indulgence of the spectators is entirely at an end. It is a violation of fair play, which they cannot admit of. This man is to them, in every respect, as good as he: they do not enter into that self-love by which he prefers himself so much to this other, and cannot go along with the motive from which he hurt him. They readily, therefore, sympathize with the natural resentment of the injured, and the offender becomes the object of their hatred and indignation. He is sensible that he becomes so, and feels that those sentiments are ready to burst out from all sides against him.

The emphasis of sympathy in the *Moral Sentiments* and the focus on self-interest in *The Wealth of Nations* have been highlighted as inconsistent by those in the German Historical School. This gave rise to a debate called the 'Das Adam Smith' problem. However, many today regard these two aspects in Smith's thinking as internally consistent and a coherent part of his theory of human behaviour (Tribe, 2008). Indeed, Smith emphasised that sympathy 'cannot, in any sense, be regarded as a selfish principle', and went on to stress the importance of 'imaginary change of situation' for individuals to share the perspective of others. Smith (1759, p. 164) outlined this by suggesting that:

> When I condole with you for the loss of your only son, in order to enter into your grief I do not consider what I, a person of such a character and

> profession, should suffer, if I had a son, and if that son was unfortunately to die: but I consider what I should suffer if I was really you, and I not only change circumstances with you, but I change persons and characters. My grief, therefore, is entirely upon your account, and not in the least upon my own.

Smith's writing has significantly influenced today's Neoclassical economics, but also shaped some of the contemporary critiques against it. By seeking the behavioural logic in human nature, Smith naturalises the motivations and actions of economic agents, as opposed to Marx and Veblen who have historicised it, albeit in very different ways (see following sections). Smith may not have reduced all economic and social phenomena to the behaviour of individuals, but many of his writings at least in part reflect a variant of 'methodological individualism' (see Box 2.1 and also Milonakis and Fine, 2008, p. 109). Nevertheless, authors such as Sen have taken up Smith's conceptions of human motives and behaviour, as well as of their roles in society, as ways to critique Neoclassical economics. For example, Sen has pointed out that the Neoclassical logic of rational choice outlined above conflates choice with welfare, and ignores motives for individual choice other than self-interest, including sympathy and commitment, an argument closely related to Smith. Sen (1977, pp. 335–336) further pointed out that:

> A person is given *one* preference ordering, and as and when the need arises this is supposed to reflect his interests, represent his welfare, summarize his idea of what should be done, and describe his actual choices and behavior. Can one preference ordering do all these things? A person thus described may be 'rational' in the limited sense of revealing no inconsistencies in his choice behavior, but if he has no use for these distinctions between quite different concepts, he must be a bit of a fool. The *purely* economic man is indeed close to being a social moron.

Marx, agency, and class

Marx's methodology is different from the positivist methodology based on deductive reasoning that characterises Neoclassical economics. For Marx, humans are social animals in the sense that the way individuals act and relate to each other can only be understood in a specific social context, which changes over time. Moreover, Marx identified production and how it develops as the basis of his materialist conception of history. Note that far from economic or technological determinism, production is understood to be at the centre of the system, which simultaneously encompasses social, political, and historical processes. From this perspective, individuals are defined by class relations, a collective expression of the whole system of social production, and how a group of persons are identified within it. In the Preface to *Capital Vol. I*, Marx stated that he is dealing with individuals (Marx, 1976, p. 92):

> in so far as they are personifications of economic categories, the bearers of particular class-relations and interests. My standpoint, from which the development of the economic formation of society is viewed as a process of natural history, can less than any other make the individual responsible for relations whose creature he remains, socially speaking, however much he may subjectively raise himself above them.

Also, in the Preface to *A Contribution to the Critique of Political Economy*, Marx (1971, p. 5) stated that:

> In the social production of their existence, men inevitably enter into definite relations, which are independent of their will, namely relations of production appropriate to a given stage in the development of their material forces of production. The totality of these relations of production constitutes the economic structure of society, the real foundation, on which arises a legal and political superstructure and to which correspond definite forms of social consciousness. The mode of production of material life conditions the general process of social, political and intellectual life. It is not the consciousness of men that determines their existence, but their social existence that determines their consciousness.

These passages are often misinterpreted as a technologically deterministic and teleological reading of history in which human agency is reduced to purely reflecting the personifications of economic categories and the laws of motion of economic systems. However, Marx's materialist conception of history need not mean that individuals do not have choices or 'freedom' to act, and indeed individual agencies actively shape material conditions as much as they are shaped by them. Indeed, Marx emphasises how material conditions, which are the result of human activities past and present, constrain agency. This dialectical conception of class is reflected in following quote from the *Eighteenth Brumaire of Louis Bonaparte* (Marx, 1973, p. 146):

> Men make their own history, but they do not make it as they please; they do not make it under self-selected circumstances, but under circumstances existing already, given and transmitted from the past.

In a commodity-producing society, there is a class of direct producers and a class of those who appropriate part of the product of the labour of others: what Marx called the 'surplus value' (see Chapters 4 and 7). In a capitalist society, this relation takes place, in *essence*, between classes of capital and wage-labour, whereby the former controls the means and conditions of production as well as the product. This *essential* class relation, founded in the production of surplus value, is mediated by a wide range of formal and informal social relations, institutions, and practices, and therefore take specific social, political, ideological, and cultural expressions, including subjective perceptions about status and positions.

Marx criticised his contemporary political economists for their representation of the economy as consisting merely of voluntary exchange between equal parties, which he labelled the 'fetishism of the commodity' (Marx, 1976, p. 163). This criticism, of course, applies to today's mainstream economics as well (see Chapter 5). Instead, Marx exposes the structural forces hidden behind the commodity form, which underpin the social relations and compels individuals within their class positions. For Marx, how production or consumption are organised, and hence how people behave, must be explained by examining the structure and historical specificity of the social system, rather than merely understand these outcomes as a result of individual choices and optimisation exercises (however constrained or modified). Patterns of consumption or the nature of the production process are not driven by transhistorical 'rational human nature', but are underpinned by how people relate to each other in a particular society at a particular historical moment. Marx's approach to the role of individuals in society is therefore in sharp contrast to the methodological individualistic and ahistorical rational choice framework of Neoclassical economics.

Veblen and institutions

Veblen is associated with the development of Institutional economics and Evolutionary economics. Unlike today's New Institutional economics (see Chapters 13 and 15), which has incorporated the methodological individualist rational choice framework, the (Old) Institutional economists of the early twentieth century were critical of Neoclassical economics. Veblen (1898, p. 389) considered prevailing approaches to economics in the late nineteenth and early twentieth centuries to be unsatisfactory in the way they conceived of human actions and their role in social change (see also Chapter 5):

> In all the received formulations of economic theory, whether at the hands of English economists or those of the Continent, the human material with which the inquiry is concerned is conceived in hedonistic terms; that is to say, in terms of a passive and substantially inert and immutably given human nature ... The hedonistic conception of man is that of a lightning calculator of pleasures and pains, who oscillates like a homogeneous globule of desire of happiness under the impulse of stimuli that shift him about the area, but leave him intact. He has neither antecedent nor consequent. He is an isolated, definitive human datum, in stable equilibrium except for the buffets of the impinging forces that displace him in one direction or another.

Instead, Veblen proposed a conception of human action shaped by habits, traditions, conventions etc.:

> [I]t is the characteristic of man to do something, not simply to suffer pleasures and pains through the impact of suitable forces. He is not simply a bundle of desires that are to be saturated by being placed in the path of the forces of the environment, but rather a coherent structure of propensities and habits which seeks realization and expression in an unfolding activity.

This is not to deny that individuals have desires, but for Veblen (1898, pp. 390–391), these are:

> the products of his hereditary traits and his past experience, cumulatively wrought out under a given body of traditions, conventionalities, and material circumstances; and they afford the point of departure for the next step in the process. The economic life history of the individual is a cumulative process of adaptation of means to ends that cumulatively change as the process goes on, both the agent and his environment being at any point the outcome of the past process. His methods of life to-day are enforced upon him by his habits of life carried over from yesterday and by the circumstances left as the mechanical residue of the life of yesterday.

The idea that human agency is shaped, not by preferences or rational choice, but rather by aspirations, institutions and culture and so on, is in contrast to the rational choice perspective embedded in Neoclassical economics. Furthermore, Veblen provided a distinctive evolutionary interpretation of social and economic changes, which is in contrast to Marx's material conception of history discussed in the previous section. For Veblen, what explains economic processes are not primarily material changes (say, relations of production or capital accumulation) but rather what he called 'the human material of the industrial community'. The latter was the basis for his evolutionary analysis of society in that (Veblen, 1898, p. 387):

> when taken as items in a process of cumulative change or as items in the scheme of life, these productive goods are facts of human knowledge, skill, and predilection; that is to say, they are, substantially, prevalent habits of thought, and it is as such that they enter into the process of industrial development.

Veblen's objection to human agency 'rationally' maximising 'utility' is most famously demonstrated in his notion of 'conspicuous consumption' (see Chapter 5). In his *Theory of the Leisure Class: An Economic Study in the Evolution of Institutions*, Veblen (1997, p. 24) described the emergence of an upper class in the nineteenth century whose consumption patterns are driven more by the demonstration of their social esteem and power than by accumulation of wealth based on individual 'rational' behaviour:

> the end sought by accumulation is to rank high in comparison with the rest of the community in point of pecuniary strength. So long as the comparison is distinctly unfavourable to himself, the normal, average individual will live in chronic dissatisfaction with his present lot; and when he has reached what may be called the normal pecuniary standard of the community, or of his class in the community, this chronic dissatisfaction will give place to a restless straining to place a wider and ever-widening pecuniary interval between himself and this average standard. The invidious comparison can never become so favourable to the individual making it that he would not gladly rate himself still higher relatively to his competitors in the struggle for pecuniary reputability.

Veblen recognises that material needs for reproduction remain important motives for consumption, although even these are shaped by 'emulation' (Veblen, 1997, pp. 24–25):

> The desire for added comfort and security from want is present as a motive at every stage of the process of accumulation in a modern industrial community; although the standard of sufficiency in these respects is in turn greatly affected by the habit of pecuniary emulation. To a great extent this emulation shapes the methods and selects the objects of expenditure for personal comfort and decent livelihood.

Keynes, uncertainty, and the macroeconomy

Keynes is considered the founder of modern macroeconomics. Yet Keynes's conception of the macroeconomy was very different from today's Neoclassical macroeconomics seeking 'microfoundations' and also significantly different from some of the subsequent 'reinterpretations' of Keynes (see Chapter 6). In contrast to Neoclassical macroeconomics, which interprets society as no more than a sum of its individual members, Keynes insisted that individuals do not act in isolation and that economic agents interact with one another in such a way that generates its own dynamics that cannot be reduced to models of atomised agents. Keynes's critique of Neoclassical economics forms part of the viewpoint known as the 'fallacies of composition', which arises when reasoning and concepts valid at the micro-level is falsely applied to the macro-level. In the move from micro- to macroeconomics, reasoning and concepts are transformed due to interdependencies between economic agents. In the Preface to the French edition of the *General Theory of Employment, Interest and Money*, Keynes (1936, p. xxxii) specified that:

> I am chiefly concerned with the behaviour of the economic system as a whole, — with aggregate incomes, aggregate profits, aggregate output, aggregate employment, aggregate investment, aggregate saving rather than with the incomes, profits, output, employment, investment and saving of particular industries, firms or individuals. And I argue that important mistakes have been made through extending to the system as a whole conclusions which have been correctly arrived at in respect of a part of it taken in isolation.

A particularly famous demonstration of the fallacy of composition is what was later termed the 'paradox of thrift'. Keynes challenged the so-called Say's L, which postulates that each act of supply involves the creation of an equivalent demand for output. The widely received argument during Keynes's time (which remains influential today) was that the mere act of individuals saving 'always involves investment'. In the *General Theory*, Keynes (1936, p. 84) wrote that:

> although the amount of his own saving is unlikely to have any significant influence on his own income, the reactions of the amount of his consumption on the incomes of others makes it impossible for all individuals

> simultaneously to save any given sums. Every such attempt to save more by reducing consumption will so affect incomes that the attempt necessarily defeats itself.

Similarly, in his *Treatise on Money*, Keynes dismissed the 'abstinence' theory in classical economics. He argued that the mere existence of savings from individual 'abstinence is not enough by itself to build cities or drain fens', but instead that '[i]t is enterprise which builds and improves the world's possessions'. Keynes (1930, pp. 148–149) went on to argue that:

> For enterprise to be active ... there must be an expectation of profit ... but their power to put their projects into execution on terms which they deem attractive almost entirely depends on the behaviour of the banking and monetary system.
>
> In general, the 'fallacies of composition' argument calls for the need to understand different levels of economic dynamics and the interdependencies between them. The paradox of thrift outlined above shows that an increase in savings which may be 'optimal' for individual agents can lead to a fall in aggregate expenditure and demand, and further to a decline in output and employment. A similar argument can be made for a fall in wages, which again might mean less cost and expansion of production for an individual firm. But for Keynes, wages do not only represent costs of production, but also income for workers. Since workers with less wages will spend less on consumption, aggregate demand and hence production is likely to contract.

Keynes also rendered probability theory inadequate as a guide to model economic decision-making under uncertainty, in contrast to the Neoclassical approach to risk. He argued that for future changes in the economy 'there is no scientific basis on which to form any calculable probability whatever. We simply do not know.' Having proposed 'a variety of techniques' to 'behave in a manner which saves our faces as rational, economic men', Keynes (1937, p. 214) went on to suggest that they are:

> based on so flimsy a foundation, it is subject to sudden and violent changes. The practice of calmness and immobility, of certainty and security, suddenly breaks down. New fears and hopes will, without warning, take charge of human conduct. The forces of disillusion may suddenly impose a new conventional basis of valuation. All these pretty, polite techniques, made for a well-panelled Board Room and a nicely regulated market, are liable to collapse. At all times the vague panic fears and equally vague and unreasoned hopes are not really lulled, and lie but a little way below the surface.

For Keynes, 'rational, economic men' are not those who maximise expected returns by attaching probability to unknown future events in the Neoclassical sense. Individuals resorting to 'herd behaviour' or aligning their interests with collective behaviour are equally 'rational' in the face of risk and uncertainty. This once again reinforces Keynes's privileging of systemic dynamics in the macroeconomy over the isolated optimising behaviour of atomised individuals.

Conclusion

This chapter has outlined a range of different approaches to understanding human behaviour, contrasting the Neoclassical model, in which individual economic agents make rational, optimising decisions which conform to a strict set of mathematical assumptions, with other approaches originating from Smith, Marx, Veblen, and Keynes. The latter emphasise the contextual, moral, cultural, institutional, and historical influences over behaviour. Whilst some approaches, such as Behavioural economics, continue to employ some of the concepts and tools of Neoclassical economics, other approaches take a more radical point of departure to shed light on multiple aspects of behaviour that Neoclassical economics does not address. This can serve to highlight some of the limitations of Neoclassical conceptions of the rational individual as the key building block of economics, as well as alternative ways of thinking about economic decision making and behaviour that may be more relevant in the real world.

Discussion questions and seminar activities

For further engagement, the following topics might be discussed:

- Where do preferences come from?
- When you go shopping, is your choice based on your self-interest? How about when you vote in an election?
- Did you buy a lottery ticket last week? Was your decision based on calculating the odds for the winning prize?
- What does it mean to say that 'humans are social animals'? How do different schools of economic thought understand human agency?

Further reading

An excellent summary and critique of the Neoclassical rational choice framework can be found in Hargreaves-Heap et al. (1992). Hodgson (2007) is a useful overview of different notions of individualist methodology in the mainstream.

Alternative strands of economic thought are best approached by reading the original text. Concise extracts of key sources are collected in a reader edited by Medema and Samuels (2013). Many of the texts discussed in this chapter are also available online:

- Smith, *The Wealth of Nations*: http://www.econlib.org/library/Smith/smWN.html
- Smith, *The Theory of Moral Sentiments*: http://www.econlib.org/library/Smith/smMS.html

- Marx, *Capital Vol. I*: https://www.marxists.org/archive/marx/works/1867-c1/index.htm
- Marx, *A Contribution to the Critique of Political Economy*: https://www.marxists.org/archive/marx/works/1859/critique-pol-economy/index.htm
- Veblen, *The Theory of the Leisure Class*: http://www.gutenberg.org/ebooks/833
- Keynes, *The General Theory*: http://www.hetwebsite.net/het/texts/keynes/gt/gtcont.htm

Sen (1977, 2010) engages sympathetically with Smith and discusses his legacies in modern debates on rationality in mainstream economics and beyond. Fine and Saad-Filho (2010) provide a concise overview of Marx's methods and political economic analysis. For a discussion on approaches to class analysis with focus on development, see Campling et al. (2016).

Snowdon et al. (1994) provide an excellent overview of schools of thought in macroeconomics. For a more detailed exposition of Keynes's approach to macroeconomics, see Trevithick (1992). Heilbroner (2000) offers an engaging account of Keynes's life and thoughts in Chapter 9 'The Heresies of John Maynard Keynes'.

References

Brennan, G., & Tullock, G. (1982). An economic theory of military tactics: Methodological individualism at War. *Journal of Economic Behavior and Organization, 3*, 225–242.

Campling, L., Miyamura, S., Pattenden, J., & Selwyn, B. (2016). Class dynamics of development: A methodological note. *Third World Quarterly, 37*, 1745–1767.

Fine, B., & Saad-Filho, A. (2010). *Marx's 'Capital'* (5th ed.). London/New York: Pluto Press.

Fine, B., Johnston, D., Santos, A. C., & Waeyenberge, E. V. (2016). Nudging or fudging: The world development report 2015. *Development and Change, 47*, 640–663. https://doi.org/10.1111/dech.12240.

Hargreaves-Heap, S., Hollis, M., Lyons, B., Sugden, R., & Weale, A. (1992). *The theory of choice: A critical guide*. Malden: Blackwell.

Hargreaves-Heap, S., & Varoufakis, Y. (2004). *Game theory: A critical introduction* (2nd ed.). London: Routledge.

Heilbroner, R. L. (2000). *The worldly philosophers: The lives, times, and ideas of the great economic thinkers* (7th ed.). London: Penguin.

Hodgson, G. M. (2007). Meanings of methodological individualism. *Journal of Economic Methodology, 14*, 211–226. https://doi.org/10.1080/13501780701394094.

Hodgson, G. M. (2012). On the limits of rational choice theory. *Economic Thought, 1*, 94–108.

Infantino, L. (2014). *Individualism in modern thought: From Adam Smith to Hayek*. London/New York: Routledge.

Kahneman, D. (2003). Maps of bounded rationality: Psychology for behavioral economics. *The American Economic Review, 93*, 1449–1475.

Kahneman, D. (2012). *Thinking, fast and slow*. London: Penguin.

Kahneman, D., & Tversky, A. (1979). Prospect theory: An analysis of decision under risk. *Econometrica, 47*, 263–291. https://doi.org/10.2307/1914185.

Keynes, J. M. (1930). *A treatise on money volume II: The applied theory of money*. New York: Harcourt, Brace and Co.

Keynes, J. M. (1936). *The general theory of employment, interest, and money*. London/Basingstoke: Macmillan.

Keynes, J. M. (1937). The general theory of employment. *Quarterly Journal of Economics, 51*, 209–223.

Kreps, D. M. (1990). *A course in microeconomic theory*. New York/London: Harvester Wheatsheaf.

Kreps, D. M. (1991). *Game theory and economic modelling* (New ed.). Oxford: Oxford University Press.

Loewenstein, G., Asch, D. A., Friedman, J. Y., Melichar, L. A., & Volpp, K. G. (2012). Can behavioural economics make us healthier? *BMJ, 344*, e3482. https://doi.org/10.1136/bmj.e3482.

Marx, K. (1971). Preface to a contribution to the critique of political economy. In *Historical materialism*. London: Pluto Press.

Marx, K. (1973). The Eighteenth Brumaire of Louis Bonaparte. In *Surveys from exile: Political writings volume 2*. Harmondsworth/New York: Penguin.

Marx, K. (1976). *Capital: Critique of political economy: Volume One*. London/New York: Penguin Classics.

Medema, S. G., & Samuels, W. J. (Eds.). (2013). *The history of economic thought* (2nd ed.). London/New York: Routledge.

Milonakis, D., & Fine, B. (2008). *From political economy to economics: Method, the social and the historical in the evolution of economic theory*. London/New York: Routledge.

Santos, A. C. (2011). Behavioural and experimental economics: Are they really transforming economics? *Cambridge Journal of Economics, 35*, 705–728. https://doi.org/10.1093/cje/beq049.

Sen, A. K. (1977). Rational fools: A critique of the behavioral foundations of economic theory. *Philosophy & Public Affairs, 6*, 317–344.

Sen, A. (2010). Adam Smith and the contemporary world. *Erasmus The Journal of Philosophical Economics, 3*, 50–67.

Simon, H. A. (1979). Information processing models of cognition. *Annual Review of Psychology, 30*, 363.

Smith, A. (1759). *The theory of moral sentiments*. London: A. Millar/Library of Economics and Liberty.

Smith, A. (1776). *An inquiry into the nature and causes of the wealth of nations* (5th ed.). London: Methuen & Co., Ltd/Library of Economics and Liberty.

Snowdon, B., Vane, H. R., & Wynarczyk, P. (1994). *A modern guide to macroeconomics: An introduction to competing schools of thought*. Aldershot/Brookfield: Edward Elgar.

Trevithick, J. A. (1992). *Involuntary unemployment: Macroeconomics from a Keynesian perspective*. New York: Pearson Education Limited.

Tribe, K. (2008). Das Adam Smith Problem' and the origins of modern Smith scholarship. *History of European Ideas, 34*, 514–525. https://doi.org/10.1016/j.histeuroideas.2008.02.001.

Tversky, A., & Kahneman, D. (1981). The framing of decisions and the psychology of choice. *Science, 211*, 453–458. https://doi.org/10.1126/science.7455683.

Veblen, T. (1898). Why is economics not an evolutionary science? *Quarterly Journal of Economics, 12*, 373–397.

Veblen, T. (1997). *The theory of the leisure class*. Project Gutenberg. http://www.gutenberg.org/ebooks/833

von Neumann, J., & Morgenstern, O. (1944). *Theory of games and economic behavior*. Princeton: Princeton University Press.

3 WHAT IS THE ROLE OF MATHEMATICS IN ECONOMICS?

Ourania Dimakou

Introduction

Nowadays economics is researched and taught with an integral highly mathematical component. From the onset of their studies economics students are taught to perceive economics as a technical field that cannot be mastered without a vigorous grasp of mathematics. In almost all UK universities, for instance, an A-level in mathematics is a prerequisite for an undergraduate degree in economics, more so than an A-level in economics (let alone an A-level in social sciences).

From the introductory undergraduate level, students are introduced to microeconomics with the algebraic or graphical exposition of demand and supply curves, consumer's preferences and firm's production functions. Microeconomics textbooks begin with the optimising behaviour of individuals. Individuals, or, interchangeably, consumers or households, are presumed to maximise their utility, subject to prevailing prices. This gives rise to the demand for consumer goods and supply of labour. Firms maximise profits subject to prevailing technology and input and output prices. This gives rise to the supply of goods and demand for labour.

Macroeconomics textbooks are similarly characterised when it comes to the technical and model-building aspect, although noticeable changes have been witnessed in recent years mainly as a result of the consolidation of macroeconomics around microeconomic principles. While older textbooks at the undergraduate level would start with the aggregate variables of the economic system and the classic IS/LM model, new generation books emphasise the micro-foundations of macroeconomics from the outset.

As the level of progression increases, so does the degree of mathematical advancement and sophistication. Currently, there is no field in economics without a technical/mathematical constituent. Often this growing trend in economics curricula is accompanied by a dedicated course (or set of such courses) on mathematical economics. At the same time, statistics and econometrics are nowadays enjoying high prominence within economics curricula. Take, for example, the following quote from a prominent undergraduate microeconomics textbook (H. Varian, *Intermediate Microeconomics*, 7th edition, 2005):

> The conventional first chapter of a microeconomics book is a discussion of the 'scope and methods' of economics. Although this material can be very interesting, it hardly seems appropriate to ***begin*** your study of economics...

Instead, Varian starts with an example of a model for a market, for 'economics proceeds by developing models of social phenomena' (ibid.). While a model is a legitimate simplification of reality, within economics textbooks, the emphasis is often on the first word (simple) rather than the second (reality). In other words, there is rarely an acknowledgement or a discussion with regards to the relation (or lack thereof) between a model, its simplicity, and the reality it is assumed to address. Varian then goes on to construct a model that explains the determinants of prices of apartments in a college town.

From the first paragraph of Varian's celebrated book, (micro)economics is defined in terms of how it studies its subject (through models), while a discussion of scope and methods of the (sub-)discipline is considered secondary. Here we take the opposite view and, through our discussion of the importance of maths in economics, embark on a journey about methods of inquiry, scope, and content of economics.

This chapter has two aims. The first is to trace the evolution of the mathematisation of economics: when and how did the mathematisation of economics take place and how does it continue to do so at exponential rates? We will see that mathematics has not always been at the core of the discipline. Classical political economists, for instance, despite their differences, rarely used mathematics to express their ideas. And for a long time, the field was unpersuaded, even hostile, to mathematical representations of the economic. The second is to discuss implications and critiques of a mathematical formalisation of economics. What does this mean for the conceptualisation of the economic, our understanding of economic phenomena and prescriptions for economic policy? In essence, we delineate the ways through which the triumph of a particular form of reasoning, i.e. mathematics, displaces content, reduces substance, and precludes other methods of inquiry.

Before we proceed, it is useful to start with a brief discussion of what we mean by methods. Methods in economic investigation refer to systematic ways and techniques through which the subject is approached and analysed. Although different methods can be employed independently of the overall research agenda of a theory or a school of thought, they inevitably reflect a particular stance on how the realm under study is perceived. That is to say, although we can distinguish method from content, both are interrelated in complex and bi-directional ways. The fundamental relation between the two relates to the nature of our subject matter and how we think we can study it.

The prominence of mathematics in economics is closely related to the deductive method of reasoning. According to this logic of enquiry, one starts from a set of assumptions/axioms (e.g. optimising individuals with a given preference structure) and draws out conclusions through logical reasoning. This differs from the inductive method of reasoning, whereby close observation of reality comes first. With the latter, reality is historically and socially situated. To reiterate, however, this is not to say that logical deduction can only be undertaken by the use of maths (e.g. Ricardo or Menger). Nor that an inductive approach would necessarily be amathematical. Nonetheless, mathematics is akin to logical reasoning and this was indeed the particular method that emerged within mainstream economics through the marginalist revolution. This reached its peak with the formalist revolution of the 1950s and onwards. Such a development of the discipline would not have happened without changes in the conceptualisation of the realm of economics.

The rest of the chapter proceeds as follows. We begin with a brief discussion on the role of mathematics in today's economics teaching and research (the section 'Role of Mathematics in Contemporary Economics'). The following section 'How Did Economics Become so Mathematical?' traces the elevation of mathematics historically, while the section 'Contrasting the Mainstream Approach to Smith, Ricardo, Marx, and Keynes' outlines approaches and methods that do not rely on mathematical formalisation. The final section, 'Concluding Remarks: Consolidating Mathematics in Economics and Its Implications', discusses the implications that mathematisation has on the discipline.

Role of mathematics in contemporary economics

Mathematics is now an integral part of economics both in teaching and, even more so, in research. Undergraduate programmes in economics usually entail a couple of dedicated courses in mathematics for economists, as well as econometrics, while maths is also integrated into the core subjects of the discipline: microeconomics and macroeconomics.

An introductory course in maths for economists would cover topics in analysis of functions and algebra, while moving on to focus on differential and integral calculus, and optimisation, as well as probability theory and distributions. More advanced courses would cover matrix algebra, game theory, and dynamic (intertemporal) optimisation, among other topics. These mathematical tools have various applications in both microeconomics and macroeconomics, as well as in statistics and econometrics.

Conventional microeconomics is preoccupied with the so-called consumer and producer theories. Axiomatic preference theory is analysed, before moving on to the crucial question of utility maximisation. The latter is taught in many different settings, such as maximising utility between two different goods, subject to a budget constraint, or maximising utility across leisure and consumption, or consumption and savings. Either way, the fundamental preoccupation of consumers (or households or individuals, all treated the same) is some sort of utility optimisation, given set constraints. Utility maximisation, as mathematically indistinguishable, is in principle applied to both decisions across different items at a specific point in time, as well as over time. On the producer side, microeconomics teaches us profit maximisation (or its dual problem of cost minimisation, subject to a production function). The firm is faced with a production function and is assumed to convert factors of production (usually labour and capital) into final goods with the aim of maximising its profits (that is, total revenues minus costs of production).

The central organising concept in microeconomics (and also, indeed, in macroeconomics) is the concept of equilibrium (see Chapter 6). Bringing together the optimising behaviour of the consumer and the firm provides us with the equilibrium point of that transaction, and aggregating across individuals and firms we can derive the market or the economy equilibrium. For example, utility maximisation with regards to leisure and consumption derives the demand for goods and supply of labour, while profit maximisation gives us the supply of goods and demand for labour schedules. All these schedules are a function of the relative price (the real wage in this example), and the intersection of the demands and supplies obtains the equilibrium in the labour and goods markets. That is, that level of the real wage whereby the demand and supply of labour are equated, and the same for the demand and supply of goods. Equilibrium is understood as market clearing and the price adjustment mechanism is essential for the establishment of the equilibrium. Thus, the two fundamental principles in microeconomics are that of optimisation and equilibrium.

Microeconomics is further concerned with different market structures and how the firm's optimal behaviour may be differentiated, under distinct competitive settings (from perfect competition to monopoly to oligopoly and so on). Some of these settings require different mathematical techniques, such as game theory. The outcomes under different institutional settings are usually compared in terms of economic (Pareto) efficiency, which allows for statements along the lines of the best (most efficient) allocation of scarce resources. Further topics in microeconomics discuss regulatory intervention (e.g. taxation) with an eye to bringing out Pareto improvements, as well as uncertainty and insurance behaviours. Bringing in uncertainty in decision-making opens economics to the study of probability theory and probability distributions. More advanced microeconomics modules usually entail further in-depth elaboration of the same topics. In particular, advancement in the teaching of microeconomics is synonymous with advancement in the use of more formal and complex maths.

Macroeconomics also entails an integral mathematical component, depending on the level at which it is being taught. Introductory macroeconomics courses concentrate on aggregate behaviours and variables, employing mainly algebraic and graphical tools, as, for instance, when analysing the Neoclassical or the IS/LM model. The same principles and mathematical tools, described above, are also employed, particularly when building macroeconomic models from microeconomic principles, which has become the main trend in research since the 1970s, with teaching following closely, especially at more advanced levels. Dynamic programming (optimisation), as part of the advancement of DSGE modelling, has also become widespread in advanced courses, including computational methods and computer programming as many of these complex models require numerical solutions (as opposed to analytical ones), and special software has been developed in assisting that (e.g. DYNARE).

In addition, statistical mathematics, which forms the basis for econometrics, is also part of the training of economists with topics including: probability and measure theory, probability distributions, integration and mathematical expectation, matrix algebra, set theory and complex analysis, stochastic processes, as well as statistical methods (measures of association, estimation, statistical inference, and advanced techniques of regression analysis).

Nonetheless, the use of this mode of analysing and teaching economics is only recent. The following section traces the developments that led to the dominance of mathematics in economic reasoning.

How did economics become so mathematical?

From classical political economy to the marginalist revolution

The history of economic thought, and history of the mathematisation of economics, in particular, is purposely overlooked in contemporary economics programmes. It is also rarely debated within orthodox journals, and when so, it is conventionally portrayed as a 'cumulative, inevitable and, indeed, *natural*' (Mirowski, 1991, p. 145) process. It also usually proceeds in ahistorical terms: the process of mathematisation becomes synonymous to *progress* in the discipline of economics in and of itself. The passage from old to new theories (say, new growth theory, New Institutional economics, new Schumpeterian, new Keynesian…) is marked by increased mathematical formalism, improvement of technique, hence elegance and rigour. Substance is secondary. Conversely, inadequacies in older theories are portrayed especially through their lack of rigour. Furthermore, the biggest impediment to *progress* is identified as lack of mathematical (or even computational) tools.

However, this does not reflect the history of economic thought appropriately. The evolution of economics mathematisation was not a natural, inevitable process. The period prior to the Marginalist revolution, the Classical political economy epoch, was characterised by contributions from Smith, Ricardo, Malthus, Mill, and Marx. Despite their huge differences, commonalities characterise both their approaches to economic theorising and their subject matter. These economists were predominantly concerned with the long-run development and dynamic nature of the economic system, situated within its wider social, political, and historical context. And while their conclusions, conceptualisations, and methods differed, they share a holistic and collectivist (class-based) mode of analysis.

This is not to say that classical political economy was not influenced by developments in other sciences, including natural sciences, and in particular Newtonian ideas. Many classical political economists, including Ricardo, Mill, and Marx, sought to identify the underlying social laws of capitalism. Smith, for instance, was explicit in his *magnum opus* regarding his quest for an understanding of the nature and causes of the wealth of nations (Milonakis, 2017). And, although Smith is known as the father of laissez-faire and individualistic principles, there are plenty of instances in his work where he deviates from these, in favour of historical and class-based analyses.

In the period of Classical political economy, there also existed scattered voices in support of mathematical reasoning in economics (such as Quesnay, Canard, Condorcet, and Cournot).[1] All of these precursors looked to the physics of motion (mechanics) to guide them in their analogies with economics, particularly with regard to price ratios and values. However, such attempts largely failed and fell into oblivion. For despite the Newtonian influence, Classical political economists never considered the tools and methods of physics as relevant for economics. Expressed differently, the influence of the natural sciences, as well as the French Enlightenment, on Classical political economy had mostly to do with the idea of whether the social cosmos is also governed by societal laws. This, however, is distinct from introducing techniques (such as laws of mechanics) into the field of political economy.

Marginalism and its main contributors

The last decades of the nineteenth century witnessed what came to be known as the Marginalist revolution. The movement entailed a set of pioneers, who independently, even if simultaneously, put forth a different approach to economic inquiry. At the forefront of this process were Jevons (in Britain), Walras (in France), and Menger (in Austria). Their followers include Edgeworth and Pareto (in Europe) and Fisher (in the US).

These economists introduced the concepts and methods that are familiar in today's economics, particularly microeconomics. As a result, since 1870, mathematical analysis began to be used more widely in economics, following the examples of physics. Economics aspired to a scientific basis, with rapid displacement of the term 'political economy'. To understand how this process took place, we need to have a look at the broader changes introduced at the conceptual and substantive level, which made the transition into mathematical expression possible (or *natural*).

What marked this rupture? The marginalists were all trained in a natural science (and the same held true for the precursors in the classical epoch). But it was the first time that the aim to transform economics 'into a mathematical *science* on a par with natural sciences becomes a programmatic proclamation' (Milonakis, 2017, p. 1374). This entailed, first, a shift in mode of analysis (how the subject can be studied) away from a holistic, collectivist, and broadly historico-inductive mode towards a more individualistic, abstract, and deductive one. Second, it entailed a separation of positive ('what it is') from normative ('what it ought to be') theory. Third, it entailed a parting between the economic and the non-economic. Preoccupation with positive analysis of the economic was seen as the essence of 'pure science' and synonymous with value-free theory (Milonakis, 2017).

Consequently, these changes in how economics was conceived had important implications, both for the discipline's subject matter, precluding in essence the classical themes of growth and change in the historic and social nature of capitalism, and for the mode through which these themes were to be studied (class-based analysis which take account of the dynamism of the system and in which social organisation is at the fore). Non-economic factors (from morals to justice, distribution, well-being) were no longer considered part of the subject matter of scientific or 'pure' economics. In contrast, the focus on individual economic behaviour strips the human from its social and historical context and narrows the object of study to the problem of an optimal (equilibrium) allocation of given resources. The scope of economics turns to viewing the economy as market relations, with market outcomes, especially in terms of demand and supply, underpinned by individual optimising behaviour (see Chapters 2 and 5). Further, with the organising principle of equilibrium, marginalists were supporters of the classical theme of laissez-faire. However this was now promoted on grounds of efficiency, instead of capital accumulation.

The transitions briefly described above, in the unit and mode of analysis and the aim of scientific economics, are essential as they lay the basis for abstract and, in particular, mathematical analysis. For while concepts such as dynamism, long-run development, distribution, social motives, and class interests are very hard to be considered appropriate for mathematical expression, this is not the case for the new ones introduced by marginalists. In what follows we briefly discuss the main pioneers of the marginalist revolution.

Jevons

Jevons was a meteorologist and chemist who rejected the economics of Mill and Ricardo. He believed that economics was intrinsically mathematical as it dealt with quantities. His basis was a special version of Bentham's philosophy of utilitarianism.

As stated in his *Theory of Political Economy* (1871), his aim was to 'treat the economy as a calculus of pleasure and pain' and to sketch out '… the form which the science … must ultimately take' (Screpanti and Zamagni, 2005, p. 174). These premises highlighted his belief that value (and price) are subjective, depending entirely on utility and especially on the benefit from the last unit consumed by the individual. This became the core marginalist principle and a major break from classical political economy. Values (and prices) are understood as both individual and subjective. The value of things depends on whether and how much they are desired. So, the value of an object is such, because it is considered an end for individuals and because it arises from a process of choice. This stands in sharp contrast to the more objective theory of value of Smith, Ricardo, and Marx, based on costs and conditions of production, irrespective of individual choices (demand).

For marginalists, the individual has two sole characteristics: first, the *homo economicus* derives utility from consumption of goods and, second, s/he acts rationally, with the aim of maximising utility or more generally self-interest. With such a utility theory of value, the price of a good is determined in the sphere of exchange; what we are willing to pay for an extra unit is determined at the margin by the pleasure it gives us. Thus, equilibrium price determination derives directly from a series of fundamental motive forces, or the 'mechanics of utility and self-interest'. This reveals a direct analogy from static mechanics imported into economics. In addition, the very notion of a marginal utility has a mathematical counterpart in differential calculus (through derivatives).

Jevons adopted the same conceptual apparatus in the sphere of production, which gave rise to the notion of marginal diminishing returns, based on the assumption of substitutability among inputs of production. Similarly for his theory of labour supply, whereby the individual derives disutility from work, itself increasing with the amount of labour supplied. The same mathematical expressions of differential calculus and static mechanics apply.

A note on the mathematical method is worth making at this point, as this becomes commonplace with the increasing formalisation and dominance of Neoclassical and mainstream economics. Jevons assumes that the worker works autonomously (owning the means of production), as this ensures the divisibility of labour that is required for the application of marginal calculus. Therefore, waged employment, which implies discrete changes in hours worked (and hence is not differentiable), is excluded, despite this being the dominant form of labour relation under capitalism. This illustrates that, at times, the mathematical expression imposes restrictions on the economic phenomena under study, and, although vastly overlooked, the resolution of mathematical tractability versus realism is not necessarily balanced or satisfactory (although Jevons was aware of this limitation, contemporary economics still operate under the assumption of divisible labour in utility functions).

Walras and Menger

Walras formalised the economy as a whole with the theory of general competitive equilibrium. His focus expanded to all markets that constituted the whole of the economy and the links between these, providing us with the first general prototype of abstract theory (*Elements of Pure Economics*, 1874–1877). Markets are interlinked, ensuring that all choices are compatible. A general equilibrium is achieved when all relative prices are such that all individuals have maximised their objectives simultaneously. Hence, a system of simultaneous equations must be solved. In his conception, the economy is made up of many individuals (who operate either as consumers or as producers and entrepreneurs) and there is no space for the notion of social class. In essence, there is no fundamental difference between consumers and entrepreneurs (they could be randomly reassigned), and there are no capitalists, in that capital is owned by the workers and competition eliminates all profit (above the rate of return on capital). In this setting, Walras is preoccupied with the existence of equilibrium in a pure idealised system: will there exist a set of (relative) prices that will simultaneously equate all demands and supplies? Unlike Jevons, Walras was not a utilitarian and utilities were introduced at the end to bolster the model.

Menger is also considered one of the pioneers of the marginal revolution, reaching the same conclusions with regard to the principle of marginal utility, and is an exceptional example of a supporter of the abstract and individualistic methodology, while, at the same time, opposing the use of mathematics. He played a major role in the 'methods fight' against the German historical school.[2]

The marginalist revolution laid the foundations for economics as scientific, based upon the principles of methodological individualism, equilibrium, and marginal analysis, appropriate for mathematical expression and reasoning. Nonetheless, the latter was not adopted immediately, and the full potential of the mathematisation of economics was completed about 70–80 years later, with the take-off of what has been termed the formalist revolution (beginning in the 1950s) and the full dominance of a hegemonic paradigm in which mathematics have become the essence of economics.

From pluralism to Arrow and Debreu

The end of the nineteenth and the first half of the twentieth centuries saw the rise of large corporations, trade unions and labour laws, collective movements and technological dynamism, as well as the ideology of socialism. The First World War and the Bolshevik Revolution transformed the role of the state, giving way to unparalleled degrees of central planning and state control and a retreat from free markets. A further blow to the free-market ideal resulted from the 1929 crash and the ensuing Great Depression. The real economy seemed far removed from well-functioning markets and harmonious equilibria among asocial individuals.

Intellectually, the first part of the twentieth century can be thought as a period of pluralism. Concurrent to the processes of establishing the marginalist (Neoclassical) principles and methods, other approaches to economics prevailed. The Old (American) Institutionalism and historical schools (especially in Germany) were grounded on empirical and inductive methods and focused on broader societal issues, such as monopolisation, distribution, and labour relations instead of a main preoccupation with efficient resource allocation. And there was opposition to the mathematisation of marginalist economics from within the Neoclassical field as well. Marshall was leading this process, particularly in Britain, with the influence of his *magnum opus* (*Principles in Economics*, 1890) in setting the basis of Neoclassical economics. For, albeit a mathematician as well as a Neoclassical economist, he confined the mathematical expression to the appendices of his work, while opting for verbal discourse and diagrammatic exposition in the main text.

In the wake of the Great Depression, Keynes's General Theory (1936) came to offer both a response to the phenomenon of massive unemployment and an attack on the prevailing marginalist theories that were unable to address, let alone account for it. Keynes will be discussed in the section 'Contrasting the Mainstream Approach to Smith, Ricardo, Marx and Keynes', but it is worth noting here that he offered a distinct focus and methodology by adopting a more inductive reasoning and viewing the economy as a holistic entity that could not be decomposed into, nor derived from, its individual constituent parts (Fine and Dimakou, 2016, ch. 1).

Despite the pluralism of that period, the critique of Neoclassical principles and the establishment of macroeconomics as distinct from microeconomics led by Keynes, a rediscovery of Walras's general equilibrium theory by some mathematicians in Vienna promoted the resurgence of the mathematisation of scientific economics at the beginning of the 1930s. This was part of the broader development in the natural sciences, with the separation of mathematics (especially from physics) under Hilbert's programme (1918), which sought to re-establish mathematics on an axiomatic and logical basis with a life of its own. The work of this group, which included Karl Menger, von Neumann, Wald, and Morgenstern, was mostly concerned with pure mathematical technique, rather than its application to economic problems. For this purpose, the problem of the existence of Walras's general equilibrium was a good starting point. Besides mathematicians, some economists also took interest in the problems of general equilibrium (Hotelling and Hicks for example).

The formal mathematisation process was further enhanced with the establishment of two institutions, namely the Econometric Society (in 1930) and the Cowles Commission (in 1932), marking the second programmatic proclamation, now on the other side of the Atlantic, for the reformulation of economics on a mathematical basis. These institutions included researchers, such as Frisch, Fisher, Hotelling, Tinbergen, Koopmans, Arrow, Debreu, and many others from the Vienna Circle, who had migrated to the US in the ascent of Nazism. The proclamation of the Econometric Society is telling in setting the aim for economics, particularly in opposition to American Institutionalism (and its empirical approach):

> ... as an international society for the advance of economic theory in its relation to statistics and mathematics ... The main object ... would be to promote studies that aim at a unification between the theoretical-quantitative and the empirical-quantitative approach to economic problems... penetrated by a constructive and rigorous way of thinking similar to that which has come to dominate in the natural sciences. (Proclamation of the Econometric Society, 1930)

Developments during the 1940s sustained the ongoing process of the mathematical formalisation of economics, as well as systematic data collection and statistical analysis. The involvement of economists, amongst other scientists, in the war effort led to the development of new mathematical techniques, not least as part of the planning for resources shift from civilian to military production, as well as for analysing intelligence and military strategies, bringing economics closer to operational research and engineering. The militarisation of economics further enhanced the systematic collection of data, leading to the first step towards the systems of national accounts. The Cowles Commission, after having moved to Chicago, turned its focus on new methods of statistical analysis. The economic system is portrayed as a probability distribution. General equilibrium theory, as a system of simultaneous equations derived from individualistic optimisation, provided the theoretical basis for the development of statistical techniques (simultaneous equation estimation, 2SLS, etc.) to test the theory with data. And in the late 1940s, the focus for such research shifts to the RAND Corporation,[3] which produced work on systems analysis, as well as game theory, a body of mathematical analysis centred on problems of rational choice.

The *Theory of Games and Economic Behaviour* (1944) by von Neumann and Morgenstern reflects the epitome of the axiomatic mathematics of this time (Backhouse, 2002). Samuelson's *Foundations of Economic Analysis* (1947) was also published, marking the end of the Marshallian tradition in economics. However, and unlike the work of von Neumann and Morgenstern, Samuelson's foremost mathematical influence came from the previous century's physics (thermodynamics), thus 'representing a step back in the direction of the physics envy of the nineteenth century' (Milonakis, 2017, p. 1382). The mathematics of constrained optimisation that Samuelson introduced attained a central role in the discipline for decades to come.

Undoubtedly, the climax of the formalist revolution came with the proof of existence of general equilibrium by Arrow and Debreu (1954), employing Brouwer's fixed-point theorem from topology (first used by von Neumann[4]). At the peak of economics' formalist upheaval: 'general equilibrium theory had ceased to make any descriptive claim about actual economic systems and had become a purely formal apparatus about a quasi economy' (Blaug, 1998, p. 14). Yet, this was precisely the goal of the formalisation of economics, rather than perceived to be a weakness. Indeed, for Debreu (who was a member of the Bourbaki group[5]):

> An axiomatized theory first selects its primitive concepts and represents each one of them by a mathematical object ... Next assumptions on the objects representing the primitive concepts are specified, and consequences are mathematically derived from them. The economic interpretation of the theorems so obtained is the last step of the analysis. According to the schema, an axiomatized theory has a mathematical form that is completely separated from its economic content. If one removes the economic interpretation of the primitive concepts, of the assumptions ... its bare mathematical structure must still stand. (Debreu, 1986, p. 1265)

The description of the economy by Debreu (1959) (see Box 3.1), for instance, attests to what Blaug (2003) describes as the *absolute* preference for the form of an economic argument or concept over its content, and hence substance.

Box 3.1: Debreu's description of the economy

A complete description of an *economy E* is now possible; it consists of:

> For each consumer, his consumption set X_i and his preference pre-ordering $\prec i$.
> For each producer, his production set Y_i.
> The total resources ω.

A *state* of the economy *E* is a specification of the action of each agent, i.e., for each consumer (resp. producer) a specification of his consumption x_i (resp. production y_i) in the commodity space. Thus a state of *E* is an $(m + n)$-tuple $((x_i), (y_i))$ of points of R^l. It can be represented by a point of $R^{l(m+n)}$. Formally:

> *An economy E is defined by: for each i = 1, ..., m a non-empty subset X_i of R^l completely preordered by $\prec i$; for each j = 1, ..., n a non-empty subset Y_j of R^l1; a point ω of R^l.*
> *A state of E is an (m + n)-tuple of points of R^l.* Debreu (1959, p. 75)

During the post-war boom, Keynesian macroeconomics, on the one hand, and (formalist Neoclassical) microeconomics, on the other, evolved separately, allowing for the coexistence of continuing methodological and contextual dissonances, while also reflecting a schizophrenic representation in teaching. Nonetheless, the consolidation of the Keynesian revolution to general equilibrium microeconomics was only a matter of time with the demise of Keynesianism from the early 1970s onwards.

With the rise of monetarism and New Classical economics in the 1970s, the mathematisation of economics, in both teaching and research, was rendered more systematic. Macroeconomics was consolidated around general equilibrium microeconomics, with added theoretical elements, notably rational expectations. Rational expectations are individualist, model-consistent and based on the notion of the future as calculable risk. In the 1980s, Real Business Cycle (RBC) theory took macroeconomics to further extremes with the 'collapse' of macro on micro and the short onto the long run. Formalisation was further enhanced and the research programme became more quantitative and more specific, if not narrow. The ultimate goal of (macro)economics transformed to 'fit stylised facts' (that is, the observed statistical properties of macroeconomic aggregates). And in the consensus that materialised after the 1990s, whereby the RBC paradigm is tweaked by the addition of a couple of new Keynesian (market imperfections) elements, this agenda was reinforced. Macroeconomics came to be analysed under the rubric of the dynamic stochastic general equilibrium (DSGE) paradigm. The latter is an umbrella of mathematical models that command full convergence on general equilibrium from micro-foundations and principles in a 'dynamic' context, in which the *homo economicus* maximises utility not only within a given period, but also intertemporally, over time. The long-run equilibrium is static in essence (albeit movable by stochastic disturbances), while the short-run fluctuations come about as a result of optimal responses to exogenous stochastic shocks. In a sense, the DSGE framework can be viewed as an extension of the general equilibrium of the 1950s, yet remaining static in nature, with the dynamics of the equilibrium unaddressed (Fine and Dimakou, 2016, ch. 1). In parallel with developments in scholarship, advanced mathematical and quantitative techniques became core to the teaching of economics, especially at higher levels, including dynamic programming (both as a mathematical optimisation and a computing method) as well as analysis of recursive models and stochastic processes.

Contrasting the mainstream approach to Smith, Ricardo, Marx, and Keynes

Contrary to general belief, mathematical formalism is not the only way to conduct economic theorising. There is a long tradition from different schools of thought and economists that attests to this. In what follows, we present briefly the approaches of the classical political economists, Smith and Ricardo, Marx and Keynes.

Smith

Smith is considered the pioneer of Classical Political Economy. All classical writers were writing at a time when political economy was not distinct from the other social sciences and, consequently, the subject of political economy could not be considered in isolation from social, sociological, political, historical, and psychological dimensions. Classical writers would navigate with ease between the economic and the non-economic, historical narrative and theoretical discourse, and would incorporate social and other dimensions in their argumentations. This understanding of political economy (that is, of economics as a social science, and not narrowly as the science of the economy) is also reflected in the methods of analysis undertaken, albeit with different emphases (Milonakis and Fine, 2009).

Smith's approach to economic theorising can be seen as pluralist, if not, at the same time, eclectic. It has been recognised that he has made extensive use of both deductive and inductive methods and in his discourse, the historical, theoretical, philosophical and social were intergraded. "There is scarcely a page of *The Wealth of Nations* where history and theory are sundered apart' (Milonakis and Fine, 2009, p. 19). His combined work is a broader inquiry into the science of society. And this is pursued with a combination of distinct angles in a multidisciplinary frame, evident, for instance, across the macro-dynamic theory of economic development and the micro-theory of market exchange, as well as the individualistic (theory of market exchange) and holistic (distribution of product) modes of reasoning, and the deductive and the inductive methods. Smith's use of the abstract/deductive method was done, without however using mathematics and without being axiomatic, rather rooted in the empirical sphere. At the same time, he also made use of empirical and historical records for illustrative purposes.[6]

For example, in arguing his thesis of the division of labour, Smith (*The Wealth of Nations*, p. 10) provides his observations of a visit to a pin-making factory:

> One man draws out the wire, another straights it, a third cuts it, a fourth...; to make the head requires two or three distinct operations; to put it on is a peculiar business, to whiten the pins is another; it is even a trade by itself to put them into the paper; and the important business of making a pin is, in this manner, divided into about eighteen distinct operations.... [An average factory of ten workers] could make among them upwards of forty-eight thousand pins in a day. Each person, therefore...might be considered as making four thousand eight hundred pins in a day. But if they had all wrought separately and independently, and without any of them having been educated to this peculiar business, they certainly could not each of them have made twenty, perhaps not one pin in a day.

Ricardo

Ricardo, on the other hand, while he is acknowledged as both continuing and advancing the political economy of Smith, provided the first methodological schism, elevating the abstract/deductive method in economics, while maintaining commitment to a holistic, class-based approach. Although rooted in the realities of his time, Ricardo's main work is mostly devoid of any historical or empirical references, and excessively supported by abstraction and hypothetical examples that allowed, through the deductive method, to derive his conclusions. One celebrated such numerical example is the hypothetical trade setting for showing that Portugal has absolute (but not comparative) advantage in the production of both wine and cloth relative to England. Schumpeter has termed this tendency of applying results from simplified, hypothetical models, themselves derived from restrictive assumptions, to the solution of practical problems the 'Ricardian Vice' (Milonakis and Fine, 2009).

Marx

Marx is seen as drawing on the more holistic and abstract aspects of the methods of Smith and Ricardo, together with a radical reconstitution of the theory of value. In opposition, Marginalism can be understood as offspring of the individualistic aspects of Smith, and the deductivism of Ricardo (as well the individualistic utilitarianism of Bentham), with an aim of breaking away from classical political economy.

The explicitly stated aim of Marx's work can be seen from the much-quoted: 'The philosophers have only interpreted the world, in various ways; the point, however, *is to change it*' (cited in Milonakis and Fine, 2009, p. 33). In pursuit of this goal, Marx's main contribution is to explain the workings of the capitalist system and its laws of motion. Marx's approach and method is built of three edifices: classical political economy, German philosophy, and French utopian socialism. As a continuation from the first, Marx takes the labour theory of value and the collectivist mode of reasoning, and extends and redevelops Ricardo's abstract method. The second brings in Hegelian dialectics and Feuerbach's materialism, while the last influence reflects his emphasis on social justice and alternative forms of collectivist ownership. Given the rich roots of Marx's theorising and methodology, we cannot place his method along the usual inductive vs deductive division. This may well be the reason why Marxist thought and method has inspired research frameworks in many fields, e.g. art history, cultural studies, philosophy, historiography, and all the social sciences (minus economics!).

Marx makes use of the method of dialectics, applied not only in the formation and process of ideas, as in Hegel, but in the whole world. That is, the natural, historical, and intellectual world is represented as a process, in continuous movement, change, and transformation, by means of contradiction among tendencies and counter-tendencies. Thus, his method is materialist dialectics, and is sought to show how through the process of thesis-antithesis-synthesis the true essence of the world can be revealed (Milonakis and Fine, 2009).

Marx (Marx, *Poverty of Philosophy*, cited in Pilling, 1980) criticises the 'ahistorical' perception of the theoretical constructs of Classical political economy (of both Smith and Ricardo), in the sense of the immediacy and universality imposed to economic laws (in treated as natural ones) and its categories.

> Economists express the relations of bourgeois production, the division of labour, credit, money, etc. as fixed immutable, eternal categories ... Economists explain how production takes place in the above mentioned relations, but what they do not explain is ***how these relations themselves are produced***, that is the historical movement that gave them birth ... these categories are as little eternal as the relations they express. They are historical and transitory products.

He is also critical of the empiricism in their work. Marx starts from the premise that the emergence and development of the various concepts and relations at the core of a particular epoch need to be traced and explained. As such, he embraces abstraction, as an important technique of inquiry, but such abstraction derives from real and concrete materials, corresponding with reality, rather than 'pure' or formal generalisations which are later appended to empirical regularities.

Marx starts with the 'simplest social form', the commodity, and slowly develops all the economic categories, and how these *grow*, to then approach reality on a lower level of abstraction (Pilling, 1980). He does so following a holistic, organistic, and dynamic approach, hence rejecting both individualistic ahistorical analysis, as well as equilibrium as an organising concept. Marx's method is based on an organistic approach, which implies that society is viewed as a system of internally related entities, not only to one another but to the social whole (itself consisting of structures, practices, institutions, etc.). Such relations are developing and give rise to the basic economic concepts. For example, the word "'Dynamic' for Marx has a quite different meaning than in mainstream (Neoclassical) economics. It is not simply the passage of logical time or a moving equilibrium. Rather it means historical coming into being, while continuously changing and developing.

His (materialist) dialectical logic contrasts formal logic, not least in exposing its limitations. For example, with regard to the principle of contradiction (that a statement cannot be true and false at the same time), formal logic is there to make sure that such fallacies are excluded. In contrast, dialectical logic aims to express and understand contradictions, as these reflect the development of reality, rather than eliminate them (Pilling, 1980). Concepts are meant to be fluid and continuously changing and abstractions, as well, cannot be fixed. In as much as the mathematical deductive approach to economics is based on formal logic and fixed categories (themselves derived from formal, as opposed to real, abstraction), then mathematical techniques are not appropriate to capture Marx's structure and method. Having said that, Marxian economics can (and have) been rendered compatible with mathematics in Analytical Marxism, which also abides with the principle of rational choice.

Keynes

For Keynes, mathematics and equilibrium were of little significance. His approach to mathematics and statistics/ econometrics, and his broad theoretical ideas, relate to his philosophical positions with regards to the (economic and social) world and the arguments one can draw about it, as well as to his view on the objective of economic analysis, which

> is, not to provide a machine, or a method of blind manipulation, which will furnish an infallible answer, but to provide ourselves with an organised and orderly method of thinking out particular problems ... It is a great fault of symbolic pseudo-mathematical methods of formalising a system of economic analysis ... that they expressly assume strict independence between the factors involved and lose all their cogency and authority if this hypothesis is disallowed ... Too large a proportion of recent 'mathematical' economics are merely concoctions, as imprecise as the initial assumptions they rest on, which allow the author to lose sight of the complexities and interdependencies of the real world in a maze of pretentious and unhelpful symbols. (Keynes, 1936, pp. 297–298)

In other words, Keynes saw economics theorising as 'purpose-built', rather than 'pure' (Walrasian) theory, while, at the same time, he was critical of both the illegitimate application of mathematical analysis and the elevation of the latter as the greatest form of economic reasoning (O'Donnell, 1990).

Keynes's theoretical innovations are well-recognised, what is less so, is their philosophical underpinnings. In short, Keynes started his *General Theory* (GT) from the premise that the whole need not be the sum of its constituent parts, that is, the behaviour of parts could be constrained by overall relationships and the whole could have a separate life of its own (Harcourt, 1992). Thus, his macroeconomic relations are not grounded on optimising individualistic behaviour and his holistic and organistic method shares more with Classical political economists, as well as historical schools, than the Neoclassical economics he sought to attack. Equally important, his theories of probability, expectations and, more broadly, the future are concerned with fundamental uncertainty, as opposed to calculable risk. Keynes (J. M. Keynes, *Collected Writings* 1973 XIV 112 and 122) was amongst the first to consider non-numerical probabilities seriously and contend that these were the major type of probabilities in real life:

> The calculus of probability ... was supposed to be capable of reducing uncertainty to the same calculable status as that of certainty itself ... This false rationalisation follows the lines of the Benthamite calculus. The hypothesis of a calculable future leads to a wrong interpretation of the principles of behaviour which the need for action compels us to adopt.

In other words, if the economy is a historical process heading for an uncertain future, optimising behaviour is irrelevant, expectations, undoubtedly of great significance, are neither individualistic nor rational. Rather, they reflect collective beliefs, conventions and rules of thumb. Consequently, mathematical tools and models that reflect these measurable individualistic optimising behaviours (concerning either the present or the future) are of little use.

Keynes's thought can be illuminated by his interest in philosophy and the evolution in his own methodological understanding, especially while drafting the GT (Milonakis and Fine, 2009). Apart from the influence of his father and Marshall, Keynes benefited from the circle of Cambridge philosophers (B. Russell, G. E. Moore, L. Wittgenstein, P. Sraffa, F. Ramsey). Keynes's philosophical development brought a substantial change in his thinking during the 1930s, particularly with the gradual rejection and moving away from Russell's analytic philosophy (and its atomistic and deductive methodology), allying more with Moore's common-sense philosophy and Wittgenstein. In doing so, Keynes raises reservations on the ability of reductive symbolic analyses to gain in precision (relative to everyday language) and the possibility of reducing complex entities to the level of simples. At the same time, he embraces the notion of vagueness of concepts as a means of reflecting the ambiguities and uncertainties of life. This view reflects both his scepticism towards the applicability of mathematics and econometrics in economics, his disbelief in fixed meanings, and spatial and temporal homogeneity, and his recurring reference on the vagueness of economic concepts (in the GT) and fundamental uncertainty. The simplification and precision that mathematics require, for example, may end up leaving concepts empty of meaning. And for him 'those writers who try to be strictly formal generally have no substance', while 'in writing economics one is not writing either a mathematical proof or a legal document' (cited in Milonakis and Fine, 2009, p. 277).

In his discourse, Keynes employs verbal argumentation drawing from both common and abstract concepts, induction and empirical evidence, facts of experience and common-sense logic. He also uses mathematical expressions (and diagrams), for clarification, without, however, allowing for mathematics to become the 'master', neither to substitute for substance nor to represent precise numerical magnitudes. For mathematical reasoning is useful in its symbolic, rather than its numerical, character (as cited in O'Donnell, 1990, p. 43, from Keynes's 1932 draft);

> This [equation for liquidity preference], and the preceding equations, are symbolic, not objective equations, since ρ etc. stand for a complex of numbers and are not themselves numbers.

In that sense, the GT draws from his philosophical concerns and his view of the economy as an organic unity of interdependencies. As such, it can be seen as open-system theorising with important implications for policy recommendations (Chick and Dow, 2005). This openness can be seen to have many dimensions, as in non-economic factors, the interplay between micro and macro, and the treatment of time, while at the same time it is absent from the models being developed within mainstream economics, which are based on closed systems with the aim of providing an equilibrium solution while satisfying internal consistency. In doing so (Keynes, 1936, p. 3):

> The characteristics of ... the [neo]classical theory happen not to be those of the economic society in which we actually live, with the result that its teaching is misleading and disastrous if we attempt to apply it to the facts of experience.

Concluding remarks: consolidating mathematics in economics and its implications

The mathematisation process has had long-lasting implications for the nature of economics, and the emergence of the mainstream as the dominant school of economic thought, including through the paradox of its narrowed scope but wider applicability (see Chapter 16). In what follows we discuss those implications, while bringing to the fore various criticisms that have been made in relation to the dominance of mathematical deduction in economic analysis.

First, economics has become more technical and deductive, while the orthodoxy of the discipline is hostile to any other form or method of investigation, setting the standards for the validity of economic research solely when conducted following the formal mathematical deduction method. Rigorous theory is to be thought of, and taught, in the form of models. Economic theory becomes synonymous to model-building: start with a set of assumptions, regarding primitive concepts and individual behaviours, more or less based on marginalist principles, and use logical mathematical reasoning to derive outcomes. Any other form of inquiry is excluded as 'unscientific', together with any factors (economic and non-economic) that are not amenable in mathematical form.

Second, is the disassociation, or eclectic association, between formal theory and evidence, together with a distinctive approach toward empirical verification. The deductive theoretical model should be 'confronted with the data' in predominantly ex-post ways. Evidence is to be understood as data gathering and data analysis. This captures both the way observation proceeds (mainly in terms of quantifiable measures), and the way it is related to theory, employing some form of falsification test. This echoes the influence of Friedman's (1953) work on the methodology of positive economics, whereby the model is simply a tool in the service of producing testable hypotheses. The realism of assumptions, as mere instruments, does not matter. Rather it is the predictions of the model that are relevant for ex-post testing and empirical refutation. Put it simply in the well-known dictum of Friedman 'Truly important and significant hypotheses will be found to have "assumptions" that are wildly inaccurate descriptive representations of reality, and, in general, the more significant the theory, the more unrealistic the assumptions (in this sense)' (Friedman, 1953, p. 14).

Those two central implications form the basis for the fundamental criticisms of the mathematisation of economics, relating to the realism of assumptions and individual behaviour/motives, as well as its association to, and hence relevance for, real-world problems.

Mathematical model-building since 1950s has been increasingly not only unable but also uninterested in representing reality, becoming preoccupied with its own internal needs and questions. Internal (mathematical) consistency takes precedence over external consistency. Indicative, if not unique, in this respect is Arrow and

Debreu's proof of existence of general equilibrium, for both what it entails and what it excludes; what it asks and what it does not. The proof was attained under the strictest of assumptions, such as no increasing returns to scale, a high degree of gross substitutability across all goods and services, existence of forward markets for all goods and services, etc. Nonetheless, with absolute preference of form dominating content, the tractability of an elegant solution overshadows the realism of the conditions necessary to guarantee its existence. What is more, the two further internal problems of this endeavour, namely that of uniqueness and stability of the discovered general equilibrium have been tackled with limited success. Particularly for the latter, the analysis ignores how the equilibrium may come about in historical time. Nonetheless, the proof of existence ranks as the highest of the economic scientific method, because of its rigour (mathematical form and reasoning), rather than the empirical validity of its premises or usefulness of its application in reality. Preoccupation with the above quest (under what conditions (if any) does there exist a solution (a relative price vector) that simultaneously clears all markets?) goes hand in hand with a lack of preoccupation of how both the question, and its answer, relate to real economic systems and processes.

Besides the strain of mathematical formalism on realism, the increasingly narrow method that elevated economics to its alleged 'scientific' status, also distinguished it from other social sciences and led to the narrowing of its subject matter and substantive content, while at the same time increasing its universal applicability (see also Chapter 16). However, the narrowing of the discipline's subject matter is not exclusively a consequence of the mathematical-deductive approach. For while there is nothing wrong with mathematics per se, which can indeed clarify exposition and mechanisms, there are limits to what can be analysed through mathematical models. This applies equally to concepts, analytical categorisations, and relationships between concepts. The mathematical formalisation of mainstream economics requires social phenomena and concepts to be reduced to fit a rigid theoretical premise, which imposes concrete, universal and measurable definitions. Furthermore, there is an innate difficulty in modelling systemic factors, social motives, class interests, and processes, without stripping these down and narrowing their original intended content or meaning. In contrast, Keynes embraced the 'vagueness' of concepts, not as an inability of precise measurement, but as a means of incorporating the uncertainties of economic life and the changing meanings of concepts across time, space, and context. And Marx rejected the universal nature of concepts and relations, seeking to introduce them as historically determined, emerging from the social relations of the mode of production.

A further critique pertains to the trans-historical and universal premise of mainstream economics and its representation through mathematical models. Mathematical functions entail a universality and stability of relationships that are unlikely to be found in social phenomena and relations that take place in open systems, characterised by systemic processes and social change. However, with the theoretical premise of social phenomena being solely derived from the individual's optimising behaviour, it becomes sensible to analyse them through mathematical representations. For the formalist revolution, the commitment to a particular form of mathematical modelling implies a particular form of theoretical and conceptual content (Lawson, 2015).

In relation to the widening of positive instrumentalism, the basis of testing theoretical predictions empirically (through estimation and hypothesis testing) is problematic in many accounts. First, it presumes that evidence (data) is theory-free. However this is not correct, as evidence is not collected in a theoretical vacuum. Measurement constructs are derived on the basis of (explicit or implicit) analytical categories. For example, what does or does not count as GDP? Why are non-marketed goods excluded? How are indices of corruption or trust (or happiness, or pain) quantified and constructed? Beyond measurement problems and despite advances in econometrics, statistical methods applied to reveal the properties of, for instance, macroeconomic data, are also contingent upon the theories that demand them to be studied in that way. For example, starting from the premise that the evolution of, say, GDP over time can be decomposed into a long-run, secular trend and a cyclical component, how do we extract the trend from the cyclical variation? Both the need and the way to do so depends on the presumed theoretical distinction between the short and the long run, and their relation. Simply put, data are neither natural nor objective nor exogenously given. This point also relates to the positive versus normative separation within 'pure' economics. Second, at a more fundamental level, this positivist empiricism that mainstream economics elevated to the fore, shares some link to Ricardo's approach and to Marx's criticism to it (see the section 'Contrasting the Mainstream Approach to Smith, Ricardo, Marx, and Keynes'). Using and judging a theory (model), and its predictions, on how well it matches 'appearances' (what we nowadays call 'stylised facts') implies focus on predictive strength, rather than preoccupation with the discovery of the true social relations underpinning those appearances (Fine, 1980).

Nonetheless, this approach to economic analysis is taken to the extreme with the rise of New Classical economics, RBC theory and DSGE modelling, as evidenced in the section 'How Did Economics Become so Mathematical?'. Much, if not all, of the criticisms discussed above were heavily exposed by the Global Financial Crisis (GFC) in 2007/08, which highlighted the inadequacies of the dominant paradigm. Indeed, the DSGE models had nothing to say about the possibility, let alone the likelihood or implications of the crisis. The reason why the New Consensus Macroeconomics (NCM) was unable to answer questions in relation to the financial crisis is straightforward. By construction, the New Keynesian DSGE models precluded the possibility of bankruptcy, solvency, and even liquidity problems. The financial sector was assumed to play a passive intermediation role, and macroeconomic stability was assumed to be simply a by-product of inflation stability (the so-called divine coincidence). The assumptions of NCM precluded the posing of many, if not all, of the relevant questions the crisis brought to the fore. Put more generally, the concepts and methods that have been adopted in mainstream economics are instrumental to both the implications and the conclusions of their economic theory, and to the scope and nature of the recommendations that can be derived from such an approach. Or, as the well-known quote by P. Krugman puts it: 'The economics profession went astray because economists, as a group, mistook beauty, clad in impressive-looking mathematics, for truth...' (Krugman, 2009).

Nonetheless, and despite some critical reflections within the academic profession in response to the 'crisis in the discipline', a closer examination only shows at best a mild reconsideration in response to the GFC, with the attempted inclusion of some of the realities previously ignored, notably a financial sector, or inequalities and real rigidities, as add-ons in otherwise unchanged DSGE models. Furthermore, when it comes to the methodological stance, commitment to the mathematical deductive mode of reasoning, even if with added complexity, is never challenged, and the victory of technique over substance prevails. This is still prominent in teaching where mathematical solving receives disproportionate attention relative to substantive understanding, despite dissatisfaction from the student body (not least through *Rethinking Economics*) and partial adjustments to curricula.

Discussion questions and seminar activities

Debate:

Is it possible to be an economist and not understand how to do maths?

Discussion questions:

- Do you agree with Krugman's statement that economics went astray because it mistook maths for truth?
- What are the main limitations of the mathematical approach in economics?

References

Arrow, K. J., & Debreu, G. (1954). Existence of an equilibrium for a competitive economy. *Econometrica, 22*(3), 265–290.

Backhouse, R. (2002). *The Penguin history of economics*. London: Penguin.

Blaug, M. (1998). Disturbing currents in modern economics. *Challenge, 41*(3), 11–34.

Blaug, M. (2003). The formalist revolution of the 1950s. *Journal of the History of Economic Thought, 25*(2), 145–156.

Chick, V., & Dow, S. (2005). The meaning of open systems. *Journal of Economic Methodology, 12*(3), 363–381.

Debreu, G. (1959). *Theory of value: An axiomatic analysis of economic equilibrium*. New York: Wiley.

Debreu, G. (1986). Theoretic models: Mathematical form and economic content. *Econometrica, 54*(6), 1259–1270.

Fine, B. (1980). *Economic theory and ideology*. London: Edward Arnold.

Fine, B., & Dimakou, O. (2016). *Macroeconomics: A critical companion*. London: Pluto Press.

Friedman, M. (1953). *Essays in positive economics*. Chicago/Cambridge: Chicago University Press/Cambridge University Press.

Harcourt, G. C. (1992). On Keynes's method in economic theory. In M. Sebastiani (Ed.), *The notion of equilibrium in the Keynesian theory*. London: Palgrave Macmillan.

Keynes, J. M. (1936). *The general theory of employment, interest and money*. London: Palgrave Macmillan.

Krugman, P. (2009). How did economists get it so wrong? *The New York Times*. www.nytimes.com/2009/09/06/magazine/06Economic-t.html?_r=1&emc=eta1. Last accessed 2 September 2009.

Lawson, T. (2015). *Essays on the nature and state of modern economics*. London: Routledge.

Milonakis, D. (2017). Formalising economics: Social change, values, mechanics and mathematics in economic discourse. *Cambridge Journal of Economics, 41*(5), 1367–1390.

Milonakis, D., & Fine, B. (2009). *From political economy to economics: Method, the social and the historical in the evolution of economic theory*. London: Routledge.

Mirowski, P. (1991). The when, the how and the why of mathematical expression in the history of economic analysis. *Journal of Economic Perspectives, 5*(1), 145–157.

O'Donnell, R. M. (1990). Keynes on mathematics: Philosophical foundations and economic applications. *Cambridge Journal of Economics, 14*(1), 29–47.

Pilling, G. (1980). *Marx's capital: Philosophy and political economy*. London/Boston: Routledge & Kegan Paul.

Screpanti, E., & Zamagni, S. (2005). *An outline of the history of economic thought* (2nd ed.). Oxford: Oxford University Press.

von Neumann, J. (1947). The mathematician. In R. Heywood (Ed.), *Works of the mind*. Chicago: University of Chicago Press.

4 HOW ARE THINGS PRODUCED?

Susan Newman

Introduction

For Adam Smith, the origins of the wealth of nations can be found in the rapid accumulation of capital made possible by the expansion of scale and scope of production based upon its organisation: the division of labour. It is therefore unsurprising that early scholars of the political economy of capitalist development such as Smith, Mill, and Marx were preoccupied with the question of how things are produced. Indeed, both the extent of interest in, as well as the answers to, the following questions set apart different schools of thought within economics: How are things produced? Who decides what, how, and how much is produced? How are these decisions made? What role does production play in the economy?

The rupture in economic thought by the Marginalist revolution and rise of Neoclassical economics in the 1870s saw attention shift away from the processes of production towards exchange on the market. As we will discuss further, ideas such as the social division of labour that pertain to the organisation of production gave way to choice, contract, and exchange as central concepts of economic theory. Students of economics would increasingly see firms represented as a set of cost and revenue curves rather than an organisation. Moreover, the Marginalist revolution saw a revolution in value theory from one anchored in the labour process (where the value of a commodity was created by the labour expended in its manufacture) to value being determined by the subjective judgement of consumers (a good is worth as much as someone is willing to pay for it) (see Chapter 5). This reorientation in economic thought is especially apparent when we look at standard microeconomic textbooks such as *Intermediate Microeconomics* by Varian (2010) where any discussion of how things are produced is preceded by 17 chapters on market exchange and consumer choice theory. When the subject of production is broached, it is discussed within chapters titled 'Technology' (Chapter 18), 'Profit Maximisation' (Chapter 19), 'Cost Minimization' (Chapter 20), 'Cost Curves' (Chapter 21), 'Firm Supply' (Chapter 22), and 'Industry Supply' (Chapter 23). Chapter 32 of Varian (2010), entitled 'Production', contains no actual discussion of the process of production; rather it locates considerations of the level of production within the general equilibrium framework.

In addition to the stark differences between the understanding of production and its role in the economy between Classical political economists and Neoclassical theorists, a number of other theories of the firm and production emerged both as theoretical critiques of existing orthodoxy as well as in response to apparent changes in the organisation of production. At the time of writing *The Wealth of Nations*, the Industrial Revolution in Britain was still very much in its naissance and Smith would have observed the restructuring of production by small enterprises organised as sole proprietorships in the main. It would be another 100 years before the joint stock company began to emerge as a dominant form of industrial enterprise. The concentration of production in this way influenced Marx's analysis of production and the capitalist firm. The dominant presence of the vertically integrated multinational corporations (MNCs) in the organisation of global production formed the context for the contract theory of the firm and later competence theories that will be examined in this chapter. Since the 1990s have seen a new wave in the restructuring of production with the continued dominance of MNCs in the organisation of production and global trade, together with the increased disintegration and outsourcing of productive processes such that the production of a single product can involve numerous (small) firms all over the world. The rise of transnational supply chains sees production stretched across multiple national boundaries. This change has prompted the emergence of a 'new' set of concepts deployed in the understanding of production in the world economy. This chapter will thus examine the internal logic of various theoretical approaches to understanding production as well as how new ideas gained purchase as production itself was being restructured at the level of the global economy.

Neoclassical production theory

The Neoclassical approach to the question of how things are produced has its origins in the work of Marginalist theorists such as Menger, Clark and, later, Wicksell. These theorists developed the idea of a production function (see Equation 4.1) to describe how a firm decides on the quantity of inputs employed and output produced. According to Neoclassical producer theory, only firms (we will return to the question of what constitutes a firm as a distinct institutional form later) produce things and they do so in order to maximise profits. In order to proceed with the approach of methodological individualism, that is, to treat firms as unitary and distinct entities, the dominant view of the firm as a small enterprise organised as a sole proprietorship was formed. Whilst this view arguably reflected the historical context in which the Classical economists were theorising, its main purpose was to allow the unproblematic aggregation of individual firms to the level of an industrial sector and further. In this way, the economy as a whole could be modelled by an aggregate production function that behaved in the same way as the representative firm.

A firm is not able to produce endlessly in its pursuit of profit. It faces a number of constraints. First, it is constrained by market forces that determine the cost of inputs/factors of production and the price it can charge for its output. Second, its decisions are constrained by the behaviour of its competitors. In giving an introductory overview of Neoclassical producer theory, most textbooks set aside these two constraints by appeal to perfect competition. A firm is a price taker in the markets for both inputs and its output. If it chooses to charge a higher price than its competitors it will lose all its sales and if it charges less then it will reduce potential profits. The focus of Neoclassical theory then turns to a third constraint, 'technology'.

The production function

> Nature imposes the constraint that there are certain feasible ways to produce output from inputs: there are only certain kinds of technological choices that are possible. (Varian, 2010, p. 332)

Prevailing 'technology' determines all feasible combinations of inputs and outputs that are defined by a **production set**. The envelope of this set is the production function (see Equation 4.1) which gives the maximum level of output for a given combination of inputs (see Figure 4.1). While the production set is exogenously determined, firms are free to choose from it a particular combination of inputs for a given level of output known as a **technique of production**. Available techniques of production are typically depicted by isoquants. In the same way that contours on a map trace out the coordinates of longitude and latitude of the same elevation, isoquants connect different combinations of inputs (x_1, x_2, ...) that are sufficient to produce a given level of output (y). Figures 4.2a and 4.2b depict what are known as 'well-behaved' isoquants – isoquants that are convex in shape and do not cross at any point.[1] Each point on the isoquant gives a possible production technique for a given level of output, for example, $f(x_1, x_2) = f(z_1, z_2) = y_1$. A much-cited example of 'well-behaved' isoquants are those drawn from the Cobb-Douglas production function given in Equation 4.2 and graphically represented in Figure 4.1.

$$f(x_1, x_2, x_3 \ldots) = y \quad (4.1)$$

where x_i are levels of inputs used and y the level of output produced, over a certain period.

$$f(x_1, x_2) = A x_1^a x_2^b \quad (4.2)$$

where a and b measure the output response to a change in each input and A is the scale of production, it tells us how much output we get if we used one unit of each input, A is also referred to as the technology coefficient as any proportional increase in output for any given level of inputs is attributed to qualitative technological change.

Typically, a and b are chosen such that a + b = 1. In this way, the production function is said to exhibit constant returns to scale (a unit increase across all inputs increases the level of output by the same proportion regardless of the overall level of output) and diminishing returns to a single

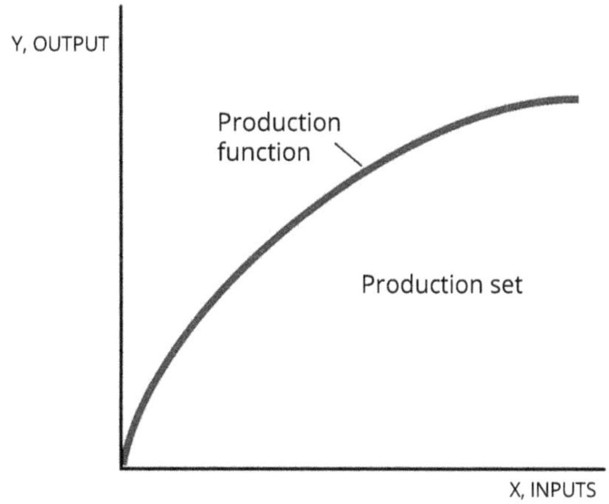

Figure 4.1 The Neoclassical production function

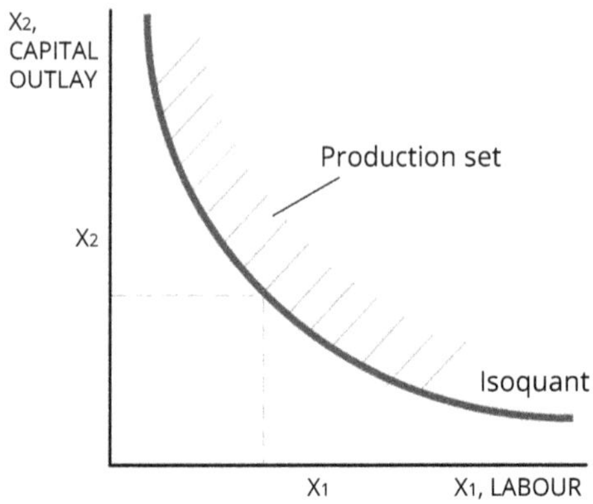

Figure 4.2a Convex isoquant showing the production set available to a producer

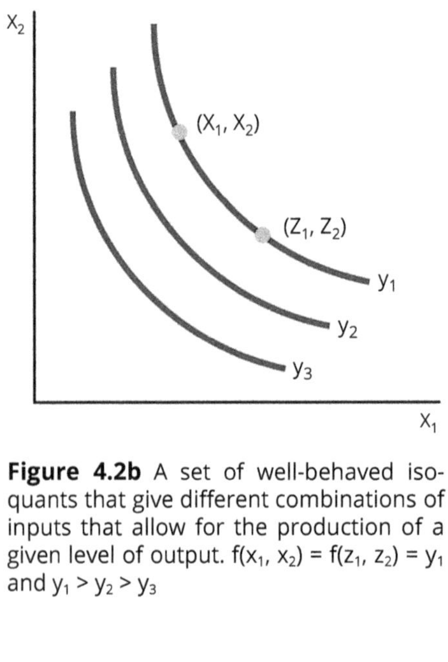

Figure 4.2b A set of well-behaved isoquants that give different combinations of inputs that allow for the production of a given level of output. $f(x_1, x_2) = f(z_1, z_2) = y_1$ and $y_1 > y_2 > y_3$

factor (i, we increase one factor of production whilst keeping the others constant, the increase in output associated with the increase in output will decrease as we increase the level of said input). In the real world, the assumption of constant returns to scale cannot hold in many firms owing to the prevalence of fixed factors and costs. It is generally impossible to reduce production below a minimum level of production that makes a particular technique possible. For example, a firm might be able to reduce two factories to one but it may not be able to reduce one factory to half a factory. In the real world, production processes often exhibit increasing returns to scale and in some cases, decreasing returns. Whilst arguably unrealistic, the assumption of constant return to scale allows for the definition of homothetic production sets – isoquants for different levels of output are simply scale models of each other.

Whilst technology is central to the Neoclassical understanding of production, it is conceived of in a very different way from our general understanding of technology. Within the Neoclassical model, technology or technological change is both narrowly defined as something that brings about quantitative changes in output (productivity-enhancing changes), and also a broad set of changes that goes beyond the development and application of engineering or scientific knowledge. For example, technology here would include the relations between workers and management, relations amongst workers, and the legal and institutional framework within which the firm operates, such as minimum wage legislation, labour law including health and safety and limits to the length of the working day, and the legal recognition/limitation of trade unions and workers' organisation more generally.

Firms choose to produce at a level of output that maximises profits, which is the difference between revenues (price × quantity of output sold) and the cost of producing. Under notional perfect competitive conditions, firms are said to be price takers, which means that maximising profits is analogous to minimising costs. This problem can be expressed mathematically as:

$$\min_{x_1, x_2} w_1 x_1 + w_2 x_2$$

subject to the technical constraint imposed by the production function:

$$f(x_1, x_2) = y$$

where x_1 and x_2 are two factors of production (e.g. labour and capital) and w_1 and w_2 are their price (e.g. wage and interest rates).

This exercise yields a cost function $c(w_1, w_2, y)$ which measures the minimal costs of producing y units of output when factor prices are (w_1, w_2). The average and marginal cost curves for a Cobb-Douglas production function are illustrated in Figure 4.3. The marginal cost refers to the cost of producing one additional unit of output and is given by the first derivative of the cost function ($\partial c/\partial y$). Whilst more complexity can be introduced to the model, for example the removal of the assumption of perfect competition in favour of monopoly or oligopoly market structures, the decision of the firm can be boiled down to the choice of technique and quantity of output associated with minimum costs. This takes the firm miles away from the concept of a dynamic, innovative, risk-taking entrepreneur championed by liberal ideologues.

Value and distribution in neoclassical economics

As discussed further in Chapters 5 and 9, the Marginalist revolution saw the replacement of various labour theories of value espoused by Marx and classical political economy with a subjective theory of value where a commodity is worth as much as individual consumers are willing to pay for it. Thus, the theory of production became oriented around the cost of production. Producers will produce as long as the cost of production is lower than the price that people are willing to pay with buyers and sellers brought together according to the supply and demand schedules of the equilibrium framework. Further, the Marginalist theory of value links the price of goods to their absolute scarcity. Menger applied the logic of Marginalism to the problem of input prices. While final goods are directly valued on the basis of their utility to the final consumer, intermediate inputs are valued on the basis of their usefulness in the

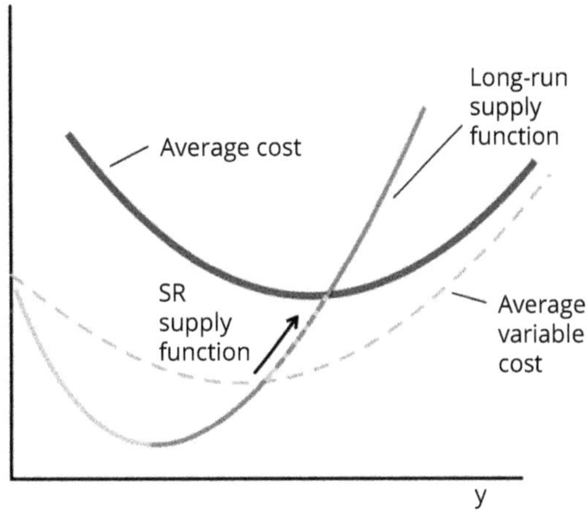

Figure 4.3 Cost and supply curves for a perfectly competitive firm

production of consumable goods. Inputs furthest upstream of the supply chain which are fixed in supply, such as land and labour, are determined on the basis of their scarcity, essentially like rents in Ricardo's theory. When it comes to labour, each individual is understood to have a maximum supply of labour and can choose, on the basis of her/his own preferences, between work and leisure and hence how much labour they will put on the market. Conversely, when an individual chooses leisure they are essentially buying back some of their own labour time at the market equilibrium wage rate. The Marginalist explanation of wage rate determination was provided by Clark (see Chapter 7). In a competitive market economy, labour, along with other inputs, receive a return that is in proportion to their contribution to production: its marginal product. Of course, in reality it is impossible to separate the contribution to production of one input since the absence of one necessary input would reduce output to zero regardless of the application of other inputs. In stark contrast to Marx's theory of value, which is premised upon the exploitation of workers by capitalists, the Marginalist/Neoclassical theory of distribution is free of value judgement. The profit flow to the capitalist simply reflects the marginal product of capital given her/his choice of technique. The firm is simply equating the marginal products of labour and capital to the wage and average profit rate when it chooses the lowest-cost technology. This implies that the wage and profit rate are determined by the scarcity of labour and capital (see Chapter 7 for an elaborate treatment of competing theories of income distribution).

Alternative approaches

Transaction costs/contract theory of the firm

Ronald Coase put forward an alternative theory of the firm in his paper 'The Nature of the Firm', published in 1937, in response to what he considered to be serious limitations in the explanatory power of the Neoclassical theory of producer choice. Coase's main criticisms were that Neoclassical producer theory failed to explain the origins of the firm. Why do firms exist? Why should production be organised in a firm rather than via the market? Why would an entrepreneur hire people rather than contracting people via the market to do the same job? Would one big firm work as well as a market economy in coordinating production and distribution? Coase's answer to these questions was based on his observation that procuring or selling on the market incurs costs over and above the price of the good itself. These 'transaction' costs include search and information costs, bargaining costs, the cost of monitoring and enforcing agreements, and the cost of competitors getting to know trade secrets, and all add up to increase the cost of producing through the market. Thus, entrepreneurs, as cost minimisers, will seek to 'internalise' these costs by directly employing workers and vertically integrating different stages of production when search and information costs, and costs associated with making and enforcing contracts exceed the countervailing costs of operating as a firm. Coase posited that there was an optimal firm size where the benefits from internalising transaction costs are not overcome by efficiency losses associated with increasing overhead costs or the ability of entrepreneurs to make decisions that result in the efficient allocation of resources as the firm gets bigger.[2]

Coase's explanations and predictions for larger firm sizes appeared to be borne out in the reality of the time. Coase was writing at a time when Fordism was in its ascendance. Fordism refers to an organisation of production based on the intricate technical division of labour and the vertical integration of production of standardised products for mass consumption. The term was named after Henry Ford and the first mass-produced automobile, the Model T manufactured by the Ford Motor Company between 1908 and 1927. We will discuss the division of labour when we look at Adam Smith's contribution to theorising production and its role in the economy. Coase was writing in a period when mass production in the US and Western Europe was organised by large integrated MNCs where few, if any, productive or ancillary activities of production were outsourced.

Competence-based theories of the firm

The competence-based approaches[3] to the theory of the firm, most closely associated with the works of Penrose (1959) and Nelson and Winter (1982), emerged out of a critique of Neoclassical economic theory of producer choice as well as the contract theory of the firm developed by Coase which critics saw as a continuation rather than a break from Neoclassical theory owing to its analytical reliance on comparative statics, methodological individualism, and a continued focus on exchange rather than the processes of production itself. These ideas found popularity in Industrial Organisation and Strategic Management Studies in the 1970s and 1980s and we are more likely to find them explained in the standard textbooks for these fields rather than within economics. However, proponents of the approach claim intellectual heritage in the work of Adam Smith, namely the idea that dynamic growth and development takes place with productivity enhancements that come out of the process of learning-by-doing (also known as dynamic economies of scale) made possible by the division of labour. We will resume, and develop, our discussion of Smith's analysis of production in the next section. Here we will outline some of the key concepts of the competence-based and evolutionary approaches of the firm and how they approach the questions of why and how production is organised within a modern capitalist society.

Whilst many proponents of competence and evolutionary approaches accept that the existence of the firm solves the problems associated with transaction costs, this in and of itself is insufficient as an explanation of the integrity, cohesiveness and endurance of the firm. One might expect that, as legal and information systems become more developed and trustworthy, it would become cheaper for the firm to externalise (outsource) an increasing number of production-related activities. This is indeed what we have seen since the 1990s as multinationals have increasingly refocused their activities on so called 'core competences' and outsourced much of their production and ancillary activities. This will be discussed further in this chapter in the section on global value chains. Competence theorists also argue against the notion of a representative firm and emphasise the heterogeneity across firms in terms of their size, ownership and organisational structures.

From the perspective of the competence approach, firms exist as repositories of skills and tacit knowledge gained through organisational learning. Whilst Adam Smith arguably focused the improvement of manual dexterity associated with specialisation afforded by the technical division of labour, competence-based theorists stress the centrality of knowledge itself and the non-material and unexchangeable factors that enhance productivity and the productive potential of a nation. The nineteenth-century economist List argued that 'the productive powers of a nation are greater than the sum of the productive powers of the individuals within it, considered in isolation, because of the productive benefits provided by the national infrastructure and culture' (Hodgson, 1998, p. 40). The competence-based theory of the firm applies this thesis to organisations. Subsequent theorists, Knight and then later Penrose, emphasised the role of knowledge in their theories of the firm in relation to the pervasiveness of uncertainty and how knowledge is intimately tied to the internal organisation of the firm. Knight (1921, pp. 268–269) argues that '[w]hen uncertainty is present the task of deciding what to do and how to do it takes ascendancy over that of execution, the internal organization of the productive groups is no longer a matter of indifference or a mechanical detail. Centralization of this deciding and controlling function is imperative, a process of "cephalization", such as has taken place in the evolution of organic life, is inevitable, and for the same reasons as in biological evolution.' The competences that both shape and are thus born out of the evolution of the organisation of a firm in response to its wider economic environment, cannot be given a market value. This reason, rather than transaction costs, explains the existence, integrity, cohesiveness, and endurance of the firm, as well as heterogeneity amongst firms.

Penrose echoes the role that a firm's organisation plays in responding to uncertainty, and stresses the tacit and elusive nature of knowledge and skills. There is much knowledge that cannot be codified and transmitted via manuals or formally taught. Rather, it results from learning through personal experience. '[E]xperience itself can never be transmitted; it produces a change – frequently a subtle change – in individuals and cannot be separated from them.' It 'shows itself in two ways – changes in knowledge acquired and changes in the ability to use knowledge' (Penrose, 1959, p. 53). This is in stark contrast to Neoclassical economics, where knowledge is treated as capital that can be given a monetary value and exchanged as well as accumulated.

Just as Coase's ideas were developed in relation to the economic reality of the day, competence theories of the firm have become increasingly influential as production has been restructured on a global scale over since the 1990s as multinational firms have been reducing their capital stock and productive capacities whilst outsourcing production as well as ancillary activities to supplier firms operating on principles of 'just-in-time' where production responds rapidly to changing market demands. There is also growing interest in technology and knowledge in shaping competitive advantages of firms in an increasingly competitive global environment. This will be discussed further in the final section on global value chains.

Smith – the division of labour as the source of the wealth of nations

Aspects of Smith's conceptualisation of production, its organisation and role in economic and social life, have informed each of the approaches covered in this chapter. For example, Neoclassical producer theory places emphasis on exchange and the role of the market, which Smith understood as critical to economic dynamism. His views on the role of knowledge and technology also provided the starting point for competence-based models of the firm. We will see in the next sections that Marx was also heavily influenced by Smith and developed his theories through critical engagement with Smith's ideas. In addition, Smith highlighted the geographical organisation of production that lies at the centre of global value chain, global commodity chain, and global production network analysis.

Smith was interested in the origin of 'the wealth of nations': How do countries get rich? How are surpluses generated so that they can be used to expand wealth and the material well-being of the population? His answer lay in the division of labour and the productivity gains that accrue from this. Using his famous example of the pin factory, Smith illustrated how production could be divided into specialised tasks – what he called the 'detail division of labour'. Smith identified three ways in which this would increase productivity: first, workers specialising in a single task would develop increased dexterity through learning-by-doing; second, a reduction in time lost from passing from one task to another; and, third, through the invention of machinery specialised to particular tasks. Smith saw the division of labour not only limited to within the factory walls but as a process by which different aspects of complex production processes can be separated into different production points across different firms and even different geographical locations – this he called the social division of labour. In this way, he anticipates the rise of transnational supply chains centuries later.

In contrast to Neoclassical economics, in Smith's account, technology and innovation are endogenous to the division of labour. Moreover, Smith presented a dynamic theory of capitalist accumulation illustrated in Figure 4.4. The division of labour is both determined by and supports the size of the market. The number of potential consumers of an industry's product can increase with population growth as well as transportation and technology that support trade and therefore make the product available to more people. But critically, the process of economic growth is self-supported – cumulative and causal – when wages increase with the course of

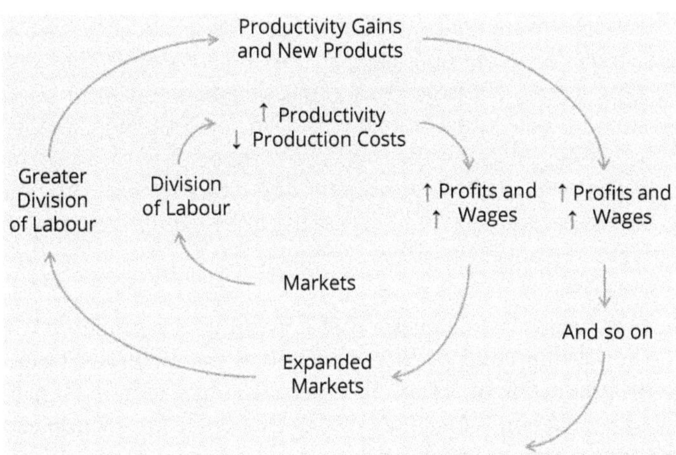

Figure 4.4 Capital accumulation: the virtuous spiral of economic development

economic development, as do patterns of demand from workers towards mass-produced goods which expands the market and provides the conditions for the further social division of labour, expansion of capital, and potentially increasing in the rate of capital accumulation. Whilst capitalist production is organised around the pursuit of profit, the functional distribution of income – between wages and profits – matters. Smith put forward the importance of encouraging capitalist interests that served both self and society. He recognised the structural advantage that capitalists had over workers in setting wages as well as the important social role that wages play in allowing workers to reproduce themselves as well as their role in providing demand for the expansion of markets and further division of labour. In fact, Smith associated high wages and high worker standards of living with a growing capital stock.

Smith made the distinction between value-in-use and value-in-exchange. Smith's labour theory of value explained the rate of exchange between products as reflecting the ratio of the average time it takes to produce each of them (see Chapter 9). Competition on the market and the ability for labour switch between the production of different products would ensure that they exchange in proportion to the labour required to produce them. But not all labour is 'productive labour' according to Smith.[4] In order to contribute to the creation of surplus (profits) that can be reinvested in the expansion of production, labour had to contribute to tangible goods and vendible goods. Labour employed in services that are immediately consumed is thus 'unproductive' – it cannot command a surplus.

Whilst Smith stressed the role of the market in expanding the wealth of nations, he also recognised its limits in terms of improving livelihoods for the majority of society. He was not the dogmatic champion of laissez-faire policies ascribed to him by many contemporary commentators. In addition, he was an advocate for workers' education provided for by the state in order to combat the deleterious effects of factory life which often involved mundane and repetitive tasks.

Marx – capitalist production as exploitation

> [T]he historical movement which changes the producers into wage-workers, appears, on the one hand, as their emancipation from serfdom and from the fetters of the guilds, and this side alone exists for our bourgeois historians. But, on the other hand, these new freedmen became sellers of themselves only after they had been robbed of all their own means of production, and of all the guarantees of existence afforded by the old feudal arrangements. And the history of this, their expropriation, is written in the annals of mankind in letters of blood and fire.[5]

For Marx, the answer to the question of how things are produced is historically contingent. The starting point of Marx's analysis is the question of how society is organised in the production of things. All societies produce to meet human needs and desires but how production is organised distinguishes different societal epochs. Marx refers to the specific ways in which production is organised in societies as 'modes of production'. Marx identifies different historical modes of production: primitive communism, Asiatic, Antique or Ancient, and Feudalism. Each of these is structured according to class relations (for example, landlords and serfs under feudalism) and appropriate corresponding categories of analysis can be attached to these.

To illustrate the historical distinction between the capitalist mode of production from what came before, Marx develops Smith's distinction between value-in-use and value-in-exchange. Use-values are connected to the usefulness of things and all societies produce use-values. All societies produce use-values but capitalist societies differ from preceding societies because production is organised along distinct class-based divisions between workers and capitalists in the production of commodities – things produced by labour for exchange through the market. Exchange-value is the ability to exchange one commodity with another and is unrelated to the physical properties of things in the way that use-values are (see also Chapter 9). Furthermore, and as discussed in Chapter 8, Marx explains the emergence of money as a social relation that can provide the basis for systematic market exchange as the universal equivalent. Whilst there has always been exchange amongst and between societies, production primarily for exchange is what typifies capitalism.

Under capitalist relations, a producer is separated from the means of production – land and the tools and machines required for production which Marx referred to as capital. In England, under feudalism, landless peasants had free access to common for arable and livestock farming. The movement of Inclosure Acts between 1604 and 1914 created private property rights to land previously held in common. This displaced peasants from common land and forced them into waged work which underpinned the reconfiguring of the structure of society according to workers and capitalists defined by their control, or lack of, over the means of production. A worker owns and sells their labour power with little control over conditions of work such as the length or type of contract and has little control over the labour process or product. Workers in today's so-called gig economy do not choose to be on zero-hours contracts but have these imposed upon them. They have the freedom to refuse to sell their labour, but this is a partial freedom given the alternative of starvation and social deprivation. Capitalists, on the other hand, have a monopoly over the means of production and control workers and the product of their labour through their command of wage payments and ownership of, or command over, the tools and raw materials. Note that this separation between labour and the means of production is universal in the Neoclassical model, where labour is viewed as an input like any other.

Under capitalism, individuals' capacity to work is commodified. Workers sell their labour power to a capitalist for a wage. Like any other commodity, labour power also has use-value which is the creation of other use-values. Marx builds on Smith's labour theory of value and develops it into a theory of capitalist exploitation. When exercised as labour, labour power creates new value from which the capitalist can appropriate a surplus. Capitalists can do this because of their position of structural advantage in society. The simplest way for capitalists to extract surplus is through exploitation, where workers work more hours than required to produce the value of their wage. In stark contrast to the marginal theory of distribution, the distribution between capital and labour is determined not by factor productivity but by power relations. Absolute surplus can be increased by extending the working day without a commensurate increase in wages, intensification of work through the application of discipline through supervision, penalties or indirectly through a system of wages based on piece rates, or as a by-product to technological change that allows the reorganisation of the labour process such as to eliminate of 'pores' in the workday. As discussed in Chapter 13, this can also be done through the extension of work to the whole working-class family in the case of social reproduction.

Marx's analysis explains the tendency for the concentration of capital and the rise of monopolies owing to the tendency for the rate of profit to fall. As the limits of absolute surplus appropriation are reached, capitalists seek to maintain profit levels by reducing the value of labour power by appropriating productivity gains that arise out of the augmentation of labour with machines and other forms of technical change. This raises the technical composition of capital (e.g. more machines for every worker). But since it is only (living) labour that produces surplus value, as the share of labour falls, so does the rate of profit. To secure profits, capitalists seek to consolidate into bigger units. Some capitalists will go out of business and others will take over their assets. This process would appear to explain the waves of mergers and acquisitions that punctuate the history of capitalism.

Marx was less optimistic about the impact of capitalist development on the majority of the population than Smith. Whilst Smith recognised some of the potential negative impacts of the factory system on the quality of workers' lives, by the time that Marx was writing in the second half of the nineteenth century, the degree of exploitation in factories had intensified. Work was a dangerous and unfulfilling occupation. Marx saw the only sustainable solution to the plight of workers to be the dismantling of the capitalist mode of production and its class structure to be replaced by a democratic, egalitarian, classless society organised along the principles of 'from each according to his ability, to each according to his needs'.

Global value chains: the global division of labour

The period since the 1990s has seen dramatic changes in how production is organised globally. These shifts can be characterised by a shift from Fordist forms of production, where standardised products are produced in large vertically integrated factories for mass consumption to post-Fordist production characterised by 'flexible specialisation' where firms hold small inventories, and operate on low levels of capital stock, low equipment dedication, high product differentiation and short product runs to respond quickly to changes in market demand. These production systems are characterised by vertically disintegrated supply chains where each firm specialises on a single stage of production. They are organised and governed by multinational corporations that outsource much of their production to supplier firms along these chains. The dispersion of the chains across national boundaries has also been increasing. Trade in intermediate goods, parts and components, has been on the rise and according to UNCTAD (2013), 80 per cent of global trade now takes place in value chains linked to transnational corporations.

Economists have tended to explain the rise of global value chains as the result of trade liberalisation, the ICT revolution that has reduced the costs and risks of coordinating complex production processes at a distance, and wage differentials between countries that have made it profitable to relocate certain components of production. Mainstream economic theories of off-shoring production are based upon the extension of the Heckscher-Ohlin model (Krugman et al., 2014).

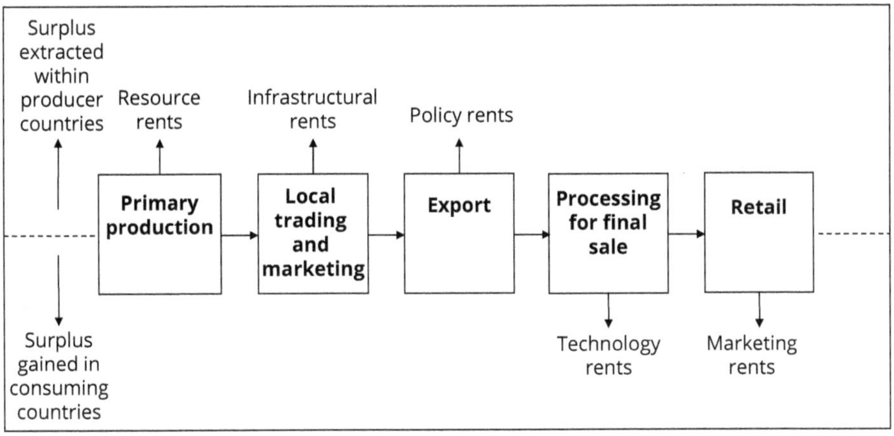

Figure 4.5 Example of a possible rent distribution along a simple global value chain

A strand of analysis, collectively referred to here as Global Value Chains (GVC), has developed outside of mainstream economics which stresses the vertical nature of production and pays particular attention to the nature of the interactions between economic actors or agents along transnational supply chains.[6] Rather than a coherent approach, the chain concept applied to the study of commodity markets has been utilised and developed within a large number of academic disciplines, generally outside of economics. These include geography, sociology, business studies, management studies, and development studies to name but a few. Approaches have therefore varied depending on the nature of the questions asked that determine the focus on a particular type of relationship along the chain and its outcomes. For example, management and business studies focus on coordination and control of supply chains by key actors and the implication of this on efficiency of the production and marketing system. They are interested in transaction costs and focus on exchange at the nodes of a supply chain. Other approaches stress the role of power and governance structures in determining chain outcomes such as the distribution of income or 'value' along chains (see Figure 4.5). Global Production Network approaches that developed within the subdiscipline of economic geography stress that the chains need to be understood as embedded within the social and institutional environments where they operate.

Different chain approaches have also drawn from a wide and eclectic range of theories to explain the phenomenon and to identify policies for industrial development and upgrading. Some approaches have incorporated aspects of transaction cost- and competence-based theories of the firm discussed above. Others have based analyses on more radical political economy approaches such as structuralism and dependency theory to explain unequal distributions of income along chains.

Conclusion

This chapter provided an introduction to Neoclassical theory of the firm as a theory of production and compared this to a set of alternative conceptualisations and theories of production across the history of economic thought. Table 4.1 provides a summary

Table 4.1 Summary of the approaches to the question of how things are produced covered in this chapter

	Unit of analysis	Analytical focus	Analytical approach	Key concepts include	Suggested texts
Neoclassical theory of the firm	The individual firm	Exchange	Comparative statics	Profit maximisation	Varian (2010)
Contract theory of the firm	The individual firm	Exchange	Comparative statics	Transaction costs	Coase (1937, 1992) and Williamson (1979)
Competence approach to the firm	The individual firm	Organisation and governance of production	Stress path dependence and dynamic change	Organisational learning	Hodgson (1998), Nelson and Winter (2002)
Adam Smith	Individual enterprise and the Economy as a whole	Production and exchange	Generalising from real historical experience	The division of labour	Foley (1999)
Marx	The economic system as a whole in relation to its constituent parts	Macro coherent economic system	Historical/ Dialectical Materialism	Capitalist exploitation	Fine and Saad-Filho (2010)
GCC/GVC/ GPN	Individual firms connected through input–output relations	Organisation and governance of production	Eclectic with various emphases on: Value-added accounting, critical sociology & political economy.	Transaction costs, organisational learning, industrial structure, industrial upgrading	Bair (2005) and Dicken (2015)

of some of the key themes and approaches that have been discussed. Whilst in Neoclassical economics the firm is the main analytical unit considered, it offers no explanation for either the emergence of, or the organisational form of the firm. The analysis is narrowly oriented around exchange. The contract theory of the firm emerged as a critique of the Neoclassical theory to explain the emergence of firms as a response to the pervasiveness of transaction costs. Rather than a break from Neoclassical economics, this approach retains the latter's key framework and categories of analysis. Competence-based theories of the firm have their intellectual roots in the work of Smith and stress the relationship between the organisation of a firm and firm specific characteristics such as knowledge and technology that cannot be exchanged on the market.

By contrast to these theories of the firm, Classical political economists such as Smith and Marx located and analysed production and how it was organised within an understanding of the capitalist economy as a whole. Whilst Smith saw the progressive potential of capitalist growth in raising living standards for all, Marx's analysis of capitalism revealed the class basis for the organisation of production with the exploitation of workers at the heart of it. Whilst Smith and Marx were theorising during specific historical times based upon their contemporary observations of how economies worked, by taking a historical and systemic approach to the study of production, they were able to anticipate many of the trends in the organisation of production today including the nature of technological development and its adoption in production, the significance of multinational corporations in the organisation of production and the rise of transnational supply chains.

Discussion questions and seminar activities

- Answer the following from each of the approaches outlined in this chapter:
  - What role do firms play in the economy?
  - Where do they come from/why do they exist?
  - What motivates their behaviour?
  - What factors make a firm successful?
- How is firm success related to size? Smith distinguished between productive and unproductive labour according to their contribution to economic growth and development. Consider the activities included in contemporary calculations of GDP. Which of these would be considered productive and which unproductive? Further, are there any economic activities that have been omitted from a measure of GDP that contribute to a countries growth and development? (Hint: consider the issue of social reproduction in Marx's framework.)
  - Take a look at the National Accounts for a country of your choice. If you were Smith, would you advise the country to produce different things? Contrast this to the view from Neoclassical economics.
- Watch *Panorama* - 'Amazon: The Truth Behind the Click', a BBC documentary about Amazon shopping (2013), available at https://www.youtube.com/watch?v=UQATFbLvlHk. Working in groups, provide an interpretation of this workplace using Classical and Marxist theories.
- Watch (part of) the 2004 documentary, *The Take*, by Naomi Klein and Avi Lewis. How would proponents of each of the perspectives outlined in this chapter (Neoclassical economics, Smith, contract theory of the firm, competence-based theory of the firm, and Marx) explain and assess the role of worker-operated enterprise in economic growth and development?

Further reading

Bair, J. (2005). Global capitalism and commodity chains: Looking back, going forward. *Competition & Change, 9*(2), 153–180.

Coase, R. H. (1937). The nature of the firm. *Economica, 4*(16), 386–405.

Coase, R. H. (1992). The institutional structure of production. *The American Economic Review, 82*(4), 713–719.

Dicken, P. (2015). *Global shift: Mapping the changing contours of the world economy*. London: Sage.

Fine, B., & Saad Filho, A. (2010). *Marx's capital* (5th ed.). London: Pluto Press.

Foley, D. (1999). *Notes on the theoretical foundations of political economy*. Mimeo.

Hodgson, G. (1998). Evolutionary and competence-based theories of the firm. *Journal of Economic Studies, 25*(1), 25–56.

Knight, F. H. (1921). *Risk, uncertainty and profit*. New York: Houghton Mifflin.

Krugman, P. R., Obstfeld, M., & Melitz, M. J. (2014). *International economics*. Harlow: Pearson.

Nelson, R. R., & Winter, S. G. (2002). Evolutionary theorizing in economics. *Journal of Economic Perspectives, 16*(2), 23–46.

Nelson, R. R., & Winter, S. G. (1982). *An evolutionary theory of economic change*. Cambridge: Belknap Press/Harvard University Press.

Penrose, E. (1959). *The theory of the growth of the firm*. Oxford: Oxford University Press.

UNCTAD. (2013). *World Investment Report 2013: Global value chains: Investment and trade for development*. New York/Geneva: United Nations.

Varian, H. (2010). *Intermediate Microeconomics: A Modern Approach*. Eighth Edition, W.W. Norton: London.

Williamson, O. E. (1979). Transaction-cost economics: The governance of contractual relations. *The Journal of Law and Economics, 22*(2), 233–261.

5 HOW AND WHY ARE THINGS CONSUMED?

Mary Robertson

Introduction

Consumption is the end purpose of almost all economic activity. We work to produce things to be consumed, or to facilitate consumption in some way. This is most obvious for jobs directly involved in the production of goods. But it is also true of retail and logistics, which together serve to organise the acquisition of things to consume, and of the financial services sector, which facilitates consumption. There is even a growing tendency to see public services and care work through the prism of consumption, with students increasingly regarded as consumers of education services, for example.

Given the centrality of consumption to the economy, it is surprising that economists have tended to pay it scant attention as a subject in its own right. Among the Classical economists, it is only Marx who had anything substantive to say about the content of consumption (see below). Smith (1999) described the 'natural progress of opulence', by which he meant the progressive satisfaction of consumption needs under capitalism, from subsistence through convenience and luxury. But consumption does not feature in the index of *The Wealth of Nations*. Ricardo engaged with consumption through the prism of its impact on economic growth, and thus confined himself to questions as to its size relative to overall investment, and whether consumption was productive or unproductive. Similarly, in Keynes's *General Theory*, consumption features only in the aggregate, as a macroeconomic flow.

Within mainstream economics, consumption is subsumed under a particular model of human choice that consigns the objects, processes, and consequences of consumption to a black box. The key assumption of this model is that human beings are rational and self-interested, which, with the aid of some auxiliary assumptions, allows choices to be modelled using Marginalist techniques for optimisation (see Chapter 2).

This model of human behaviour has assumed a central role in the theoretical framework of Neoclassical economics. However, the extension of the model to explain a seemingly infinite number of everyday and life decisions that have nothing to do with consumption – a process that has been described as 'economics imperialism' – reinforces the point that Neoclassical consumer theory is, at root, a theory of choice rather than consumption (see Chapter 16).

The range of alternative approaches to consumption exists outside of the Neoclassical tradition. Only some of these are direct responses to the shortcomings of the Neoclassical model, others pre-date its invention. Nonetheless, it is helpful to group them in terms of how they differ from that model. One group of alternatives persists in reducing consumption to choice, but questions the specific claims made about human decision-making by the rationality postulate. A second group of alternatives seeks to move beyond the question of choice by theorising consumption more holistically.

This chapter begins by introducing Neoclassical consumer theory, covering its theoretical components, recent developments, and criticisms. It then moves on to look at a range of alternatives, emphasising how they incorporate or focus on some of these aspects missing from the Neoclassical approach.

Neoclassical consumer theory

The standard approach in Neoclassical economics is to treat consumption decisions as choices that people make on the basis of their preferences. In making such decisions, consumers are regarded as rational utility maximisers, choosing goods subject to prices and budget constraints in order to maximise utility (see Chapter 2).

The utilitarian roots of neoclassical theory

The origins of the behavioural assumptions underpinning Neoclassical consumer theory lie in the nineteenth-century school of moral philosophy known as utilitarianism. Utilitarianism holds that the morally best state of affairs is the one that secures the greatest happiness for the greatest number. It is an ethical outlook that embodies a particular perception of human nature as hedonistic, that is, as driven fundamentally by the pursuit of happiness or utility. As one of its founding thinkers, Bentham (1907, p. 4), put it:

> Nature has placed mankind under the governance of two sovereign masters, pain and pleasure. It is for them alone to point out what we ought to do, as well as to determine what we shall do.

To understand this conception of human nature, it is important to stress, first, that happiness is considered to be entirely subjective. The individual is the absolute arbiter of what gives her/him utility and no attempt is made to explain why or how one's preferences come about. It follows that individuals must be trusted to decide for themselves what is best for them, allowing the theory to make no substantive claims about what is good for people beyond the maximisation of happiness. Second, utilitarianism is an individualistic theory, meaning that the utility of each individual must be taken into account and equally weighted. It should also be emphasised, however, that this does not necessarily imply that individuals are selfish. It is perfectly compatible with the theory for individuals to derive utility from the happiness of others. Economists call this 'other-regarding preferences'.

The utilitarian thesis that individuals are utility maximisers was incorporated into economics by early thinkers such as Mill. However, in using utility maximisation as the foundation for a theory of consumption, economists have often reduced the sources of utility to consumer goods, leaving non-material sources of utility and other-regarding preferences de facto excluded. The result is that utility maximisation comes to be defined in terms of choices over different bundles of goods.

The second assumption that Neoclassical consumer theory takes from utilitarianism is that human beings are instrumentally rational in pursuing their own utility (see Chapter 2). Someone is instrumentally rational if s/he uses the best available means to achieve her/his ends. In this context, at least, the assumption of rationality encompasses both perfect information about the range of choices available, and the perfect capacity to choose optimally across these choices. Like the treatment of utility as wholly subjective, instrumental rationality excludes any grounds for the substantive criticism or judgement of people's choices. It is concerned only with how effectively those choices are pursued.

Subjective utility maximisation and instrumental rationality form the conceptual foundations of Neoclassical consumer theory. According to this approach, consumers are sovereign. Unpicking preferences and the concept of utility is not regarded as a job for economists, which is limited to the analysis of spending power. This gives rise to a tautology that is at the heart of the Neoclassical approach to consumption: people choose what they like, and people like what they choose. The first part of the tautology comes from the assumption that people will always act rationally to maximise their own utility. The second part of the tautology comes from the proposition that utility is defined subjectively and that individuals are always instrumentally rational, as it implies that people's actual choices can be taken as their 'revealed preferences'.

This basic framework can be found in embryonic form in the work of early economists such as Mill. However, it took the Marginalist revolution of 1870, as a result of which these assumptions were made explicit and specified through formal axioms, for it to be developed into a fully fledged Neoclassical theory of consumption.

The model

The Marginalist revolution shifted economists' attention from ethical debates about human nature to the pursuit of a formal model of consumer decision-making. The challenge was to specify a utility function $u^i(x_1, x_2, x_3, \ldots x_n)$ for the *i*th consumer and for the goods, $x_1, x_2, x_3, \ldots x_n$ from which properties of consumption behaviour could be derived.

Turning the behavioural assumptions outlined in the previous section into a utility function of the form $u^i(x_1, x_2, x_3, \ldots x_n)$ for the *i*th consumer and for the goods, $x_1, x_2, x_3, \ldots x_n$ required a number of additional assumptions to be made about the nature of preferences and rationality.

1. Preferences must be complete, meaning that preferences cover all possible consumption bundles and any two bundles of goods can be compared.
2. Preferences must be transitive, so that if a person prefers x to y and y to z they will also prefer x to z. This allows all goods to be ranked in relation to each other.
3. It is assumed that consumers have non-satiable or monotonic preferences and therefore that they always want more of a good.
4. However, it is also assumed that consumers derive diminishing marginal utility from each good, that is, that the utility derived from an additional unit of a good

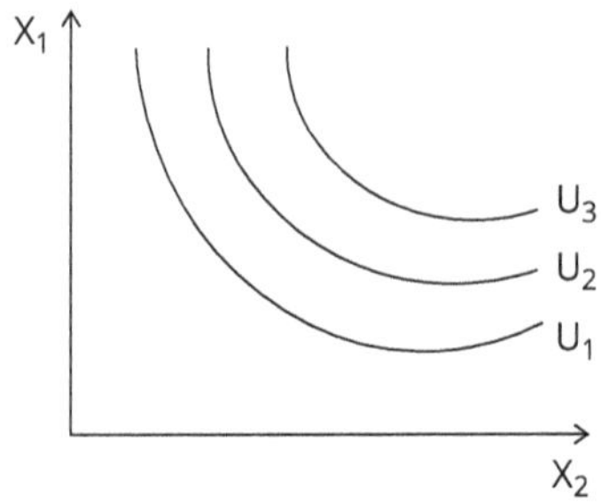

Figure 5.1 Indifference curves

diminishes as the quantity increases. This implies that consumers prefer a mix of goods to lots of one and a little of another.

Together these assumptions give rise to well-defined utility functions, which can be represented graphically in the form of indifference curves drawn in an (x_1, x_2) space. Indifference curves represent the different combinations of x_1, x_2 between which the consumer is indifferent. Or, to put it differently, indifference curves represent the different combinations of x_1, x_2 from which the consumer derives the same amount of utility. Utility is therefore equal along each of the curves in Figure 5.1 below. The shape of the indifference curves is given by assumptions 1–4 on the previous page. The completeness and transitivity assumptions ensure that the indifferent curves are smooth and continuous. Utility increases as the curves move outwards, reflecting monotonicity. And the curves are convex because of the assumption of diminishing marginal utility, and its implication that a mix of goods is better than large amounts of just one.

To close the model, it is necessary to introduce a budget constraint, which is defined in terms of the different combinations of goods a consumer can buy at given prices and budget. It is represented by the straight line in Figure 5.2. The slope is determined by the relative prices of x_1, x_2 with the slope getting steeper the cheaper x_1 is relative to x_2. The slope reflects the fact that, as x_1 gets cheaper, more of x_1 can be bought by substituting away from a given amount of x_2, which implies a steeper slope.

The assumption that individuals are instrumentally rational utility maximisers dictates that they will consume on the highest possible indifference curve within their budget constraint. It is clear from Figure 5.3 that the highest possible indifference curve the consumer can obtain is that tangent to the budget constraint at point A. Consumers will therefore choose to consume the bundle of goods at that point of tangency. The tangency implies that, at the point of consumption, the relative marginal utility of the goods in the bundle are equal to their relative prices and that, under the assumption of perfectly competitive markets, the consumer is fulfilling the condition for optimisation set out in Chapter 2.

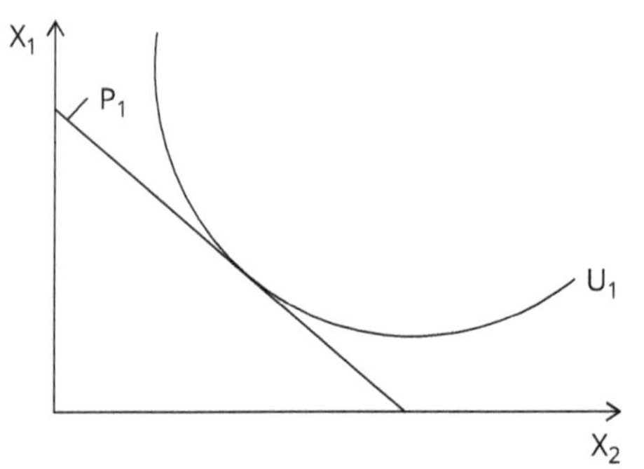

Figure 5.2 Indifference curve and the budget line

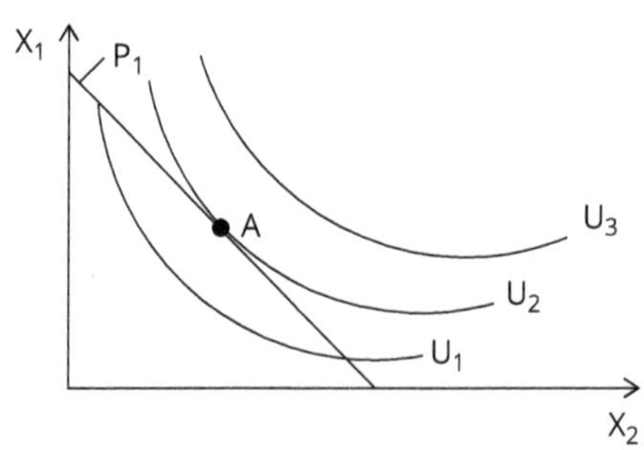

Figure 5.3 Utility maximisation with a given budget constraint

That, in essence, is what Neoclassical economics has to say about consumption.[1] At this stage it is worth making several points about the model. First, consumers differ across preferences, which, remember, are treated as wholly subjective, and across budgets, but the way in which people make consumption decisions is formally the same. The particular shape of each individual's utility function and indifference curves will differ from person to person, but within the model each individual consumes where relative prices are equal to relative marginal utilities. Second, the model is symmetrical to the model of production presented in Chapter 4 in which firms maximise profits subject to a production function. Indifference curves are formally identical to the isoquants that represent production functions, with levels of utility here substituting for levels of output there. This technical apparatus that forms the core of Neoclassical economics, and the formal similarity between Neoclassical theories of consumption and production have led to the argument that the content of Neoclassical economics is led by the technical requirements of its apparatus rather than the demands of the subject matter (Fine and Milonakis, 2009).

Third, it was mentioned earlier that, while the model is at heart a theory of choice or decision-making, a by-product of it serving as the basis for a theory of consumption was the gradual disappearance of non-material sources of utility from the theoretical framework. In other words, economists tended to think of utility as something caused by purchased goods and services. From the 1970s, however, the scope of the theory broadened out, as economists began to apply the model to non-consumption decisions. This is the focus of the next section.

The scope of the model – economics imperialism

The pioneer of extending the theoretical framework of Neoclassical consumer theory to non-market decision-making was Becker, who advocated, and practised, an 'economic approach' to all social science, seeking to explain a whole range of decisions using the framework of rational utility maximisation. One famous example is his characterisation of education as an investment. Education, he argued, should be understood as creating 'human capital' because investing time and money in education makes us more employable and gives us higher earning potential (see also Chapter 7). He used the same technological apparatus described above to build a model in which an individual's level of education reflects the point at which the marginal cost of expending additional time and money on education is equal to the marginal wage increment resulting from that education.

Becker made a career of applying rational utility-maximising behaviour to increasingly far-flung areas of human life, including the decision to commit a crime, the decision to get married, the decision to have children, and even how much time one should spend with one's children (Becker, 1976). His efforts won him a Nobel Prize in economics in 1992, for 'having extended the domain of economic theory to aspects of human behaviour which had previously been dealt with – if at all – by other social science disciplines such as sociology, demography and criminology' (Becker, 1992).

However, the Neoclassical explanatory framework was often at odds with the methodologies of the other disciplines to which Becker's subject matter traditionally belonged. Sociology, criminology, and anthropology, for example, tend to put much more emphasis on social structures such as power, class, and the state. The imposition of the highly individualistic rational economic agent on this subject matter was consequently often greeted with hostility, leading some to dub Becker's expansion of the scope of the economic approach 'economics imperialism' (Fine and Milonakis, 2009).

Despite this kickback, the approach has been popularised more recently in the form of such books as *Freakonomics* (2009), which offers an 'economic theory of everything'. Freakonomics popularised the rational, utility-maximising approach by using it to explain obscure observed phenomena such as underused gym memberships. In doing so, it served to present all manner of behaviour as optimal, often counter-intuitively. If Becker represented a form of disciplinary imperialism, Freakonomics was the extension of the rational, utility-maximising framework to the realm of the trivial (see Chapter 16).

Probing the assumptions of the neoclassical model

It is clear from this exposition that Neoclassical consumer theory relies on a number of assumptions. The nature of these assumptions merits further consideration, as do the implications for the explanatory power of the model.

Human beings are utility-seekers

Pettit (2001) suggests that many experience a conflict between the account economists give of our motivation, and the understanding of our motivation we arrive at through introspection. Many, if not all of us will feel driven by more complex motivations than utility-seeking, including: the desire to do what is morally right even if it goes against our self-interest; providing for the happiness and good fortune of others; and doing what is good for us even if that does not involve actions that are immediately desirable.

Pettit's point is often echoed by students newly initiated in Neoclassical theory. However, recall that we saw above that there is nothing inherent in the concept of utility to attach it, in particular, to selfish or materialistic motivations. In its original meaning, utility was defined so broadly as to be able to accommodate all manner of preferences, including moral ones, other-regarding ones and higher pleasures. The de facto selfish and materialistic nature of the Neoclassical consumer resulted from the way in which the concept of utility was deployed as part of a theory of market-based consumption, but this outcome was accidental rather than necessary. There is therefore a sense in which Pettit is technically incorrect. The Neoclassical emphasis on consumer sovereignty, and the tautology at the heart of their theory – people choose what they prefer and prefer what they choose – both imply that the theory is fundamentally open and non-prescriptive as to the content of preferences.

That said, the reader may wish to pause and reflect on how convincing this is. Technically, the concept of utility may be defined in the broadest sense, especially outside of market-based consumption. However, we saw above that Neoclassical economists, having first narrowed the scope of their theory in order to focus on consumption, then proceeded to broaden it out again, extending their model of decision-making to non-market situations through the economic approach of Becker and, latterly, Freakonomics. The question emerges whether, as the scope of the theory has been extended, the content given to the concept of utility has been similarly so. It is true that

Becker displays a willingness to talk about altruism and similar emotions (see, for example, Becker, 1992). But doubts remain as to whether such motivations are incorporated into his models successfully. In Becker's (1976) model of the decision to have children, for example, parents are assumed to derive utility from the quantity and the quality of children (the latter proxied by the amount spent on each child), with the final quantity and quality of children determined by the point at which marginal utility is equal to marginal cost. No doubt many parents will find this an intuitively problematic account of the kind of pleasure they derive from their relationship with their child.

Human beings are perfectly rational

Neoclassical economics' rationality assumption also requires further examination in light of an abundance of real-world examples of what seems to be evidently irrational behaviour, such as addiction. Again, it is important to remember here that an explanation not making intuitive sense does not in itself mean that it is not true – many made the same objection when it was discovered that the world is not flat. One explanation is that the rationality assumption is not meant to be interpreted literally; it is an assumption made for analytical purposes. Satz and Ferejohn (1994) argue that these analytical purposes are legitimate because in a perfectly competitive market, people behave 'as if' they were rational. This is because market competition shakes out inefficient behaviour and makes observed outcomes equivalent to those in which agents are perfectly rational. Of course, this explanation does not work for examples like Freakonomics, when Neoclassical consumer theory is applied to non-market decisions.

An alternative approach is to point to the wide-ranging empirical fit of the model. The trick of Freakonomics, for example, is to show that all manner of seemingly irrational behaviour can be made sense of through the theory. However, the fact that the rational choice model can be made to fit a range of scenarios does not imply that the model offers a true explanation. As Lazear (2000) has argued, the explanatory narrowness of the theory allows it to offer an explanation of a broad range of phenomena, but that same narrowness also means it is unable to think broadly about any particular problem. As a result, it may miss key aspects of a given problem that have explanatory import.

In addition to observable irrationalities in human behaviour, most people accept that there are limitations on human cognitive function. Attempting to reconcile this with the Neoclassical assumptions of perfect information and perfect rationality has had a significant impact on the discipline, as reflected in the number of Nobel Prize winners whose work has involved challenging the rationality assumption in this way. Nobel Prize winner Simon, for example, focused on human beings' cognitive limitations, arguing that human beings are, in reality, only boundedly rational and consequently are more likely to engage in behaviour that is merely satisfactory rather than optimal (Simon, 1978). The hugely influential information-theoretic economics, which was motivated by the feeling that perfect information is too stringent an assumption in most real-life settings, won a Nobel Prize for its pioneers, Akerlof, Spence, and Stiglitz in 2001 (see Stiglitz, 2001). Two psychologists, Kahneman and Tversky, won the Nobel Prize in economics for their research demonstrating 'the susceptibility to erroneous intuitions of intelligent, sophisticated, and perceptive individuals…[which]…became a standard reference as an attack on the rational-agent model' (Kahneman, 2003). Grappling with the rationality assumption has therefore spawned a number of new schools of thought, one of which, behavioural economics (see also Chapter 2), is discussed below. As we shall see, these new schools of thought vary significantly in the extent to which they break with the technological apparatus of Neoclassical economics

'Technical' assumptions

The third set of assumptions the Neoclassical model makes about human behaviour, in addition to utility-seeking and rationality, is that preferences are complete, transitive, non-monotonic and convex. As with the other assumptions, it is reasonable to question how accurately they capture human decision-making. Most textbooks will attempt to defend these auxiliary assumptions as intuitively appealing, arguing, for example, that we do tend to prefer more of things to less (see Varian, 2003). However, the historical emergence of those assumptions as part of a disciplinary drive to formalisation, along with the fact that economists have spent decades playing around with those assumptions to explore the implications for the technical properties of the model, suggest that these assumptions are made in order to guarantee well-defined utility functions and, therefore, a tractable model. But this does not necessarily undermine the explanatory power of the model. The extent to which economics needs mathematics and formal modelling – both of which necessarily impost technical constraints on our theories – is a fraught debate that is addressed in Chapter 3.

Preference formation

A fourth set of assumptions is that preferences are fixed and exogenously given. It is enough to appeal to intuition or personal experience to establish that our tastes, needs and desires evolve in the course of our lives and therefore that our preferences are not fixed. However, the changing nature of preferences is so evident that to present it as a criticism of Neoclassical consumer theory risks becoming a 'straw man' argument. The real question is whether it is justified to assume that preferences are fixed for the sake of theorising them.

A number of arguments could be made to defend such an assumption, ranging from theoretical tractability or elegance, to respect for consumer sovereignty and the desire among economists to avoid paternalistic judgements of people's preferences. However, treating preferences as fixed is less justifiable if they are liable to change in response to factors internal to the theory. We need to be careful here. The Neoclassical model of consumption excludes by assumption the possibility that consumption may change in response to anything other than an alteration in relative prices and/or the budget constraint. But some have argued that this exclusion from economic theorising of other factors that may shape preferences and consumption is unjustified. Fine and Leopold (1993), for example, argue that, far from being given within a sovereign consumer, preferences are determined by social factors and processes, some of which, at least, should fall within the remit of economics. Fine and Leopold suggest that there is no inherent reason why social processes of preference formation cannot be investigated by social scientists, and that in failing to do so, Neoclassical economics leaves us with a weak and impoverished understanding of consumption.

Undifferentiated goods

The final set of assumptions concerns the nature of goods in the Neoclassical model. It is assumed for the sake of the model that goods are indistinguishable from each other except in terms of their price, their capacity to cause utility, and the properties of their efficient distribution (as with club goods, public goods, and natural monopolies). But in real life goods are hugely diverse, and in ways that are relevant to many questions pertaining to consumption. The consumption of fossil fuels and junk food, and access to basic necessities such as water and shelter, for example, all raise important sets of questions that the Neoclassical framework not only has no tools to answer, but cannot even comprehend.

In this instance, the assumptions have implications for the scope of the explanatory power of the model. Neoclassical economics offers, at its heart, a theory of decision-making and of the outcomes of exchange processes in perfect markets. But consumption encompasses a broader array of processes, practices, and phenomena than decision-making and market exchange, including those that shape demand, allow demand to be realised as consumption, and determine the consequences of that consumption.

Alternative approaches

Developments in decision theory - behavioural economics

One set of alternatives has sought to moderate the assumption that people are perfectly instrumentally rational, and thus respond to criticisms that the assumption is too stringent. Behavioural economics (see also Chapter 2) uses cognitive psychology and evidence drawn from experiments and surveys to identify and explain the ways in which human behaviour diverges from that predicted by the rational, utility-maximisation framework. It has tended to emphasise, among other things, behavioural traits such as: the importance of habit and rules of thumb; that doing the 'right thing' matters; and that people care more about a loss than they value an equivalent gain – what economists call 'loss aversion'. For an example, these properties of individual behaviour and how they differ from what would be predicted by the Neoclassical model, see Box 5.1.

Box 5.1: The ultimatum game

Split the group into an equal number of proposers and responders. Every proposer is given £10. The proposer then decides how to divide the money between themselves and a responder. The responder then decides whether to accept or reject the offer. If they accept the offer, you both get the proposed amount. If they reject the offer, you both get nothing.

From the point of view of a Neoclassical responder, more is better than less and some is better than nothing, and no other considerations enter the picture. The Neoclassical proposer, for their part, is similarly motivated and so has no incentive to offer any more than a minimal positive sum. The Neoclassical model would therefore predict that every proposer would offer the smallest possible unit to the responder - namely, 1p or £1 - and that the responder would accept it.

Research finds that only four in 100 people offer less than 20 per cent and more than half of all responders reject offers that are less than 20 per cent. This is a significant divergence from the Neoclassical prediction. Recall that the responder in the Neoclassical model prefers something to nothing so has no incentive to reject any non-zero offer. But these results suggest that, in real life, people care about fairness and are often willing to sacrifice a small monetary gain for themselves to punish a proposer they believe has been unfair. The real life proposers seem to either share this concern for fairness or to be aware of other agents' capacity for spite and to factor it into their decision-making.

Two sub-categories of behavioural economics borrow experimental and neuroscientific methods from the natural sciences. Experimental economics uses lab-based experiments to investigate the properties of individual preferences and the properties of individuals' decision-making processes (Starmer, 1999). Neuro-economics uses brain imaging to gather evidence about the neurobiological mechanisms through which individuals make decisions.

The break that behavioural economics makes with the deductive, a priori method of theorising that characterises Neoclassical consumer theory is notable. However, the size of this break should not be exaggerated. First, behavioural economics and its spin-offs are, like Neoclassical consumer theory, theories of decision-making rather than of consumption more precisely or concretely understood. In its data gathering and application, behavioural economics considers non-consumption as well as consumption decisions, raising questions about how adequate they can be as theories of consumption. Second, while behavioural economics employs a richer and more grounded conception of individual decision-making than the axiomatic method of Neoclassical economics, it retains, nonetheless, an analytical focus on utility maximisation, albeit in the context of constraints. Third, behavioural economics also retains from Neoclassical economics: a focus on the individual rather than the social as its unit of analysis; the use of equilibrium to structure its models; and the evaluation of the model's outcomes in terms of efficiency, albeit with more openness and understanding of deviations from efficiency.

Veblen – the theory of the leisure class

Veblen was a Norwegian-American economist and sociologist whose 1899 book, *The Theory of the Leisure Class*, made a landmark contribution to the study of consumption. Despite writing the book before the formalist revolution had fully taken hold of economics, Veblen was critical of its ahistorical and axiomatic approach to explaining individual behaviour, arguing that economists should study how behaviour evolved in the course of historical change, Veblen (1994, p. xxvi):

> Instead of studying pleasures and pains, or satisfactions and sacrifices, on the supposition that these 'real forces' determine what men do, economists should study the processes of human behaviour at first hand. For this purpose, the important psychological categories are not the felicific calculus and the association of ideas, but propensities and habits.

On the basis of such a study, he then argued that the era in which he was writing was characterised by social stratification corresponding to the division of labour between those who had to work for a living and those who could live without working. The latter are free to engage in conspicuous consumption, the objects of which become endowed with status and social glorification. One result is that members of the leisure class are revered rather than resented, Veblen (1994, p. 83):

> the wife, who was at the outset the drudge and chattel of the man ... has become the ceremonial consumer of goods which he produces. But she still quite unmistakably remains his chattel in theory; for the habitual rendering of vicarious leisure and consumption is the abiding mark of the unfree servant.

Another is that individuals not in the leisure class seek to emulate those who are, by themselves engaging in conspicuous consumption. Veblen (1994, p. 111) stressed that they may do so even when they have to forego other goods to the point of hardship:

> As increased industrial efficiency makes it possible to procure the means of livelihood with less labor, the energies of the industrious members of the community are bent to the compassing of a higher result in conspicuous expenditure, rather than slackened to a more comfortable pace.

Veblen represents a significant departure from the Neoclassical theory of consumption. He is certainly criticising the Neoclassical notion of rationality but, unlike Behavioural economics, he is not simply tweaking assumptions, but taking a fundamentally different starting point. That starting point is the set of historically developed social and economic institutions, and the social stratifications that they create. In Neoclassical terms, he is grappling with the question of preference formation, but he breaks with Neoclassical economics by arguing for the socially determined nature of preferences, demonstrating that people derive utility from socially endowed properties of goods, and explaining how those properties arise in terms of social formations.

The resulting theory, and its implications, are very different to those of the Neoclassical model. Whereas the Neoclassical model sees consumption primarily as the satisfaction of material desires, for Veblen, consumption is cultural; it is constitutive of an individual's identity rather than a reflection of an individual's wants. Veblen's view of individuals as socially constituted leads him to understand consumption habits collectively, as properties of classes rather than individuals. This is evident in the way that trying to bolster one's social status through conspicuous consumption characterises the consumption habits of the working class as a whole. Veblen is describing how consumption habits are shaped by cultural refractions of economic inequalities, mediated by perceptions of status and image.

One implication is for the impact of consumption on people's well-being. Veblen makes it clear that the pursuit of status through conspicuous consumption does not correspond to rational utility maximisation. On the contrary, for Veblen, trying to emulate the consumption habits of the leisure class is decidedly irrational because it requires them to work harder and solidifies their role in capitalism's division of labour. A further implication follows for the role consumption plays in capitalist society. Whereas in the Neoclassical model consumption serves to meet human need, Veblen views conspicuous consumption as a mechanism for social control. By neutralising resentment over capitalism's division of labour and incentivising the working class to continue working hard rather than questioning the justice of the division of labour, conspicuous consumption serves to perpetuate capitalism.

Perhaps unsurprisingly, Veblen also departs from Neoclassical economics in taking a critical attitude towards consumption practices. Recall that the Neoclassical model is neutral with regard to the content of preferences and what brings utility, as reflected in both the concept of consumer sovereignty and the failure to differentiate goods except with respect to price and their capacity to cause utility. Veblen, by contrast, adopts a sarcastic, mocking tone throughout *The Theory of the Leisure Class*, leaving the reader in no doubt that he does not view conspicuous consumption as a good thing.

Commodity fetishism

Veblen was not the first to view ideology as important in shaping utility and consumption. Marx had done so too. But whereas Veblen traced that ideology to the esteem in which the ruling class is held, Marx located it at the heart of the capitalist organisation of production and distribution. Neoclassical theory is not tied to a particular historical period: rational utility maximisation is presented as a transhistorical, innate human quality. Marx, by contrast, was concerned with the different ways in which societies organise human labour to provide for human needs and wants. What distinguishes capitalism is that these needs and wants are provided for in the form of commodities. A commodity is 'an external object, a thing which through its qualities satisfies human needs of whatever kind' (Marx, 1991, p. 125) that is exchanged on a market. Marx places the commodity at the centre of his analysis.

A commodity can be understood in terms of its use-value – how it satisfies human need – and its exchange-value – its monetary value on the market (see Chapter 9). Because capitalism is a system of generalised commodity production and exchange, which means that human needs and wants can only be fulfilled through the purchase of commodities, Marx argues that, under capitalism, exchange-value dominates use-value. He means by this that what distinguishes commodities in terms of their usefulness or desirability is subordinated to their exchange-value on the market.

Marx sees this one-sidedness reflected in Neoclassical economics, with its reduction of goods to price and an abstract notion of utility. Viewed through this lens, the Neoclassical model is an example of 'commodity fetishism'. Because workers encounter the product of their labour and satisfy their needs in the anonymous context of the market, the powerful set of social relations which underpin the production and exchange of every commodity are concealed under capitalism. Commodities appear to the worker as independent of the production process that uses their labour. The power embodied in these social relations instead appears to inhere in objects, and commodities appear more powerful than they are.

In stark contrast to the Neoclassical and behavioural approaches to consumption, Marx provides an analysis of the distinctive nature of consumption under capitalism. Whereas the ultimate concern of Neoclassical economics is with the properties of the distribution arising from a market exchange when certain behavioural assumptions are made, Marx asks how a capitalist system, understood as a system of generalised commodity production, provides for human needs and with what consequences. The objects of consumption are understood, not in terms of optimising decisions, but as the items and conditions generally perceived to be necessary for a socially acceptable living standard in a particular historical context.

Marx argued that capitalist development is a process of commodification, through which more and more aspects of life are incorporated into market relations and provided for through a commodified relationship. Prior to capitalism, for example, the majority of people fed themselves in the non-commodified form of subsistence farming. In our lifetimes we have seen aspects of domestic work that were traditionally left to women commodified through the invention of such things as washing machines and ready meals. Marx argued that these changes had profound consequences for human and social relationships because with commodification grew commodity fetishism, and the growing alienation of people from each other and from the product of their labour.

Marketing and manipulation

Marx, like Veblen, challenges the notion of consumer sovereignty at the heart of Neoclassical economics by viewing consumption practices as irreducibly social. Finding no home in mainstream economics, this idea has evolved through disciplines such as marketing, which studies the moulding and manipulation of desires through advertising. The founding belief of this approach is that symbols and images play an essential role in shaping people's preferences and consumption behaviour. There are several reasons for this. First, our ability to gather and process information is limited, thus we economise by relying on signs and information widely and easily available through public discourses. Second, we are social beings who form our needs, desires, and attitudes relationally, learning and interpreting through interaction with others. Consequently, it is argued, Ozanne and Murray (1995, p. 522):

> Consumption does not merely arise in response to fundamental human needs or use values (utility); it is social activity that integrates consumers into a specific social system and commits them to a particular social vision.

Marketing theorists then go on to show how this role for symbols and images is exploited by advertising to manipulate people's preferences and consumption practices. In Marxist terminology, 'advertising has aided and exploited commodity fetishism by suggesting that commodities have magical properties – that is, that buying a product will increase the consumer's social status or attractiveness' (Science Encyclopedia, 2016). The result is that sometimes 'it is the image ... not the consumer, that is sovereign' (Firat et al., 1995, p. 47).

The marketing approach to consumption provides a useful counter-weight to Neoclassical conceptions of consumer sovereignty. The risk, however, is that, Fine (2007, p. 1):

> (t)aken to its extreme, the use value of a commodity can float free of its material properties. It is the interpreted sign value that matters, and value as such and its associated relations are rendered analytically redundant.

The allegation is that, by giving primacy to the social and discursive formation of preferences, the range of cultural meanings that may be attached to goods become too open-ended, such that both consumer sovereignty and the material aspects of consumption fall out of the analysis. Holt (2002) calls this the 'cultural authority narrative', according to which 'omnipotent corporations use sophisticated marketing techniques to seduce consumers to participate in a system of commodified meanings' (Holt, 2002, p. 71). Fine (2005, p. 2) calls it the 'hidden persuaders' argument, saying, '[g]iven a radical twist, the sovereign consumer is deposed and becomes victim to the manipulative hidden persuaders in pursuit of what are deemed to be artificially created, even false, needs.' In other words, commodity fetishism and its descendants have been criticised for going too far in the other direction, failing to acknowledge the extent to which human beings are capable of rational, reflective, autonomous thought or the sway held by material realities over human understandings. More recent developments have tried to bridge this gap, as we see in the next section.

The systems of provision approach

The Systems of Provision (SoP) approach, founded by Fine and Leopold (1993) and subsequently developed by Fine (2005, 2007, 2012), was a response to dissatisfaction with both 'the devil of Neoclassical economics and the deep blue sea of postmodernism' (Fine, 2012, p. 1). If the former treats preferences and goods as given and assumes that the consumer is motivated by utility derived from the physical properties of the good, and the latter disregards the physical properties of both the good and the consumer entirely and treats both as flexible and capable of reconstructions, then the SoP approach seeks to bridge the gap between the two by attaching the construction of meaning to a material chain of provision. In other words, Fine argues that consumption is shaped by culturally endowed meanings, but that these meanings emerge out of the material circumstances and chain of activities through which a particular good is provided, what he calls a SoP.

The SoP approach therefore organises the economy into commodity-specific systems defined by the (concrete and specific) structures, agents, processes and relations involved in the provision of the good. These SoPs are then analysed along the entire chain of provision, from financing through to production, marketing and consumption. It is held that these material circumstances of provision give rise to a distinct and unique consumption culture which shape the consumption practices attached to the good produced in each SoP. In Fine's (2012, p. 2) own words:

> consumption could be usefully (if not fully) addressed through identification of different and differentiated sops organised along specific commodity lines. Such specifics involve tracing back from consumption and consumer through the material practices by which they are reproduced and transformed as an integral whole, or system.

What Fine is advocating is that studies of the culture of consumption of a particular good be linked to studies of the material provision of that good in order better to explain the former and to tease out the interactions between the two. He says, 'the SoP approach allowed, and deliberately intended, the strengthening if not the (re)introduction of the material to the (cultural) study of consumption' (Fine, 2012, p. 3).

An example may help to understand the approach. Robertson (2016) uses it to explain the rise in popularity of owner-occupied housing over other housing tenures in the UK since the 1980s. She argues that support for financial and other advantages associated with owner-occupation were important, as was under-investment in alternatives. However, these developments made themselves felt via changes in the consumption culture around housing, which was mediated by government discourses, and changes in shared meanings and imagery around housing. The SoP approach's emphasis on the interaction between the cultural and the material is captured by Robertson's attention to the way in which the material conditions of provision both generate and hold in check the cultural meanings used to interpret them.[2]

In terms of the preceding discussion, the SoP approach seeks to improve on Neoclassical economics by explaining preference formation. However, in contrast to the marketing approach, the SoP approach also recognises that individuals do not simply internalise social discourses but rather interpret them reflexively in light of their material experiences. The material and the cultural are linked because to be plausible and effective the meanings and beliefs that people attach to goods must correspond in some way to their material experiences of those goods. And to understand and explain these material experiences, we have to look at the operation of the entire chain of provision, or SoP. There is also common ground with Marx in viewing cultures of consumption as complex and good-specific because they are 'deeply rooted in social forces, structures and processes that interact with one another to give rise to complex outcomes' (Fine, 2005, p. 4).

The SoP approach is the only theory we have looked at that places the differentiation of goods centre stage, as is reflected in Fine's insistence that consumption cultures are SoP-specific and that specific SoPs must be investigated concretely. As it is sometimes put, whereas Neoclassical economics employs a form of horizontal theorising, examining the choice process over a range of given goods, the SoP approach analyses consumption vertically, by tracing consumption of a specific good back along the chain of provision that facilitated it.

In both of these respects, the SoP approach would seem to offer a much richer understanding of consumption than that provided by Neoclassical economics. However, that richness comes at a price. First, the approach is very labour-intensive. An adequate study of an entire SoP will need to engage in a detailed, empirical investigation of the particular SoP under study, and then draw on insights from a range of different disciplines and theories to explain its operation. All this places a very heavy burden on the researcher. Second, the approach's insistence that SoPs are time-, location-, and commodity-specific means that applications of the approach are significantly narrower in scope than the highly general conclusions of Neoclassical economics. Whatever one thinks of the particular claims made by Neoclassical consumer theory, it has proved to have very wide applicability. The SoP approach, by contrast, is a method through specific questions about consumption can be answered, but one that is ill-equipped to reach generalisable findings. The extent to which this matters, and whether generalisability should be an objective of theorising, is, of course, a matter for debate.

Conclusion

We have seen that mainstream economics has an odd relationship with consumption. On the one hand, consumer theory is the bedrock of Neoclassical economics, the foundation on which all of its other theories are built. On the other hand, Neoclassical economics often seems as if it has little to say about consumption as such, with major insights into actually existing consumption practices coming from outside the discipline. This conclusion brings out the fundamental differences across the different approaches discussed, by contrasting their answers to three key questions.

First, *what should a theory of consumption be about?* Neoclassical economics treats consumption as synonymous with decision-making and develops a theory of decision-making that is broad in scope and widely applicable to a whole range of non-market as well as market decisions, as demonstrated by economics imperialism. The Neoclassical approach is also based on, and intended to serve as, a universal account of human nature. Neoclassical economists do not limit the scope of their theory to a particular era, location, or form of social and economic organisation, but rather hold it to apply it to all people for all time.

Behavioural economics shares these features with Neoclassical economics, but all of the other approaches we considered differ from it in some way. Both Veblen and the marketing approach are interested in how consumption preferences are formed, though they highlight different influences (the hierarchical social structures found in certain societies during particular historical epochs and the ability of certain agents to manipulate perceptions and desires, respectively). Both Marx and the SoP approach take a broader perspective of consumption than Neoclassical economics insofar as both are concerned with how human needs are created and provided for in a generalised system of commodity production and exchange. However, their scope of applicability is narrower. Marx is explicit that his analysis only applies to capitalist societies, while SoP analyses take place at the level of particular sectors in particular economies.

Second, *what conception of human nature underpins the theory?* In the Neoclassical model, agents are self-interested utility-seekers with perfect rationality. Further, these traits are seen as unchanging and universal, characteristic of all people in all times and places. Behavioural economics is similarly universalist, but introduces cognitive impairments and non-rational behaviour into its assumptions about agents, for example, allowing for moral motivation or for sub-optimal decision-making.

For the other approaches, by contrast, agents are socially and historically embedded. This means that their behavioural traits are malleable, the product of their social context in particular times and places. This malleability also creates more scope for irrational behaviour understood, not merely as modest violations of optimising behaviour as it is in behavioural economics, but as actively contrary to self-interest. This is evident, for example, in Veblen's account of workers enduring hardship in order to emulate the consumption patterns of the leisure class, or in the marketing approach's account of people being manipulated into consuming things they don't really need.

Finally, *what role is played by formal techniques such as mathematics?* Neoclassical economics give a high priority to rigour and mathematical neatness, arguably to the point of allowing technical imperatives to subordinate empirical ones (see Chapter 3). The other approaches, by contrast, are discursive and historically engaged, arguably to the point of messiness and intractability.

Discussion questions and seminar activities

This chapter has highlighted a range of issues which can be further explored in seminar discussions and activities:

- Does Neoclassical economics provide a realistic account of human decision-making? Does it matter?
- Which characterisation of individuals do you think is more accurate, that provided by Neoclassical economics or that provided by Behavioural economics?
- Given the examples presented in Box 5.1, why do Neoclassical economists persist in characterising people as rational economic agents? (Consider theoretical usefulness, ideology, aggregate behaviour.)
- What aspects of consumption does behavioural economics leave out? Does it matter?
- What other forms of conspicuous consumption can you think of (hint: consider advertising and branding)? What are the similarities and differences between these forms of conspicuous consumption and those associated with the leisure class?
- What grounds does Veblen have for adopting a critical stance towards the utility people derive from conspicuous consumption?
- How susceptible are you to advertising and marketing? Think of examples.
- What role does advertising play in a capitalist economy?
- To what extent does the presence and effectiveness of advertising undermine the explanatory power of the Neoclassical model?
- 'Freedom of choice characterises our society by its absence in its important aspects and its presence at a superficial level' (Himmelweit, 1977, p. 34). Discuss this statement in relation to Neoclassical and Marxist approaches to consumption.
- When might it be useful to have a good-specific, vertical analysis of consumption? Consider from the point of view of policymakers, consumers, and researchers.
- To what extent is there a trade-off between theoretical tractability and generalisable results, on the one hand, and explanatory truth on the other? Why does this trade-off arise? How do you think it should be settled and why?

- Identify the similarities and differences between Neoclassical production and consumption theory. What, if anything, do the similarities imply about the two theories?
- Frank et al. (1993) argued that economics students are more likely to display such traits than people who have never studied economics, and therefore that the behavioural traits of rational economic man could be learnt.
- Divide the class into proposers and responders and play the ultimatum game. To what extent do the results conform to economic theory? Now do the same experiment on people who have never studied economics. How do the results differ?
- Compare and contrast Marx and Neoclassical economics' treatment of social relations. What are the strengths and weaknesses of each?
- Think of some examples of goods and services that have been commodified and consider how they have impacted on social relationships.

References

Becker, G. S. (1976). *The economic approach to human behaviour*. Chicago: University of Chicago Press.

Becker, G. S. (1992). *The economic way of looking at life*. Nobel Lecture.

Bentham, J. (1907). *An introduction to the principles of morals and legislation*. Oxford: Clarendon Press.

Fine, B. (2005). Addressing the consumer. In F. Trentmann (Ed.), *The making of the consumer: Knowledge, power and identity in the modern world* (pp. 291–311). Oxford: Berg.

Fine, B. (2007). From sweetness to McDonald's: How do we manufacture (the meaning of) foods? *The Review of Social & Economic Studies, 29*(2), 247–271.

Fine, B. (2012). *Consumption matters*. Mimeo.

Fine, B., & Leopold, E. (1993). *The world of consumption*. Abingdon: Routledge.

Fine, B., & Milonakis, D. (2009). *From economics imperialism to Freakonomics*. Abingdon: Routledge.

Firat, F. A., Dholakia, N., & Venkatesh, A. (1995). Marketing in a post-modern world. *European Journal of Marketing, 29*(1), 40–56.

Frank, R., Gilovich, T., & Regan, D. (1993). Does studying economics inhibit cooperation? *Journal of Economic Perspectives, 7*(2), 159–171.

Himmelweit, S. (1977). The individual as the basic unit of analysis. In F. Green & P. Nore (Eds.), *Economics: An anti-text*. London: Macmillan.

Holt, D. B. (2002). Why do brands cause trouble? A dialectical theory of consumer, culture, and branding. *The Journal of Consumer Research, 29*(1), 70–90.

Kahneman, D. (2003). Experiences of collaborative research. *American Psychologist, 58*(9), 723–730.

Lazear, E. P. (2000). Economics imperialism. *The Quarterly Journal of Economics, 115*(1), 99–146.

Levitt, S. D., & Dubner, S. J. (2009). *Freakonomics: A rogue economists explores the hidden side of everything*. New York: Harper Perennial.

Marx, K. (1991). *Capital* (Vol. 1). London: Penguin.

Ozanne, J., & Murray, J. (1995). Uniting critical theory and public policy to create the reflexively defiant consumer. *American Behavioural Scientist, 8*(4), 516–525.

Pettit, P. (2001). The virtual reality of homo economicus. In U. Maki (Ed.), *The economic world view* (pp. 75–97). Cambridge: Cambridge University Press.

Robertson, M. (2016). *(De)constructing the financialised culture of owner-occupation in the UK, with the aid of the 10Cs.* Mimeo.

Satz, D., & Ferejohn, J. (1994). Rational choice and social theory. *Journal of Philosophy, 91*, 71–87.

Science Encyclopedia. (2016). *Consumerism – Consumerism and mass production*. http://science.jrank.org/pages/8818/Consumerism-Consumerism-Mass-Production.html. Last Checked 16 Oct. 2016.

Simon, H. A. (1978). *Rational decision-making in business organisations*. Nobel Lecture.

Smith, A. (1999). *The wealth of nations*. London: Penguin.

Starmer, C. (1999). Experiments in economics: Should we trust the dismal dcientists in white coats? *Journal of Economic Methodology, 6*, 1–30.

Stiglitz, J. E. (2001). *Information and the change in the paradigm in economics.* Nobel Lecture.

Varian, H. R. (2003). *Intermediate microeconomics: A modern approach* (6th ed.). London: Norton.

Veblen, T. (1994). *The theory of the leisure class*. New York: Dover Publications.

6 DO ECONOMIES REACH EQUILIBRIUM?

Rob Calvert Jump

Introduction

Do economies reach equilibrium, and how would we know if they do? What would be the characteristics of equilibrium? Would it correspond to an efficient, or a fair, allocation of resources? Is it even useful to organise theory around an equilibrium concept? On the one hand, these are questions of economic theory that have been debated at length throughout the history of economic thought. On the other hand, these are questions of actually existing economies, as theoretical constructs are meaningful to the extent that they can be confronted with reality.

The idea of equilibrium took a long time to emerge in economic theory. Prior to the eighteenth century, economics was never entirely separate from ethics and theology, and equilibrium as a theoretical concept was not a major point of reference. This began to change with theorists like Cantillon, Steuart, Quesnay, and Smith. With Quesnay, in particular, the first explicit model emerges emphasising the interdependence of economic activity, the *tableau économique*. This describes a circular flow of income and expenditure between landowners, farmers and manufacturers. Disentangling the different flows in Quesnay's *tableau* is quite difficult for a reader used to the algebra of contemporary economics, but it does serve to illustrate the interdependency of incomes and expenditures in a complex multi-sectoral economy. With Smith (1890, p. 11), we have the most famous statement in English of this interdependency:

> In almost every other race of animals each individual, when it is grown up to maturity, is entirely independent, and in its natural state has occasion for the assistance of no other living creature. But man has almost constant occasion for the help of his brethren, and it is in vain for him to expect it from their benevolence only ... It is not from the benevolence of the butcher, the brewer, or the baker that we expect our dinner, but from their regard to their own interest.

This is as concise a statement as any of the interdependency of economic activity, and leads to a basic problem in economic theory: if human activity is collective, but humans do not act with a view to the collective benefit, how are activities coordinated?

Equilibrium, as an organising concept in economics, is closely associated with the question of coordination. There are, however, almost as many definitions of equilibrium as there are types of model. *The New Palgrave: A dictionary of economics* (Vol. 2) (Milgate, 1987, p. 179) takes the following line:

> At the most elementary level, 'equilibrium' is spoken about in a number of ways. It may be regarded as a 'balance of forces', as when, for example, it is used to describe the familiar idea of a balance between the forces of demand and supply. Or it can be taken to signify a point from which there is no endogenous 'tendency to change': stationary or steady states exhibit this kind of property. However, it may also be thought of as that outcome which any given economic process might be said to be 'tending towards', as in the idea that competitive processes tend to produce determinate outcomes. It is in this last guise that the concept seems first to have been applied in economic theory.

This last definition of equilibrium, as a state towards which an economy tends, can be found in both Smith and Ricardo. For Smith, writing at the end of the eighteenth century, coordination in capitalist economies was achieved by the 'truck and barter' of market exchange. On the one hand, competition between buyers and sellers in a single market would lead to a uniform price being established for each commodity. On the other hand, capitalists would move their production from commodities yielding low profits to commodities yielding higher profits, a process that would end in a uniform rate of profit.

The equilibrium price is therefore, as Smith put it, 'the central price, to which the prices of all commodities are continually gravitating' (Smith, 1890, p. 44; see also Chapter 9). For Smith, this process of gravitation might be retarded indefinitely by a lack of competitive pressure, but Ricardo was of the opinion that 'the principle which apportions capital to each trade in the precise amount that it is required, is more active than is generally supposed' (Ricardo, 1951, p. 90). In any case, through Smith and Ricardo we have a plausible explanation of the process by which free competition ensures a degree of coordination in capitalism, and a general conception of equilibrium as a state towards which an economy tends.

This chapter examines the Neoclassical approaches to equilibrium and disequilibrium that superseded the classical political economy of Smith and Ricardo, and are still important in the popular undergraduate and graduate textbooks. A number of alternative approaches, which are usefully left out of the popular textbooks, are then discussed. As well as considering the different ways in which equilibrium has been understood across different theoretical approaches, I also comment on the relative importance of equilibrium within different approaches.

Neoclassical approaches

Smith and Ricardo argued that competition between capitalists would force prices towards an equilibrium, although neither economist actually referred to the 'central price, to which the prices of all commodities are continually gravitating', in this manner. The use of the word equilibrium appears to have been popularised by Mill in the middle of the nineteenth century, although his treatment of the concept did not go much beyond the discursive theories of Smith and Ricardo.

Whilst mathematical treatments of equilibrium did exist in the early nineteenth century, most notably in the work of Isnard and Cournot, its use as an organising concept in formal economic models only emerged fully with the Neoclassical revolution. After the Marginalists had popularised the use of marginal utility in economic theory, Marshall and Walras respectively developed the theories of Neoclassical partial and general equilibrium. Marshall and Walras were also the first to discuss the stability properties of Neoclassical equilibria at any length, and their basic ideas concerning the stability of equilibrium still make it into the popular textbooks. The best treatments of the topic are contained in Gravelle and Reese (2004) and Mas-Colell et al. (1995), which discuss Walras's and Marshall's stability theories in some detail. The following section discusses these theories, after which the contemporary Neoclassical approach is considered.

Marshall and Walras

Marshall and Walras laid the foundations for equilibrium analysis as it is understood in contemporary undergraduate and graduate textbooks. Walras, whose work preceded that of Marshall, focused on the economy as a whole in his general equilibrium analysis. His main interest was the interdependency of different markets, and he discussed this problem at various levels of complication. In comparison, Marshall focused on the existence and attainment of equilibrium in single markets under *ceteris paribus* assumptions, and was comparatively less concerned with the interdependence of different markets. Beyond these differences in scope, equilibrium was central as an organising concept for both theorists, where the attainment of equilibrium implies market clearing. As partial equilibrium is considerably more straightforward than general equilibrium, I will focus on this for the most part.

The first edition of Marshall's *Principles of Economics* appeared in 1890. Its purpose was to synthesise the insights of the Marginalist school with the older insights of Smith and Ricardo. Thus, in the Preface to the first edition, Marshall states that, 'The present treatise is an attempt to present a modern version of old doctrines with the aid of the new work, and with reference to the new problems, of our own age' (Marshall, 2013, p. xix). Marshall summarised Smith and Ricardo's theories as a supply curve linking price and quantity produced, and the Marginalist theory as a demand curve linking the same variables. The result is the well-known Marshallian cross, illustrated in Figure 6.1.

Partial equilibrium in Marshall's model is simply where the supply and demand curves cross. Mathematically, therefore, Marshallian partial equilibrium is the solution to a pair of simultaneous equations. This is one of the best-known examples of the static method in economics, where there is no obvious ordering of events, and no obvious causal structure. In Figure 6.1, the price is not determined first, and then quantity determined by the supply or demand curve; the equilibrium price and quantity are determined simultaneously.

Figure 6.1 Marshall's partial equilibrium diagram, following Marshall (1890)

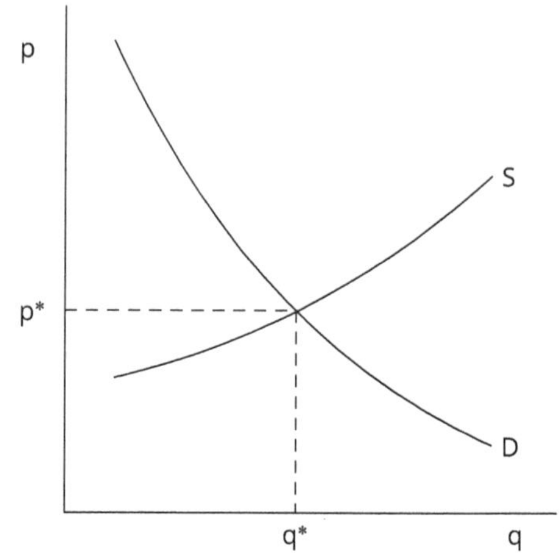

The first edition of Walras's *Eléments d'Économie Politique Pure* was published in 1874. Whilst Marshall focused almost exclusively on partial equilibrium, Walras focused single-mindedly on general equilibrium – simultaneous equilibrium in all markets. Like Marshallian partial equilibrium, Walrasian general equilibrium is the solution to a system of simultaneous equations linking commodity prices and quantities produced. We therefore have a very simple definition of equilibrium in the Marshallian and Walrasian systems: the solution to a system of simultaneous demand and supply equations. But do such equilibria satisfy the earlier definition of a state towards which an economy tends? In other words, is it plausible to assume that the economy in Figure 6.1 actually reaches its partial equilibrium?

Issues of stability are fundamentally concerned with the passage of time, and any stability analysis of a static model has to impose some ordering of events on the underlying simultaneous equations. Both Marshall and Walras proposed dynamic processes whereby one could study the stability or otherwise of partial and general equilibrium. Interestingly, the two processes are quite different, and in some cases can give different results. I will consider Marshall's process first, and Walras's process second, and then examine a simple case in which their outcomes differ.

Marshall's process supposes that, in any given period, the quantity of output is fixed. Given this quantity, we can read off a 'demand price' from the demand curve, which is the maximum price customers are willing to pay, and a 'supply price' from the supply curve, which is the minimum price sellers are willing to charge. This is illustrated in Figure 6.2, where market output is fixed at q^m, and the demand price p^d is greater than the supply price p^s. Whilst we do not know exactly which price will reign on the market at q^m in Figure 6.2, we can reasonably assume that it will be greater than p^s, in which case sellers are receiving a greater revenue than the minimum amount needed to supply q^m. The implied high profits encourage production to increase in the direction of the equilibrium output $q*$. The reader can confirm for themselves that an equivalent argument applies whenever market output is greater than $q*$, and therefore the partial equilibrium is stable. Thus, Marshall (2013, p. 288):

Figure 6.2 Stability analysis with Marshall's process

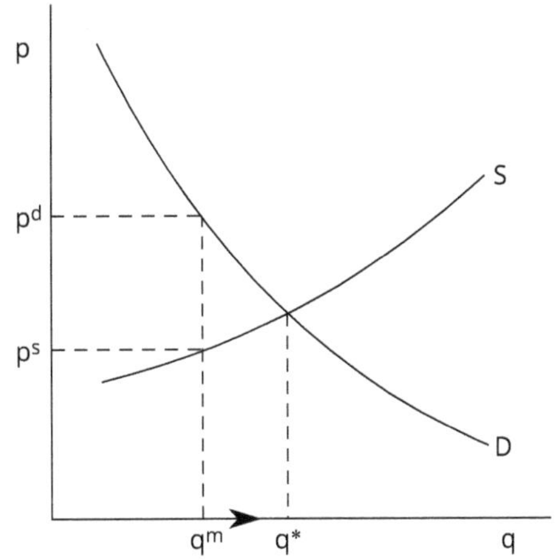

> When demand and supply are in stable equilibrium, if any accident should move the scale of production from its equilibrium position, there will be instantly brought into play forces tending to push it back to that position; just as, if a stone hanging by a string is displaced from its equilibrium position, the force of gravity will at once tend to bring it back to its equilibrium position.

Marshall's adjustment mechanism is similar to Smith and Ricardo's adjustment of capitals in response to differential profit rates, despite their notions of equilibrium being rather different, and the foregoing can be compared to Smith's description of the central price towards which, 'the prices of all commodities are continually gravitating'.

Walras's process supposes that the market price is fixed in any given period, rather than the quantity of output. Given the market price, we can read off quantity demanded from the demand curve, which is the amount customers wish to purchase, and quantity supplied from the supply curve, which is the amount sellers wish to offer. This is illustrated in Figure 6.3, where the market price is fixed at p^m, and the quantity demanded q^d is greater than the quantity supplied q^s. At this point, Walras assumed that no trade would actually take place, but instead, via a *tâtonnement* process, an auctioneer or market maker would adjust price in the direction of excess demand, defined as the difference between quantity demanded and quantity supplied. Thus, Walras (1954, p. 172):

> the attainment of equilibrium prices requires a rise in the prices of those commodities the effective demand for which is greater than the effective offer, and a fall in the prices of those commodities the effective offer of which is greater than the effective demand.

In Figure 6.3, q^d is greater than q^s at p^m, and therefore the market price rises in the direction of the equilibrium price p∗. The reader can confirm for themselves that an

Figure 6.3 Stability analysis with Walras's process

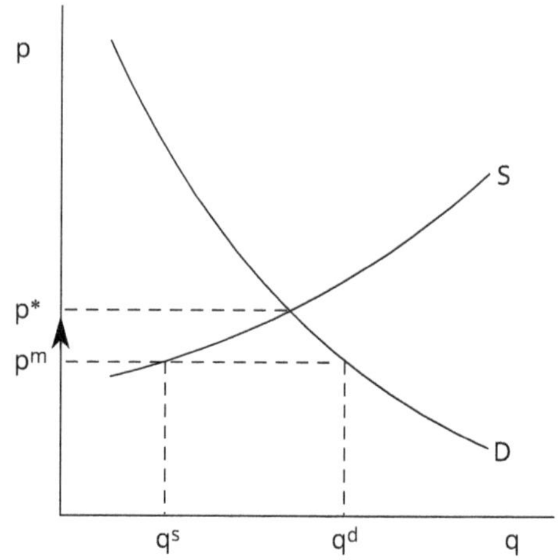

equivalent argument applies whenever the market price is greater than p∗, and therefore the partial equilibrium is stable.

So in our simple example, with a downward-sloping demand curve and upward-sloping supply curve, the Marshallian and Walrasian disequilibrium processes give the same result. Consider, however, the partial equilibrium illustrated in Figure 6.4. Here we have a situation in which both the demand curve and the supply curve are downward sloping, with the demand curve steeper than the supply curve around the equilibrium. This might be relevant in situations where increasing returns to scale are important, for example. Marshall's process is illustrated in the left-hand panel, assuming the market output is initially below its equilibrium. As the demand price is greater than the supply price at this output, we should expect output to increase over time, ensuring stability. Walras's process is illustrated in the right-hand panel, assuming that the market price is initially equal to the demand price in Marshall's process. As quantity demanded is greater than quantity supplied, excess demand is positive, and we should expect the market price to increase over time, moving the economy further away from its equilibrium.

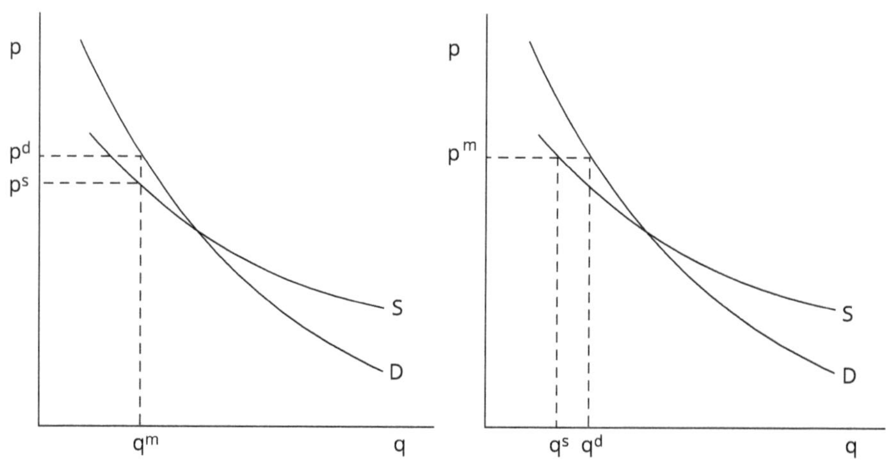

Figure 6.4 Stability analysis in the Marshallian and Walrasian adjustment processes

In the partial equilibrium illustrated in Figure 6.4, the Marshallian process leads us to believe that the partial equilibrium is stable, whilst the Walrasian process leads us to believe that the partial equilibrium is unstable. Only in the former case, therefore, does the partial equilibrium satisfy Smith and Ricardo's definition of equilibrium as a state towards which the economy tends. Despite this anomalous case, both Walras and Marshall were relatively optimistic about the ability of real-world economies to reach Neoclassical equilibria. Thus Walras (1954, pp. 224–225), for example, argued that,

> It never happens in the real world that the selling price of any given product is absolutely equal to the cost of the productive services that enter into that product, or that the effective demand and supply of services or products are absolutely equal. Yet equilibrium is the normal state, in the sense that it is the state towards which things spontaneously tend under a regime of free competition in exchange and in production.

Notably, and presumably as a result of this optimism, 'crises' as explicitly disequilibrium phenomena only gain a fleeting mention in his *Eléments d'Économie Politique Pure*.

Contemporary Neoclassical theory

The starting point of contemporary approaches to the stability of Neoclassical equilibrium models was Paul Samuelson's formalisation of the Walrasian *tâtonnement* process in 1941. This casts Walras's price adjustment rules in the form of differential equations, with the time derivative of the price vector a function of excess demands. As a result, the stability of Neoclassical equilibria can be studied in a fairly straightforward fashion, and it quickly became clear that the local and global stability of general equilibrium under *tâtonnement* requires gross substitutability between all commodities. This means that a rise in the price of one good increases the demand for every other, which rules out strong income effects.

Why are strong income effects problematic for the stability of Neoclassical equilibria? Consider an initial state of equilibrium, and a small increase in the price of a single commodity. Strong substitution effects mean that consumers shift their expenditure to other commodities, making the excess demand for our original commodity negative, and thus its price decreases. The equilibrium is therefore stable. Strong income effects, however, mean that the rise in price might increase the incomes or net wealth of some consumers, which will increase their demand for the commodity. The excess demand is then positive, and thus the price of our commodity increases further, making the equilibrium unstable.

The foregoing is linked to the so-called anything goes theorems of Sonnenschein, Mantel, and Debreu in the 1970s, where the same issues lead to the possibility of multiple Walrasian equilibria. These results, and the famous cyclical *tâtonnement* process of Scarf (1960), resulted in a large number of economists losing faith in the ability of Neoclassical general equilibrium theory to describe real-world economies. However, an opposite reaction led to a sustained effort to improve the available models of disequilibrium. The major outcomes of this research programme were the various *non-tâtonnement* processes, and two of the most successful – the Edgeworth process and the Hahn process – still make it into the popular textbooks. The best textbook treatment is contained in Varian (1992), and the best dedicated treatment is contained in Fisher (1983).

The Edgeworth and Hahn processes are relatively complicated and use sophisticated mathematics to determine the stability of Neoclassical equilibria. They are relatively successful compared to the Walras and Marshall processes, although it is not always the case that the equilibrium reached is independent of the path taken to reach it. Despite these successes in modelling disequilibrium processes, by the early 1980s, the equilibrium method had expanded from microeconomics to embed itself in macroeconomics as the 'New Classical' revolution, and the question of equilibrium stability largely faded from view. Indeed, over a century after the initial contributions of Walras and Marshall to the stability of Neoclassical equilibria, the authors of the contemporary 'gold standard' graduate textbook in microeconomics can argue that, Mas-Colell et al. (1995, p. 620):

> A characteristic feature that distinguishes economics from other scientific fields is that, for us, the equations of equilibrium constitute the center of our discipline. Other sciences, such as physics or even ecology, put comparatively more emphasis on the determination of dynamic laws of change ... The reason, informally speaking, is that economists are good (or so we hope) at recognizing a state of equilibrium but are poor at predicting precisely how an economy in disequilibrium will evolve.

The perceived theoretical importance of equilibria, and a perceived inability of theory to deal with disequilibria, has led to contemporary theory dealing with dynamics as a sequence of moving equilibria. This 'temporary equilibrium' method descends from the work of Hayek, Lindahl, and Hicks in the 1930s, and is almost universally used in the real business cycle models and New Keynesian models that dominate contemporary macroeconomics. The basic idea is illustrated in Figure 6.5. Instead of an equilibrium which does not change over time, around which a dynamic disequilibrium process evolves, the economy is always assumed to be in equilibria which themselves change over time. So in Figure 6.5, our supply curve is in three different positions at three different dates, corresponding to a change in fundamentals, expectations, or endogenous state variables (such as the quantity of capital). As a result there is a sequence of temporary equilibria: q_1, q_2, and q_3.

In general, and particularly in contemporary macroeconomics, there is little concern with the stability of the temporary equilibria at each date. This is closely related to the outlook of Mas-Colell and his co-authors, in which states of equilibrium take theoretical priority over states of disequilibrium. With Walras and Marshall, therefore, we have plausible disequilibrium processes which may or may not ensure that an economy reaches a Neoclassical equilibrium. Despite this, both theorists were optimistic that their equilibria constituted states towards which economies would actually tend, consistent with Smith and Ricardo's older definition. In the post-war period the study of disequilibrium processes advanced rapidly, but this research programme fell out of favour during the New Classical revolution, and the dominant contemporary

Figure 6.5 Temporary equilibria in a single market

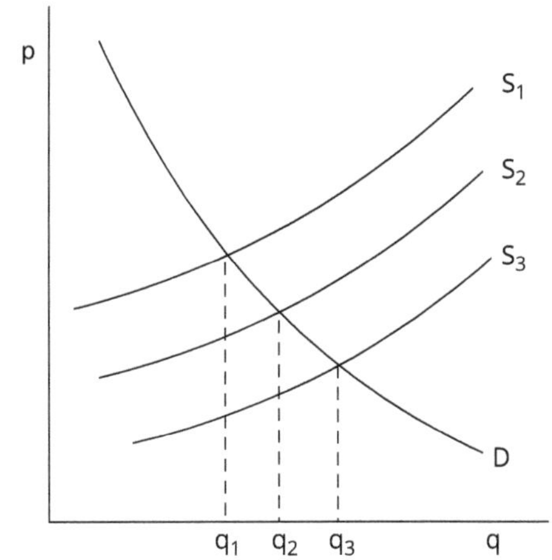

theories – whether New Classical, New Keynesian, or otherwise – tend to assume that economies are always in equilibrium.

The importance of this theoretical shift cannot be emphasised enough. In macroeconomics it is associated above all with the work of Lucas, one of the major progenitors of the New Classical economics that emerged in the 1970s. The idea that economies should be considered as though they are always in equilibrium – and, in New Classical macroeconomics, that equilibrium implies market clearing – makes equilibrium the central organising concept in modern economics. It is associated, although it does not always imply, the existence of 'natural' or 'non-accelerating inflation' rates of unemployment, and the association of non-market clearing with the existence of market power and monopoly. Importantly, this equilibrium approach has carried over to the New Keynesian orthodoxy that dominates macroeconomics in the early twenty-first century. There are, however, alternative approaches, which we turn to next.

Alternative approaches

The Neoclassical approaches considered above dominate the undergraduate and postgraduate textbook treatments of equilibrium and stability. In the second half of this chapter, I consider three alternative approaches: the Marxist approach, the Keynesian approach, and the Hayekian approach. These approaches rarely make it into the textbooks. Equilibrium as an organising concept tends to be less important in these approaches, and all three tend to be more sceptical about the ability of economies to reach equilibria, whether Neoclassical or otherwise.

The Marxist approach

Marx, like Smith and Ricardo, did not make great use of equilibrium as an organising concept. Where states of equilibrium can be identified in Marx's theory, their definition and characteristics are, unsurprisingly, somewhat different to those in Walras's and Marshall's theories. On the one hand, Marx had a complicated labour theory of value which went beyond that of Smith or Ricardo, and results in a transformation problem relating values to prices of production (see Chapter 9). On the other hand, almost the entirety of the second volume of his *magnum opus*, *Capital*, is concerned with the ability of multi-sectoral economies to reproduce themselves over time. Marx used 'reproduction schemes' to examine this question, which resemble, to some extent, Quesnay's *tableau économique*.

Underlying Marx's reproduction schemes is the circuit of capital, which describes the flow of money and commodities between various activities,

$$M \rightarrow C \ldots P \ldots C' \rightarrow M'.$$

Here, M denotes an initial value of money, and C denotes commodity inputs purchased with M. Production takes place, yielding a greater value of physical capital C', which is finally sold for a greater value of money, M' (see Chapter 4). Within this circuit, Marx divides the total product into two major sectors, or 'departments'. The reproduction schemes are then relatively straightforward. The first department only produces means of production, but requires means of production and articles of consumption in fixed proportions, whilst the second department only produces articles of consumption, but again requires means of production and articles of consumption in fixed proportions. The proportion of means of production and articles of consumption in total output must then equal the proportion needed for total inputs for the economy to remain in a state of simple reproduction.

This type of analysis, including the slightly more complicated case of 'accumulation and reproduction on an extended scale', were analysed by Marx using numerical examples. Throughout, the relative prices of the various articles of consumption and means of production are assumed to be fixed. Thus, Marx (1956, p. 397):

> The question that confronts us directly is this: How is the *capital* consumed in production replaced in value out of the annual product and how does the movement of this replacement intertwine with the consumption of the surplus-value by the capitalists and the wages by the labourers? It is then first a matter of reproduction on a simple scale. It is furthermore assumed that products are exchanged at their values and also that there is no revolution in the values of component parts of productive capital.

Later, in book three of *Capital*, Marx discussed the role of demand and supply, and competition between capitalists, in equalising prices and profit rates within the circuit of capital. This discussion owes a great deal to Smith and Ricardo, and as a result it is possible, if this is deemed useful, to interpret Marx as an equilibrium theorist – even if, like Smith and Ricardo, he did not refer to simple and extended reproduction in this manner. This interpretation of Marx is closely associated with the work of Michio Morishima (1973, 1977, 1989), although it is not always a popular interpretation within contemporary Marxist theory. Fine and Saad-Filho (2004, p. 64), for example, correctly point out that Marx, 'never draws the implication, as in general equilibrium theory or for the proponents of laissez-faire, that different producers and consumers are harmoniously co-ordinated through the market at high levels of employment of resources'.

Given this, it is perhaps unsurprising that Marx did not describe in great detail how the circuit of capital might be maintained in a stable state, and the largely Ricardian description of competition between capitals was left to the third volume of *Capital*. Instead, in the second volume we find the following passage, Marx (1956, p. 50):

> If capital stops short in its first phase M–C, money capital assumes the rigid form of a hoard; if it stops in the phase of production, the means of production lie without functioning on the one side, while labour power remains unemployed on the other; and if capital is stopped short in its last phase C'–M', piles of unsold commodities accumulate and clog the flow of circulation.

This is the basis of Marx's theory of crisis, developed in the *Theories of Surplus Value*, and discussed in Chapter 10 of this textbook. And in the first volume, after a lengthy discussion of profits, wages, and accumulation, we find a description of the business cycle, Marx (2003, pp. 592–596):

> The course characteristic of modern industry, viz., a decennial cycle (interrupted by smaller oscillations), of periods of average activity, production at high pressure, crisis and stagnation, depends on the constant formation, the greater or less absorption, and the re-formation of the industrial reserve army or surplus-population ... Taking them as a whole, the general movements of wages are exclusively regulated by the expansion and contraction of the industrial reserve army, and these again correspond to the periodic changes of the industrial cycle.

This passage forms one of the first 'real' theories of the business cycle, as opposed to a theory driven by monetary factors, and is clearly a dynamic process which is not obviously tending towards a state of stability. The theory was formalised by Goodwin in 1967 as a system of non-linear differential equations. In the Goodwin model, the employment rate increases with the rate of profit, as capitalists accumulate. However, the profit rate subsequently decreases with the employment rate, as workers' bargaining power increases and the share of income going to labour increases. Although the resulting system has an equilibrium in which the employment rate and labour share are constant, this equilibrium is not in fact stable, and unless the system starts off in equilibrium it will constantly cycle around it. This is illustrated in Figure 6.6, which plots simulated time paths for the employment rate and labour share in the Goodwin model (Goodwin, 1967).

If we take Goodwin's formalisation as a reasonable interpretation of Marx's theory of the business cycle, then states of simple and extended reproduction can be considered as states of potential equilibria, rather than equilibria in the older sense – as states towards which an economy will actually tend. Thus, in the second volume of *Capital* we are told that capitalist production, Marx (1956, p. 499):

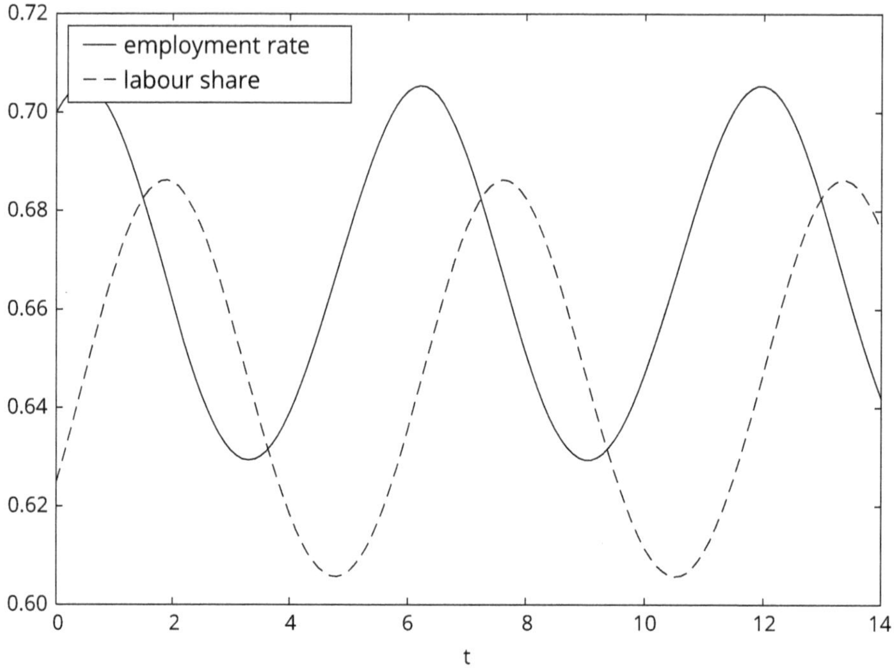

Figure 6.6 Simulated time series in the Goodwin model

> engenders certain conditions of normal exchange peculiar to this mode of production and therefore of the normal course of reproduction, whether it be on a simple or on an extended scale – conditions which change into so many conditions of abnormal movement, into so many possibilities of crises, since a balance is itself an accident owing to the spontaneous nature of this production.

And in the third volume of *Capital* we are told that, 'The industrial cycle is of such a nature that the same circuit must periodically reproduce itself, once the first impulse has been given' (Marx, 1972, p. 489).

Equilibrium was not, therefore, a particularly important organising concept for Marx, and where it can be identified (as with simple and expanded reproduction) it is arguably not a state that an actual economy is likely to reach. Whilst Walras and Marshall knew that Neoclassical equilibria could be unstable in theory, but were relatively optimistic about their stability properties in practice, Marx knew that simple and extended reproduction was possible in theory, but did not think that actual capitalist economies would reach these states in practice.

The Keynesian approach

As with Marx, the definition of equilibrium in Keynes's economics is somewhat different to its definition in Neoclassical economics. Whilst some of his earlier work used an explicitly dynamic method, the *General Theory of Employment, Interest, and Money*

(1936) returned to the static method. In particular, and unlike a number of his contemporaries, Keynes tended to rely on verbal discussion of simultaneous equations. The model of the *General Theory* is designed to explain the level of output as a whole, rather than prices and outputs in single markets or systems of markets. In this way it is profoundly different to the Neoclassical approach.

The determination of equilibrium in the *General Theory* is relatively clear. Investment increases to the point at which the marginal efficiency of capital is equal to the interest rate, and the level of output is determined by a multiplier mechanism operating on this level of investment through the marginal propensity to consume out of current income. The level of output directly determines the level of employment, which in turn impacts the demand for money and therefore the interest rate. 'Thus the position of equilibrium will be influenced by these repercussions; and there are other repercussions also' (Keynes, 1936, p. 249).

Passages like the foregoing directly lead to the Hicks-Hansen IS-LM interpretation of the *General Theory*, illustrated in Figure 6.7. The IS curve gives each combination of output and the interest rate at which saving equals investment, and the LM curve gives each combination of output and the interest rate at which money demand equals money supply. Equilibrium is then where the IS and LM curves cross. This is reminiscent of the Marshallian cross considered above, and it is possible to construct a disequilibrium adjustment process, analogous to the Marshallian adjustment process for partial equilibrium, to study how the economy approaches its IS-LM equilibrium (e.g. Varian, 1978). This disequilibrium aspect of the Neoclassical synthesis used to be fairly popular, particularly in graduate textbooks such as Patinkin (1965), but tends to be downplayed in modern textbooks.

Regardless of the disequilibrium stability of IS-LM equilibrium, it is not entirely clear that a simple, simultaneous equation model is what Keynes had in mind.[1] It is certainly the case that the marginal propensity to consume, the position of the investment schedule, and the extent of liquidity preference jointly determine the level of national output, employment, and the interest rate in the *General Theory*. However, it is not obvious that Keynes considered these determinants to be stable over time, which calls into question the relevance of the static IS-LM apparatus. On the one

Figure 6.7 The textbook IS-LM model

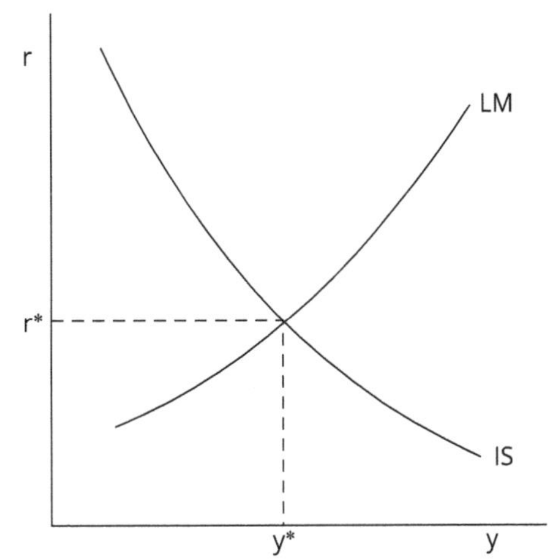

hand, 'there is not one of the above factors which is not liable to change without much warning, and sometimes substantially' (Keynes, 1936, p. 249). On the other hand, we are told that:

> In particular, it is an outstanding characteristic of the economic system in which we live that, whilst it is subject to severe fluctuations in respect of output and employment, it is not violently unstable. Indeed it seems capable of remaining in a chronic condition of sub-normal activity for a considerable period without any marked tendency either towards recovery or towards complete collapse. (Ibid.)

It is this tension between the 'severe fluctuations' in Keynes's vision of capitalism, which are nonetheless 'not violently unstable', which makes his equilibrium method so interesting. What Keynes appears to be grasping at is a theory of bounded, possibly chaotic, fluctuations, and this was the route taken by post-war Keynesian business cycle theory. Inspired by the Stockholm School, Kalecki's business cycle models, and Keynes's *General Theory*, theorists such as Samuelson, Hicks, Phillips, Kaldor, and Goodwin constructed models made up of difference and differential equations in the 1940s and 1950s to describe the 'severe fluctuations' that characterised pre-war capitalism.

As with Goodwin's formulation of Marxist business cycles discussed above, a key element of post-war Keynesian business cycle models was the generation of endogenous fluctuations which never approach a stable equilibrium. However, instead of the accumulation of capital determining employment and class struggle determining profitability, the Keynesian models tended to rely on interactions between accelerator mechanisms in investment and multiplier mechanisms in consumption to drive the business cycle. The Hicks (1950) model, for example, has a locally unstable equilibrium under empirically plausible parameterisations, but output is limited above by a ceiling, as output can only expand to a level consistent with full employment of available resources. Figure 6.8 plots a simulated time series for aggregate demand produced by this model, where the ceiling is clearly visible.

Other models yield cycles caused by more complicated forms of non-linearity, with non-linear investment or savings functions playing an important role. Later, Goodwin presented and discussed a number of non-linear multiplier accelerator models in the vein of Hicks (1950), and theorists such as Day and his co-authors (Day and Shafer, 1986) examined the existence of chaotic dynamics in Keynesian business cycle models. As with Goodwin's Marxian business cycle model, these models have equilibrium solutions, but these are not equilibria by Smith and Ricardo's definition. Instead, the models cycle around these equilibria indefinitely, producing endogenous fluctuations.

In the Marshallian and Walrasian traditions, states of equilibrium are theoretically prior to states of disequilibrium. Adjustment processes have been studied in some depth, but contemporary Neoclassical economics tends to construct temporary equilibrium models – particularly in macroeconomics. For Keynes and Marx, the role of equilibrium is more subtle. For Marx, equilibrium is a logical possibility, but economies are unlikely to ever reach such states. For Keynes, although the *General Theory*

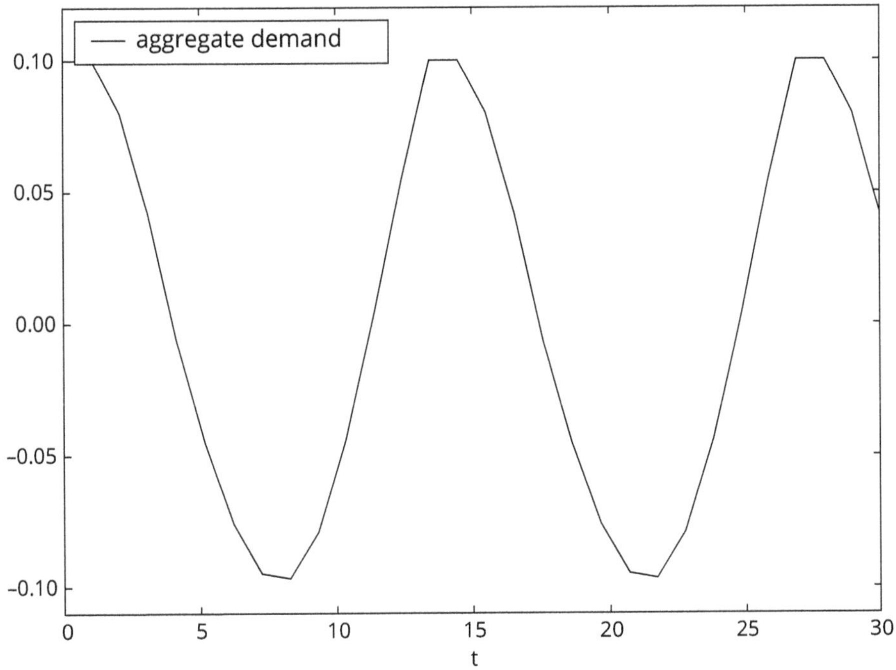

Figure 6.8 Simulated time series in the Hicks (1950) model

itself concentrates predominantly on states of unemployment equilibrium, whether these equilibria actually constitute points of rest is ambiguous. This led to a considerable post-war literature on disequilibrium business cycles, mainly driven by instability in investment expenditure. This literature does not tend to make it into contemporary undergraduate or postgraduate textbooks, where temporary equilibrium models, often of the rational expectations variety, predominate. This is the case despite the dominant contemporary macroeconomics being relatively Keynesian, and despite the relative ease of incorporating endogenous fluctuations and chaotic dynamics into temporary equilibrium models (Benhabib, 1992).

The Hayekian approach

Hayek's economic theory is the final alternative approach to equilibrium and disequilibrium that I will consider. Unlike Marx and Keynes, Hayek's definition of equilibrium, particularly towards the beginning of his career, was largely Neoclassical. In particular, he considered the full utilisation of available resources to be a basic equilibrium condition. However, as time went on Hayek developed a detailed theory of business cycles that relegated Neoclassical equilibria to a position of potential equilibria, in much the same manner as Marxist and Keynesian equilibria can be interpreted.

The main presentations of Hayek's business cycle theory are contained in his *Monetary Theory and the Trade Cycle* (first published in German in 1929) and his *Prices and Production* (first published in English in 1931). In both books, Hayek is primarily concerned with the movement away from an initial state of Neoclassical equilibrium.

This movement must be due to monetary factors, according to Hayek, as an expansion of the money supply is the only way that investors can finance an expansion of production beyond the level consistent with existing saving. In fact, as the money supply expands, and the interest rate consequently falls, it becomes profitable for investors to finance activities that take longer lengths of time to come to fruition. So, according to Hayek, if the interest rate is high we would expect to see production processes which yield a revenue fairly quickly – light manufacturing, for example. If the interest rate is low, we would expect to see production processes that take longer to yield a revenue – the construction of skyscrapers, perhaps.

The lengthening of the average period of production induced by a reduction in the interest rate should alter the prices of investment goods relative to consumption goods, as resources are diverted from the latter to the former. This, according to Hayek, will eventually lead to an increase in the price of consumption goods, and consumers will resist this decrease in their standard of living. Thus, according to Hayek (1935, pp. 88–89):

> It is highly improbable that individuals should put up with an unforeseen retrenchment of their real income without making an attempt to overcome it by spending more money on consumption ... The prices of consumers' goods will therefore rise relatively to the prices of producers' goods. And this rise of the prices of consumers' goods will be the more marked because it is the consequence not only of an increased demand for consumers' goods but an increase in the demand as measured in money.

In turn, this should lead to a shortening of the period of production, and the consequent fluctuations in relative prices is a defining characteristic of Hayek's business cycle theory.

Whether the foregoing should be interpreted as a stable disequilibrium adjustment process, similar to the Walrasian and Marshallian processes, or a theory of persistent fluctuations, similar to the Goodwin model and Keynesian business cycle models, is not obvious. Whilst the Marxist and Keynesian theories have been formalised as both static and dynamic models, and the different interpretations can be compared relatively easily, equivalent literatures do not exist in Austrian economics. More so than any other school of thought, Austrian economics has resisted the use of formal mathematical techniques in economic theory, and even contemporary treatments (e.g. Garrison, 2001) rely on verbal and graphical reasoning. A major debate within Austrian economics did take place in the 1970s and 1980s, however, concerning the ability of economies to reach equilibrium. On one side, economists such as Kirzner (1997, p. 62) argued that Neoclassical economics is fundamentally correct in its focus on equilibrium, but misunderstands the importance of entrepreneurial knowledge discovery in the attainment of equilibrium. Thus,

> Entrepreneurial discovery is seen as gradually but systematically pushing back the boundaries of sheer ignorance, in this way increasing mutual awareness amongst market participants and thus, in turn, driving prices, output and input quantities and qualities, toward the values consistent with equilibrium (seen as the complete absence of sheer ignorance).

As a result, Kirzner's interpretation of the Austrian approach, 'while sharply differing from the mainstream competitive equilibrium model, does not necessarily see that model as totally irrelevant' (ibid.).

On the other side of the debate, economists such as Lachmann (1976) were not only sceptical of the ability of economies to reach stable states, but called into question the relevance of equilibrium theorising in general. Instead, capitalist economies should be viewed as 'a continuous process without beginning or end, propelled by the interaction between the forces of equilibrium and the forces of change' (Lachmann, 1976, p. 60; Vaughn, 1992). This kind of approach follows the later Hayek, particularly his famous paper on the role of knowledge in economics (Hayek, 1937), and certain passages from *The Pure Theory of Capital* (1941). Thus, Hayek (1941, p. 17):

> When it is used in contrast to equilibrium analysis in general, [dynamics] refers to an explanation of the economic process as it proceeds in time, an explanation in terms of causation which must necessarily be treated as a chain of historical sequences. What we find here is not mutual interdependence between all phenomena but a unilateral dependence of the succeeding event on the preceding one. This kind of causal explanation of the process in time is of course the ultimate goal of all economic analysis, and equilibrium analysis is significant only in so far as it is preparatory to this main task.

Thus equilibrium theorising was arguably central to Hayek's early work, but its importance steadily declined as post-war Austrian economics matured. Interestingly, Hayek's insistence on the importance of causal, historical explanations in economics, and Lachmann's championing of this view, brings Austrian economics into contact with Post-Keynesian theory, particularly via the work of Shackle (1973, 1974). This unexpected point of contact between the followers of Hayek and Keynes reinforces the difficulty of interpreting their original work, and the difficulty in answering the questions they asked.

Concluding remarks

There is a tradition in economics, which is particularly pronounced in contemporary macroeconomics, of treating equilibria simply as properties of models, rather than properties of the real world. Thus Machlup (1958, p. 11) argues that:

> Equilibrium as a tool for theoretical analysis is not an operational concept; and attempts to develop operational counterparts to the construct have not been successful. Some of the variables in a model usually have statistically operational counterparts; in rare instances all have. But even in this event the *compatibility* between the variables is always a question of the assumed interrelations and of the limitation of the model to the variables selected. The 'real world' surely has infinitely more variables than any abstract economic model, and their 'actual' interrelations are neither known nor, I fear, knowable (partly because they probably change

unpredictably over time). It follows that the equilibrium between selected variables could not be observed even if each of the variables had an observable counterpart in the real world.

However, if we bear in mind the original definition of equilibrium in economics, as a state towards which economies tend, then we can recognise its fundamental empirical importance. Capitalist economies either tend towards stable states, and are only displaced from those states by exogenous shocks, or they generate endogenous fluctuations that do not disappear over time. It is not clear which of these is a better description of real world economies, and neither is it clear if one description is valid for every time and place. However, the vast majority of contemporary textbooks treat capitalist economies as if they always tend towards stable states, and focus overwhelmingly on equilibrium as a central organising concept. This has not always been the case in the history of economic thought, and this chapter has considered some of the major alternatives.

The choice of alternatives has been guided by historical importance, and there are other alternatives to textbook theory that have not been considered here. Evolutionary economics became increasingly important during the second half of the twentieth century, and evolutionary game theory is widely used in contemporary microeconomics. This approach is also used in agent-based computational economics, which emerged in the 1970s and has been widely used in financial economics and macroeconomics. Historical and institutional economics were major contenders to Neoclassical theory in the first half of the twentieth century, particularly in areas such as labour economics, and these approaches make little use of equilibrium reasoning. More recently, time series econometricians have proposed and studied purely statistical definitions of stability, which can be used as operational definitions of equilibrium. The interested reader can consult the reading list below for further information on these approaches, as well as the Neoclassical, Marxist, Keynesian, and Hayekian approaches to equilibrium and disequilibrium.

Discussion questions and seminar activities

This chapter has discussed a range of issues concerning the stability of capitalist economies. For further engagement in class, the following questions might be considered:

- The Neoclassical theories of equilibrium discussed at the beginning of this chapter suppose that the demand and supply curves are fixed – i.e. they are unaffected by events that take place outside of equilibrium. Do you think this is realistic? Which disequilibrium events might affect the demand or supply curves?
- Compare and contrast the Marxian, Keynesian, and Austrian business cycle theories. Which, if any, do you think is an adequate characterisation of contemporary economies?
- How might we amend the simple Neoclassical models of disequilibrium considered in this chapter to allow for monopoly and oligopoly? Is it possible for a market dominated by a single price-setter to be in disequilibrium?

The following activities could also be used in class:

- In groups, compare post-war time series of US and UK unemployment rates – these data are easy to access from the FRED database or similar. Is there an obvious equilibrium in either series? Is there an obvious business cycle in either series? What might this tell us about the stability, or otherwise, of capitalist economies?
- Divide the class into pairs, and play a repeated version of the ultimatum game in which the players take turns to be the proposer. Do proposal and acceptance behaviours settle down to an equilibrium – i.e. a repeated pattern of play?
- The theories of equilibrium and disequilibrium considered in this chapter ignore environmental issues. Consider the level of food waste, or plastic packaging, created as a by-product of the food industry. In groups, discuss whether or not this can be maintained indefinitely, whether or not it constitutes an equilibrium, and how we might extend the concept of equilibrium to allow for environmental issues.

Further reading

For a discussion of Marshall's and Walras's disequilibrium processes, aside from the textbook discussions noted above, the reader can consult Blaug (1985, pp. 405–408). For a discussion of the various differences between Marshall's and Walras's economics, de Vroey's work is a good place to start (De Vroey, 2012). By far the best discussion of post-war Neoclassical disequilibrium theory is contained in Fisher (1983). This is a largely forgotten literature, which is worth being aware of. A selection of the work on complexity and chaos in temporary equilibrium models, particularly of the rational expectations variety, is contained in Benhabib (1992). This body of work is also relatively unpopular today, although it appears to be making a slight comeback after the 2008 crisis. The reader might also consult Kirman (1989) for a useful summary of uniqueness and stability problems in Neoclassical general equilibrium theory.

The equilibrium interpretation of Marx is closely associated with the work of Morishima (1973, 1977, 1989) and can be traced to von Bortkiewicz's work on the transformation problem at the beginning of the twentieth century (Freeman, 1995). As mentioned in the text, one dissenting view is Fine and Saad-Filho (2004). There is a considerable literature on the Goodwin model. Veneziani and Mohun (2006) provide a lengthy discussion of the model and give a large number of references. Important early extensions of the original model include Desai (1973), Desai and Shah (1981), and Pohjola (1981). An interesting equilibrium formulation of the Goodwin model is presented in Mehrling (1986), where the class struggle is formalised using game theory. This approach is arguably under-studied, although game theory is also used in the Analytical Marxist tradition – see Veneziani (2012) for a survey.

For the IS-LM model, particularly the validity of IS-LM equilibrium, one should read the original Hicks (1937) paper in conjunction with Hicks (1980). As noted in the text, Patinkin (1965) discusses the role of disequilibrium in the Neoclassical synthesis, and Leijonhufvud (1968) takes a more radical disequilibrium approach to the economics of Keynes. In contrast, the reader can refer to Krugman (2000) for a defence of the IS-LM model (in the context of 'small models' in general), although not as an interpretation of the *General Theory*. The post-war business cycle literature is thoroughly treated in Gabisch and Lorenz (1987). This is essential reading for anyone interested in the subject. This also covers Kalecki's business cycle theory, which has not been considered in the main text. The reader might also like to consult Haberler (1937) for a survey of pre-Keynesian business cycle theory.

Garrison (2001) is a prominent example of contemporary Austrian economics. Vaughn (1992) provides a good discussion of the debate on equilibrium and disequilibrium within Austrian economics. Caldwell (1998) provides an overview of Hayek's movement from equilibrium theory to disequilibrium theory, and chapter 11 of Roncaglia (2005) provides a useful overview of Menger, Mises, and Hayek. Thornton (2005) is an interesting paper examining the relevance of skyscraper construction to Austrian business cycle theory. The reader might also be interested in the work of Shackle, particularly Shackle (1973) and Shackle (1974), as an example of the overlap between Post-Keynesian and Austrian economics. There are also a number of existing studies of equilibrium and disequilibrium in the history of economic thought. Mosini (2007) is a particularly useful collection of essays, with a large number of further references, and has been useful in writing the present chapter.

Nelson and Winter (1982) is a classic reference in evolutionary economics, and a skim through the pages of the *Journal of Evolutionary Economics* is a good way of getting a feel for the literature. In terms of agent-based modelling specifically, one can refer to the second volume of the *Handbook of Computational Economics* (Tesfatsion and Judd, 2006). Historical and institutional economics are more dispersed, and the former in particular is not a particularly popular approach (although economic history is, of course, a separate and vibrant discipline). For a useful interpretation of institutional economics, one could refer to Hodgson (1998). Finally, Hendry (1995) is an extremely useful reference for issues of stability and equilibrium in econometrics, although any textbook on time series econometrics would be adequate for this purpose.

References

Benhabib, J. (1992). *Cycles and chaos in economic equilibrium*. Princeton: Princeton University Press.

Blaug, M. (1985). *Economic theory in retrospect* (4th ed.). Cambridge: Cambridge University Press.

Caldwell, B. (1998). Hayek's transformation. *History of Political Economy, 20*(4), 513–541.

Day, R., & Shafer, W. (1986). Keynesian chaos. *Journal of Macroeconomics, 7*(3), 277–295.

De Vroey, M. (2012). Marshall and Walras: Incompatible bedfellows? *European Journal of the History of Economic Thought, 19*(5), 765–783.

Desai, M. (1973). Growth cycles and inflation in a model of the class struggle. *Journal of Economic Theory, 6*(6), 527–545.

Desai, M., & Shah, A. (1981). Growth cycles with induced technical change. *Economic Journal, 91*(364), 1006–1010.

Fine, B., & Saad-Filho, A. (2004). *Marx's Capital*. London: Pluto Press.

Fisher, F. (1983). *Disequilibrium foundations of equilibrium economics*. Cambridge: Cambridge University Press.

Freeman, A. (1995). Marx without equilibrium. *Capital and Class, 19*(2), 49–89.

Gabisch, G., & Lorenz, H. (1987). *Business cycle theory: A survey of methods and concepts*. Berlin: Springer.

Garrison, R. (2001). *Time and money: The macroeconomics of capital structure*. London: Routledge.
Goodwin, R. (1967). A growth cycle. In C. Feinstein (Ed.), *Socialism, capitalism and economic growth*. Cambridge: Cambridge University Press.
Gravelle, H., & Reese, R. (2004). *Microeconomics*. Harlow: Pearson Education.
Haberler, G. (1937). *Prosperity and depression*. Geneva: League of Nations.
Hayek, F. (1929). *Monetary theory and the trade cycle*. Translated from German by N. Kaldor and H. M. Croome (1933), New York. Harcourt, Brace & Co.
Hayek, F. (1935). *Prices and production*. New York: Augustus M. Kelly.
Hayek, F. (1937). Economics and knowledge. *Economica, 4*(13), 33–54.
Hayek, F. (1941). *The pure theory of capital*. Chicago: The University of Chicago Press.
Hendry, D. (1995). *Dynamic econometrics*. Oxford: Oxford University Press.
Hicks, J. (1937). Mr Keynes and the 'classics': A suggested interpretation. *Econometrica, 5*(2), 147–159.
Hicks, J. (1950). *A contribution to the theory of the trade cycle*. Oxford: Oxford University Press.
Hicks, J. (1980). IS-LM: An explanation. *Journal of Post Keynesian Economics, 3*(2), 139–154.
Hodgson, G. (1998). The approach of institutional economics. *Journal of Economic Literature, 36*(1), 166–192.
Keynes, J. (1936). *The general theory of employment, interest and money*. London: Macmillan.
Kirman, A. (1989). The intrinsic limits of modern economic theory: The emperor has no clothes. *The Economic Journal, 99*(395). Supplement: Conference papers, pp. 126, 139.
Kirzner, I. (1997). Entrepreneurial discovery and the competitive market process: An Austrian approach. *Journal of Economic Literature, 35*(1), 60–85.
Krugman, P. (2000). How complicated does the model have to be? *Oxford Review of Economic Policy, 16*(4), 33–42.
Lachmann, L. (1976). From Mises to Shackle: An essay on Austrian economics and the Kaleidic Society. *Journal of Economic Literature, 14*(1), 54–62.
Leijonhufvud, A. (1968). *On Keynesian economics and the economics of Keynes*. New York: Oxford University Press.
Machlup, F. (1958). Equilibrium and disequilibrium: Misplaced concreteness and disguised politics. *The Economic Journal, 68*(269), 1–24.
Marshall, A. (2013). *Principles of economics*. Basingstoke: Palgrave Macmillan.
Marx, K. (1956). *Capital* (Vol. 2). London: Lawrence & Wishart Ltd.
Marx, K. (1972). *Capital* (Vol. 3). London: Lawrence & Wishart Ltd.
Marx, K. (2003). *Capital* (Vol. 1). London: Lawrence & Wishart Ltd.
Mas-Colell, A., Whinston, M., & Green, J. (1995). *Microeconomic theory*. Oxford: Oxford University Press.
Mehrling, P. (1986). A classical model of the class struggle: A game-theoretic approach. *The Journal of Political Economy, 94*(6), 1280–1303.
Milgate, M. (1987). Equilibrium: Development of the concept. In *The New Palgrave: A dictionary of economics* (Vol. 2). London: The Macmillan Press Limited.
Morishima, M. (1973). *Marx's economics*. Cambridge: Cambridge University Press.
Morishima, M. (1977). *Walras' economics*. Cambridge: Cambridge University Press.
Morishima, M. (1989). *Ricardo's economics*. Cambridge: Cambridge University Press.
Mosini, V. (2007). *Equilibrium in economics: Scope and limits*. London: Routledge.

Nelson, R., & Winter, S. (1982). *An evolutionary theory of economic change*. Harvard: Harvard University Press.

Patinkin, D. (1965). *Money, interest, and prices*. New York: Harper Row.

Pohjola, M. (1981). Stable, cyclic and chaotic growth: The dynamics of a discrete-time version of Goodwin's growth cycle model. *Journal of Economics, 41*(1), 27–38.

Ricardo, D. (1951). *The works and correspondence of David Ricardo, Volume 1: On the principles of political economy and taxation*. Cambridge: Cambridge University Press.

Roncaglia, A. (2005). *The wealth of ideas*. Cambridge: Cambridge University Press.

Samuelson, P. (1941). The stability of equilibrium: Comparative statics and dynamics. *Econometrica, 9*(2), 97–120.

Scarf, H. (1960). Some examples of global instability of competitive equilibrium. *International Economic Review, 1*(3), 157–172.

Shackle, G. (1973). *Epistemics & economics: A critique of economic doctrines*. Cambridge: Cambridge University Press.

Shackle, G. (1974). *Keynesian Kaleidics*. Edinburgh: Edinburgh University Press.

Smith, A. (1890). *An inquiry into the nature and causes of the wealth of nations*. London: George Routledge and Sons.

Tesfatsion, L., & Judd, K. (Eds.). (2006). *Handbook of computational economics, Volume 2: Agent-based computational economics*. Amsterdam: North-Holland.

Thornton, M. (2005). Skyscrapers and business cycles. *The Quarterly Journal of Austrian Economics, 8*(1), 51–74.

Varian, H. (1978). The stability of a disequilibrium IS-LM model. In *Topics in disequilibrium economics*. Basingstoke: Palgrave Macmillan.

Varian, H. (1992). *Microeconomic analysis*. New York: W.W. Norton.

Vaughn, K. (1992). The problem of order in Austrian economics: Kirzner vs. Lachmann. *Review of Political Economy, 4*(3), 251–274.

Veneziani, R. (2012). Analytical Marxism. *Journal of Economic Surveys, 26*(4), 649–673.

Veneziani, R., & Mohun, S. (2006). Structural stability and Goodwin's growth cycle. *Structural Change and Economic Dynamics, 17*(4), 437–451.

Walras, L. (1954). *Elements of pure economics*. London: George Allen & Unwin Ltd.

7 HOW IS INCOME DISTRIBUTED?

Jo Michell

Introduction

In the two and a half centuries since Smith wrote *The Wealth of Nations*, economists' interest in income distribution has waxed and waned. The topic has drifted in and out of fashion, driven by historical developments and shifting theoretical and political sands. The Classical thinkers attempted to explain how income was divided among capitalists, landlords, and workers – the classes described by Smith as the 'three great, original, and constituent orders of every civilised society' (1776/1976, p. 265). Ricardo declared Political Economy to be 'an enquiry into the laws which determine the division of the produce of industry among the classes who concur in its formation' (1820, pp. 278–279). Marx recast Ricardo's model as a system driven by conflict between workers and capitalists over the distribution of income.

The Marginalist revolution of the 1870s replaced the Classical idea of a *surplus* accruing to capitalists and landowners after wages are paid, with the factor rewards theory of Jevons, Clark, Marshall, and others. For the Marginalists, income distribution is determined by the relative contribution to production provided by each factor of production (labour, land, and capital). The income received by the owners of these factors is determined in competitive markets in the same way as the price of goods. In return for the use of factors of production, owners receive a reward equal to the marginal contribution of that factor to the production of utility-providing consumption goods. In competitive markets, the real wage will then equal the marginal productivity of labour at the current level of employment.

The Marginalists rejected the class-based analysis of the Classical authors: individuals are no longer seen as capitalists or workers but as owners of factors of production which may be held in any combination or proportion – reflecting in part the changing reality in which capitalists might also own land, or better-paid workers might save for their retirement by accumulating financial assets.

For some of the Marginalists at least, income distribution, like goods pricing, was seen as the outcome of impersonal 'natural laws' – not something that policy could or should aim to influence. For Clark, the Classical idea that employers have a structural advantage over workers in the wage bargaining process is therefore not only false but dangerous because it could lead to attempts to influence income distribution rather than relying on the market mechanism. This view was widespread in the early twentieth century: despite high income inequality, discussion of distribution was largely confined to the fringes of the discipline.

With the stock market crash of 1929 and the onset of the Great Depression, economists' focus shifted to the problems of the slump. The publication in 1936 of Keynes's *General Theory* marked the start of macroeconomics as a distinct discipline. But income distribution still received relatively little attention. In 1939, Keynes declared the stability of the share of wages in national income to be 'a bit of a miracle' (1939, p. 49), while offering little explanation as to the cause. By 1957, Kaldor had included stability of the wage share as one of his stylised 'facts' of economic growth. But interest in the issue was growing among the followers of Keynes in Cambridge. The ideas of Kalecki in particular were attracting attention. Kalecki, who had independently discovered the same key principles as Keynes, had developed a macroeconomic theory in which aggregate demand and income distribution both played important roles.

From the 1950s onwards there was growing polarisation of views on income distribution. Neoclassical ideas about growth and distribution coalesced around Solow's (1956) model in which the long-run distribution between capital and labour is assumed fixed. Less orthodox economists – who saw themselves following in Keynes's footsteps – grew increasingly critical of the Neoclassical vision of long-run full employment and competitive markets. Solow provided a theoretical explanation for Kaldor's stylised facts just as Cambridge Keynesians (including Kaldor) were developing new ideas about the interplay between growth and distribution.

Solow's use of an aggregate production function was a particular focus of criticism from the Cambridge Keynesians and Italian economists such as Sraffa and Garegnani. In what came to be known as the Cambridge Capital Controversies, the Cambridge UK economists argued that Solow's approach suffered from logical inconsistencies and should be abandoned. Defence of the Neoclassical approach was centred at Harvard (in Cambridge, Massachusetts). While the Neoclassical economists eventually admitted defeat on technical terms, the implications of the debate for economic theory remain unresolved. Nonetheless, Solow's Neoclassical aggregate production function became the standard model of growth and distribution, while discontented critical economists continued to look for alternatives.

Income inequality declined in the advanced capitalist nations from the end of the Second World War until the 1970s. From the 1980s onwards, however, inequality rose sharply and once again began to attract economists' attention. During the 1990s and 2000s, orthodox economists used the Marginalist approach to try to explain how changes in technology and increasing global trade were affecting income distribution – while heterodox economists continued to develop ideas which retained Classical influences.

The publication of Piketty's *Capital in the 21st Century* in 2014 marked the point at which discussion of inequality returned to centre stage in economics. Piketty and his colleagues presented data showing how, after a period of growing equality following the Second World War, inequality of income – and *wealth* – was rising once again. In a break from the modern economics tradition, Piketty set the analysis in a sweeping historical narrative. As a result, it was hailed by some as a return to the style of Classical economics.

Classical analysis of distribution

Smith

What laws govern the division of national income between workers, capitalists and landlords? Partial answers were given by early thinkers such as Cantillon and Quesnay, but a systematic analysis is arguably first developed by the Classical thinkers, starting with the publication of Smith's *The Wealth of Nations* in 1776. Smith's central question was *what determines the wealth of nations?* His answer is that wealth accumulates because capitalists, instead of consuming their profits, use their income to increase the productive capital stock. This leads to greater employment of workers and a greater division of labour – Smith thought this is the ultimate source of productivity increases. The process is guided not by collective deliberate thought or planning, but by an *invisible hand.* But how does this invisible hand decide how much income is given to the capitalist as profits, or taken home by the worker as wages? And what of the landlord?

This division of income is known as the *functional distribution* of income – because it is done on the basis of economic *function.* This can be contrasted with the *personal distribution* which describes how income is allocated within groups – such as the distribution of wage income among workers, or the distribution of profits between corporations. The Classical economists focused on the *functional distribution* because competition was thought to equalise incomes *within* classes: profit rates would be equalised by competition between capitalists, while workers would compete for work and move between employers to equalise wage rates. Different mechanisms were thought to be involved in determining the division between income *types*: wages, profits and rents. Identifying these mechanisms and analysing the implied outcomes was an important element of Classical economic analysis.

The distributional theories of the Classical writers are intertwined with their theories of *value* and *price* (see Chapter 9). One of Smith's important contributions is the idea that the amount of labour required to produce a commodity can be used as an *objective* measure of *value* – a way to compare the 'quantities' of otherwise incomparable items.[1] In primitive societies, Smith argues, labour time of production also determines *exchange values*: prices. In a famous example, Smith describes a simple economy in which hunters use only their own labour to catch animals. In this economy, if it takes twice as long to catch a deer as a beaver, then these will be exchanged at a ratio of two beaver to one deer.

Smith then considers the more realistic case where goods are produced using not only labour but also using capital and land. As discussed in Chapter 9, Smith introduces the distinction between the *natural prices* of commodities and *market prices* – the observed rates of exchange between different commodities in the market. Smith believed that market prices are determined by the transitory forces of supply and demand but will always tend to converge towards natural prices.

Smith provides two different – and incompatible – accounts of what determines the natural price of a commodity. The first is the labour required to produce the commodity. In places, Smith appears to suggest that labour is not only an objective *measure of value* but also the *cause of value.* In contrast with earlier thinkers who saw land or accumulation of gold as the source of wealth, Smith argues that labour is the ultimate source of wealth in human societies.

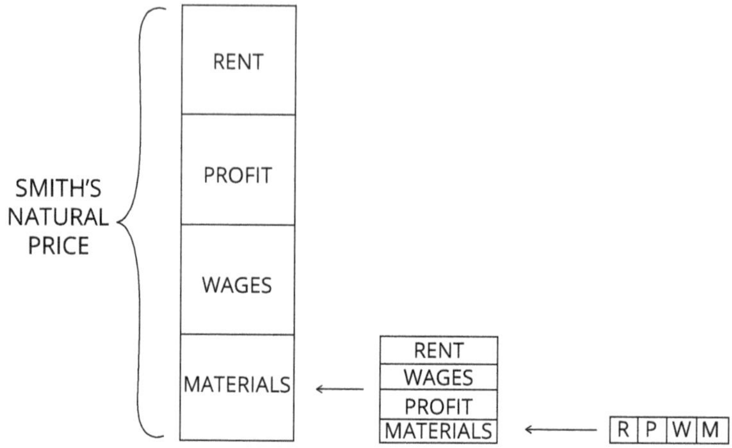

Figure 7.1 Smith's 'adding-up' theory of prices

Smith's second method to determine the natural price of a commodity involves dividing the *value added* in production – the difference between the price paid for material inputs and the price received for selling final goods – between the three factors of production: value added is equal to the sum of wages, profits, and rents. To illustrate, consider a firm that purchases commodities as inputs to the production process – either raw materials or partially manufactured intermediate goods. After production, the firm sells the newly produced goods, pays labour the going wage, and pays rent for its premises; what remains is profit. The division of output between costs (wages, rent, and commodity inputs) and profits is now accounted for – if not explained – with the exception of the cost of the commodity inputs. But the value added in the production process of the commodity inputs can also be divided up in the same way: into wages, profits, rents – and commodity inputs. By following the chain of inputs all the way back to the production of raw materials, *all* output can allocated to wages, rents, and profits. Smith's approach is sometimes called the 'adding-up' theory of prices. The *natural price* of a commodity is then just the sum of the three *natural prices* of the factors of the factors used in its production. This is illustrated in Figure 7.1.

Smith briefly discusses what determines this *natural price* (or *natural rate*) for each of the three types of income – wages, profits, and rents – but does not provide conclusive answers, at least in the case of profits and rents. In the case of wages, Smith argues that a worker's subsistence consumption requirements determine the *natural price of labour*: 'the lowest which is consistent with common humanity' (1776/1976, p. 86).[2] Smith is ambiguous about the extent to which the determination of the distribution of income involves conflict. The overall picture is one of harmony: by following their own self-interest, individuals unwittingly serve the greater good. But Smith also makes sharp comments about the tendency for capitalists to try to impose monopolies, artificially inflating their share of total output: 'People of the same trade seldom meet together, even for merriment and diversion, but the conversation ends in a conspiracy against the public, or in some contrivance to raise prices' (ibid., p. 145) Smith is likewise critical of landlords, arguing that rent is a 'monopoly price' and that: 'landlords, like all other men, love to reap where they never sowed, and demand a rent even for the natural produce of the earth' (ibid., p. 67). Smith's account of subsistence wage determination therefore hints at the idea of a *surplus*: value produced by labour but appropriated by other factors of production.

Ultimately, Smith fails to provide a complete account of the distribution of income, and the inconsistencies in his account leave his view open to a range of interpretations. But in his suggestion that labour is the source of value, Smith lays the foundation for Ricardo (see also Chapter 9).

Ricardo

Ricardo takes Smith's labour theory of value as his starting point, but points out that it is inconsistent with Smith's *adding-up theory* of prices and distribution. Smith treats the amount of labour used to produce a commodity as the *natural price* of that commodity. But the adding-up theory of prices shows that labour receives only part of the market price of the commodity as its reward, with the remainder going to profits and rents. This inconsistency, sometimes characterised using the distinction between *labour embodied* and *labour commanded*, is illustrated in Figure 7.2. If the true price of a commodity is determined by the labour required to produce it, then it should be possible to sell the commodity and use the proceeds to hire labour equal to that required to produce the commodity – this is the *labour commanded*. But a sum of money equal to the sales price of a commodity will hire *more* labour than is required to produce that commodity, because in the *adding-up theory*, labour receives only a

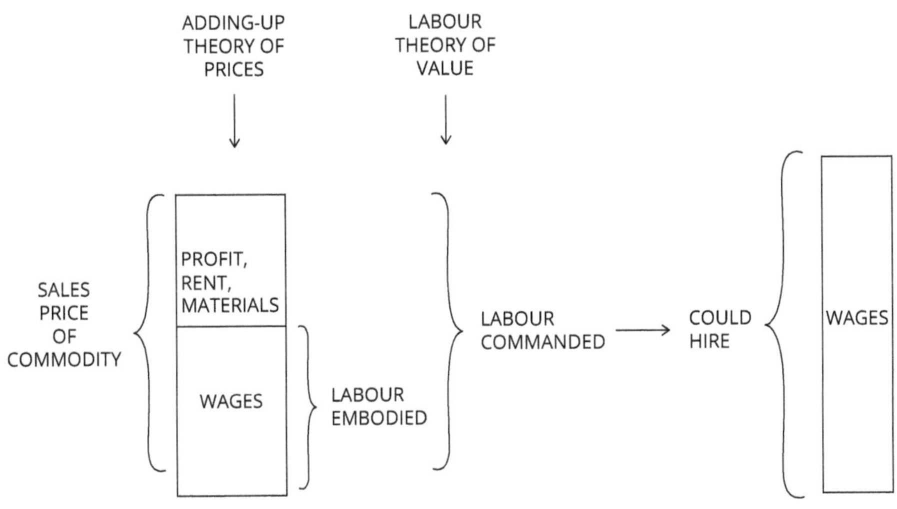

Figure 7.2 The 'adding-up' theory of prices versus the labour theory of value

fraction of the sales price. The *labour commanded* by the commodity exceeds the *labour embodied* in it – the labour used for production. This inconsistency leads Ricardo to criticise Smith and to abandon the 'adding-up' theory of price. Ricardo instead argues that the cost of labour – the wage – is irrelevant and the exchange value of commodities is determined by the labour time required for production: 'the value of a commodity ... depends on the relative quantity of labour which is necessary for its production, and not on the greater or less compensation which is paid for that labour' (1817, p. 5).

With the 'adding-up' theory discarded, Ricardo needed another way to determine shares of national income. To find the answer, he focused on a question which to Smith had not appeared very important: how is a growing population to be fed? Ricardo's friend, the Reverend David Malthus, had recently published his pessimistic *Essay on Population* 1798 which predicted mass hunger due to what he saw as the inescapable tendency for population growth to exceed the rate at which food production could be increased. Ricardo was writing at a time when tariffs on imported grain – known as the Corn Laws – prevented imports of cheap grain from continental Europe. This kept the price of grain high, allowing landlords to collect high rents for the use of agricultural land.

The landlord is therefore more prominent in Ricardo's account of the distribution of income than in Smith's. Ricardo was concerned that by keeping the price of food high, landlords forced capitalists to pay high wages – high enough for a subsistence standard of living – therefore depriving them of the profits which are the ultimate source of accumulation. Since wages would be spent entirely on high-priced grain, the landlord would be the only beneficiary. In the long run, Ricardo believed that the cost of food production would increase, causing rents to rise while squeezing profits and bringing accumulation to a halt.

In dealing with the problem of the landlord, Ricardo introduces a crucial innovation into economic theory: marginal analysis. Ricardo, drawing on the ideas of Malthus, notes that as new land is brought into cultivation, or as currently cultivated land is worked more intensively, the additional crop yield for a given increase in labour and tools tends to decline. Ricardo formalises the idea that the marginal product of labour in agriculture declines as more labour is applied.[3] This insight is the key to Ricardo's theory of distribution.

Like Smith, Ricardo assumes that workers are paid a subsistence wage. They receive enough money to buy the goods necessary to keep themselves alive but little more. The share of income going to the workers is then fixed, with the division of the remainder between capitalists and landlords still to be determined. This is where Ricardo's assumption of declining marginal productivity in agriculture comes into play.

Ricardo assumes that agricultural production is in the hands of capitalist farmers. Like Smith, he assumes that free movement between sectors by capitalists and workers will equalise wages (at subsistence levels) and profit rates. An upper limit is set, however, to the rate of profit by the productivity of the lowest quality *marginal* land.

Since marginal productivity falls as land cultivation increases, the marginal *cost* of producing enough food to keep a worker alive rises: more capital and labour are required to produce the same amount of food. With growth of the working

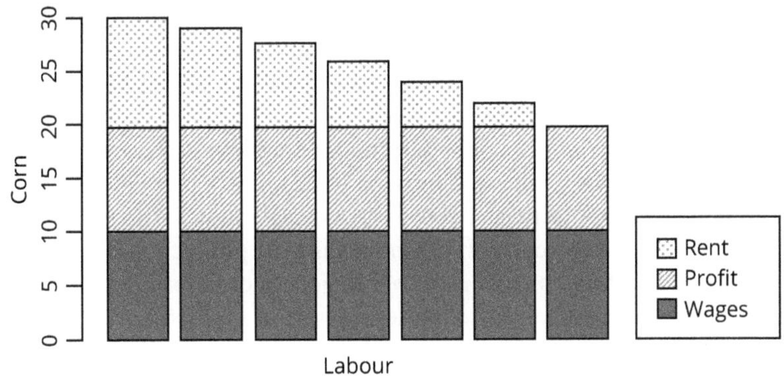

Figure 7.3 Ricardo's model of distribution

population the cost of subsistence per worker rises. As a result, the money wage must also rise – but since wages are spent entirely on subsistence income, the landlord is the only beneficiary of rising food prices.

A straightforward way to understand Ricardo's system of distribution is to use agricultural output (corn) as the unit of measure. Figure 7.3 shows the relationship between units of labour applied to agricultural production and output. The vertical bars show the quantity of corn produced by each unit of labour. Given Ricardo's assumption that the marginal productivity in agriculture declines, the height of the bars declines as additional labour is applied.

Since Ricardo assumes that workers use tools in fixed proportions, the capital–labour ratio is fixed. And since Ricardo assumes that marginal productivity in manufacturing industry is *constant*, and industrial production (clothes, tools, and so on) is undertaken only to supply the needs of workers, both agricultural and industrial, the ratio of workers in agriculture to workers in manufacturing is also constant. As a result, the number of bars can also represent labour in the industrial sector and the volume of capital in use.

While the height of the bars represents the marginal productivity in agriculture at each scale of production, the total area of the bars represents the corresponding total agricultural production. Ricardo's model provides an elegant way to determine the division of this product between the workers, landlords, and capitalists. Since workers receive a fixed subsistence income (in corn) this can be represented as a fixed quantity, *W*, of each bar.[4] The workers' share in income is then given by the shaded area. What remains is to determine the division of the surplus between capitalists and landlords.

The rent on land will vary with quality: higher-productivity land will command a higher rent. Note that Ricardo's definition of the rate of profit *excludes* rent as a cost: the surplus is what remains after costs of production are paid and this surplus is divided between rent and profits. Since the capital–labour ratio is assumed constant, the rate of profit can therefore be represented by the ratio of profits, *P* to wages: *P*/*W*.

Consider the limiting case where capitalists pay *no* rent on marginal land. The lowest-quality land currently under cultivation generates no rental income for landlords. This is represented by the rightmost bar in Figure 7.3. The entire output remaining after paying the subsistence wage is received as profits by the capitalist. The profit on marginal land is equal to the entire 'surplus' produced on it. Since the rate of profit is equalised by competition, this ratio must be equal on each plot of land, so that *total profits* can be drawn as a rectangle, above the rectangle representing wages. Further, since capitalists can move not only within agricultural production but also between agriculture and manufacturing, which is *not* subject to diminishing returns, the output produced on marginal land determines the rate of profit (the ratio of profits to wages) in industry as well as in agriculture. Once the subsistence wage and the rate of profit are determined, the remainder of the surplus accrues to landlords as rent, and Ricardo has a complete account of the distribution of income between the three classes. Total rent is shown as the dotted area in Figure 7.3.[5]

In introducing the assumption of diminishing returns in agriculture, Ricardo is able to construct a fully determinate model of the distribution of income. As lower-quality marginal land is brought into production, the rate of profit falls and the share of income going to the landlords increases. Without the repeal of the Corn Laws, Ricardo concludes, rent will squeeze out profits entirely, bringing capitalist accumulation to a halt.

Marx

Like Smith and Ricardo, Marx's starting point for his theory of income distribution is the idea that human labour is the ultimate source of wealth and income. Marx (1867/1976) focuses on how this can be reconciled with the existence of profit. Like Ricardo, Marx highlights the flaw in Smith's reasoning: the incompatibility between the *labour embodied* and *labour commanded* versions of his price theory. Marx returns to the issue that if profits are positive, these two magnitudes cannot be equal. If all commodities exchange in the market at their value (defined as labour *embodied*) how can capitalists make a profit? To see the problem, consider the productive process of a capitalist firm. The firm buys two inputs: *means of production* (machines and raw materials) and *labour*. If the firm purchases means of production which took 30 hours of labour to produce and purchases 70 hours of labour to work on these materials, the firm must pay 100 hours' worth of commodities. But the value of the finished goods is also 100 hours of labour! If the finished goods are sold at their value, profit will be zero.

Marx acknowledged that zero-sum games were possible. If a capitalist can sell commodities at a price in excess of the value of those commodities, s/he will make a profit. But this gain will be matched by a loss on the part of the buyer. Deviations of prices from values can explain profit for individual firms, but cannot explain how the capitalist class as a whole is able to generate a profit.

Marx solves the puzzle by drawing a distinction between *labour* and a distinct commodity which he calls *labour power*. Labour power is the ability to *perform labour*. When capitalists hire workers, what they purchase is not *labour* but *labour power*. Workers don't sell their labour, instead they sell their ability to do a day's work (their labour power). The labour cost of the ability to do a day's work is the subsistence wage:

the *cost of producing* labour power is the labour required to produce the subsistence commodities consumed by a worker.

The crucial point is that the value of labour power, the labour needed to produce it, is *less* than the labour performed by a worker – and therefore less than the value of the commodities produced using that labour power. If the working day is twelve hours long, Marx argues, the value of *labour power* may only be four hours. To keep a worker alive and able to work may require commodities which take only four hours labour to produce. But that worker can work for twelve hours. The capitalist purchases *labour power* worth four hours but obtains *labour* worth twelve! The difference is what Marx calls *surplus value*. After production is complete, the capitalist is in possession of commodities worth twelve hours of labour but has only given up commodities worth four hours. The capitalist has generated *surplus value* worth eight hours. Marx defines the *rate of surplus value* as the ratio of surplus value to labour power. In the example above this is equal to 8/4 = 2.

The distinction between labour and labour power is Marx's solution to the puzzle of profits. The ability to pay workers less than they produce allows the extraction of surplus value by capitalists. And this surplus value is the source of profit. Surplus value is possible because labour power is a unique commodity: it is the only commodity which produces new value. Since the purchase price of labour power is less than the value produced, it is the only source of surplus value and therefore profits. For Marx, the ultimate source of profit can therefore be traced not to market exchange, but to the productive process (see Chapter 4).

Marx's theory of income distribution is therefore a theory of exploitation in production. Unlike Ricardo, Marx was relatively unconcerned about the role of landlords. This was perhaps because, by the time Marx was writing, Ricardo's key assumption of diminishing returns in agriculture was looking increasingly implausible: agricultural productivity was instead rising and food prices were falling.

Marx's primary concern was instead the struggle between capitalists and workers. Capitalists, in competition with one another, constantly attempt to lower costs and increase profits by increasing the rate of surplus value. Workers confront capitalists, by demanding higher wages or a shorter working day, which will instead lower the rate of surplus value. Since profits are the source of capital accumulation, these conflicts over distribution have important implications for economic growth and development (see Chapter 10).

Mill

Mill was Marx's contemporary and, like Marx, was a socialist. But Mill's evolutionary socialism was of a quite different kind to that of Marx. While Marx thought that revolution would be the result of crisis and workers overthrowing capitalism, Mill believed in a gradual transition towards a more equitable society.

Mill is a key link between the Classical thinking of Ricardo and the Neoclassical theory of Marshall and others. While Mill presented his ideas as a continuation and evolution of Ricardo's, he made a number of important breaks which anticipate the subsequent Marginalist revolution. In particular, Mill moved away from Ricardo's labour theory of value towards a system where price is determined by the long-run costs of both labour and capital, the supply of which may vary as a result of the decisions of individuals.

But perhaps Mill's most significant contribution is his distinction between the *laws of production* and *laws of distribution*. Mill writes, 'Political Economy informs us of the laws which regulate the production, distribution, and consumption of wealth' (1844/1967, p. 313). While Mill followed Ricardo in viewing the laws of production (such as diminishing marginal productivity in agriculture) as immutable physical facts, he parted company on the resulting implications for income distribution. In Mill's view, there is no direct connection between the laws of production and the laws of distribution. The latter, he argues, are governed by particular social and institutional arrangements and can therefore be adjusted to meet the will of society. In adopting such a position, Mill was able to continue developing economic theory along the lines taken by Ricardo and his followers, while drawing quite different conclusions about policy.

Like both Smith and Ricardo, Mill was suspicious of landlords, but he went much further in his proposals on how to deal with them, proposing a tax on increases in unearned land income; over time, this would lead to the gradual nationalisation of land. Mill also backed the formation of trade unions as a way to increase the strength of workers and raise the share of wages in national income. To overcome the Malthusian tendencies towards overpopulation, Mill advocated making contraception widely available. Where his predecessors saw only the unavoidable if regrettable consequences of natural laws for the poorest, Mill saw ways to change the rules of the game in their favour.

And Mill, like his predecessors, saw the growth and development of capitalism eventually drawing to a halt, but unlike the pessimism of Ricardo he saw this as a reason for optimism. With the Malthusian problem of population solved by birth control, there would be a tendency for wages to rise and profits to fall. As a result, accumulation would slow down and the system would gradually converge on a steady state in which the distribution of income is broadly egalitarian. Mill believed that in the advanced economies of his day, further growth in output and population was not desirable: instead, the primary problem was one of distribution.

Marginalism

The emergence of Marginalist theory in the 1870s saw a significant break with the Classical tradition. Marginalist theory takes Ricardo's insight about declining marginal productivity in agriculture and applies it to a wider range of economic phenomena. This provides a way to introduce the demand for goods as a determinant of price. This approach contrasts with that of the Classical writers who saw prices as largely determined on the supply side by the cost of production, with demand determined mainly by necessity, convention and social factors. Early Marginalists such as Jevons (1871) and Böhm-Bawerk (1890) argued that demand is instead determined by the subjective values individuals place on goods, which in turn reflect the *utility* obtained from consumption. The Marginalists applied Ricardo's idea of diminishing marginal returns to the utility of consumption. As consumption of any particular good increases, the *additional* utility obtained decreases. As a result, the price that individuals are willing to pay for additional units of consumption of a particular good falls as the quantity consumed increases. Individuals will then choose to consume any good in the quantity at which the additional utility gained is equal to the utility foregone in payment (see Chapter 5).

This principle was then applied to the demand for, and pricing of, factors of production, leading to a Marginalist theory of distribution. Ricardo's principle of diminishing returns didn't apply only in agriculture, it was argued, but in *all* areas of production: any factor of production will be subject to diminishing marginal productivity as its use increases. Firms will therefore use any factor of production up to the point where the additional output generated is equal to the required payment. In a competitive system, all factors of production (land, labour, and capital) receive an income equal to their marginal contribution to production. Since the ultimate aim of production is to obtain utility from consumption, the demand for a factor of production, and therefore its compensation, reflects the utility it ultimately provides through consumption.

For the Marginalists, the distribution of income is the result of voluntary market interactions between individuals as they try to obtain the greatest possible utility from consumption. Ricardo and Marx's vision of landlords, capital and labour conflicting over their shares in national income is replaced by Marshall's vision of capital and labour cooperating voluntarily, with each receiving a reward in proportion to their contribution: 'Capital in general and labour in general co-operate in the production of the national dividend, and draw from it their earnings in the measure of their respective (marginal) efficiencies' (Marshall, 1820/2013, p. 451).

While Jevons focused on the demand for factors of production, under the assumption that supply is essentially fixed in the short run (the population of workers is employed to their maximum physical capacity), Marshall's contribution was to introduce decision-making about the supply of factors of production into the analysis. Rather than assuming that all workers work the maximum possible number of hours, Marshall instead argued that individuals face a decision over how much labour to sell. Against the utility gained from consuming one's wages must be weighed the *disutility*, or the unpleasantness, of working. As the marginal increase in the utility of consuming one's wages decreases with hours worked, so the marginal disutility of work increases.

Jevons derived the negative relationship between the demand for labour and the wage, the labour demand curve, on the basis of the diminishing productivity of labour. Marshall added the upward-sloping labour supply curve. The point at which the supply curve cut the demand curve gave the market-determined level of employment and the associated real wage. If demand for a particular good increased, the real wage offered would likewise increase, and the point at which it offset the unpleasantness of additional work rose, bringing forth an increase in labour supply.

Marshall also considered the supply and demand for *capital*: if the demand for capital is determined by the additional production it will enable, what determines the supply? For Marshall, the answer is thrift: the return on capital is *interest*, and interest is the *reward for waiting*.[6] Just as the worker balances the utility of the wage against the disutility of work, the capitalist must balance the utility of immediate gratification against the disutility of waiting. As the rate of interest increases, so does the willingness of the capitalist to wait. The supply curve for 'capital' is upward-sloping. The intersection with the downward-sloping marginal productivity curve determines the volume of investment, the rate of accumulation, and the income of capitalists.

Despite having laid the foundations for a complete Marginalist theory of income distribution, Marshall remains cautious. Firstly, he follows Ricardo in viewing rents on land as determined purely by the variations in productivity between different quality areas of land. Since no discomfort has to be endured by the landlord in making land available for cultivation, no optimising supply decision is involved – unlike the case of the owner of capital. Marshall also notes that the reaction of capital investment to changes in saving rates will be slow, so that at any point in time, many capital goods will earn 'quasi-rents' in addition to 'the interest of capital'. Even when it comes to wages, Marshall is unwilling to make the jump from describing the decision-making processes of capitalists and workers to declaring this a full account of the determination of labour's income.[7]

Clark, an American who independently discovered many of the same principles as Jevons and Marshall, did not share Marshall's concerns. He argued that the marginal productivity theory was not just how things *are* but also how they *should be*. Clark's purpose was to 'to show that the distribution of the income of society is controlled by a natural law [which gives] to every agent of production the amount of wealth which that agent creates' (1902, p. v). Clark saw the theory not only as a technical description of how markets function, but also as an *ethical* position. Only when the distribution of income was determined purely by the marginal contributions of factors of production would it be just. For Clark, wages set in a competitive market reflect the contribution to collective well-being of the labour performed. Workers' income is exactly what is deserved.

In addition to Jevons, Böhm-Bawerk, Marshall, and Clark, important contributions to the Marginalist distribution theory were made by Wicksteed, Walras, and Wicksell, among others, concerning the substitutability of factors of production and the so-called adding-up problem. The latter was the issue of proving that if all factors were remunerated according to their marginal contributions, this would exhaust the total output produced. Marshall's caution on declaring the issue of income distribution closed turned out be warranted; some lines of inquiry introduced more problems than they solved. For example, Wicksell's attempt to incorporate the time of production into the theory of the rate of interest unearthed difficult conceptual problems that would subsequently be the focus of criticism from the UK Cambridge economists (see the Introduction above).

One line of criticism of the newly developed Marginalist theory of distribution focused on the assumption of competition. While Marshall assumed 'competitive markets', the precise meaning of the term had not yet been defined and there were inconsistencies in Marshall's arguments. He thought that costs decreased with the scale of enterprise, but this implies that larger firms can undercut less cost-effective small firms with the implication that capitalism tends towards an oligopolistic or monopolistic structure.

This led to the development of the Marginalist theories of *imperfect competition* by Robinson (1933/1969) and *monopolistic competition* by Chamberlin (1923). Robinson's theory replaced the assumption of price-taking firms with a downward-sloping marginal revenue curve, which became the standard textbook 'monopoly' model, while Chamberlin's model formalised a spectrum of market structures from pure competition to pure monopoly with the real world lying somewhere in between. Although often discussed together, a key difference between the two theories is that Robinson saw her model as reintroducing the Classical idea of labour exploitation. Monopoly power allows firms to pay workers less than their marginal product. Chamberlin had a different perspective, and instead saw his formalisation of a hybrid market structure as a fundamental reconstruction of value theory in which concepts such as labour exploitation had little meaning. Robinson would later disown what was arguably her most influential contribution to economics, while Chamberlin's model was ignored for decades until it was revived by New Keynesian economists.[8]

The macroeconomics of distribution

While the increasingly dominant Marginalist approach reduced income distribution to a narrow technical issue, others continued to develop alternative ideas, often drawing on the Classical thinkers for inspiration. Radical writers such as Hobson (1902) and Luxemburg (1913/1951) carried on in the Classical tradition, exploring the macroeconomic implications of unequal income distribution. Veblen's (1899) *The Theory of the Leisure Class* gave a searing critique of Neoclassical models, arguing that a central feature of human society is imitative behaviour of the wasteful consumption of the rich by the poor (see Chapter 5).

The publication of Keynes's (1936) *General Theory* marked a watershed in the evolution of economic theory. Keynes showed that capitalist economies could become stuck in situations of persistently high unemployment. This was thought impossible by the early Marginalists without outside interference to prevent the functioning of the market mechanism: an important implication of the Marginalist theory of distribution is that, in competitive markets, any factor of production with a positive price must be scarce and therefore fully employed.

The central idea of the *General Theory*, that total spending in an economy may be insufficient to purchase all of the output produced at full employment, had been suggested by earlier thinkers. Ricardo's friend Malthus thought that 'general gluts' of commodities were possible but could never quite explain why. Marx wrote about the tendency of capitalism towards monopoly and the resulting potential for problems of 'realisation of the surplus' (see Chapter 10). While Keynes didn't explicitly consider long-run income distribution in the *General Theory*, he did reject Marshall's assertion that the marginal disutility of labour determines the supply of labour and therefore the level of employment and the real wage. Keynes argued instead that employment was determined by total spending in the economy and that workers were not in a position to determine their real wage – they couldn't price themselves back into employment.

Keynes's key innovation, the principle of effective aggregate demand, was independently discovered by the Polish economist Kalecki. Kalecki's theoretical system *did* include both a theory of income distribution and a macroeconomic role for it. Kalecki drew on writers such as Luxemburg who, like Marx, saw the tendency towards monopoly as leading to excess saving or insufficient spending (e.g. Kalecki, 1954/1990).

Another critique of the Marginalist approach to distribution derived from Sraffa's (1960) demonstration that a system of equilibrium prices could be determined with no need to rely on Marginalist principles and therefore without a direct role for factor demands (see Chapter 9).[9] Sraffa's critique casts doubt on the logical validity of the method of deriving a demand curve for a factor of production from its marginal productivity, and thus on the Marginalist theory of distribution as a whole.

These two lines of criticism formed the basis for what would come to be known as the *Post-Keynesian* theory of distribution (Kregel, 1979).[10] Kalecki's theory can be summarised neatly in the statement that 'workers spend what they get and capitalists get what they spend'. Using simple accounting, Kalecki showed that if workers consume all of their wage income, then all spending on capital investment will accrue to capitalists as profit. This has powerful implications. Capitalists can increase their share of national income by raising investment spending. Alternatively, if capitalists instead choose to spend their money on luxury consumption, this won't affect their profit income, at least in the short run.

Kalecki developed early models in the Marginalist tradition using Robinson's imperfect competition framework. He subsequently abandoned this approach and instead assumed that marginal costs would tend to be fairly constant over a large range of output. The implication is that distribution between profits and wages is determined by the markup of prices over labour costs imposed by firms. Given different spending propensities from capital and labour income, shifts in income distribution caused by changes in the markup will affect aggregate demand. A shift from wages to profits will lead to lower spending on consumption and therefore lower demand and output.

Subsequent Post-Keynesian thinkers drew on Keynes, Kalecki, and Sraffa to develop distinctive theories of income distribution. While the emphasis varied, a number of common features can be identified. Following Sraffa, the Marginalist theory of distribution was rejected as logically incoherent. Following Keynes, the notion of a 'supply' of savings and 'demand' for borrowed funds for investment, leading along Marshallian lines to an equilibrium *natural rate of interest*, was rejected. In an economy with an elastic supply of bank credit, it is argued, lack of savings cannot constrain investment. Instead, investment spending is the primary factor determining growth and employment, with saving determined as a residual.

What determines the volume of investment in the absence of the marginal productivity theory? Keynes used the term 'animal spirits' to capture the notion that while past costs, current interest rates, and expected profits all matter, there is also an element of collective psychology involved in the investment decision, so there is ultimately no mechanistic way to determine investment spending. Since this decision lies with business owners, in what is assumed to be an oligopolistic market structure, the Post-Keynesian theory restores the Classical notion of a *surplus* of profits over wages determined by asymmetric bargaining power between capital and labour and reflected in the markup of prices over wage costs.

The Post-Keynesian approach therefore differs significantly from Marginalist theory. Incomes are not directly related to the productivity of factors of production, and the distribution of income is instead determined as a result of social and political factors as well as the market power of firms. Clark's view that Marginalism provides a just 'natural law' of distribution is rejected.

Distribution in modern economics

Following the Marginalist revolution, the nascent economics of imperfect competition struggled to make headway and orthodox economists reverted to their earlier reliance on competitive markets. By the 1950s, the Solow growth model and its descendants had come to dominate thinking about long-run processes of accumulation and distribution. This model assumed that the economy could be represented by a single *aggregate production function* (see Chapter 4). It became conventional to assume long-run full employment and competitive markets, so that factor incomes were determined along Marginalist lines. The commonly adopted assumption of a Cobb-Douglas production function implies that the distribution between capital and labour is fixed.[11]

Despite protests by those inspired by Sraffa's criticisms of the logical deficiencies of marginal productivity theory, the aggregate Cobb-Douglas production function became the standard tool of macroeconomic theory, and was used extensively as the basis for empirical exercises that tried to identify the determinants of growth by estimating the parameters of the assumed production function. These growth accounting exercises imposed the restriction that the distribution of income between capital and labour *couldn't change* over the period under investigation. As a result, shifts in income distribution would instead be interpreted as changes in quantities of factors, or shifts in productivity.

While the economics profession had essentially declared the issue of the *functional distribution* to be closed, awareness was growing that the factors determining the *personal distribution* remained largely unexplored. The post-war economics of income distribution therefore reverses the position of the Classical writers. The Classical thinkers assumed that incomes of each factor type would be equalised by competition, i.e. that a uniform wage rate and profit rate would prevail, and that the main question was therefore how the functional distribution is determined. Post-war economists took the opposite view. With the functional distribution issue settled by marginal productivity theory, what remained was to explain the distribution of income *within* income types, such as the distribution of wages. Further, empirical evidence showed that the Classical assumption was wrong: wage rates and profit rates were *not* uniform but appeared to conform to fairly stable but asymmetric distributions. This phenomenon was first discovered by Pareto (1897) who found that incomes generally fit a *lognormal distribution*. This means that income distribution is substantially unequal with a small number of individuals receiving incomes which are multiples of the mean.

Attempts to explain this phenomenon fall into a number of different categories. In a comprehensive survey, Sahota (1978) notes that these can be divided into two broad groups: theories based on the belief than individual and social choices can affect income distribution, and theories based on the belief that income inequalities are somehow 'pre-ordained'.

In much discussion of personal income distribution, it is either explicitly or implicitly assumed that the correct focus is *wage* distribution. A key recurring theme is that variance in ability will lead to variance in wages, in line with the marginal productivity theory. Debate then revolves around the determinants of ability. Some theorists assume that such differences are mainly genetic, with evidently unpalatable conclusions. More nuanced thinkers note that education and training are key determinants of skill and ability. An important step was taken by Gary Becker (1967) when he introduced the concept of *human capital.* Becker's key idea is that individuals make an optimising decision on how much to 'invest' in education. Since education is costly, this cost must be compared to the expected future increases in income that result from the skills obtained from that education. The decision on whether to invest in education is then an analogue to the decision of the capitalist in Marshall: the loss of utility from reducing consumption in order to pay for education is compared to the expected increase in future income resulting from that education, and the optimal level of education is chosen. The implication is that wage inequality is the outcome of the optimising decisions and preferences of individuals. Those who are willing to wait eventually receive higher incomes while those who prefer instant gratification remain stuck on lower incomes.

Becker's theory faced substantial criticism for taking an unrealistic view of human "rationality", for its failure to consider social, family and environmental factors in the development of skills, and for its failure to consider the role of non-wage income and inherited wealth.

Another proposed explanation for personal income inequality was based on so-called *life-cycle theories*, which attempt to model the way that individuals' behaviour changes over their lifetime in response to their income. Over a person's lifetime, income usually follows a hump-shaped pattern: it is low in the early stages of life and increases as earnings rise throughout a person's working life, followed by a substantial drop in income as individuals reach retirement age. If what matters are *lifetime earnings*, rather than earnings at any point in time, and assuming that people can borrow and save to increase consumption during low-income periods of their life, then measures of income inequality at a point in time will overstate the problem of income inequality. Instead, they capture differences between people at different stages of their lives.

Despite the development of these and other theories to explain the inequality of personal incomes, none appeared conclusive and interest in the subject waned to the point that, in 1980, Robinson wrote:

> The whole subject is so embarrassing that in fact it is scarcely mentioned. There is no treatment at all of the determination of the distribution of income in orthodox teaching, and precious little about its consequences. What to the general public appears one of the most interesting of all questions is simply left out of the syllabus. (1980/1985, p. 160)

Seventeen years later, in a Presidential Address to the Royal Economic Society entitled *Bringing Income Distribution in from the Cold*, Anthony Atkinson, who arguably did more than any other economist to keep interest in the subject alive, made a similar point, although in characteristically gentler language: "The title of this Presidential Address is chosen to highlight the way in which the subject of income distribution has been marginalised. For much of this century it has been very much out in the cold" (Atkinson, 1997, p. 297).

With income inequality within advanced economies rising from the 1980s onwards, the 1990s saw a revival of interest in the subject. The key individualist elements already identified (education, human capital, rational choice) were incorporated into more sophisticated Marginalist supply-and-demand models which depicted the interplay between individual choices, technological change, and the availability of education. By the 2000s, it was almost universally accepted among orthodox economists that rising inequality was the result of *skill-biased technical change* (SBTC). This hypothesis views rising inequality as the result of changes in technology which increase the demand for skilled labour. Since educational standards were not keeping pace with technology, a shortage of skilled workers leads to rising wage differentials between these workers and the more abundant low-skilled workers.

Despite almost universal adoption of this hypothesis, in the years preceding the 2008 crisis, the evidence became increasingly difficult to reconcile with the theory. Measures of educational achievement rose in the US, implying an increase in the supply of skilled labour. At the same time, wage inequality continued to rise. Economists therefore began to consider the possibility that other factors, in particular institutional and political factors, might be the cause of rising inequality. In 2007, Nobel Prize winner Paul Krugman admitted he had changed his mind on this issue: "[I]nstitutions, norms and the political environment matter a lot more for the distribution of income and impersonal market forces matter less than Economics 101 might lead you to believe" (2007, p. 145).

The publication of Piketty's *Capital in the 21st Century* (2014) marked an important shift in the debate, as well as becoming a surprise bestseller. Piketty and his co-authors assembled a substantial dataset covering both functional *and* personal income distributions for a number of countries. Piketty showed that income inequality had followed a U-shaped pattern in countries such as the US and the UK. Inequality fell during the Second World War from its the previously high level reached in the 1920s, remained subdued until the 1980s, and then began to rise rapidly once more.

Piketty's book was hailed by some as a return to the Classical tradition. However, the explanation provided by Piketty for these trends is Marginalist. The results are derived from a modified Solow growth model in which the Cobb-Douglas production function is replaced by the more general *constant elasticity of substitution* (CES) form, which allows for shifts in the functional distribution of income. Piketty argues that a combination of high saving rates and low growth have combined to produce a falling labour share of income alongside growing wealth-to-income ratios. In the wake of Piketty's book, there has been a substantial revival in interest in the topic. At the time of writing this chapter, it is too early to offer an overall assessment of the outcome of this revival.

Conclusion

Two hundred years after Ricardo set out to determine 'the laws that determine the division of [income]', the issue remains unresolved. The idea that Marginalism provides a 'natural law' of distribution has proved persistent among some sections of the profession. In 2004, Nobel Prize winner Lucas wrote: 'Of the tendencies that are harmful to sound economics, the most seductive, and in my opinion, the most poisonous, is to focus on questions of distribution' (Lucas, 2004). But decades of high inequality in many advanced nations have not only rekindled academic interest in the subject. It has also become an important political issue. There is a growing sense that Marginalist theory alone is insufficient to explain the inequality of recent decades. As economists once more grapple with the complex interplay between global trade, technological change, monopoly power, and the declining bargaining power of workers, the shadow of the Classical thinkers is yet to be fully shaken off.

Discussion questions and seminar activities

- Can you define the following terms clearly?
  - (a) Rent
  - (b) Wages
  - (c) Profit
  - (d) Interest
- What is the difference between *income* and *wealth*?
- What factors determine the distribution of income:
  - (a) Between wages, profits, interest, and rents?
  - (b) Between those receiving *high wages* and those receiving *low wages*?
  - (c) Between different countries?
- Explain the difference between the marginalist theory of distribution and the surplus theory of distribution.
- J. S. Mill proposed a tax on all future increases in rent. Is this a good policy? Try to identify some pros and cons of this policy.
- Income inequality increased in many countries in the 1980s and 1990s. What might have caused this increase?

References

Atkinson, A. B. (1997). Bringing income distribution in from the cold. *The Economic Journal, 107*(441), 297–321.

Becker, G. S. (1967). *Human capital and the personal distribution of income: An analytical approach* (Woytinsky Lecture no. 1). Ann Arbor: Institute of Public Administration, University of Michigan. Reprinted in *Human capital* (2d ed.). New York: Columbia University Press (for Natl. Bur. Econ. Res.), 1975, pp. 94–144.

Chamberlin, C. H. (1923). *Theory of monopolistic competition*. London: Oxford University Press.

Clark, J. B. (1902). *The distribution of wealth*. London: The Macmillan Company.

Hobson, J. A. (1902). *Imperialism: A study*. New York: James Pott & Company.

Jevons, W. (1871). *The theory of political economy*. Reprint. Edited by R. D. Collison Black. Harmondsworth: Penguin Books.

Kaldor, N. (1955). Alternative theories of distribution. *The Review of Economic Studies, 23*(2), 83–100.

Kaldor, N. (1957). A model of economic growth. *The Economic Journal, 67*(268), 591–624.

Kalecki, M. (1954/1990). Theory of economic dynamics: An essay on cyclical and long-run changes in capitalist economy. In J. Ostatynski (Ed.), *Collected works of Michal Kalecki*. Oxford: Oxford University Press.

Keynes, J. M. (1936). *The general theory of employment, interest and money*. London/Basingstoke: Macmillan & Co.

Keynes, J. M. (1939). Relative movements of real wages and output. *The Economic Journal, 49*(193), 34–51.

Kregel, J. (1979). Income distribution. In A. Eichner (Ed.), *A guide to post Keynesian economics*. London/Basingstoke: Macmillan.

Krugman, P. (2007). *The conscience of a liberal*. New York: W.W. Norton & Company.

Lucas, R. E. (2004, May). *The industrial revolution: Past and future* (pp. 5–20). Federal Reserve Bank of Minneapolis: *The Region*.

Luxemburg, R. (1913/1951). *The accumulation of capital*. London: Routledge & Kegan Paul.

Malthus, T. R. (1798/1888). *An essay on the principle of population*. London, Reeves & Turner.

Marshall, A. (1820/2013). *Principles of economics* (8th ed., Palgrave classics in economics). Basingstoke: Palgrave Macmillan.

Marx, K. (1867/1976). *Capital: A critique of political economy, Volume I* (B. Fowkes, Trans.). New York: Penguin.

Mill, J. S. (1844/1967). Essays on some unsettled questions of political economy. In J. M. Robson (Ed.), *The collected works of John Stuart Mill, Volume IV*. London: Routledge & Kegan Paul.

Pareto, V. (1897). *Manual of political economy.* English translation of *Manuale di Economia Politica, 1906.* New York: Augustus M. Kelley Publishers.

Piketty, T. (2014). *Capital in the twenty-first century*. Cambridge, MA: Harvard University Press.

Ricardo, D. (1820). Letter to Malthus dated 9 Oct. in Ricardo, David. 1951–73. In P. Sraffa (Ed.) with the collaboration of M. H. Dobb, *The works and correspondence of David Ricardo* (Vol. VIII). Cambridge: Cambridge University Press.

Robinson, J. (1933/1969). *The economics of imperfect competition* (2nd ed.). New York: St. Martin's Press.

Robinson, J. (1956). *The accumulation of capital*. London: Macmillan.

Robinson, J. (1980/1985). *Spring cleaning*, Mimeo, Cambridge; Published as: The theory of normal prices and the reconstruction of economic theory. In G. R. Fiewel (Ed.), *Issues in contemporary macroeconomics and distribution*. London: Macmillan.

Sahota, G. (1978). Theories of personal income distribution: A survey. *Journal of Economic Literature, 16*(1), 1–55.

Smith, A. (1776/1976). An inquiry into the nature and causes of the wealth of nations. In R. H. Campbell & A. S. Skinner (Eds.), *The Glasgow edition of the works and correspondence of Adam Smith* (Vol. II). Oxford: Oxford University Press.

Solow, R. (1956, February 1). A contribution to the theory of economic growth. *The Quarterly Journal of Economics, 70*(1), 65–94.

Sraffa, P. (1960). *Production of commodities by means of commodities*. Cambridge: Cambridge University Press.

Veblen, T. (1899). *The theory of the leisure class*. London: The Macmillan Company.

von Böhm-Bawerk, E. (1890). *Capital and interest, a critical history of economic theory*. London/New York: Macmillan.

Woodford, M. (2003). *Interest and prices: Foundations of a theory of monetary policy*. Princeton: Princeton University Press.

8 WHAT IS THE ROLE OF MONEY IN ECONOMICS?

Peter Hughes and Annina Kaltenbrunner

Introduction

Money has taken many different forms over history and across space. In some places, small cowrie shells have been used as money. On the island of Yap, massive stones acquired the role of money, involving dangerous sea travel and transportation to bring them to the island. In Western traditions, gold and silver are strongly linked with money. Today, pieces of paper, cheap metal and plastic are used as money. As we continue into the twenty-first century, we can envisage 'cashless societie' where rather than relying on physical money, people and economies increasingly use computerised systems and database entries as money. At the same time, financial technologies have created new financial instruments, such as cryptocurrencies, which some have considered new forms of money.

These opening remarks raise fundamental issues which need to be addressed by economic theories analysing money, three of which will be discussed in this chapter adopting a history of economic thought approach. First, Why do we need money? What are its functions? Economics often approaches issues related to money by asking why it exists in the first place. Money is a complex and a costly institution for an economy to operate. So the presumption is that it provides some sort of service. Second, What is money? What is its nature and what forms does it take? Above, we listed several different forms of money used across different contexts. Any theory of money needs to be able to address these differences and indicate what these things have in common to make them money. The third question is, Where does money come from? Its emergence. For example, does money arise purely to facilitate commodity exchange between individuals or is it also related to credit and financial operations? And how important are the actions of the state in creating money?

Different schools of economic thought have answered these three questions very distinctly and by doing so represent fundamentally different views of money and the underlying economy. These different views have crucial implications for economists' interpretation of the operations of commercial banks, the role of the state with regard to money, and the nature and effectiveness of monetary policy.

First, Neoclassical economics, rooted in the monetary thought of Classical political economists such as Hume, Smith, and Ricardo, has a very limited role for money. Based on the rational expectations, efficient market paradigm, money is primarily used to facilitate transactions and to deal with market imperfections and frictions in the 'real' economy (operations related to the production and exchange of commodities embedded in the physical world). Changes in monetary factors will have no impact on this 'real' economy, at least in the long run (the (long-run) Classical dichotomy). This also implies that any increase in money supply leads to a proportionate increase in the price level as the underlying 'real' economy remains unchanged (the Quantity Theory of Money). As to the nature and emergence of money, in Classical and Neoclassical economics, money is considered a commodity which is produced like other commodities. This means that there is no role for private commercial banks and/or the state in the production and governance of money.

Second, authors in the tradition of Schumpeter and Keynes put the existence of credit and the financial system at the heart of the theory of money. Money is not a commodity itself but an inherently social relation which emerges from the interaction between debtors and creditors. Its role is to act as unit of account and, in the Keynesian tradition, it emerges to protect against the implications of a fundamentally uncertain world. This, however, endows the state with a crucial role in the creation and management of money and gives a peculiar, and potentially powerful, role to the private banking system.

Finally, the Marxist approach to money takes a slightly different angle from the other two approaches outlined above. In line with Marxist ontology, it revolves around considerations of value and social structures and takes what could be considered an intermediate position between those who consider money a commodity in its own right and those which locate money in the social relations of financially sophisticated credit economies. In line with its methodology it adopts a historical materialist approach, where the functions and forms of money depend on the current structure of the economy system.

This chapter discusses these three main schools of thought and their approach to money. In line with the key questions posed in the beginning, the discussion is structured according to their different conceptions of the functions, forms, and emergence of money.

Classical and Neoclassical theory of money: a commodity view of money

The Neoclassical view of money begins with the Classical economists' rejection of the sixteenth- and seventeenth-century idea of Mercantilism. Mercantilism argued that the accumulation of precious metals via exports should be the main aim of national economic policy. The accumulation of these precious metals represented the wealth of the nation. The Classical economists of the eighteenth century argued against this. Hume (1752) and Smith (1776), for example, held that the role of money (still largely seen as precious metals) was only to facilitate exchange and trade and that the appropriate measure of wealth in the economy was real output. Hume was an early advocate of the Quantity Theory of Money, an idea that states that money has a specific role to facilitate trade and that the quantity of money, relative to the size of the real economy, impacts only on the price level within an economy. Anticipating what would later become known as the Classical dichotomy, he argued that if money flows into an economy (earned through trade) then this will not impact on the industry of that economy. Hume argued that this increase in money in an economy leads to inflation and nothing more. The Classical economist Ricardo (1817) retained the Quantity Theory of Money, but moved the debate within economics towards the idea that money was a commodity, subject to the same market forces as other commodities. Its value derived from the costs of extracting the precious metals used as money.

Today, the Quantity theory of Money idea is most closely associated with Fisher (1930) and Friedman (1956). Fisher put forward a Quantity Theory of Money equation: MV = PT (with M as total stock of money; V the velocity of circulation, how many times a single unit of money is used in a certain time period; P the general price level; and T the total number of transactions). Fisher's equation establishes a clear relationship between the monetary economy and the real economy. MV representing the total effective supply of money for an economy, PT represents the total demand for money in the economy for transactions. Velocity and the number of transactions are largely assumed to be given (or determined by other factors), so any short-term change in the supply of money can only impact on the price level.

These ideas were re-examined by the Neoclassical economists in the late nineteenth century. Jevons (1896) explored the role of money in addressing frictions in the market system (echoing ideas from Smith a century earlier). However, it was Menger (1892) who took much of these classical thoughts and developed the Neoclassical approach to money, providing the best and clearest view of money from this tradition. He structured his explanation according to: what money was; its role in the economy; and where it came from. This theory is the basis of the discussion below.

The Neoclassical approach (following Menger) begins with the idea that everything in the economy can be contracted perfectly and goods and services exchange freely and without frictions. Humans are rational and able to make decisions effectively based on accurate assessments of choices that they make. This view of the economy and humans obviously does not correspond to reality, but it is the starting point and the benchmark for the mainstream approach to money. According to this view, the important factors in the economy are real elements (goods, services, capital, etc.). Real variables determine all significant economic outcomes. In such a case, money has limited use. This is often why mainstream economics ignores the presence of money – it's considered trivial in these theories. This trivialising of money within Neoclassical economics is captured through the idea of the neutrality of money. If money is understood to be neutral in the economy, then the only aspects of the economy that money can affect are nominal variables (prices, inflation, wages). These nominal variables have no impact on the important (real) aspects of the economy, so money could be safely ignored. This gives rise to the Classical dichotomy, according to which the 'real' and the 'nominal' sectors of the economy operate separately from one another. Box 8.1 discusses this view for the role and nature of the interest rate in Neoclassical economics.

The above view of the economy is taken as the benchmark. In practice, the economy does not conform to this theoretical ideal. Neoclassical economists (partly) acknowledge this and theories have been developed to explain the divergence from this idealised outcome through reference to various 'frictions' and 'transaction costs'. Money is seen as a way of dealing with these frictions that produce inefficiencies and sub-optimal outcomes.

Box 8.1: The interest rate in Neoclassical economics

The interest rate in Neoclassical economics has nothing to do with money as discussed here. As money acts a veil for real activity (see main text), the interest rate is not a monetary phenomenon but instead a reflection of real factors. The interest rate is simply a price, determined by the demand for and supply of assets used for savings and investing. Savings are a store of wealth where income exceeds consumption. Investment is used to create new real factors and is related to the marginal productivity of capital. If the marginal product of capital (the return from the investment) is larger than the cost of acquiring saved assets form others, then investment goes ahead. The interest-rate is only the marginal price of these saved assets that brings this market into equilibrium.

Table 8.1 The functions of money in Neoclassical economics

Medium of Exchange	Commodity which agents are willing to accept in exchange for goods and services – allows trade to go ahead
Store of Value	Commodity which is able to maintain purchasing power over time – can be used as savings
Unit of Account	Commodity which is a single, common denominator of the relative value of all goods – allows different goods and services to be compared and prices denoted in common terms

In this view, money performs three essential functions summarised in Table 8.1. Anything able to perform these functions in an economy would be defined as money. Anything able to perform some of these functions but not all of them, or anything not able to consistently perform these functions would be considered 'near' money.

Given Neoclassical economics' disproportionate focus on market exchange (see also Chapters 5, 6, and 7), the most important function of money is its ability to make trading easier and more efficient, that is its medium of exchange function. The other functions of money are derived from this first function. Because money can be used as a medium of exchange in the future, it also becomes the best commodity to store value for future transactions. The store of value is a store of generalised purchasing power, where people can use money to buy commodities in the future. Similarly, because everybody wishes to use the same commodity in trading, it becomes the common way to price all goods and services (or a unit of account). These functions help to reduce the costs of transacting and address the frictions involved with trading. By having a common unit of account, the pricing and comparisons of trading options becomes more efficient. By having a store of value, consumption of goods and services can be smoothed and transactions spaced out over time.

This 'exchange' view of economic processes is also reflected in the way Neoclassical economics sees the emergence of money. The argument goes as follows. Before the development of money, barter was the main form of trade. Barter involves the direct exchange of goods and services, without some intermediary (i.e. money). However, barter suffers from a number of frictions or 'transaction costs'. These difficulties are summarised with the concept of 'double co-incidence of wants'. Any exchange under barter requires each party to be willing to accept those exact goods on offer, at an agreed ratio (price), in exchange for those goods/services they are offering. If either is unwilling to exchange, the exchange doesn't happen. In this case, the exchange does not have the co-incidence of wants.

The direct exchange of real goods and service in barter also faces other difficulties and frictions. Firstly, the bundles of goods on offer must be in the correct amounts to allow trade in whole units (no dividing a live chicken to make change); the quality of each item traded must be checked (you get good chickens and bad chickens), and the trade must be done in a timely fashion otherwise items can degrade in quality (chickens die). This can lead to complex chains of exchanges where each party makes multiple exchanges to arrive in a situation where each individual exchange can be completed. In this system of barter, a single commodity that is widely accepted would solve the problem of double coincidence of wants. In any exchange, a person who was looking to trade away items would always be willing to accept payment in this special commodity. This special commodity becomes what we call money. Thus, money is the commodity which functions as medium of exchange.

The commodity that develops into a widely accepted commodity-money does so through a competitive process within the bartering system. At the beginning of the process, we start with all traders carrying goods they wish to exchange. It is helpful to think of a large mediaeval fair with a large number of small traders each meeting in person and bartering. Each type of good has a specific combination of characteristics that are all useful for being traded. The seven characteristics that are important for a traded good to become widely used are listed below (Table 8.2). There is a large co-dependence between many of these characteristics

Each commodity now has two sources of demand. Firstly, what we could call the 'intrinsic' or 'use' demand. This describes the demand from the traders to acquire and consume that good. But now, with an eye towards future trading, each commodity also has a demand related to its usefulness in trading – a 'trading/money/transaction' demand.

As bartering continues, traders begin to accept certain goods in trade because of their usefulness for future trading. They accept the good because they believe they can use it later to trade for goods they wish to have. Any commodity that could be considered poor in any of these characteristics would often be quickly dismissed by traders as having nothing beyond its use value. In this specific economy, the good with the

Table 8.2 Characteristics of money

Portable	Can be transported easily.
Divisible	Can be split up into smaller pieces to use for smaller trades.
Identifiable	Can be quickly and easily classified.
Uniform	Each example of this good is similar and easy to check the quality.
Durable	Able to last over different time periods without degrading in quality or changing.
Scarce	Limited in availability.
Acceptable	Others willing to accept it in exchange for other goods.

best combination of these characteristics becomes gradually more and more widely used and accepted until it becomes the universal money – the good that everybody uses as medium of exchange.

This does not mean that the commodity that evolves into money has a perfect combination of all these characteristics. All it needs is the best combination of characteristics out of the available goods in that economy at that time. Some economies could have no commodities that are very suitable for money, but they just end up with an inferior form of money. What defines the 'best' combination is also sensitive to the specifics of that economy. What this can mean is that the best commodity can change over time as the needs of the economy changes. Sometimes durability could become more important, sometimes portability.

Typically metals like gold, silver, or electrum (a naturally occurring alloy of gold and silver) are seen as having the best combination of these characteristics. Where gold and silver was available (or other precious metals) it was often selected in this competitive process as the money in that economy. Whilst ways were found to visually disguise less valuable metals as gold and silver, true gold was often easily identifiable through its weight. Gold and silver also benefit from having limited use as a consumable commodity.

This process reveals and explains another important characteristic of the Neoclassical view of money. In this view, money is essentially one commodity among others, that is Neoclassicals adopt what we call a commodity view of money. Money starts as a traded commodity much like every other commodity and evolves into the institution of money over time because of a specific combination of characteristics. Any commodity can act as money within an economy. The exact commodity used in each context depends on the available commodities. If an economy has access to gold in sufficient quantities, gold is often the commodity with the best combination of characteristics that make it a good money. If an economy lacks access to gold, then another commodity, with a different (not necessarily worse) set of characteristics would arise as money.

This all leaves very little role for the state. The state is not required to have any role in this system, though when the state is considered it is often seen as a rent-seeker, taking control of the creation of money to earn rent through the process of seigniorage (the profit earned between the face value of a currency and cost of producing it).

The implications for monetary policy arising from this position are as follows. The state has no need to contribute to the development and operation of a money system. Money exists because it is individually efficient for all members of that economy to use it. It becomes self-sustaining through the actions of individuals. The state becomes important once it takes control of the issuance of money as a rent seeker. As the monopolistic issuer of money, the only role the state has is to ensure that a correct amount of money is in existence in the economy. The correct amount of money can be defined as the amount of money (as a medium of exchange) that allows the efficiency gains from money to be realised. A money that fails to be issued in an appropriate amount would soon be replaced by an effective alternative (if the rational competitive process in the economy was allowed to proceed).

Lastly, we should also consider what implications the Neoclassical view of money has for the role of commercial banks. In advanced sophisticated modern economies, private sector banks are often associated with money. In the Neoclassical, commodity view of money, commercial banks are passive agents. The banks respond to the transaction demands of the real economy which is then accommodated by the central bank. So in this conceptualisation of money, banks are merely intermediaries between the real economy and its desire for the efficiency gains from using money, and a state that issues money and collects rent (through seigniorage).

Schumpeter, Keynes, and Post-Keynesian theories of money: a credit view of money

The previous section discussed one strand of economic thinking, emanating from Classical political economists such as Hume and Ricardo that was further developed by authors like Menger, Fisher, and later Neoclassical economists, for whom money is a commodity like any other. Responding to our three questions we showed that for these authors money is needed to deal with frictions in the market exchange, that is, money is primarily a medium of exchange. Money is essentially a commodity like many others and emerges to deal with the inefficiencies of barter exchange between private individuals. Money, and consequently monetary policy, have no impact on the 'real' economy which means that there is little role for banks and the state in its emergence and governance.

For a second strand of economic thinking, pioneered with the work of Schumpeter and Keynes, money emerges from the social relations of debt and credit. This means that money is largely credit money. These debt relations are formed over historical time with a future that is not known to economic agents. This, in turn, gives a primary role to commercial banks and the state in the emergence and governance of money.

Both Schumpeter and Keynes developed their ideas during the inter-war period characterised by severe monetary and financial instability. Whereas Schumpeter's credit view of money is part and parcel of his broader theoretical apparatus on economic development, innovation and the business cycle and has become a key influence for what has become known as evolutionary economists, Keynes's work on money has influenced a range of scholars concerned with issues of a monetary production economy, financial instability, and monetary policy which form part of the Post-Keynesian School (e.g. Chick, Davidson, Dow, Minsky, etc.).

For Schumpeter (1939, 2017), money is essential to set off the production process. In contrast to Neoclassical static equilibrium analysis, this production process takes place over historical time, that is, it lasts over several periods. This means that initial advances of money to entrepreneurs are a sine qua non of a modern capitalist economy. These advances allow them to buy before they are selling and hence to initiate the (innovative) production process. Money is what denominates these financial advances and, consequently, can be used to settle them again in future periods. Rather than the outcome of individual equilibrium decisions, in a world characterised by historical time, money is needed to bridge unexpected (disequilibrium) outcomes of individual decisions and/or time lags between individual receipts and disbursements (Messori, 2004). Thus, in Schumpeter's credit view of money, money is what acts as a unit of account and means of payment of credit relations, it is credit money. For Schumpeter, the 'essence' of money is not what specific form it takes (a commodity,

Box 8.2: Keynes and the interest rate

For Keynesians the interest rate is a compensation to part with the protection against uncertainty. In its narrowest interpretation, liquidity preference theory is a theory of the determinants of the interest rate. In order to part with the liquidity of money agents need to be offered a return q; that is, the interest rate. For Schumpeter, the interest rate is the price that must be paid to acquire immediate purchasing power in the form of control over production goods. Its level is determined by the demand and supply in the credit market and it is paid as a share of the profits that arise from development.

a banknote, etc.), but its ability to clear claims and counter-claims of credit and debit relations (Michell, 2014).

Keynes comes to a similar conclusion though rather than focusing on the dynamic and cyclical nature of the capitalist production processes, he places particular emphasis on the fundamental uncertainty and risk which is created through the passing of time (Keynes, 1936, 1971). In the idealised conditions envisioned in Neoclassical economic models, this problem is absent; agents know the past, present and future. If prices are not completely foreseeable in advance, their variation follows probabilistic patterns. Agents can learn these patterns, and even make rational trades to hedge against price risk. In Keynes's view, economic agents do not know and cannot know full economic reality before it unfolds. The future can be only imperfectly hedged, and only then with other agents who themselves are taking unknown risks. A money that holds its value through time is the only protection against this uncertainty. It explains why money exists in Post-Keynesian thought. See Box 8.2 to see a reflection of this view in Keynes's theory of the interest rate.

Keynes himself divides the reasons for holding money into three motives. Firstly, the transaction motive, which is the need for cash for the current transaction of personal and business exchanges. The transaction motive can be further divided into the income and business motive depending on which unit is implied in the transaction. The transaction motive is not very different from the Neoclassical view of money as primarily a medium of exchange determined by current income. Keynes's contribution to monetary economics becomes clearer in the other two motives, the precautionary motive and the speculative motive. The precautionary motive refers to the desire to hold money as a protection against any sudden or unforeseen expenditures or opportunities. This includes the need to meet any financial obligations denominated in that same money. As such, the precautionary motive shows most clearly the role of money in a world of uncertainty. Finally, Keynes defined the speculative motive as 'the object of securing profit from knowing better than the market what the future will bring forth' (Keynes 1936, p. 170). For Keynes, this referred particularly to the ability to take advantage of changes in expected price (and hence interest rate) developments in capital markets.[1] The asset which best fulfils these motives is money, that is, it has the highest liquidity premium. Money's return is pure liquidity for which it is held despite offering no pecuniary returns. The amount of resources an individual wishes to retain in the form of money in different set of circumstances is called liquidity preference (Keynes, 1936, p. 166).

From this it becomes clear that for Keynes money is an asset, among many others, that has certain properties and fulfils specific functions. Its return can be compared to the return of other assets, which will determine economic agents' demand for money. Keynes defines these properties in his 'own rate of return' equation in Chapter 17 of the General Theory as follows:

$$(q-c)+a+l$$

Four main elements determine the net benefit of holding an asset. First, its yield or output q, which is measured in terms of direct satisfaction or capacity to produce saleable output. Second, carrying costs c which arise from the need to house or store the asset safely. Third, the expected appreciation a, which is the expected appreciation of an asset relative to the numeraire (which turns out to be money given its highest liquidity premium). Finally, an asset may have a liquidity premium l which is the ease of conversion into money without loss (Chick, 1983, p. 298). These attributes define a spectrum of assets among which wealth holders can choose, ranging from capital assets, which offer a high yield but little liquidity and high carrying costs, to money for which the yield, carrying cost, and expected appreciation[2] are nil, but which offers the highest liquidity premium. Assets with different liquidity premia have to offer different monetary returns to compensate for their relative illiquidity measured against a reference asset, i.e. money.

The question which now arises is why does money have the highest liquidity premium? In other words, what are the functions and properties of an asset which give it the highest liquidity premium and ability to fulfil the motives listed above? According to Keynes, this depends on an asset's ability to fulfil three functions: to act as unit of account, to store of wealth, and as a medium of exchange.[3] The three functions are defined in the same way as in Neoclassical economics. The unit of account function is the use of money as a common denominator of relative value; store of wealth allows purchasing power to be maintained over time; the medium of exchange function permits trade to take place using money as an intermediary.

In contrast to Neoclassical economics, which prioritises the medium of exchange function, for Post-Keynesian economists, the primary function of money is to act as a store of value. In Keynes's writings, money is held because it is a secure abode of purchasing power which transfers wealth in a world of uncertainty and allows meeting contractual obligations. The stability of money to act as unit of account, and therefore a store of value, is guaranteed by two properties of money in a capitalist society: zero or negligible elasticities of production and substitution. While the former assures money is not replaced by another asset when its price rises, the latter makes sure that a rise in the price of money will not lead to increased production.

This view of money shows that in Keynesian economic thought, in contrast to Neoclassical economics where money is a commodity, money is primarily credit money. As in Schumpeter's theory, it is the unit of account which denominates contractual relations between economic agents and the means of payment which settles those relations. Thus, in Keynesian thought, money is an inherently social phenomenon and will be determined by factors such as power and trust. Moreover, given the fundamental role of money in Keynesian economic thought, monetary dynamics permeate all areas of economic life. Keynesian theories are those of a monetary production economy. Neutrality of money cannot hold at any point.

The final question which arises then is how in Keynesian economic thought an asset comes to act as money. How does money emerge? This, in turn, is closely tied to the question of what qualifies as money, that is, what is the nature and forms of money? As we have seen above, in Neoclassical economics, money is a commodity. Most frequently, gold became the most widely accepted commodity and hence money. In Keynesian economic thought, the unit which denominates credit relations between private economic actors, and hence the unit which is required to repay these obligations, is considered to be money. Graeber (2012) argues that this credit view of money predates that of financially sophisticated economies and shows that historically the means to settle debt, and hence money, have been as varied as shells, coins, or even humans. However, in today's financially sophisticated economies, and the ones analysed by Keynes and Schumpeter, this debt largely comes in the form of bank lending (and the corresponding deposits as will be shown below).

In line with the analytical structure of this chapter, this view of money then has important implications for the role and importance of commercial banks and the state for the emergence and governance of money, and the nature and effectiveness of monetary policy. These issues stand at the core of the Post-Keynesian school thought, as will be seen below, with important differences in the nuance of the argument.

In contrast to Neoclassical economics, where banks are largely passive intermediaries of funds, commercial banks assume a crucial role in Keynesian economics. First, as seen above, commercial bank debt, that is our deposits, are considered money in that school of thought. More than that, through their ability to make loans banks are seen to create money – that is, money is endogenous. Rather than being constrained by prior savings or an increase in the exogenously issued quantity of money by the central bank, it is the loans extended by commercial banks which create deposits and hence money in a financially sophisticated economy. Post Keynesians differ whether in their loan providing activity, commercial banks purely react to demands by the real economy (horizontalists) or have their own liquidity preference (structuralists), but the reality that loans create deposits and that these loans and deposits can be considered money is one core element of Post-Keynesian economics.

However, if credit relations are what underpins money, the latter becomes an inherently social phenomenon and its acceptability dependent on its issuer's credibility to honour its commitments. Agents must be able to rely on its value stability and social acceptability to repay back its debt. In the first instance, this engenders agents' trust in the banking system and their ability to access their deposits (banks' liabilities). For many Post-Keynesian authors the most important institution which guarantees the value stability and wide acceptability of money is the state.

Modern states almost invariably have a monopoly on the issue of currency, that is fiat money. Because it has no basis in any 'real' factor, fiat money depends on the beliefs and expectations of the people holding it. The guarantee of value stability and honouring of commitments by the state is secured by its ability to generate (future) tax revenues and potentially draw on the central bank as lender of last resort. The thesis that what ultimately supports money's value is the state and its taxing powers has been most forcefully put forward by the Chartalist approach coined by the German economist Knapp. Today it is prominently represented by the Modern Monetary Theory (MMT), which postulates that given that the government is the sole supplier of money, it has unlimited ability to pay for things and/or fulfil outstanding and future obligations. As a consequence, a government cannot go bankrupt and has full monetary autonomy. However, even for Post-Keynesians who acknowledge the existence of private bank money, the state maintains a fundamental role in securing the value of this money through rules and regulation of the banking system and by accepting and supporting this privately issued money.

Finally, this view of monetary dynamics has important implications for the role of monetary policy and the central bank. As discussed above, in modern economies, the financial system nowadays creates a widely accepted money. Rather than exogenously determined by the central bank, the money supply is largely the outcome of lending decisions by the private banking system. This has important implications for the conduct of monetary policy. For example, rather than targeting the quantity of money in the economy, central banks nowadays target the interest rates which in turn affects bank behaviour. Similarly, as also discussed above, the rules and regulations governing the private banking system become crucial to secure the value of money.

Finally, this however also shows that money, and the credit relations it underpins, can be a fundamental source of 'disturbance' to the real economy. If bank credit, and hence the money supply, is elastic to credit demand by the private sector, this can lead to the build-up of imbalances and fragilities in creditor–debtor relations. More concretely, extensive credit supply during boom-phases can lead to the build-up of high debt levels which cannot be honoured during moments of downturn. The role of the financial sector in contributing, and/or exacerbating the cyclical nature of capitalism, has been important in Schumpeter's work but found particular fame in Minsky's work (Minsky, 1986).

Marxist theory of money: a historical materialist perspective

Marx's theory of money starts with the historical emergence of money. Similar to Neoclassical economics, this emergence is located in the process of commodities exchange where one commodity enables the exchange of others. However, in contrast to Neoclassical economics (and indeed (Post-) Keynesian economics to an extent) Marx does not start his analysis with the question of 'what money does', but he is interested in 'what money is'. He answers this question with the proposition that money is the 'universal equivalent' and a commodity with its own value.

In Marxist political economy, commodities are products with two properties: to satisfy a particular desire or need of human being, that is their use-value embodied by the actual amount of labour used to produce this commodity; and to be exchanged for other products, which is their exchange-value. The fact that commodities have these two values generates an inherent contradiction. Money emerges from this contradiction.

Box 8.3: Marx and interest rates

Although the sources for interest payments must arise in the circuit of capital, the determination of the interest rate itself is determined by social conventions and norms in Marxist political economy. In contrast to the rate of profit which is based on the generation of surplus value, for Marx the interest rate is a purely monetary phenomenon which is determined by the laws of supply and demand for money capital as well as institutional factors.

For Marx, money is the 'universal equivalent' at which exchange values are expressed. Each unit of money value can be regarded as expressing a certain amount of labour time. More than that, 'labour time embodied in use value can only be validated socially in the form of money, and thus exchange values mediated by the market' (Lucarelli, 2010, p. 200).

As long as abstract labour is validated socially, money as the universal equivalent has its own independent value. Thus, as pointed out above, for Marx money is more than just a unit of account or medium of circulation, it is a commodity with its own – labour-time-embodied – value. Importantly though, the emergence of money as the universal equivalent is only made possible because the value of all commodities is expressed by the common unit of labour time. It is this condition which allows money to represent all commodities in their exchange-values. The fact that money, a commodity with its own value, becomes to denominate all other commodities, also creates a distinction between value and price. 'Price is the amount of money that a commodity commands in a particular situation. Value is the amount of labour time embodied in a particular commodity' (Foley, 1983, p. 6) (see also Chapter 9). As with Neoclassical economics, the question then arises which commodity is chosen at the expense of all other commodities to act as this universal equivalent. Similar to its view of the interest rate (see Box 8.3), for Marx this is due to social customs and norms. In Marx's time, gold represented the universal equivalent. Paper money was seen as a symbol for gold.

Once Marx had defined the essence of money, that is, what it really is, he went on to set out the different types of functions money could assume. Similar to the other approaches previously discussed, he divided these in three main functions: measure of value (unit of account), means of circulation and the abstract representation of value itself, that is 'money as money'. In this latter role, money can again take on three functions: store of value; means of payment or deferred payment in the form of credit; and world money. However, in contrast to Neoclassical and (Post-) Keynesian theory, and in line with his methodological approach, these different functions were derived in a logical sequence. In a nutshell, it was seen above that the 'universal equivalent' expresses the value of other commodities. From this it can be seen that for Marx money's first function is to act as measure of value and to set prices. Once prices are set they are 'realised' in the market, which means money becomes used as means of circulation. These two functions are internal to the market process. At times though, money must leave this process, for example to act as a hoard (store of value) between buying and selling decisions or to act as credit to tide over fluctuations in the production process. This is when money functions 'as money', that is, it represents an independent form of value (Lapavitsas, 1994). As will be discussed in more detail below, this shows the crucial and deeply endogenous role of money in capitalist accumulation, often expressed in Marx's general circuit M-C-M'.

A final important aspect of Marx's basic monetary theory is the relationship between these functions and the forms money can take (commodity money, credit money, fiat money, etc.). Here Marx argued that money's different functions are closely related to its evolving forms, each dependent on the specific state of capitalist development. Money as a measure of value relates to rudimentary exchanges and can be performed by any commodity (e.g. salt, shells, and indeed gold). As seen above, more sophisticated and generalised market processes lead to the emergence of money as means of circulation, which in turn leads to the advent of metallic coins and state fiat money. Finally, the functions of money as an abstract representation of value, in particular that of means of deferred payment, mainly correspond to the most recent, financially sophisticated stage of capitalism (Lapavitsas, 1991, 1994). Thus, commodity money is only one historical form of the universal equivalent. As capitalism evolves, the other forms of money, such as bank credit money, become more dominant forms (Lucarelli, 2010).

It is important to note though that while other forms of money can become more dominant, in its essence, money remains a commodity in Marxist economic thought. This is so because other forms of money suffer from key weaknesses. State supported fiat money, for one, is nearly exclusively a means of circulation. The state can expand its quantity nearly endlessly, but has trouble adjusting its quantity downward. The resulting inflation will ultimately destroy the state issued fiat money, re-asserting the prominence of commodity circulation and as one commodity as measure of value and means of circulation (Lapavitsas, 1994). Similarly, privately produced (bank) credit money can expand in speculative bouts transgressing the 'monetary constraint' and potentially causing unstable manias. When the bubble bursts, however, agents will return to the state asserted means of circulation or even a commodity value backed measure of value. The monetary constraint asserts itself (Lucarelli, 2010). This also shows that in line with (Post-) Keynesian Economics, but in contrast to Neoclassical economics, in Marxist economic thought banks are active economic agents which can 'create' money – at least to a certain extent. This also shows that through its potential influence on bank behaviour, there is a potential role for the central bank in Marxist political economy.

Another important question which arises, in particular in comparison to Neoclassical and (Post-) Keynesian approaches, is the role of the state in validating and indeed creating money. We have seen that whereas Neoclassical economics has a very limited role for the state, some (Post-) Keynesian approaches ascribe an overriding importance to state created money. What we see in Marx is that it depends on the form money takes. Whereas there is no evident role for the state in the emergence of money as universal equivalent and measure of value, its function as means of circulation, in particular if it comes in the form of fiat money, is fundamentally tied to the validating actions of the state. As means of circulation, money is guaranteed and sanctioned by the state. Although not as obvious, there is also an important role for the state in case of bank credit money. Although created in private transactions, its legitimacy and general acceptability is closely tied to the central bank issuing official reserves and acting as lender of last resort (Lucarelli, 2010).

Finally, we have seen that, in Neoclassical economics, money is, at least in the long run, understood as a veil which does not affect the underlying 'real' economy. Money is considered to be neutral. In Post-Keynesian economics, in turn, money infuses and shapes the real economy on a constant basis. This is also the case in Marxist political economy. In Marxist economic thought money is intrinsically linked to capitalist accumulation. Indeed, Marx was one of the fiercest opponents of the neutrality of money.

This is best expressed in Marx's general circuit M-C-M', when money is capital. In simplified terms, money (M) is transformed into commodities (C) (using labour power and means of production), which are then transformed back (sold) as money M' of altered value (ideally higher if capitalists can generate surplus value and realise it as profits). Money is crucial at two points of the circuit. First, money is needed to set off the circuit as capitalists borrow money to start the production process (which they pay back with the profit they generate). Second, one can see, that the main purpose of the circuit is to generate money itself; or put in line with what has been discussed above, to generate value in terms of the universal equivalent, that is money. Thus, money stands behind the very logic of a capitalist economy because the primary motivation of individual capitalists 'is the creation and realisation of surplus value as profit in its money form' (Lucarelli, 2010, p. 201).

Conclusion

This chapter has analysed three main schools of thought (Classical/Neoclassical; Keynes/Schumpeterian; Marxist) and their different views and interpretations of money. It structured its discussion around the forms, functions, and emergence of money. It showed that whereas Classical and Neoclassical economists see money largely as a commodity, which acts as a medium of exchange to deal with market frictions, Schumpeter and Keynes and authors in this tradition adopt a credit view of money, in which money's main function is to denominate and meet debt obligations and act as store of value. It emerges to deal with fundamental uncertainty and the production process therein. Lastly, Marx and his followers place the functions, forms, and emergence of money firmly in the specific historical material conditions. These different approaches to money, the chapter also showed, have fundamental implications for different schools of thoughts' varying views of the operations of commercial banks, the role of the state with regard to money, and the nature and effectiveness of monetary policy, a summary of which is presented in Table 8.3.

Table 8.3 Summary of different perspectives on money

	Antecedents	Examples of later and current proponents[a]	Main function of money	Forms of money	Emergence of money	Money and the real economy	Role of the state	Role of commercial banks	Role of monetary policy
Classical and Neoclassical	Hume Smith Ricardo	Jevons Menger Fisher Friedman	Medium of Exchange	Commodity Money	Barter Exchange	Separate (Classical Dichotomy and Neutrality of Money)	Not Essential (Rent Seeker that takes advantage of Seigniorage	Passive Intermediaries	Only impacts price level
Schumpeter and Keynes	Schumpeter Keynes	Hyman Minsky Victoria Chick Jan Kregel Basil Moore MMT	Store of Value	Credit Money	Credit Relations (Chartalists/ MMT: Taxing Capacity of State)	Inseparable (Monetary Production Economy; Liquidity Preference and investment decisions)	Essential (MMT: sole creator of money; Post-Keynesians: regulator of banking system)	Create Money (Endogenous Money)	Essential for Real Economy (target interest rates)
Marx	Marx	Suzanne de Brunhoff Duncan Foley Costas Lapavitsas Ben Fine	Measure of Value	Historically Contingent (in essence commodity money)	Historically Contingent	Inseparable (The Circuit of Capital)	Depends on form money takes	Create Money (Endogenous Money)	Essential for Real Economy

[a]*This is by no means an exhaustive list but just some examples*

Discussion questions and seminar activities

- How do different schools of thought define money? What are their views about its functions, forms, and emergence?
- Why is there no role for the central bank and/or the state in the Classical/ Neoclassical Theory of Money?
- What would you say is the main difference between the Marxist theory of money and the two other approaches (Classical/Neoclassical and Schumpeterian/Keynesian)?
- Discuss why the neutrality of money does not hold in the Keynesian/ Schumpeterian and Marxist view of money.
- Discuss the following statement: A commodity theory of money is not fit for purpose for today's financially sophisticated economies.
- Show how the three different schools of thought discussed in this chapter would account for the Global Financial Crisis? What implications would such crisis have for the real economy in these schools of thought?
- Group discussion where each group is handed a collection of low-denomination domestic coins, foreign currency and other seemingly random objects (I've used forgeries, small batteries, conkers). The groups are then asked to rank the value of these objects (to themselves) and link them to the characteristics of good money. Student groups usually hit on the idea of acceptability – forgeries do a good job of bringing this out.

References

Chick, V. (1983). *Macroeconomics after Keynes : a reconsideration of the General Theory*. Oxford: Philip Allan.

Fisher, I. (1930). *The theory of interest: As determined by impatience to spend income and opportunity to invest it*. New York: The Macmillan Company.

Foley, D. K. (1983). On Marx's theory of money. *Social Concept, 1*, 5–19.

Friedman, M. (1956). *Studies in the quantity theory of money*. Chicago: University of Chicago Press.

Graeber, D. (2012). *Debt: The first 5000 years*. London: Penguin.

Hume, D. (1752). *Essays, literary, moral, and political*. Reprinted by London: Ward, Lock, and Tyler, 1875.

Jevons, W. S. (1896). *Money and the mechanism of exchange*. New York: D. Appleton and Company.

Keynes, J. M. (1936). *The general theory of employment, interest and money*. London: Macmillan & Co.

Keynes, J. M. (1971). *Collected writings*. London: Macmillan.

Lapavitsas, C. (1991). The theory of credit money: A structural analysis. *Science & Society, 55*(3), 291–322.

Lapavitsas, C. (1994). The banking school and the monetary thought of Karl Marx. *Cambridge Journal of Economics, 18*(5), 447–461.

Lucarelli, B. (2010). Marxian theories of money, credit and crisis. *Capital & Class, 34*(2), 199–214.

Menger, K. (1892). On the origin of money. *The Economic Journal, 2*, 239–255.

Messori, M. (2004). Credit and money in Schumpeter's theory. In N. Arena, N. Salvadori, & A. Graziani (Eds.), *Money, credit, and the role of the state. Essays in honour of Augusto Graziani* (pp. 173–198). Farnham: Ashgate.

Michell, J. (2014). Book review: 'Treatise on money' by J. A. Schumpeter. *Economic Issues, 19*(2), 86–88.

Minsky, H. P. (1986). *Stabilizing an unstable economy*. London: Yale University Press.

Ricardo, D. (1817). *On the principles of political economy, and taxation*. London: John Murray.

Smith, A. (1776). *An inquiry into the nature and causes of the wealth of nations*. Oxford: Clarendon Press.

Schumpeter, J. A. (1939). *Business cycles*. New York: McGraw-Hill.

Schumpeter, J. A. (2017). *Theory of economic development*. London: Routledge.

9 HOW ARE GOODS AND SERVICES VALUED IN ECONOMICS?

Marco Veronese Passarella

Introduction

The search for the determinants and the measure of value of products of human activity – be they single basic commodities (e.g. corn), services (e.g. education), complex artefacts (e.g. large-scale infrastructures), or composite accounting entries (e.g. the annual gross domestic product) – was the key motive behind the inception of modern economic thought. The first attempts to develop a positive theory of value date back to the seventeenth and the eighteenth centuries. They trace back, in particular, to the ground-breaking works of Petty and Cantillon. However, it was the Classical political economists, notably Smith and Ricardo, who engaged to formulate a complete theory of value of goods produced and traded within a capitalist society. The latter is characterised by a 'free' labour market and the private ownership (or control) of means of production. According to Smith, Ricardo, and other Classical theorists, value is an intrinsic or objective feature of goods and it is best expressed by the cost or effort of production. Thus labour would be not only the cause of value, but also the natural measure of it – although some modifying circumstances should be taken into account in the definition of the value in exchange.

The Classical intrinsic theory of value dominated studies in political economy until the 1870s. It was then replaced by the subjective theory of value developed by the early Neoclassical economists in the last decades of the nineteenth century. The new, utility-based approach was so successful that the Classical theory was completely crowded out within three decades or so. Nowadays the vast majority of economists see value as arising from the subjective preferences of the individual consumer. These preferences are 'revealed' by the individual's observable choices. Utility is no longer regarded as a 'cardinal' (meaning measurable) magnitude, but the current theory continues to rely on the utilitarian philosophy that inspired the works of the pioneers of the Neoclassical approach (see Chapter 5). Building upon these premises, the key learning from this chapter is the different ways in which value has been understood in economics since the mid-eighteenth century. For this purpose, the rest of the chapter is organised as follows. The section 'Current mainstream approach to value' focuses on the preference-based theory of value, meaning the approach that dominates microeconomics journals, university modules, and textbooks today. The section 'Alternative approaches' is made up of three subsections. It deals with the early Neoclassical (or Marginalist) subjective approach, the Classical intrinsic theory, and current heterodox approaches to value (notably the Marxian theory, the surplus approach, and energy-based theories), respectively. Some remarks are provided in the section 'Alternative approaches to value: Marx's critique of political economy'.

Current mainstream approach to value

The current dominant view can be defined as a 'preference' or 'ordinal utility' theory of value. It states that value is defined by the utility of goods and services for the consumer. So value is not a barometer of the effort of production, let alone an intrinsic feature of a certain good or service. On the contrary, value is always individual (as it is something that shows up in the individual consumer's brain, not an inner feature of items 'out there') and subjective (as it arises from an individual choice). This means also that interpersonal comparisons of utility cannot be made. All economists need to look at, when analysing the consumer's behaviour, is his/her system of preferences. These preferences are 'revealed' or 'disclosed' by the consumer's actual, observable, choices (see also Chapter 5). However, the concept of utility is not strictly necessary to define consumption patterns for the individual consumer. As Lionel Robbins (1932) clearly stated, all is necessary is that the consumer's ends are classifiable in order of importance. Nevertheless, utility functions are still used by most textbooks to provide intuitive representation of the consumers' preferences.

The utility approach to value is not just a *positive* theory, meaning a theory that *explains* what the actual value of things 'out there' is. It is also a *normative* theory of value, meaning a theory that *states* how things should be assessed. Indeed, it is frequently used by policymakers to appraise projects and policy proposals. The problem is that if utility is individual and subjective, it can be hard to observe or measure. As a result, interpersonal comparisons are arbitrary and 'collective' (or 'social') welfare cannot be defined in general terms. Ironically, welfare economics, which was developed by Pigou (1920) and other economists of the early twentieth century to analyse well-being at the society-wide level, is grounded in the utility theory of value. As welfare economics is invoked to justify most traditional government policies (think of egalitarian policies, redistributing income from the wealthy to the poor), these turn out to lack scientific rationale. How to get out of this impasse? There are some concepts through which the utility theory of value can still be made operational, notably, the individual willingness to pay, Pareto efficiency and optimality criteria, and the compensation test. In short, a certain policy is worth doing if the maximum amount that the gainers are willing to pay to the losers (to accept the policy) is greater than the minimum amount the losers are willing to accept. No cardinal measurement of utility is necessary to appraise social well-being and make decisions. This approach is an extension of Pareto's efficiency criterion (Pareto, 1896, 1906) and was developed in the 1930s by Kaldor (1939) and Hicks (1939). When evaluating a certain change, there is a Pareto improvement when at least one individual is made better off and no one is made worse off. The Kaldor-Hicks efficiency criterion states that there is a rise in efficiency when a 'Pareto-superior state' is reached by arranging sufficient money compensation from the individuals who are made better off to those who are made worse off, so that everyone ends up no worse off than before. The standard example is the compensation for pollution paid by a factory: the latter should be allowed to pollute until it can compensate its neighbourhoods for the losses they suffer because of pollution (see Box 9.1 for a criticism of this view).

Box 9.1: Is the Kaldor-Hicks efficiency criterion really 'value-free'?

Despite its popularity, the Kaldor-Hicks criterion is not neutral. Supporting a certain government policy only when it is coupled with a corrective redistribution of income across social groups might seem a way out of the problem of the interpersonal comparisons of utilities. However, this criterion is not independent of value judgements about alternate income distributions, as it implicitly implies a preference of the policymakers for the status quo. Unfortunately, this means also that standard methods of assessment of government projects and policies, including the well-known 'cost–benefit analysis' (where benefits are inferred from the 'willingness to pay' of the individuals), are not value-free. On the contrary, those methods are grounded in a well-defined subjective, utilitarian philosophy.

Alternative approaches

Early Neoclassicals and the cardinal utility approach

The utility theory of value traces back to the so-called Marginalist revolution which took place in the last three decades of the nineteenth century and has established itself as the dominant approach in economics ever since. It was Jevons (1871), Walras (1874), Menger (1871), and especially Marshall (1890), who put marginal utility at the heart of a new way of doing economic theory that was then termed 'Neoclassical economics'.[1] As mentioned above, Neoclassical economists advocated the idea that things are valuable because the individual gets satisfaction from them. More precisely, the value of a certain good is defined by the utility the consumer gets from the last dose of it. Neoclassical authors built, in particular, upon the pioneering works of Bentham, Gossen, and other 'outsiders', in a period that was dominated by the cost-based approach to value advocated by Classical political economists. From Bentham (1789), the Neoclassicals borrowed the reduction of individual behaviour to a maximising calculus of pleasure and pain deriving from consumption (see Chapter 5). From Gossen (1854), they got both the principle of decreasing marginal utility and the principle of equality of weighted marginal utilities. Gossen's first principle implies that the satisfaction obtained from consumption decreases as the quantity consumed increases. In formal terms:

$$u_i' = \frac{du(q_i)}{dq_i} \geq 0, \text{with}\, u_i'' = \frac{d^2u(q_i)}{dq_i^2} < 0$$

where u_i' stands for the marginal utility of the *i*-th good (say, either X or Y in the second section), $u(\cdot)$ is the utility function of the consumer, q_i is the quantity of the *i*-th good, and u_i'' is the second derivative of the utility function (e.g. the derivative of marginal utility).

Gossen's second principle states that the consumer maximises her well-being when she manages to balance her marginal satisfactions per unit of value across different goods. In formal terms, the equilibrium or maximum satisfaction condition is:

$$\frac{u'(x)}{p_x} = \frac{u'(y)}{p_y} = \cdots = \frac{u'(z)}{p_z}$$

where x, y, and z are quantities of goods X, Y, and Z, respectively, and p_x, p_y, and p_z are their unit prices. Money can be now taken into consideration by assuming that z stands for the amount of gold (so that we can take its price as the *numeraire*, $p_z = 1$), be it either in form of coins or bars. If a constant marginal utility of gold-money is assumed, unit prices can be re-expressed as a direct function of marginal utility of goods. For instance, the unit price of X in terms of gold is:

$$p_x = \frac{u'(x)}{u'(z)} \cdot p_z = \frac{1}{\bar{u}_z} \cdot u'(x)$$

where $\bar{u}_z$ is the constant marginal utility of gold-money. This fundamental result was first obtained by Marshall in his *Principles of Economics* (1890). It allows bridging the gap between the utility theory of value and the determination of individual demand schedules, as it makes clear that the unit price of good X falls as the consumption of it increases (thereby reducing the marginal utility of X).[2] This is the original formulation of the Neoclassical principle of decreasing individual demand. It enabled Marshall to work out the 'consumer surplus' (or 'consumer rent'), meaning the psychological gain linked with the difference between the market price the individual consumer pays for a certain good and the price she would be willing to pay for intra-marginal doses of it. When the cardinal utility theory of value gave way to the ordinal approach, Marshall's derivation of individual demand was replaced with the modern method based on indifference curves (see Chapter 5).

Despite its popularity, the utility theory of value suffers from many limitations. We have already mentioned that the impossibility of interpersonal comparisons of utility is one of the main issues with the cardinal approach to value advocated by the early Neoclassicals. The hypothesis of constant marginal utility of money has also been questioned, because money utility is very likely to be affected by income and wealth levels of individuals. On the other hand, the current (ordinal) approach is not free from criticism either. The main issue concerns the way individual preferences are defined. Preferences cannot always be inferred by choices. For instance, individuals cannot always choose what they prefer (think of health, beauty, etc.). In addition, individual preferences are not innate and context-free, but are affected by social interactions with other individuals and the environment (see Chapter 5). Furthermore, rationality of individuals is always bounded, as they make decisions in an uncertain world. As a result, their behaviour can hardly be described by a maximisation function under constraints (see Chapter 2). Finally, both the ordinal approach and the cardinal approach to value regard prices, including input prices, as 'indexes of scarcity'. This is the fundamental assumption that lies behind the neoclassical theory of distribution (see Chapter 7). However, the scarcity-based theory of prices and distribution has been questioned by several economists since the 1960s. This is discussed further in the section on alternative approaches.

The Classical approach to value

Historians of economic ideas are still wondering whether Marginalism was a real revolution, meaning a radical change in the paradigm of economic science. While Jevons, Walras, and Menger distanced themselves from the Classical tradition, Marshall saw his own contribution as a development of Smith, Ricardo, and Mill's works. After all, the new approach was to be labelled Neoclassical. Most Marginalists, like most Classical economists before them, supported *laissez-faire* in economic policy. They also shared the view of the economy as a spontaneous equilibrium system ruled by natural-like laws. Yet differences are particularly apparent when focusing on the theory of value. In a sense, if Marginalism was a revolution, it was a rebellion against the Ricardian intrinsic approach to value. Notice that it was Marx who coined the term 'Classical Political Economy' to refer to a theoretical system based on the analysis of interactions between (and within) social classes, a theory of surplus creation and distribution, and an intrinsic theory of value. For Marx, the benchmark theory was the one developed by Ricardo, while Smith was sometimes criticised for his theoretical ambiguities.

Yet Smith was the first author who provided a complete formulation of an intrinsic theory of value. In *An Inquiry into the Nature and Causes of the Wealth of Nations* (1776), he clearly defined the 'value in use' (or 'use-value') and the 'value in exchange' (or 'exchange-value').[3] The former is associated with the want-satisfying power of a good, say X, and roughly corresponds to the early-neoclassical concept of utility. The latter is the power of purchasing other goods which the possession of X conveys.

> The word value, it is to be observed, has two different meanings, and sometimes expresses the utility of some particular object, and sometimes the power of purchasing other goods which the possession of that object conveys. The one may be called 'value in use'; the other, 'value in exchange'. The things which have the greatest value in use have frequently little or no value in exchange; and, on the contrary, those which have the greatest value in exchange have frequently little or no value in use. (Smith, 1776, ch. 4)

We can define exchange-value as the quantity of the good (or goods) Y which a unit of X can be exchanged for. In formal terms:

$$\varepsilon_{x,y} = \frac{q_x}{q_y}$$

A positive use-value is a necessary condition for a certain good to have a positive value in exchange. If no one is willing to consume it, the exchange-value of X is null. However, for Smith utility is not a proper measure of the value in exchange, let alone a source of intrinsic value (see Box 9.2).

Box 9.2: The diamond–water paradox

Smith uses the well-known 'diamond–water paradox' to explain why utility is not a reliable measure of value. In short, a pint of water is more useful than an ounce of diamonds, but the former is cheaper than the latter. As a result, value in exchange has little or nothing to do with utility of goods. The Marginalists would counter-argue that Smith should have looked at the marginal utility, meaning the relative scarcity of diamonds compared to water, to solve the paradox. However, the point is that for Smith the value in exchange must be traced back to production conditions.

Rather, a good possesses an intrinsic value because it is produced by means of human labour. More precisely, labour is the cause and the unit of measure of value, as:

> The annual labour of every nation is the fund which originally supplies it with all the necessaries and conveniences of life which it annually consumes, and which consist always, either in the immediate produce of that labour, or in what is purchased with that produce from other nations. (Smith, 1776, intro.)

However, Smith makes a further distinction for the capitalist economy between 'natural prices' and 'market prices'. The 'market price', as the observed rate of exchange between different goods in the market, will tend to converge towards what Smith terms a 'natural price': 'The natural price … is, as it were, the central price, to which the prices of all commodities are continually gravitating' (p. 634). The 'natural price' is the price that would prevail by adding up the remuneration of workers, landowners and capitalists, if these were all free to move where they get paid the most, thereby levelling their own respective remuneration rates across the economy. Such an account, however, conflicts with an attempt to build a theory of price and value on the basis of the labour required to produce a good. For Smith, nevertheless, a pure labour theory of value can be applied to a pre-capitalist economy, where there is no capitalist or landowning class:

> In that early and rude state of society which precedes both the accumulation of stock and the appropriation of land, the proportion between the quantities of labour necessary for acquiring different objects seems to be the only circumstance which can afford any rule for exchanging them for one another. (Smith, 1776, ch. 6)

But, Smith continues, a pure labour theory of value is not fit for a well-developed capitalist society:

> As soon as stock has accumulated in the hands of particular persons … the whole produce of labour does not always belong to the labourer … Neither is the quantity of labour commonly employed in … producing any commodity, the only circumstance which can regulate the quantity which it ought commonly to … exchange for … The real value of all the different component parts of price … is measured by the quantity of labour which they can, each of them, purchase or command. (Smith, 1776, ch. 6)

However, value remains an intrinsic property of goods and it is determined by production conditions despite being realised in exchange.

At the beginning of the nineteenth century, Smith's theory of value was recovered and developed by Ricardo. In a sense, Ricardo engaged to clean up Smith's theory from a few logical inconsistencies. The starting point of Ricardo's theory can be best explained by taking into consideration an abstract society where workers' real wages are only made up of corn. For the sake of simplicity, let us assume also that corn is

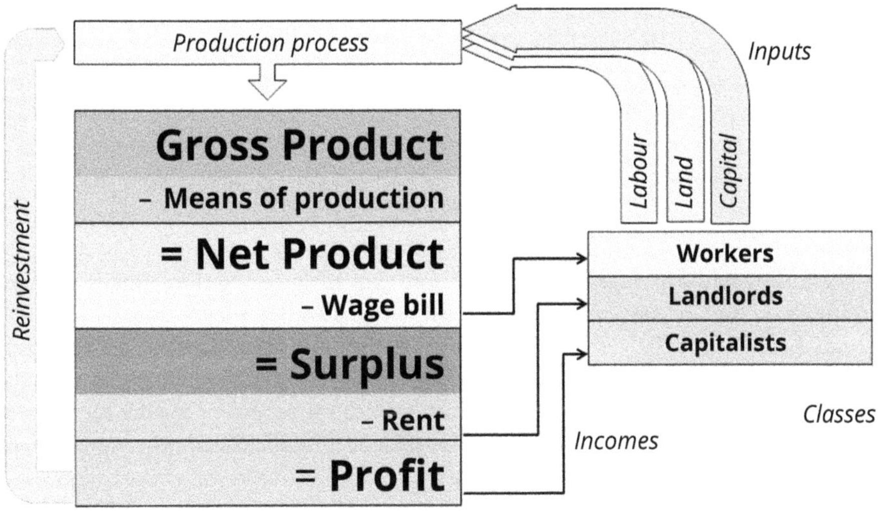

Figure 9.1 Net product is the difference between gross product and means of production (that is, corn output net of seeds in the corn industry). Surplus is what remains after wages are deducted from net product. Surplus is made up of non-labour incomes, including rent and profit

produced by means of labour only. In the corn sector, capital is advanced by capitalists in the form of a corn wage-bill paid to workers. Consequently, the rate of profit can be worked out in physical terms (meaning in corn terms, see Figure 9.1), regardless of the price system.

If a decreasing fertility of lands is assumed, so that labour productivity in the corn sector falls as both the extension and the intensity of farming increases, the rate of profit of the corn sector eventually declines. Finally, since competition between capitalists leads to the equalising of profit rates across sectors, sooner or later the general rate of profit will fall as well. Ricardo can therefore argue that tariffs, quotas and other restrictions on imported agricultural products end up squeezing the profit rate of the manufacturing sector (while inflating landowners' rents), thereby discouraging capital accumulation.[4]

Ricardo's analysis of income distribution in terms of corn is fascinating and elegant. However, it is difficult to generalise (see also Chapter 7). A different unit of measure of value is necessary to extend the properties of a corn-based economy to a society where workers afford to buy a composite bundle of wage goods. In *On the Principles of Political Economy and Taxation* (1817, and subsequent editions), Ricardo committed to generalising his point by advocating an embodied labour theory of value. In contrast to Smith, for Ricardo, labour contents can be shown to determine natural prices (and exchange rates) also within a capitalist society. In a nutshell, if labour is the only primary input in production, and competition levels out profit rates across sectors, natural price ratios mirror embodied labour ratios. The quantity of direct labour spent in the production of a certain good is, therefore, the measure of both its intrinsic value and its exchange rate with other goods:

> It cannot then be correct, to say with Adam Smith, 'that as labour may sometimes purchase a greater, and sometimes a smaller quantity of goods, it is their value which varies, not that of the labour which purchases them' ... but it is correct to say, as Adam Smith had previously said, 'that the proportion between the quantities of labour necessary for acquiring different objects seems to be the only circumstance which can afford any rule for exchanging them for one another'. (Ricardo, 1817, ch. 1)

Unfortunately, the wage bill is not the only sum advanced by the capitalists. Other means of production, say machines, are also bought and employed as inputs besides labour. Techniques of production, meaning both the number of machines per employee and production times, vary across sectors. This affects the relative value of products. As a result, price ratios no longer reflect labour content ratios, except for the very special case in which everything is produced by the same technique. Clearly this never occurs and, if it does so, it is only by chance. On the one hand, Ricardo was aware of this issue:

> I sometimes think that if I were to write the chapter on value again which is in my book, I should acknowledge that the relative value of commodities was regulated by two causes instead of by one, namely, by the relative quantity of labour necessary to produce the commodities in question, and by the rate of profit for the time that the capital remained dormant. (Ricardo, 1820, letter to McCulloch)

On the other hand, Ricardo thought that labour contents could still provide a decent empirical measure of value:

> [T]his cause of the variation of commodities is comparatively slight in its effects ... The greatest effects which could be produced on the relative prices of these goods ... could not exceed 6 or 7 per cent. (Ricardo, 1817, ch. 1)

However, this analytical issue, along with other 'external' conditions, paved the way for the replacement of the labour theory of value with the utility-based approach advocated by the early Neoclassicals.

Alternative approaches to value: Marx's critique of political economy

While abandoned by Neoclassical economists and academia, the baton of Classical theory of value was picked up by socialist thinkers of the nineteenth century, particularly by Marx and his co-writer Engels. For Marx, Classical economists were guilty of taking for granted the system of capitalism. They had failed to identify and explain its historical specificity. The analysis of capitalism's 'laws of motion' and 'internal contradictions' had to be at the heart of the critique of political economy. Focusing on the theory of value, there are three main innovations made by Marx: first, the replacement of Ricardo's 'microeconomic' theory with a social (or 'macroeconomic') approach to value; second, the clear recognition of the monetary form of value; third, the use of the labour theory of value to show that the 'surplus value' earned by the capitalists arises from the exploitation of workers in the production sphere.[5] The labour market is the fundamental institution of capitalism. Within a capitalist society, workers are free before the law.[6] To provide for themselves, they sell the only 'commodity' they possess, their own 'labour power', to industrial capitalists in exchange for a money wage. In the factory, workers spend labour to produce heterogeneous goods marked by different use-values. Accordingly, this labour takes many different concrete forms. Each concrete labour time is a fraction of the society-wide labour time. It becomes socially necessary abstract labour, and hence social value, to the extent that products are sold on the market in exchange for money. In other words, value is created *in potentia* within the production sphere, but must be then socially validated (or realised) within the circulation sphere. While circulation may well 'destroy' value (when a 'realisation crisis' occurs, due to overproduction), it cannot add value to products at the economy-wide level.

The point is that inter-capitalist (or inter-firm) trade is a zero-sum game for the capitalist class taken as a whole. The profit made by one capitalist is here offset by the loss suffered by another capitalist. Consequently, the origin of surplus value, meaning the difference between the amount of money 'advanced' by the capitalists at the beginning of the economic process and the amount they realise at the end, must be searched for in the production sphere.

> Accompanied by Mr. Moneybags and by the possessor of labour-power, we therefore take leave for a time of this noisy sphere, where everything takes place on the surface and in view of all men, and follow them both into the hidden abode of production, on whose threshold there stares us in the face 'No admittance except on business' … On leaving this sphere of simple circulation … we can perceive a change in the physiognomy of our dramatis personae. He, who before was the money-owner, now strides in front as capitalist; the possessor of labour-power follows as his labourer. The one with an air of importance, smirking, intent on business; the other, timid and holding back, like one who is bringing his own hide to market and has nothing to expect but – a hiding. (Marx, 1867, ch. 6)

> [O]ur friend, Moneybags, must be so lucky as to find, within the sphere of circulation, in the market, a commodity, whose use-value possesses the peculiar property of being a source of value, whose actual consumption, therefore, is itself an embodiment of labour, and, consequently, a creation of value. The possessor of money does find on the market such a special commodity in capacity for labour or labour-power. (Marx, 1867, ch. 6)

For Marx, an economy-wide surplus value can only arise from the *excess* of the use-value of labour power (for the capitalist class) over its value in exchange. The former is measured by the overall working day of the labourers, whereas the latter is only measured by the 'necessary' labour time. This is the time it takes to produce the bundle of consumption goods workers purchase back by spending their own wage on the market. In other words, capitalists' surplus value (or profit) arises from unpaid labour, for workers are paid a wage that allows them to consume just a share of the entire net product of the economy. The rate of exploitation of the working class is, therefore, defined by the rate of surplus labour, meaning the ratio of the surplus labour time to the necessary labour time. Having clarified this, Marx goes on and shows that the general rate of profit of the economy is a linear, positive, function of the rate of surplus labour. The general profit rate is the uniform rate which is charged over production costs if capitalists are free to move their capitals across sectors. When fixed capital (say, machines) and non-wage circulating capital (for instance, raw materials) are taken into account as inputs,[7] competition and other market forces are likely to drive relative output prices away from relative labour contents. This is the problem faced by Ricardo indeed. However, at the economy-wide level the summation of prices is always proportional to the summation of labour contents, and total profit (determined by the general rate of profit) is always proportional to total surplus labour (determined by the exploitation rate). Prices and profit are nothing but transformed forms of labour contents and surplus labour, respectively (see Box 9.3). For Marx, Ricardo's conundrum had been eventually solved, while his critique of Classical political economy had turned into a critique of capitalism and its exploitative nature.

Box 9.3: The transformation problem

The so-called transformation problem arises from Marx's attempt to find a general rule to transform 'values' of commodities (reflecting their own content of social labour) into prices of production, meaning prices prevailing in a competitive market. Such a rule would allow showing that value is produced in the production sphere and can only be redistributed (not created) in the exchange or circulation sphere. The summation of prices of production would match the summation of values, and, similarly, total profit would match total surplus value. As a result, it would be possible to claim that prices are transformed values, while capitalists' profit is transformed surplus value, meaning (unpaid) social surplus labour time expended by the working class in the production sphere. Marx provided incomplete notes and numerical examples on the process of transformation which did not allow to address this question in a satisfactory way. First-class theorists such as Bortkievitz, Böhm-Bawerk, Dobb, Lange, Pareto, J. Robinson, Samuelson, Steedman, Sweezy, and many others, have all dealt with this conundrum since the end of the nineteenth century. However, no consensus was achieved until the early 1980s, when a number of 'new interpretations' of the Marxian theory of value were proposed. While these interpretations still show some noteworthy differences between them, they are usually based on the idea that prices and values do not concern different accounting systems. On the contrary, they are linked together by the monetary expression of social labour time (MELT), now defined as the ratio of the economy-wide money value added to total direct or living labour time of the economy. Building upon the MELT concept, it is shown that a coherent rendition of the transformation process can be provided. In short, if the economy's net product expressed in prices of production is defined as $\mathbf{p}^T[\mathbf{I} - \mathbf{A}]\mathbf{q}$, the Marxian theory of value can be traced back to the claim that $\mathbf{p}^T[\mathbf{I} - \mathbf{A}]\mathbf{q} = m\ \mathbf{l}^T\mathbf{q}$, where m stands for the MELT (e.g. Duménil and Foley, 2008; Foley and Mohun, 2016). The condition above states that the money value added of a capitalist economy, not its gross value, expresses the social direct labour time expended by the workers in the production sphere, thereby confirming Marx's main insight about the original of value and surplus-value. The debate on transformation is anything but concluded.

Alternative approaches to value: Sraffa's surplus approach

Marx's rendition of the labour theory of value gave rise to one of the most long-lasting controversies in the history of economic (and philosophical) thought. The point is that Marx's explanation about how to 'transform' labour contents (or labour-values) into competition prices (or reproduction prices) was incomplete.[8] None of the repeated attempts to develop or amend it made by the Marxist theorists between the end of the nineteenth century and the beginning of the twentieth century were entirely convincing (see Box 10.3). In addition, the socialist turn of the Classical approach was regarded as politically unseemly in major Western universities. As a result, the Classical approach to value was neglected by most theoretical economists until the 1960s, when it was revamped by Sraffa's major work, *Production of Commodities by Means of Commodities. Prelude to a Critique of Economic Theory*. There are two main points made by Sraffa in this work: first, the Marginalist-Neoclassical theory of value and distribution is affected by a fatal flaw;[9] second, relative prices can be worked out without any reference to utility functions or individual preferences. For this purpose, capitalism must be regarded as a circular production process generating a physical surplus. All is necessary to define prices, meaning the set of relative prices which allow the system to reproduce over time, is the knowledge of the economy-wide technique of production. In the case of an economy with single-product industries, the set of techniques is given by the vector of labour coefficients and the matrix of interindustry coefficients. For example, in a two-industry (and two-good) economy the price system would be:

$$p_x = \left(l_x \cdot w + p_x \cdot a_{xx} + p_y \cdot a_{xy}\right) \cdot (1 + r)$$

$$p_y = \left(l_y \cdot w + p_x \cdot a_{yx} + p_y \cdot a_{yy}\right) \cdot (1 + r)$$

where a_{xx} is the quantity of good x (say, quarters of corn seeds) used as an input to produce one unit of the same good (for example, one ton of corn), a_{xy} is the quantity of good y (say, tons of iron) used as an input to produce one unit of good x (one ton of corn in our example), and so on. Notice that, unlike Sraffa, we stick to the Classical assumption that workers are paid in advance, so that profit accrues on the total capital advanced, including wages.

When $n > 2$ industries are taken into consideration, the price system can be generalised and defined in matrix terms as:

$$\mathbf{p}^T = \left(\mathbf{l}^T w + \mathbf{p}^T \mathbf{A}\right) \cdot (1 + r)$$

where $\mathbf{p}^T = [p_j]$ is the $1 \times n$ row vector of reproduction prices,[10] $\mathbf{l}^T = [l_j]$ is the $1 \times n$ row vector of direct labour coefficients, and finally $\mathbf{A} = [a_{ij}]$ is the $n \times n$ matrix of technical coefficients.[11]

We have n price equations and $n + 2$ unknowns (namely, n prices plus the wage rate and the profit rate). The system can be solved by taking the price of a certain good or the net product of the economy as the *numeraire* and by setting exogenously either w or r. As a result, prices are determined by conditions of production, as claimed by the Classicals and Marx. In addition, income distribution does no longer reflect marginal productivities of labour and capital, respectively. On the contrary, it must be defined 'from outside the system', as the profit rate and the wage rate exceeding the subsistence level both depend on several institutional factors, including class struggle and the monetary policy stance.

> The choice of the wage as the independent variable ... was due to its being there regarded as consisting of specified necessaries determined by the physiological or social conditions which are independent of prices or the rate of profits. But as soon as the possibility of variations in the division of the product is admitted, this consideration loses much of its force. And when the wage is to be regarded as 'given' in terms of a more or less abstract standard, and does not acquire a definite meaning until the prices of commodities are determined, the position is reversed. The rate of profits, as a ratio, has a significance which is independent of any prices, and can well be 'given' before the prices are fixed. It is accordingly susceptible of being determined from outside the system of production, in particular by the level of the money rates of interest. (Sraffa, 1960, ch. 5)

Finally, while Sraffa's system does not rely on the labour theory of value, and in fact has been regarded by many theorists as a rejection of it, the two approaches are not necessarily at odds. If the monetary value added of the economy is assumed to be proportional to the total direct labour, the surplus value (or profit) earned by the capitalists is proportional to the surplus labour spent by the workers in the production sphere (we refer again to Box 10.3).

Alternative approaches to value: energy-theories of value

The publication of *Production of Commodities* went along with a renaissance of political economy in the 1960s–70s. Interestingly, Sraffa's approach shares a number of features with an earlier contribution of the Hungarian-American mathematician and physicist Von Neumann (1937).[12] It is also very akin to the input–output analysis developed by Leontief (1941, 1986). The latter may well be regarded as a pioneering empirical application of Sraffa's later theoretical work. The Von Neumann-Sraffa-Leontief approach, also termed the surplus approach or NeoRicardian school, is suitable for the empirical analysis of structural interdependencies between industries. However, its popularity has been falling in North American and European economics divisions since the early 1980s. Predictably, the marginalisation of the surplus approach has gone along with a reduction in the interest in theories of value. If value is defined by individual preferences, all the economist is interested in is either the good's price within a competitive market or (if markets are absent or imperfect) individual willingness to pay for it.

While being set aside by most economists, the inquiry into the nature and causes of (intrinsic) value has been revamped within the field of ecological economics since the late 1970s (see also Chapter 14). Environmental scientists and ecological economists usually distinguish the 'instrumental value' from the 'intrinsic value' of things. Instrumental value is defined as the value reflecting the difference that a good makes to satisfaction of individual wants. It roughly corresponds to the 'marginal utility'. The intrinsic value is the value of 'maintaining the health and the integrity of an ecosystem or species, per se, irrespective of human satisfaction' (Farber et al., 2002, p. 376). Building upon this view, some scientists have proposed an (embodied) energy-theory of value, aiming either to complement or replace utility-based theories of value. Solar energy is usually regarded as the only primary (scarce) input, meaning the only source and measure of intrinsic value, whereas labour and capital are just intermediate goods or inputs. The main strength of energy theories of value is that, while anchoring value to thermodynamic laws and energy consumption, they provide a method of valuation which does not depend on consumers' preferences. In this sense, they show a clear similarity with the Classical theory and the surplus approach.[13] A second strength of energy-theories of value is that they are rather intuitive, as all goods and services require a certain amount of available energy to be produced. A third strength is that, like both the Classical and the surplus approaches, the energy-based theory provides a method of valuation that does not rely on utility-functions, demand and supply schedules, or individual preferences. Since the measure of value is independent of income distribution and prices, the energy-based approach is also unaffected by the logical flaw that marks the Neoclassical theory of price and distribution. While the energy-based approach is not free of criticisms either (see Box 9.4), it seems highly palatable for environmental scientists and policymakers,[14] and it could lead to a new renaissance of the Classical approach

Box 9.4: Open issues with energy-theories of value

From a biophysical viewpoint, there are three main issues with energy-theories of value. First, they typically consider only energy inputs and outputs, neglecting mass. Second, there are other inputs of energy in the biosphere (think of gravitational pull) in addition to solar energy. Third, when a pure solar energy flow theory of value is advocated, 'there are issues with spatial and time scales' (Patterson, 1998, p. 118). From an economic viewpoint, there are two additional criticisms. First, energy-based theories of value turn out to be 'undetermined' both socially and historically. They assume that social value is independent of the specific dominant mode of production and exchange and of the underlying social relations. Here energy-based theories share one of the weaknesses of utility-based theories of value. Second, it has been argued that the exchangeability of goods and services in definite proportions is linked to the presence of a 'third thing' that makes it possible. Yet, 'any candidate for the status of the third thing, value, must be an intrinsic property *solely* of the commodity'. By contrast, 'all natural material things [and not just human products within capitalism] are formed through processes that require available energy and so the input of such natural energy per se cannot be the third thing generating exchange ratios that are characteristic solely of commodities' (Brown, 2008, pp. 135–136). In other words, the point is not *how* the value of things can be measured *in general*, but *what* the value of a product *is* within a capitalist economy. In principle, relative values could be measured by taking any product as the unit of account. This is the reason even a peanut-theory of value, in which all commodities are denominated in direct and indirect 'peanut units' (Gintis and Bowles, 1981, p. 7) was provocatively proposed. The point is that gold, corn, salt, peanuts, and solar energy, can all act as 'money' as a means of exchange and a unit of account. In formal terms, relative prices are not affected by the unit of measure chosen. This choice per se says nothing about the source or cause of intrinsic value of products. This is the reason the definition of the *numeraire* (and the unit of measure) should not be confused with the selection of the theory of value.

Conclusion

What are the determinants and the measure of value of products was a fundamental question that marked the inception of modern economic thought (see Table 9.1 for a summary of different approaches across the history of economic thought).

The current mainstream approach regards value as arising from the individual's preferences. The latter are revealed either by the individual's observable choices or by her own willingness to pay. This approach is grounded in the utility theory of value developed by the early Neoclassicals since the end of the nineteenth century. Indeed, the current preference-based approach may well be regarded as an 'ordinalist' rendition of the idea that value is defined by the subjective utility the individual derives from the consumption of the last (or marginal) unit of a certain good. This is the usual story told by intermediate microeconomics textbooks. Yet the utility- or preference-based theory was not the dominant approach when political economy arose as an independent discipline from moral philosophy. On the contrary, for Smith, Ricardo, and other Classical theorists, value was an intrinsic (or objective) feature of goods and it was best expressed by their labour content. While progressively abandoned by economists, the labour-theory of value was used by Marx to found his critique of both the then-dominant view in economics, that is, Classical political economy, and its subject, capitalism. His line of research remained on the sidelines of the academic debate until the early 1960s when it was revamped by Sraffa. Sraffa provided both a harsh criticism of the dominant Neoclassical approach, and a logically sound rendition of Classical (and Marx's) intrinsic theory of relative prices, termed the surplus approach. The latter enjoyed great popularity in the 1960s–70s but has become neglected by most economists since the 1980s. Interestingly, the early pioneering energy-based theories of value were developed during the same period. These theories show a noteworthy resemblance with the Classical and surplus approaches. The debate around how goods and services are, or should be, valued remains open (despite microeconomics textbooks and modules being dominated by the preference-based view) and engages a plurality of disciplines.

Table 9.1 Approaches to value from the mid-eighteenth century up until today

Schools of thought	**Unit of value**	**Nature of value**	**Analysis level**	**Economic sphere**	**Political philosophy**	**Some of main theorists*****	**Period**
Utilitarians	Total utility	Intrinsic	Micro	Exchange	Mainly egalitarian	Bastiat, Beccaria, Bentham, Cournot, Galiani, Gossen, Say, Senior	1750–1880
Classicals	Production cost, individual labour	Intrinsic	Micro, Macro	Production, Exchange	Mainly conservative	J. S. Mill, Ricardo, Smith, Torrens	1770–1880
Marxists	Social labour	Intrinsic	Meso**, Macro	Production	Egalitarian	[Marx] Bortkiewicz, Dobb, Luxemburg, Rubin, Sweezy	Since 1860s
Marginalists (or Early Neoclassicals)	Marginal utility	Subjective	Micro	Exchange	Heterogeneous	Jevons, Menger, Marshall, Walras	1880–1930
*Neoclassicals**	Preference, willingness to pay	Subjective	Micro	Exchange	Mainly conservative	Allen, Hicks, Pareto, Slutsky	Since 1890s
Surplus Theorists	Reproduction cost	Intrinsic	Meso**	Production	Egalitarian	[Sraffa] Garegnani, Pasinetti, Steedman	Since 1960s
Ecological Economists	Energy cost	Intrinsic	Meso**	Ecosystem	Mainly egalitarian	–	Since 1970s

Notes: *Today's dominant approach; ** industry level; *** excluding living scholars

Discussion questions and seminar activities

Apply the different theoretical perspectives covered in the chapter to explain how you would value:

- A table
- A film
- A car
- An urban park
- A barrel of oil

What are the implications of using the different theoretical perspectives?

Can goods and services be valued without relying on the preferences of individual consumers?

What are the strengths of each approach to understanding/measuring value?

Further reading

Barber, W. J. (2010). *A history of economic thought*. Middleton: Wesleyan University Press, Chaps. 1, 3, 5, 6.

Bellofiore, R. (1989). A monetary labor theory of value. *Review of Radical Political Economics, 21*(1–2), 1–25.

Costanza, R., & Hannon, B. (1989). Dealing with the 'mixed units' problem in ecosystem network analysis. In *Network analysis in marine ecology* (pp. 90–115). Berlin: Springer.

Faccarello, G., & Kurz, H. D. (Eds.). (2016). *Handbook on the history of economic analysis Volume III: Developments in major fields of economics*. Cheltenham: Edward Elgar.

Foley, D., & Simon, M. (op. cit.). *Value and price* (G. Faccarello & H. D. Kurz, Eds.).

Hill, R., & Myatt, T. (2010). *The economics anti-textbook*. London: Zed Books, Chaps. 4, 8.

Lavoie, M. (2014). *Post-Keynesian economics: New foundations*. Cheltenham: Edward Elgar, Chap. 3.

Marx, K. (1894). *Capital. A critique of political economy* (Vol. 3). Harmondsworth: Penguin Books/New Left Review, 1981.

Screpanti, E., & Zamagni, S. (2005). *An outline of the history of economic thought*. Oxford: Oxford University Press on Demand, Chaps. 2.2, 3.1, 4.3, 5.1, 6.5, 8.3, 11.2.

Shaikh, A. M. (1998). The empirical strength of the labour theory of value. In *Marxian economics: A reappraisal* (pp. 225–251). Basingstoke: Palgrave Macmillan.

References

Bentham, J. (1789). *The principles of morals and legislation*, T. Payne. (Republished 1988, New York: Prometheus Books).

Brown, A. (2008). A materialist development of some recent contributions to the labour theory of value. *Cambridge Journal of Economics, 32*(1), 125–146.

Duménil, G., & Foley, D. (2008). The Marxian transformation problem. In S. N. Durlauf and L. E. Blume (Eds.), *The New Palgrave Dictionary of Economics*, 2nd edition. Basingstoke: Palgrave Macmillan.

Farber, S. C., Costanza, R., & Wilson, M. A. (2002). Economic and ecological concepts for valuing ecosystem services. *Ecological Economics, 41*(3), 375–392.

Foley, D., & Mohun, S. (2016). Value and price. In G. Faccarello (Ed.), *Handbook on the history of economic analysis* (pp. 589–610). Cheltenham: Edward Elgar.

Gintis, H., & Bowles, S. (1981). Structure and practice in the labor theory of value. *Review of Radical Political Economics, 12*(4), 1–26.

Gossen, H. H. (1854). *Entwickelung der gesetze des menschlichen verkehrs, und der daraus fliessenden regeln für menschliche handeln*. Braunschweig: F. Vieweg.

Hicks, J. R. (1939). The foundations of welfare economics. *The Economic Journal, 49*(196), 696–712.

Jevons, W. S. (1871). *The theory of political economy*. London: Macmillan.

Kaldor, N. (1939). Welfare propositions of economics and interpersonal comparisons of utility. *The Economic Journal, 49*, 549–552.

Kurz, H. D., & Salvadori, N. (2001). Sraffa and von Neumann. *Review of Political Economy, 13*(2), 161–180.

Leontief, W. W. (1941). *The structure of the American economy 1919–1929*. Oxford: Oxford University Press.

Leontief, W. W. (1986). *Input-output economics*. Oxford: Oxford University Press.

Marshall, A. (1890). *Principles of economics*. London: Macmillan, 1920.

Marx, K. (1867). *Capital. A critique of political economy* (Vol. 1). Harmondsworth: Penguin Books/New Left Review, 1976.

Menger, C. (1871). *Grundsätze der volkswirthschaftslehre* (Vol. 1). Vienna: Braumüller.

Pareto, V. (1896) *Cours d'économie politique*. Lausanne: Librairie de L'Université.

Pareto, V. (1906). *Manuale di Economia Politica*. Milan: Piccola Biblioteca Scientifica.

Patterson, M. (1998). Commensuration and theories of value in ecological economics. *Ecological Economics, 25*(1), 105–125.

Pigou, A. C. (1932). *The economics of welfare*. (4th ed.) London: Macmillan.

Ricardo, D. (1817). *On the principles of political economy and taxation*, Vol. I of The works and correspondence of David Ricardo, Ed. P. Sraffa with the collaboration of M. H. Dobb, 1951. Liberty Fund, Indianapolis.

Ricardo, D. (1820). Letter to McCulloch. In P. Sraffa (Ed.), *The works and correspondence of David Ricardo, 1951–52* (Vol. VIII, pp. 279–280). Cambridge: Cambridge University Press.

Robbins, L. (1932). *An essay on the nature and significance of economic science*. London: Macmillan.

Smith, A. (1776). *An inquiry into the nature and causes of the wealth of nations*. Chicago: University of Chicago Press, 1977.

Sraffa, P. (1960). *Production of commodities by means of commodities*. Cambridge: Cambridge University Press.

Von Neumann, J. (1937). A model of general economic equilibrium. In *Readings in the theory of growth* (pp. 1–9). London: Palgrave Macmillan, 1971.

Walras, L. (1874). *Eléments d'économie politique pure ou théorie de la richesse sociale*. Lausanne: Corbaz.

10 WHAT CAUSES ECONOMIC CRISES? AND WHAT CAN WE DO ABOUT THEM?

Bruno Bonizzi and Jeff Powell

Introduction

Countries' growth paths follow the cyclical fluctuations of business activity (so-called business cycles), regularly experiencing slowdown and sometimes entering recessionary periods. A crisis, in contrast, is marked by the suddenness of the descent into recession and the prolonged and often-painful nature of its duration. A crisis can be catalysed by any of a number of factors. Boom and bust in financial asset prices, particularly the stock markets, are a fact of life. Governments around the world, especially the developing world, sometimes run into difficulties servicing their debt. And currencies sometimes fluctuate dramatically, pushing domestic residents into financial troubles. Few crises, however, were as serious as the global financial crisis that started in 2007/08, which, in a way, represented a mix of all the problems described above. It started in a segment of the US financial sector, but financial losses piled up and led major financial institutions to insolvency, first in the US and then internationally. International financial investments declined dramatically, with global investors desperately trying to store their wealth into safe US government bond assets, inducing a generalised global asset price collapse and sharp depreciations of many currencies against the US dollar. Governments were forced to intervene to save insolvent banks, becoming heavily indebted in the process. As this financial meltdown unfolded, the crisis extended to the rest of the economy, consumption and investment collapsed, unemployment rose: a Great Recession ensued in the world economy. According to the International Monetary Fund (IMF, 2009), it was the worst recessionary period since the Great Depression in the 1930s.

Given the severity of these dramatic events, and the frequency of less dramatic downturns, a key task of economics should be to explain crises, and hopefully to suggest policy actions to prevent or at least limit the damage they cause. It is surprising therefore that economic theory has for a long time devoted little attention to crises, and even denied their analytical possibility. However, thanks to economists such as Marx and Keynes, crises can be understood not only as possible, but as inevitable events in an unchecked capitalist economy. Despite these contributions, the causes, the role of crisis in economic theory, and the policy implications remain subject of intense debate.

In this chapter, we will explore how crisis has been understood by economists through capitalist history. We will first look at Classical and Neoclassical economists, whose views prevailed at least until the 1930s. This group has downplayed the importance of crisis, and placed emphasis on policy errors as a source of economic disruption. We will then turn to those economists who, while employing the tools of Neoclassical general equilibrium theory, recognise that crises are possible and result from market imperfections. In the third section, we present different theories that put emphasis on crisis as an intrinsic feature of capitalism, though with different views on whether financial disruption is the cause or the symptom of a more widespread crisis. This is followed by a brief discussion of the policy implications of the differing approaches to crises taken by these schools of economic thought.

Crisis as outcome of government intervention in otherwise efficient markets: from Classical to Neoclassical economics

Classical political economists were mostly concerned in understanding the long-run tendencies of capitalism rather than its (in)stability. The Classical system is dynamic but does not experience cyclical fluctuations. The cornerstone of this view is the renowned proposition by the French economist Say (1803), according to which 'a product is no sooner created, than it, from that instant, affords a market for other products to the full extent of its own value'. Say's Law, as the proposition became known, effectively states that overproduction in a capitalist economy is impossible, and was espoused by almost all Classical political economists. Observed situations of excess supply of goods were not a violation of the law: these represented excess supply in particular sectors of the economy, which were matched by insufficient supply of other goods, rather than a problem at the aggregate level.[1] Except for these temporary imbalances, the system as a whole was rather stable.

Instability could, however, arise from bad policymaking, as the so-called Bullionist controversy showed. The Bank of England, as a result of the panic that followed the false news of a French invasion of Britain, had suspended the convertibility of currency into gold in 1797. The convertibility was not restored for about twenty-five years, during which period Britain experienced sustained price inflation. A debate ensued. On the one hand, the 'Bullionists' (among whom was Ricardo) argued that the suspension of convertibility was to blame, as it allowed excess supply of currency by the Bank. This excess supply then circulated in the economy, thereby generating inflation. On the other hand, 'Anti-Bullionists' argued that convertibility was not necessary, since the creation of banknotes by the Bank simply accommodates the needs of traders and producers, who issue bills to finance their activities, and can never be excessive. The Bullionists won the debate, and convertibility was restored, thus crediting the view that monetary policy could itself be a cause of instability.

By and large, these views did not change with the transition from Classical to Neoclassical economics. The possibility of a crisis is essentially absent in the economics proposed by the Marginalists in the second half of the nineteenth century. The Marginalist revolution shifted the focus from the aggregate level and its class division to individual producers and consumers. To the extent that such theories focus on the aggregate economy, such as in the general equilibrium theory of Walras (1954), this was simply the sum of individual, to a large extent identical, markets. This system was not well equipped to account for fluctuations of the economy as a whole. Furthermore, standard Neoclassical economics is fundamentally preoccupied with static equilibrium rather than the dynamics of the economy (see Chapter 6). In general equilibrium analysis, a powerful 'auctioneer' corrects the excess supply and demand by setting prices such that supply and demand exactly match for all goods. As all market imbalances are cleared simultaneously, there can be no intrinsic source of fluctuations and crises.

The impossibility of embedding cycles and crises in such analyses is emblematic in the efforts of Jevons (1875), a founder of Neoclassical analysis, who had to resort to a very unlikely source to explain them. Jevons linked business cycles to 'sunspots', i.e. the periodic appearance of dark spots on the surface of the sun that characterise its cyclical activity. Solar cycles last for about eleven years, a number surprisingly close to the ten and a half years that Jevons calculated to be the average period between commercial crises. This induced him to theorise that the power of radiation that changes over the solar cycle is the determinant of business confidence fluctuations. While Jevons's sunspots theory was never particularly successful, the Neoclassical system developed into a full macroeconomic model in the early twentieth century. This model distinguishes between different types of markets: money markets, labour markets, goods markets and loanable funds markets. Otherwise, this model uses standard general equilibrium analysis and reflects the following essential messages. Firstly, the analysis starts from a condition of stability: in normal conditions, all markets are assumed to be in equilibrium, there is no involuntary unemployment, and no excess supply of goods or money. Secondly, the aggregate level of output is determined, via Say's Law, by the supply side of the economy (and hence the labour market). Finally, any imbalance is corrected by price changes, e.g. if labour demand falls below labour supply – i.e. there is unemployment – the real wage quickly adjusts downwards to restore full employment (see Chapter 7). Under such conditions, changes in employment and output signify either periods of transition as the price system adjusts to clear all markets, or simply reflect a new optimal equilibrium of the economy, following a fundamental change, such as a technological improvement. In other words, crises are short-lived or are effectively not crises at all.

The impossibility to explain long and painful recessions was clearly at odds with the reality of the Great Depression. In the US, GDP fell by 28 per cent between 1929 and 1933, and unemployment rose from 3.2 per cent to more than 25 per cent. The Neoclassical model was ill-equipped to explain such catastrophic events. It is in this context that Keynes's critique of the Neoclassical model emerged. As the chapter discusses later, Keynes emphasised falling aggregate demand as the main cause of a crisis, in direct contradiction to Say's Law, and was very sceptical of the idea that the market, left to itself, would be able to restore full employment by readjusting prices. The economics of Keynes was better suited to explain the Great Depression and to provide solutions to crises, and quickly replaced the Neoclassical model. For a long time, Keynesian theory represented the general consensus in macroeconomics.

The Neoclassical and Classical views of crisis only began to slowly re-emerge in the 1960s. In 1963, Friedman and Schwartz published *A Monetary Theory of the United States* (1963), which challenged the Keynesian consensus. The central thesis of their work is that initial changes in the money supply, rather than aggregate demand, were the primary determinant of instability. Crucially, they argued that the Great Depression was a consequence of the failure of the Federal Reserve Bank, which had contracted the money supply at a time when the demand for money by the public increased following the financial crash in 1929. The money market imbalance generated the recession, as households reduced consumption and hoarded money. The Fed may not have caused the recession as such, but it was the primary culprit for its duration and severity. The government rather than the market was to blame.

A complete restoration of the Neoclassical model came in the 1970s and 1980s, with the rise of the New Classical school of macroeconomics. In New Classical models, all agents optimise their behaviour based on rational expectations, i.e. they do not make systematic errors in predicting the future, and markets are assumed to be clearing in the Walrasian tradition, with flexible prices adjusting quickly to accomplish this. Just as in the Neoclassical macroeconomic model, crises are effectively impossible in such a model of the economy. What then explains cyclical fluctuations? One suggested account is that agents are 'surprised' by policy actions. If, for example, monetary authorities intervene in the economy in a way that deviates from their usual policy rules, this could have a temporary impact on the economy (giving rise to the 'monetary equilibrium business cycle' theory). The other possibility is that these fluctuations represent a genuine response to 'real' (i.e. non-monetary) factors. The 'real business cycle' theory indeed argues that the single most important source of fluctuations in aggregate economic activity are technological shocks. The observed changes in unemployment represent the optimal response of agents modifying their labour supply (over an infinite time horizon), rather than that these would result from the insufficient demand for labour on behalf of firms. For Prescott (1999), a major proponent of this theory, the Great Depression had nothing to do with changes in demand or the money supply, but instead was argued to be the outcome of changing labour market institutions that induced people to work less.

In sum, since the golden age of Classical political economy, a large part of economic analysis has effectively dismissed the analytical centrality of economic crises. In a Neoclassical world, where all markets clear, crises are impossible, or they are the result of random short-lived miscalculations or government errors. For many economists, Say's Law remains at the heart of how the workings of the economy can be explained.

The new Keynesian classical synthesis: crises and market imperfections

As New Classical macroeconomics restored the belief that changes in aggregate demand did not cause significant fluctuations in levels of economic activity, some economists remained sceptical of its extreme conclusions about crises. As the prominent Keynesian economist Tobin (1986, p. 349) warned: 'I hazard the prediction that neither of the two species of business cycle theory offered by new classical macroeconomics will be regarded as serious and credible explanations of economic fluctuations a few years from now.' Despite this dissatisfaction, most macroeconomists were convinced by the New Classicals' claim that macroeconomics needs framing on the basis of general equilibrium theory. How to reconcile these two apparently incompatible positions? The solution was to change the microeconomic assumptions behind general equilibrium theory. Rather than starting with perfect markets that continuously cleared and perfectly rational agents, a number of economists started to introduce market imperfections. Such micro-level imperfections produced, at the macro-level, results that were similar to Keynesian economics, such as the possibility of involuntary unemployment and shortfalls of aggregate demand. For these reasons, these economists called themselves New Keynesians.

The most fundamental imperfection occurs in the price system. Partly inspired by Keynes himself, New Keynesian economists introduce rigidities in their models, as a result of which wages and prices move sluggishly rather than instantaneously. This creates a rationale for aggregate demand to determine aggregate output and employment, at least for a while. In case of a decrease of aggregate demand, prices and wages will not fall to clear the goods and the labour markets, Say's Law is violated, and involuntary unemployment persists. The problem is solved when prices and wages start to adjust, but this can take a long time. This is the reason why, as the chapter will discuss, New Keynesians advocate for policy intervention to restore the levels of aggregate demand.

For New Keynesian economists, a crisis can therefore happen as a disequilibrium phenomenon. But what causes it? In most New Keynesian models this is typically represented as an exogenous shock, as the key point of such models is to explain how the economy as a whole behaves in a crisis situation and which factors amplify the crisis. Comparatively less attention has been directed at understanding how crises may arise dynamically.

Research on market imperfections can, however, also shed light on the rise of imbalances in the economy. In particular, New Keynesian economists have emphasised the occurrence of information asymmetries, i.e. different access to information between two agents in an economic transaction. These are thought to be particularly pervasive in financial markets, where lenders typically have imperfect information about borrowers' intentions or actual performance. A type of asymmetric information that helps explain the build-up of a crisis is 'moral hazard'. It is impossible (or too costly) for lenders to properly monitor all borrowers, so borrowers have an incentive to take on excessive risk, gambling for higher personal gains (Diamond, 1984). The problem can be solved if contracts are designed so that borrowers have enough 'skin in the game', for example by providing collateral. But those financial institutions originating lending to sub-prime borrowers before the 2008 crisis clearly did not: they were not directly exposed to those mortgages, which they packaged together and then sold on the market, and furthermore many of them were such large and systemic institutions that they were effectively too-big-to-fail. Many other crises have been explained with reference to moral hazard in financial markets. In the late 1990s, currency crises in several emerging countries were blamed on the excessive foreign currency borrowing by private companies, which were counting on their governments' support (Corsetti et al., 1999).

The general point is that informational asymmetries can lead financial markets, and in turn the economy, out of equilibrium. Asset prices may grow too fast, building up vulnerabilities, which eventually lead to a crisis. Because markets do not clear instantaneously, output and employment fall. However, New Keynesians believe that eventually the economy will return to a stable path. Crises are possible, but are largely seen as a disturbance in an otherwise steady economy in the canonical models, which have become the framework of analysis of most central banks (see Box 10.1). As the prominent New Keynesian and former IMF Chief Economist Olivier Blanchard (2014, p. 28) declared: 'We in the field did think of the economy as roughly linear, constantly subject to different shocks, constantly fluctuating, but naturally returning to its steady state over time.' At least before the global financial crisis in 2008 this was the position taken by the majority of economists.

Box 10.1: The three-equations model

In the decades years before the crisis of 2008, a new consensus emerged in macroeconomic theory and policy. To a large extent this synthesised the New Keynesian approach to macroeconomics, with its adherence to market imperfection and aggregate demand as the main explanation of recessions, and dynamic general equilibrium modelling methodology as its main tool. Such a consensus is readily expressed by the usage of three key equations, representing the key ingredients of this approach (Woodford, 2003; Carlin and Soskice, 2009).

1. The first equation determines the level output as inversely related to the level of real interest rates (formally $Y_1 = A_1 - ar_0$).
2. The second equation determines the level of inflation, as the sum of past inflation plus the 'output gap', i.e. the deviation from the equilibrium level of output. In other words, if aggregate expenditure increases above the equilibrium level of output, inflation will rise (formally $\pi_1 = \pi_0 + \alpha(Y_1 - Y_e)$)
3. The third equation determines the optimal level of the (real) interest rate that central banks should set to stabilise the economy at a target level of inflation (formally $r_1 = r_s + \beta(\pi_1 - \pi^T)$).

Instability and stabilisation through this model can be explained as follows. The level of output fluctuates as a result of an exogenous shock in aggregate demand, through the first equation. Output fluctuations, through the second equation, result in inflation going above or below its target level. As a result, through the third equation, the central bank will respond by changing the level of interest rates in order to stabilise the inflation level.

The new consensus in macroeconomics therefore advised active, rule-based monetary policy as the main tool to stabilise the economy. This type of framework has been widely used by central banks adopting inflation-targeting policy objectives, and seemed to work in the 1990s until the financial crisis, a period known as the 'great moderation' for its relatively low and stable inflation and lack of severe recessions in most advanced economies. However, it became clear that the approach was insufficient to deal with severe crises such as the Great Recession, which required more substantial and 'unconventional' intervention.

Marx and Keynes: crisis as inherent to capitalism

To understand the contrary view of capitalism as an inherently crisis-prone economic system, we must go back to Marx. During his lifetime, Marx witnessed both more purely financial crises (the British banking crisis of 1847; the failure of Overend,

Gurney and Company in 1866) and the long depression of 1873–1896.[2] He also knew, as an economic historian, that these were only the most recent in a long series of crises since the genesis of the capitalist system.

With this knowledge, Marx set out to provide a scientific understanding for the dynamics of capitalism, a system which had, at its heart, a set of contradictions. One such contradiction, between the use value of a commodity (commodity as thing) and its exchange- value (commodity as money), set in the context of a system driven by the pursuit of surplus value (profit) rather than the fulfilment of need, a unique feature of capitalism, provides the conditions from which crises emerge (see also Chapter 9). In this understanding, crises are purgative, that is, they are necessary to resolve the contradictions that build up in the normal functioning of a capitalist economy. They allow for a renewal of the processes of accumulation.[3]

Unfortunately, during his lifetime, Marx never completed a fully elaborated theory of crisis, and so we are left with fragments of his discussions, predominantly in *Capital Volume III* (1991) and *Theories of Surplus Value* (1971). It is from these fragments however, that the body of Marxian crisis theory (and, indeed, much of non-Marxian crisis theory) has grown. These theories can be crudely placed into one of two camps. The first refers to a 'crisis of realisation', under which heading we can place crises of disproportionality and underconsumption (or overproduction). The second captures a 'crisis of profitability', under which are theories which focus on profit squeeze, class conflict, and the changing organic composition of capital. Many authors invoke various combinations of these dynamics, meaning that the differences between them are sometimes more of emphasis than of kind.

Crises of realisation

Disproportionality refers to the failure of the anarchic processes of a market economy to ensure a smooth growth path. In some sense, the real question is how does growth ever emerge from such a system, rather than why might it not! The profit motive is understood to reallocate investment to areas where demand outstrips supply, and therefore commodities are sold at prices above their values. However, in the real world, where both production and realisation take time, and capitalists struggle to separate out signals for their goods from other market noise (and respond accordingly), there is likely to be regular over-/underproduction, either in a single sector (usually goes unnoticed) or a series of sectors (can be the basis for a downturn, especially where the sectors are key to the economy). Disproportionality can also mark imbalances between investment and consumer goods production (or Department I and II, as they are called). There can be overproduction in investment goods relative to consumer goods (and vice versa), or, with the introduction of money and credit, there can be overproduction in both departments. Hilferding (1981, ch. 18) argued that credit may obscure emerging disproportionality, and interest rates amplify swings in profitability, falling during the early stages of a boom, and then rising as overproduction sets in. While disproportionality is undoubtedly present in some form during most crises, many would question whether or not it is the cause of the crisis or merely a manifestation of it.

More controversial is the second group of realisation crises, known as theories of underconsumption. In *Capital Volume III*, Marx (1991, p. 568) argued that 'The last cause of all real crises always remains the poverty and restricted consumption of the masses as compared to the tendency of capitalist production to develop the productive forces in such a way that only the absolute power of consumption of the entire society would be their limit.' Hilferding (1981), writing in early twentieth-century Germany, observed two big changes in the nature of the capitalist economy. The first was the formation of joint stock companies into cartels (consortiums of capitalist enterprises) and trusts (increasingly large enterprises resulting from mergers). The large modern firm is capable of carrying on part of its operations through a crisis serving only to 'exacerbate the disturbances in the regulation of prices' (1981, p. 296), passing the crisis on to the non-cartelised sectors, amplifying the disproportionalities which had created the conditions for crisis in the first instance, and resulting in overproduction. Overproduction would be perceived as underconsumption, as produced goods are unable to find consumers. The second change, particularly prominent in his adopted Germany, was the emergence of universal banks. Hilferding (1981, p. 293) believed that the intervention of such 'controlling banks' into the affairs of industry could help prevent the speculative activities which had catalysed earlier crises. This suggestion that the cyclical disruptions of the capitalist system could be mitigated through the actions of large banks was, unsurprisingly, a point of contention between 'reformist' and 'revolutionary' Marxists. However, Hilferding's exploration of the role of the credit system and speculation in promoting instability would later be taken up by theorists from Keynes to Minsky and beyond.

Shortly after Hilferding's work, capitalism experienced the decade-long Great Depression, which began in 1929. The impact on theoretical understandings of the role of crisis in the capitalist system was profound. Keynes took up the challenge that mass involuntary unemployment posed for the Neoclassical postulate of full employment and the neglect of aggregate demand. Keynes argued that the 'effective demand associated with full employment is a special case, only realised when the propensity to consume and the inducement to invest stand in a particular relationship to one another' (1936, p. 25).

Having established the central role for consumption and investment in maintaining economic activity, Keynes argued that a crisis could be linked to a sudden collapse in 'expectations as to the future yield of capital goods' (1936, p. 196). This fall was a product of human psychology ('animal spirits') in a context of fundamental uncertainty about the future (the latter drawn from the work of economists in the Austrian School, especially Frank Knight). If this collapse is accompanied by an increase in liquidity preference (the desire to hold cash rather than other financial assets), the resulting rise in interest rates could aggravate the decline in investment. Finally, this decline in investment may lead to rising unemployment and a falling propensity to consume, accelerating the downward spiral in output.

Is it right to describe Keynes's description of crisis as 'underconsumptionist'? Keynes himself argued that while underconsumption theories were 'undoubtedly right' (1936, p. 202) as guides to policy, they risked promoting redistribution and the increased consumption resulting from a higher propensity to consume at the cost of the promotion of investment. Keynes (1936, p. 202) resolved that the best course of action would be to 'advance on both fronts [consumption and investment] at once'. This led to a shift from an emphasis on underconsumption to one on surplus absorption, that is, the realisation of capitalist surplus through capitalists' own consumption and investment.

Kalecki (1939) pursued this emphasis on the importance of under-investment in the creation of conditions for crisis in the period following the Great Depression. For Kalecki (1965/1939, p. 119), 'investment [is] determined by the level and rate of change in the level of investment at some earlier time' since capitalists realise part of their profit through their expenditure on investment. Kalecki held that the growth of the capital stock is a function of past profits. At the top of the boom, the accumulation of capital equipment, with a stable level of output, makes for a falling rate of profit. This causes capitalists to pull back on investment. Kalecki had provided a link between investment and economic cycles, however, without a theory of financial fragility, he had not developed a full theory of crisis.

The development of underconsumption theory continued after the Second World War with the work of American Marxist Sweezy. Sweezy (1942, p. 184) viewed underconsumption as a special case of disproportionality, arising '… not from the … planless character of capitalism, but from the inner nature of capitalism'. That inner nature, he argued, was an inherent tendency to expand the capacity to produce consumption goods more rapidly than the demand for those same goods. This was premised on two further arguments. First, that the growth rate in consumption (from capitalists' consumption and workers' wages) would decline relative to the growth rate in the means of production. Second, citing empirical evidence, Sweezy assumed a stable relationship between growth in the means of production and growth in output of consumption goods. The combination of these two arguments results in a tendency for the growth in the demand for consumption goods to fall behind the growth in the production of consumption goods, creating the conditions for crisis, stagnation, or both.

A few years later, Austrian-born Steindl wrote his *Maturity and Stagnation in American Capitalism* (1952), in which he accepted Sweezy's conclusion about capitalism's inherent tendency to underconsumption, but rejected his reasoning. Drawing on the foundations of Keynes and Kalecki, Steindl returned to the importance of investment, linking its fall with rising oligopoly. The tendency that Marx had described towards capitalist concentration and centralisation leads to rising oligopoly across key sectors of the economy. This, Steindl argued, leads to an increase in the rate of surplus value produced, but without an increase in surplus value realised. Oligopoly prevents the elimination of excess capacity; capacity that would, in the Neoclassical model of perfect competition, be eliminated through the mechanism of increased competition of capitals. Excess capacity leads to falling investment and a fall in the rate of accumulation. As is the case with much of underconsumption theory based on the spread of monopoly, it is not clear why monopolists would continue to expand capacity in the face of insufficient demand. Both Kalecki and Steindl's work was influential on Sweezy (Toporowski, 2016). When Sweezy collaborated with Baran on *Monopoly Capital* (1968), their argument echoed that made by Steindl, emphasising the problems of surplus absorption created by the spread of monopoly, and hypothesising a role for unproductive consumption in sectors such as advertising, the military and finance in absorbing this surplus and preventing, or at least delaying, the onset of crisis.

Crises of profitability

The other major strand in Marxian crisis theory is based on a falling rate of profit leading to an 'investment strike' by capitalists, and a fall in output and employment. Unlike crises of realisation which encounter external limits to accumulation, crises of profitability assume that capitalism's chief limits are internal to its own functioning. A number of stylised arguments have been developed by writers both within and outside of the Marxian tradition as to why profits might fall. These include: class conflict leading to a rising post-war wage share (Bell and Cleaver, 1982); a 'profit squeeze' resulting from the inability of capitalists to pass on wage increases through rising prices (Glyn and Sutcliffe, 1972); and 'overcompetition' resulting from the entry of new state-backed industrial powers in Europe and Asia (Brenner, 2003).

However, the *inherent* tendency for the rate of profit to fall, as developed by Marx, was based on the premise of a rising organic composition of capital. Marx argued that competitive pressures would force individual capitalists to invest in machinery, leading to rising capital–output ratios. This rise in the value of constant capital (means of production) relative to variable capital (labour power), Marx called the rising organic composition of capital. Since capitalists' surplus value emerged from the exploitation of labour, a falling share of variable capital translated over time into falling surplus value.

One of the most prominent contemporary scholars to develop the theory of the profitability crisis is Shaikh (2016). In his dissection of the causes of the crisis of 2007–8, Shaikh starts with what could be viewed as a form of disproportionality, namely, that between production and circulation. He highlights the role of falling interest rates, financial deregulation and the general easing in credit conditions which fuelled the preceding boom. Accompanied by an attack on labour, profits rose while wages fell; the answer to maintain consumer spending was to expand household indebtedness. But what brings this credit-fuelled expansion to an end and initiates the downturn? Unlike Keynes, who traduced the turn in the boom to an unexplained change in mass psychology, Shaikh traces the shift to the inherent tendency for the rate of profit to fall. Shaikh's innovation is to emphasise the incremental rate of profit, that is, profit as a share of the most recent investment rather than as a share of the total capital stock. Using this measure, Shaikh (2016, p. 732) argues that US profit levels' remarkable growth through the late 1970s and 1980s peaked in the late 1990s. Echoing Marx and Keynes, Shaikh argues that the real net rate of profit is the material foundation which drives the 'animal spirits' of capitalists.

Profits are also central to the understanding of another major heterodox economist, Schumpeter. Schumpeter was very familiar with the work of Marx, and took up some of its key features, but took these in a different direction. In *The Theory of Economic Development*, Schumpeter (1934) starts by describing an economy which reproduces itself but does not grow, and shows that under such conditions no profits can be made. Profits arise when the economy is disrupted. This happens when some individuals, which Schumpeter calls *entrepreneurs*, come up with some innovative idea and apply it to production, supported by bank credit. These individuals, for a while, enjoy profits as the fruits of their innovation, which attracts imitators, spurring investment and therefore growth. Over time, however, profits are eroded by increasing competition and bank credit contracts, pushing some of the less capable imitators into difficulty. This is the beginning of the recession. But as painful as it is, Schumpeter views a recession as necessary. It weeds out inefficient producers and makes it possible to assimilate innovative processes into the productive structure of the economy. It furthermore generates the seeds for the next wave of innovations, as entrepreneurs seek new profits. Schumpeter therefore understands capitalism as an inherently unstable system, driven by the profit-seeking *entrepreneurs*, whose innovations generate repeated cycles of 'creative destruction'.

Crises of financial instability

The most common interpretation of Keynes's analysis of crisis emphasises the role of falling aggregate demand. Minsky (1982), built his *Financial Instability Hypothesis* (FIH), on a different reading of Keynes. Minsky argued that in Keynes's *General Theory*, we can see the impact of disequilibrating forces on the valuation of capital assets relative to output, and understand the preference of capitalist agents for more liquid positions in the face of fundamental uncertainty. Minsky (2010 [1931]) also highlights Keynes's famous condemnation of banks' pro-cyclical behaviour: '... a sound banker, alas, is not one who foresees danger and avoids it, but one who, when he is ruined, is ruined in a conventional and orthodox way with his fellows, so that no one can really blame him ...'.[4] At the same time, Minsky, echoing Marx, was critical of Keynes's resorting to mass psychology to explain sudden declines in investment or consumption activities (1982, p. 16).

Minsky developed his FIH in the 1980s, having witnessed stagflation in the United States in the 1970s, and the Latin American debt crisis that began in Mexico in 1982. Soon after its publication came the 1987 collapse of stock prices known as 'Black Monday' and the US savings and loan crisis of 1989–1991. It was clear to Minsky that capitalism, especially since the 1960s, was characterised by an increasingly complex structure of financial interrelations, and hence was a crisis-prone system, of which economists poorly understood the drivers of its volatility. Firms, governments, and households,[5] according to Minsky, assumed three postures with respect to their level of leverage. During periods of growth, he described the general position of corporations as 'hedged', that is, they retained the ability to repay out of operating profits both interest and principal on their borrowing. However, the core of Minsky's argument is that it is precisely this kind of stability that is *destabilising*. In their efforts to outcompete one another, capitalists' leverage would rise in lock-step, matched by innovation in the financial sector to mask the concomitant rise in risk. The next stage Minsky described as 'speculative', as an increasing share of corporations maintained only their ability to service the interest payments incurred on debt. The final stage, Minsky argued, is when corporations become 'Ponzi' units, losing their ability to repay either interest or principal. At this point, debt deflation (owing credit to Fisher [1911]) would take hold, as rising interest rates rendered the debt overhang increasingly unaffordable, driving corporations to the wall, and throwing workers out on the streets.

What is often missed in discussions of Minsky's FIH, are Minsky's reasons as to *why* corporations are pushed into a Ponzi posture. He cites two reasons. First, the costs of debt may become insupportable, because of endogenous rises in interest rates as banks pull back lending or central banks attempt to rein in an overheated economy. But second, and here Minsky (1982, p. 29) echoes Marx, gross capital income falls because the determinants of profit (and expectations of future profitability) have fallen. Where both factors are present, an economy may enter a deep recession. As to the determinants of profit, Minsky points to changes in productivity, foreign balance, government deficits, and the savings ratios of households.

Minsky, inspired by Schumpeter and Institutionalists, was also keen to apply the FIH to specific historical contexts. In particular, Minsky characterises the current phase of capitalism as 'Money Manager Capitalism', i.e. a phase where money managers – mutual funds and institutional investors such as pension funds and insurance companies – are the key actors driving the dynamics of the economy. Given the stake that these actors have in today's financial system, Minsky's insight has proven to be prophetic.

Dealing with crises

While there is much variation in the recommendations that emerge from different schools of thought in economics on how to respond to crises, much of this difference can be understood in light of the differences in analysis of the conditions which lead to crisis in the first place. In a Neoclassical approach, characterised by rational agents pursuing their objectives in efficiently allocating markets, crisis must by definition emerge from some kind of external shock to the system. Often this is put down to either 'negative fundamentals', that is, an act of omission on the part of the government in providing the conditions necessary for the proper functioning of the market, or the commission by that same government (or other institution such as trade unions) of an intervention which causes disequilibrium. After the GFC, Neoclassical advocates pointed the finger of blame at a range of state-led interventions, from supposedly inappropriate and overzealous lending by the federal mortgage providers Fannie Mae and Freddie Mac, to the Federal Reserve holding interest rates below the 'natural' rate of interest leading to asset price inflation. Consistent with this analysis are crisis responses which: seek to punish 'bad apples'; allow the failure of those institutions which are viewed to have sown disequilibrium; or even further deregulation to allow the forces of competition to root out problematic institutions before problems can once again emerge.

More dominant in mainstream narratives are economists trained in the new Neoclassical synthesis or New Keynesian school. Information asymmetries (or other causes of price rigidities) lie at the root of a series of market failures which have been carefully documented by this group. This can lead to what appears to be irrational behaviour, and result in prolonged disequilibrium outcomes with costly social consequences. Consistent with this analysis are recommendations which seek to address the market failures which are perceived to have played a role in the conflagration. Historically, these arguments have been used to justify the provision of deposit insurance, the creation of credit registries and the introduction of a raft of regulatory interventions to prevent market failure in financial markets. Emphasis in this group following the GFC has been on regulatory changes to banks' liquidity and capital adequacy ratios, as well as improvements in disclosure across a range of financial institutions and instruments.

New Keynesian economists also advocate active macroeconomic stabilisation in case of recessions. They primarily support the use of expansionary monetary policy, according to the inflation-targeting rules described in the section above, but also, in severe cases, fiscal stimulus. While the economy may itself eventually self-stabilise, it is argued that this can take a very long time and the welfare loss – especially in terms of high unemployment – may be too high a social cost to bear. Differences, however, exist within the school about how 'active' the government should be in stabilising the macro-economy.

For heterodox economists, crises are neither aberrations nor failures, but the outcome of the inherent instability of a capitalist economy. For Post-Keynesians, changing expectations in an environment of radical uncertainty generate cyclical rises in fragility. Responses to crisis in this group are focused on counter-cyclical regulatory measures, restraint of the financial sector and state intervention. Keynes (1936, ch. 24, II–III) famously called for the 'euthanasia of the *rentier*' through the imposition of low interest rates and the socialisation of investment. Minsky argued that central bank intervention was essential to protect commercial bank refinancing of corporates' positions, while central government deficit spending was needed to bolster demand and profits. He recognised that the result of such actions could be rising prices and anaemic growth, arguing that: 'If we are to do better it is necessary to reform the structure of our economy so that the instability due to financial structure heavily weighted with debt is diminished' (1982, p. 57). After the GFC, this school recommended a set of measures, including: counter-cyclical measures, such as varying the amount of capital that banks are required to hold at different phases of the business cycle; the restraint of private finance, through direct credit controls, caps on the size of bank balance sheets, and the use of capital controls to control cross-border financial flows; and measures beyond regulation, such as changes to central bank mandates and redistributive measures to tackle rising inequality.

For Marxian scholars, there is scepticism around any attempts to stabilise capitalism. This reflects the views of Marx (2002, p. 79) that the means adopted to address crisis come at the cost of 'paving the way for more extensive and more destructive crises, and … diminishing the means whereby crises are prevented'. Crises are necessary for the restoration of the process of accumulation in a capitalist economy. It would be mistaken, however, to assume that this translates into a call for inaction. Marxists recommend a greater role for the public and the collective across the economy. This might include calls to nationalise key sectors such as finance, utilities, and heavy industry, as well as the promotion of worker ownership of enterprises. More broadly, this analysis supports the organisation and protection of the working class so that the impact of crisis is not borne by the most vulnerable. This includes workplace organising and struggles for real wage increases, as well as the expansion of a range of public services.

Conclusion

In the wake of the GFC which began in 2008, the Neoclassical notion that unfettered markets provide both optimal and stable growth in output has lost credibility in many people's eyes. However, the opposing heterodox understanding of capitalism as a system of socio-economic reproduction inherently prone to crisis has equally failed to capture a foothold in mainstream thinking and policymaking. While the initial policy response dabbled with Post-Keynesian recommendations, this appears to be giving way to a New Keynesian project to fix perceived market imperfections with the benefit of insights from behavioural economics.

This poses an interesting question for historians of economic thought: why was the response to the Great Depression, in terms of the popular understanding of the relationship between capitalism and crisis, more far-reaching than that following the GFC? Certainly the social and economic context was different. The welfare state, despite being on the defensive after decades of neoliberal attack, served to mitigate some of the impact of the recent crisis compared to that experienced by the working class in the 1930s. Aggressive and globally coordinated expansion of central bank balance sheets has kept financial markets and institutions afloat, while also providing a rationale against the use of more redistributive fiscal measures. But the dominant ideas of the economics profession have undoubtedly played a role. Concerted efforts to weed out heterodox economists from departments around the world have weakened the research capacity and policy outreach capabilities of more radical voices in the profession. If crisis also represents opportunity, this one has yet to be realised.

Discussion questions and seminar activities

- Orthodox analyses of crisis put emphasis on problems of 'moral hazard' and 'adverse selection'. Explain these concepts. What examples of these problems do you see in the Great Recession that started in 2008?
- Why do you think that many commentators initially described the crisis that began in 2008 as a 'Minsky moment'? Do you think it was?
- What are the key differences between Neoclassical, New Keynesian, Post-Keynesian, and Marxian theories of crisis? What do you see as their strengths and weaknesses?

  How do Schumpeterian and Marxian views about declining profitability as the main driver of crisis differ?
- Watch the Keynes-Hayek rap, making a note of the economics concepts that Keynes and Hayek discuss. How do Keynes and Hayek view the underlying causes of crisis?

Further reading

Bertocco, A. (2017). *Crisis and the failure of economic theory: The responsibility of economists for the great recession* (New directions in Post-Keynesian economics series). Cheltenham: Edward Elgar.

Kindleberger, C. P. (2011). *Manias, panics and crashes: A history of financial crises* (Ed. R. Z. Aliber, 6th ed.). Basingstoke: Palgrave Macmillan.

Shaikh, A. (1978). An introduction to the history of crisis theories. In *U.S. Capitalism in crisis* (pp. 219–241). New York: URPE. [Online] Available at: http://www.anwarshaikhecon.org/index.php/publications/political-economy/421978/84-an-introduction-to-the-history-of-crisis-theories.

References

Baran, P. A., & Sweezy, P. M. (1968). *Monopoly capital: An essay on the American economic and social order*. Harmondsworth: Penguin.

Bell, P., & Cleaver, H. (1982). Marx's theory of crisis as a theory of class struggle. *Research in Political Economy, 5*, 189–261.

Blanchard, O. J. (2014). Where danger Lurks. *Finance and Development, 51*(3), 28–31.

Brenner, R. (2003). *The boom and the bubble*. London: Verso.

Carlin, W., & Soskice, D. (2009). Teaching intermediate macroeconomics using the 3-equation model. In G. Fontana & M. Setterfield (Eds.), *Macroeconomic theory and macroeconomic pedagogy*. Basingstoke: Palgrave.

Corsetti, G., Pesent, P., & Roubini, N. (1999). Paper tigers?: A model of the Asian crisis. *European Economic Review, 43*(7), 1211–1236.

Diamond, D. (1984). Financial intermediation and delegated monitoring. *Review of Economic Studies, 51*(3), 393–414.

Fisher, I. (1911). *The purchasing power of money: Its determination and relation to credit, interest, and crises*. New York: The Macmillan Co.

Friedman, M., & Schwartz, A. J. (1963). *A monetary history of the United States, 1867–1960*. Princeton: Princeton University Press.

Glyn, A., & Sutcliffe, B. (1972). *British capitalism, workers and the profit squeeze*. London: Penguin Books.

Hilferding, R. (1981). *Finance capital*. London: Routledge.

IMF. (2009, April). *World Economic Outlook*. International Monetary Fund.

Jevons, W. S. (1875). *Money and the mechanism of exchange*. London: Appleton.

Kalecki, M. (1939). *Essays in the theory of economic fluctuations*. London: Allen & Unwin.

Keynes, J. M. (1936). *The general theory of employment, interest and money*. New York: Harcourt, Brace, Jovanitch.

Keynes, J. M. (2010). The consequences to the banks of the collapse of money values. In *Essays in persuasion* (pp. 150–158). Basingstoke: Palgrave Macmillan.

Marx, K. (1971). *Theories of surplus value. Part III*. Moscow: Progress Publishers.

Marx, K. (1991). *Capital: Critique of political economy*. London: Penguin Books.

Marx, K., & Engels, F. (2002). *The Communist Manifesto*. London: Penguin.

Minsky, H. P. (1982). *Can 'It' happen again? Essays on instability and finance*. Armonk: M.E. Sharpe.

Prescott, E. C. (1999). Some observations on the great depression. *Federal Reserve Bank of Minneapolis Quarterly Review, 23*, 25–31.

Say, J.-B. (1803). *A treatise on political economy*. Philadelphia: Lippincott, Grambo & Co., 1855.

Schumpeter, J. A. (1934). *The theory of economic development: An inquiry into profits, capital, credit, interest, and the business cycle*. New York: Transaction Publishers.

Shaikh, A. (2016). *Capitalism: Competition, conflict, crises*. Oxford: Oxford University Press.

Steindl, J. (1952). *Maturity and stagnation in American capitalism*. New York: Monthly Review Press.

Sweezy, P. (1942). *The theory of capitalist development*. New York: Monthly Review Press.

Tobin, J. (1986). The future of Keynesian economics. *Eastern Economic Journal, 12*(4), 347–356.

Toporowski, J. (2016). The crisis of finance in Marxian political economy. *Science & Society, 80*(4), 515–529.

Walras, L. (1954). *Elements of pure economics*. London: Allen & Unwin.

Woodford, M. (2003). *Interest and prices: Foundations of a theory of monetary policy*. Princeton: Princeton University Press.

11 HOW DO ECONOMIES GROW?

Chakib Bourayou and Elisa Van Waeyenberge

Introduction

Some of the chapters in this book (Chapters 6, 10, and 15) deal with issues that are traditionally understood as part of Business Cycle Theory (BCT). Such analysis is often referred to as of the 'short run' as it focuses on deviations from 'potential' output. Within mainstream macroeconomic BCT, potential output corresponds to a level of economic activity at which a *given* capacity is fully utilised. In BCT, the state of the economy at which there is full capacity is sometimes referred to as the 'long run'. However, economists have also been concerned with trying to understand what drives changes in potential output (or capacity) of the economy, and this analysis, commonly referred to as 'growth theory', is also often referred to as the analysis of the long run (or the 'very long run'). So, across BC and growth theory, the use of short and long run can be somewhat confusing. This is discussed in more detail in the preliminaries below.

How economic growth should be analysed is a point of contention between mainstream and heterodox economics. Often it is theorised in mainstream economics as simply producing more output at the aggregate level as opposed to understanding growth as a process that causes fundamental changes in production, consumption and the organisation of the economy. To take an example, the widespread dissemination of ICT technology throughout the economy (the ICT revolution) would in most growth theories be analysed as productivity-enhancing technology that merely increases productivity of labour and, in turn, aggregate output. While ICT may increase productivity, however, it also causes changes in how goods are produced (i.e. new methods of production), what goods are produced (i.e. new industries), consumption patterns (at both intermediate and final goods level, e.g. online shopping), and institutions (think of the way in which, for instance, the benefit system has been overhauled in the UK). These shifts have profound effects on employment, income distribution, the demographics of production, and the fortunes of industries by creating new challenges as well as investment opportunities. Thus, growth is crucially a process of change, rather than merely doing more of the same. It has significant qualitative dimensions, over and above its quantitative measurement in terms of GDP growth rates. Nevertheless, as discussed further below, the Neoclassical growth literature, due to its attachment to 'one-size-fits-all' models of growth and the concept of steady state balanced growth, fails to consider the (qualitative) changes that growth brings. Furthermore, the (very) long-run growth path is often seen as independent from the short-run fluctuations around it. There tends to be little regard for how these two states or descriptions of the economy relate to one another.

This chapter discusses mainstream growth theory and its alternatives, with a focus on how growth and time (and the relationship between different time periods) are conceptualised. Mainstream interest in growth somewhat subsided with the marginalist revolution when attention turned to issues of static resource allocative efficiency (see Chapter 6). This was despite the reality that the dynamics of accumulation (or growth) had been a central concern for Classical political economists. After a brief hiatus, economics rediscovered an interest in growth around the late 1930s, with the seminal contributions by Harrod (1939) and Domar (1947) providing the foundations of what came to be called 'modern growth theory' (Sen, 1970).

The discussion in this chapter proceeds as follows. The next section deals first with some preliminaries trying to address the question of how time is understood in growth theory. This is followed by a discussion of mainstream growth theory, starting with the Harrod-Domar model which laid the foundations for modern growth theory. It highlights how 'old' Neoclassical growth theory arose to solve issues around the instability properties of the Harrod-Domar model, and contrasts this to 'new' Neoclassical growth theory, which attempted to explain technological change which had remained exogenous – and hence determined outside of the model – despite being the ultimate source of growth in old Neoclassical growth theory. The chapter then moves on to alternatives to mainstream growth analysis. These include original contributions by Classical political economists, post-Keynesians, Schumpeter and Evolutionary economists.

Preliminaries

The dichotomy between short and long run – between business cycles and growth – was briefly discussed above. As growth theory deals with the long-run trend or path of the economy, it is necessary to understand what is meant by this and how it relates to our understanding of time. This is a fraught (and often-overlooked) issue in economics, with different uses of the short-/long-run dichotomy characterising different schools of thought. Confusion seems to arise from use of the short/long run to refer to a period of historical (i.e. chronological) time, as compared to usage of the dichotomy to capture a theoretical proposition (or logical time). For instance, when the short run is used to refer to an economy characterised by a fixed capital stock – which is a theoretical proposition indicating logical time – the long run is the period when everything is fully flexible but potential output is fixed, and the very long run is the period where potential output can change – the subject of growth theory. These difficulties are compounded by different interpretations of an 'equilibrium' of the economy (see Chapter 6).

Attached to specific conceptualisations of time are questions of whether and how short-run movements or fluctuations affect long-run outcomes, and hence, whether short-run macroeconomic policy matters for growth. This tends to be captured in the notion of path (in)dependence. Path independence is the idea 'that there is an equilibrium position … [that is] somehow already defined, [that] is not affected by actions that individuals take and towards which the economy will generally tend to move'

(Arestis and Sawyer, 2009a, b, p. 13). Path dependency, then, reflects the notion that movements in actual output, together with the path towards equilibrium (if one exists), affect where the economy ends up.

A key aspect of logical time is that everything is reversible, so that a decision, once made, can simply be reversed, enabling the economy to return to a former equilibrium position. Within mainstream economics, being attached to logical time, this can manifest itself in two ways. Post-war Neoclassical economics tends to assume path independence, assuming that the long-run position (which the economy converges to), is unaffected by (short-run) movements and decisions in the current period, and thus the path taken by output does not affect where the economy ends up. This implies a separation between the analysis of the short run – business cycles – and the long run – growth. The two are assumed to be unrelated. Conceptions of path dependence can, however, exist when additional assumptions are made. An example would be to assume multiple long-run equilibrium growth paths together with short-run movements to change the path the economy is on, thus enabling short-run movements to have long-run effect. The assumption of reversibility is, however, still maintained, meaning that the original equilibrium path is still (theoretically) achievable with sufficient short-run movements to undo the effect of the initial movement.

In historical time, which most heterodox economics attaches itself to, such reversibility is not possible, and the possibility of path independence is precluded (except perhaps in the case of extremely small decisions which are immediately undone). Bhaduri (1993, p. 60) quotes Robinson (1980, p. 7) as follows: 'In space, it is possible to go to and fro, but time goes only one way; there is no going back to correct a mistake; an equilibrium cannot be reached by a process of trial and error … today is an ever-moving break from the irrevocable past and the unknown future.' In historical time, decisions made today affect what decisions can be made tomorrow, the results of these decisions, and the context in which they are made. When a decision is made, others make decisions and new information is incorporated (the economy is full of interdependencies). As a result, if the decision is reversed, the original situation will no longer prevail. This means that even if we return to the original quantitative position (for instance, in terms of the quantity of inputs used), the economy will now be qualitatively different. Arestis and Sawyer (2009a, pp. 13–14) sum up these issues with the analogy of a forest:

> let us suppose there is a main path through a forest, and there are side paths, which deviate from the main path but are such that following a side path would always lead one back to the main path. This is akin to the simplest Neoclassical approach in the sense that the path is already there waiting [for] someone to travel along it, that when someone leave the main path there are 'forces' leading them back to the path and that there is a unique destination. A form of path dependency could be introduced through the introduction of a second main path leading to a different destination, with side paths linking the two main paths. The final arrival point could then be said to be path dependent – the equivalent of multiple equilibria. The path dependency approach [historical time] is more akin to undertaking a journey through a forest in which there is no clearly marked

path, and it is a matter of hacking through the undergrowth (and perhaps there is no final arrival point – the forest goes on forever!). Each step taken has to build on previous steps and the position reach. There are irreversibilities: if one has hacked down some of the trees, even if one then retraces one's steps the trees do not immediately reappear and the experience of having hacked down some trees may have changed perceptions, etc.

Mainstream growth theories

While growth and development of an economy were central features of Classical economics (see below), following the Marginalist revolution of the later nineteenth century, interest in the subject waned. Furthermore, the Great Depression of 1929–1939 and the publication of Keynes's *General Theory* in 1936 shifted economic analysis to short-run aspects of the economy with the birth of what came to be called 'macroeconomics'. Interest in growth and development (see Chapter 12) within conventional economics, however, grew in the post-war period following the publications of Harrod (1939, 1948) and Domar (1947), giving rise to the so-called Harrod-Domar model.

The Harrod-Domar model is an exercise in 'equilibrium macro-dynamics'. It proposes a simple beginning to dynamic theory as the best way to initiate research into growth of the capitalist economy. This implies theorising growth along a *steady-state balanced growth* (SSBG) path. Along a *steady-state* growth path, all variables, including output, labour and capital, grow at a *constant* rate (i.e. their magnitude increases but at a constant rate). Along a *balanced* growth path, all variables grow at the *same* rate. A steady-state balanced growth path then implies a form of 'equilibrium' over time whereby all variables grow at *constant* and *equal* rates, i.e. the economy just gets bigger, but otherwise remains the same in all other respects. This means that proportions or ratios in the economy, like for instance the capital–output ratio (COR), remain constant. You could think of the economy along an SSBG path in terms of a specific picture that is being enlarged – without any other changes.

Despite various innovation in growth theory, as we will point out below, Neoclassical economics has failed to move away from an SSBG framework. Hence, Neoclassical growth theory, old or new remains fundamentally constrained by the limits of SSBG. For example, along a SSBG growth path, where all variables grow at equal and constant rates, structural change is necessarily excluded. Indeed, structural change as an essential feature of growth and development implies that the COR changes when particular sectors increase their share of GDP – industrialisation, for instance, increases the COR of an economy.

This rest of this chapter is structured as follows. First, we present the assumptions, workings and limitations of the Harrod-Domar growth model. This is followed by a presentation of the Solow-Swan model (old Neoclassical growth theory) and the AK model (new Neoclassical growth theory) that emerged in response to some of its limitations.

The Harrod-Domar growth model

Against the backdrop of dwindling interest in growth, Harrod (1939, 1948) and Domar (1947) sought to extend a Keynesian analysis of the short run into the long run by recognising that investment has a dual role of both influencing the level of aggregate demand in the current period and the capital stock of future periods, and thus potential output (and hence growth). The Harrod-Domar (HD) theory seeks to establish the conditions under which SSBG occurs and whether this growth path is stable. The model shares Keynes's scepticism about the ability of the economy to reach full employment equilibrium in the short run, and, as we illustrate below, the conditions to achieve the SSBG are extremely restrictive with small deviations from an equilibrium growth path either resulting in accelerating growth or progressively worsening contraction (the 'knife-edge' problem).

Following Harrod (1939), the HD model identifies three different growth rates: the *actual growth rate* (G_A) is the growth rate of output that the economy actually experiences. The *warranted growth rate* (G_W) is the rate of growth of output that is necessary to keep capital fully utilised (or it is the rate of growth at which investors' expectations are fully realised). The *natural rate of growth* (G_N) is the rate of growth of output that is just sufficient to employ a growing labour force. If the actual rate of growth exceeds the warranted rate of growth, plans to invest exceed plans to save, pushing the economy away from the rate of growth at which they would be equal. If the actual rate of growth falls below the warranted rate of growth, plans to invest are less than plans to save and growth falls further below its warranted level. Due to the way that expectations are formed in the model, these movements in the actual rate of growth are self-reinforcing, with an increase/decline in investment leading to further increases/declines in investment. This is known as the knife-edge problem; along the edge (when $G_A = G_W$) the economy is fine, however, either side of the edge the economy experiences accelerating expansionary or contractionary dynamics (see Fine and Dimakou [2016] for more detail).

Even if, however, output and capacity (i.e. the actual and warranted rate) grow at the same rate (G_A=G_W), this may be less than the rate of growth of the labour force, which means that the economy is growing at less than full employment. If you want the economy to grow with full employment and full capacity, then the three rates of growth, G_A, G_W and G_N, will need to be equal to each other. This gives you the condition for SSBG.

The HD model built on the Keynesian macroeconomic theory of the time. In accordance, the Harrod-Domar model held that the level of aggregate demand determined the short-run aggregate output level. The model focused on the level of investment, with the output level in any given period being determined according to the multiplier and accelerator principles. The size of the multiplier depends inversely on the marginal propensity to save *(s)*: a higher *s* means that more of the increase in income is saved and therefore less is consumed. Formally,

$$Y_t = \frac{I_t}{s} \tag{11.1}$$

Where Y = output, I = investment, s = the marginal propensity to save, and t denotes the time period.

The decision to invest is modelled by the accelerator, which states that the level of investment (and thus the level of capital stock) depends upon the expectations of whether demand (and thus output) would increase (or decrease) in this period compared to last period; and on the COR which shows the amount of capital that is needed to produce an additional unit of output (and thus, how much investment is needed to meet the new level of demand). The COR is assumed to be constant.[1] Mathematically this can be expressed as follows:

$$I_t = v\left(e\left(Y_t\right) - Y_{t-1}\right) \tag{11.2}$$

Where I_t = investment in period t; v = COR which is assumed to be constant; Y = output; e() denotes expectations, and thus e(Y_t) is the expected output level in period t. Thus, where output (and therefore demand) is expected to be greater than in the last period (e(Yt)>Yt−1), there will be an increase in investment (and vice versa). The higher the COR (v), the higher investment will be, as the increase in capital to meet the new output level has to be greater.

From Equations (11.1) and (11.2), we can express output in the current period as the product of both the accelerator and multiplier effects. This gives:

$$Y_t = \frac{v\left(e\left(Y_t\right) - Y_{t-1}\right)}{s} \tag{11.3}$$

Thus, output during a given period (Y_t) depends on the expected level of output (prior to its realisation) that the investment during that period was based upon. Therefore, the growth in output between two periods depends on the expected growth of output (the expected increase of output between two periods). As the rate of growth of output is equal to $\frac{Y_t - Y_{t-1}}{Y_t}$, the expected rate of growth can be obtained by dividing both sides of Equation (11.3) by the expected output level.

$$\frac{Y_t}{e\left(Y_t\right)} = \frac{v\left(e\left(Y_t\right) - Y_{t-1}\right)}{s * e\left(Y_t\right)}$$

As $\frac{\left(e\left(Y_t\right) - Y_{t-1}\right)}{e\left(Y_t\right)}$ is the expected rate of growth, denoted as e(g), we can rearrange as follows:

$$\frac{Y_t}{e\left(Y_t\right)} = \frac{v e(g)}{s} \tag{11.4}$$

And thus:

$$e(g) = \frac{Y_t}{e(Y_t)} * \frac{s}{v} \quad (11.5)$$

As expectations are correct in the long run ($e(Y_t) = Y_t$), the long-run rate of growth, the warranted rate of growth (G_w) is given by the following expression:

$$G_w = \frac{s}{v} \quad (11.6)$$

Along with the actual and warranted rates of growth, there is also the 'natural rate of growth', which gives the growth of the maximum level of output, at which full employment prevails. Growth in the natural rate occurs through increases in labour supply (n), and (in some versions) technological growth (m), both of which are exogenously determined.

$$G_n = m + n \quad (11.7)$$

For SSBG, G_A must equal G_W must equal G_N. Or, for SSBG:

$$m + n = s / v \quad (11.8)$$

However, given that m, n, s and v are all determined exogenously, there is no reason for this condition to hold. In the words of Solow (1988, p. 307): 'the possibility of steady growth would be a miraculous stroke of luck'.

Following the Harrod-Domar model and the restrictive nature of the conditions under which SSBG could be established (and maintained), economists looked for a way forward. Contributions sought to explore the circumstances under which SSBG would occur when one of the parameters (s, v, n, or m) became endogenised, meaning that they would be determined within the model. This proceeded along more Classical lines, with the endogenisation of the COR, or v, in the Neoclassical Solow-Swan model, and along more Keynesian lines, exploring how different income distributions bring about a savings rate, s, that satisfies the HD growth equation (Kaldor-Passinetti model). We discuss first the Solow-Swan model. This is followed by a discussion of further developments in Neoclassical growth theory that emerged in response to limitations of the Solow-Swan model. The section after that discusses more Keynesian growth models as part of an overview of non-mainstream theories of growth.

Old Neoclassical growth theory: the Solow-Swan growth model

In the Harrod-Domar model, the instability between the warranted and natural rates crucially depends on the fixed factor-proportions that are assumed. Solow (1956) and Swan (1956) questioned this assumption, independently developing growth models that, by allowing capital intensity to change, and hence G_w to adjust to G_n, produce stable growth in the long run.[2] We focus on Solow's exposition of the model because it has since become dominant.

Solow wanted to develop a model which showed that growth will be self-equilibrating, meaning that after a small deviation, the economy will return to its equilibrium position. To do so he removed Harrod's assumption about fixed factor proportions, allowing capital intensity per worker (i.e. the capital-to-labour ratio, $\frac{K}{L}$) to vary. The idea is that capital equipment (or machinery) is 'malleable' in that it can be used in any desired ratio with labour (Sawyer, 1989, p. 387). Even after decisions have been made regarding the level of capital stock, you can alter the number of people that are put to work on it in an infinite manner.

Solow's growth model is based on an Aggregate Production Function (APF) of the Cobb-Douglas type:

Insert space

$$Y = AF(K,L) = AK^{\alpha} L^{1-\alpha} \quad where\, \alpha < 1 \tag{11.9}$$

Total output in the economy (*Y*) is a function of capital (*K*) and labour (*L*) as well as technological progress (*A*), which is assumed to be exogenous. *A* is the so-called Solow residual and measures total factor productivity. The APF is meant to be a representation of the production of all firms in a country. It is assumed to be 'well-behaved', meaning that the marginal productivity of factor inputs is decreasing while returns to scale are constant (see Chapter 4 for a detailed exposition). Decreasing marginal productivity results in increases in output at a decreasing rate when a single factor input (*K* or *L*) rises. The APF in per capita terms is drawn in Figure 11.1 and Box 11.1 gives more detail on the model's assumptions and the derivation of the APF in per capita terms.

Compressing the macro-economy into an aggregate production function means that there is only one sector in the economy which produces one single good that can be used both for consumption and as input to production. The most straightforward way of thinking of this would be a corn economy, where corn can both be consumed and saved (and invested).

The use of the APF is a severe limitation of the model. The APF is based on the microeconomic concept of production (see Chapter 4), which is transposed to the macro-economy via methodological individualism, which holds that the macro-economy can be obtained merely by aggregating the results of microeconomic theory. The severe limitation of this was demonstrated by the Cambridge Capital Controversy which showed that once the model was extended to include more than one capital input the theoretical results of the single capital input APF do not hold.[3] Furthermore, empirically, it was demonstrated that all attempts to test the APF were invalid (Shaikh, 1974). This was famously demonstrated with the 'Humbug' dataset (see Box 11.2).

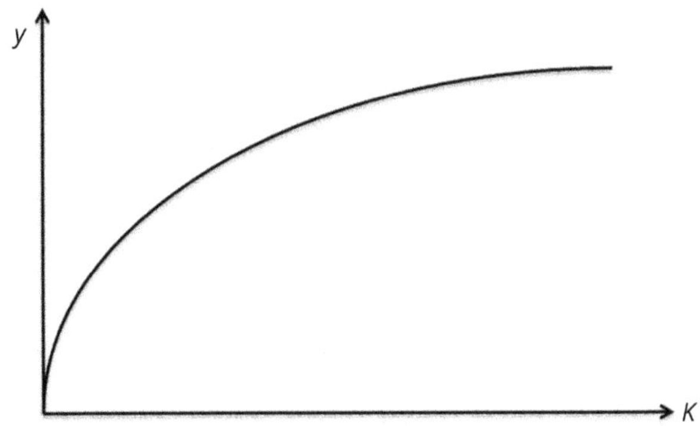

Figure 11.1 The aggregate production function in per capita form, with y as Y/L and k as K/L

The workings of the Solow growth model evolve around responses to the price mechanism reflecting relative scarcities in 'factor inputs', K and L. These alter the capital–labour ratio (k) so that the corresponding COR, v, changes to satisfies the HD equation (s/v=n). If, for instance, the labour force (L) grows faster than the capital stock (K), the price mechanism will operate in such a way as to induce the use of more labour-intensive techniques, lowering k and hence v, and vice versa. Thus, if G_N exceeds G_W, the COR, or v, will fall, raising G_W to G_N. Conversely, if G_N is smaller than G_W, the COR or v will increase, lowering G_W to G_N.

This adjustment mechanism makes two crucial assumptions. First, that the relative price of labour and capital is flexible. This presumes that there is perfect competition in the markets for labour and capital and that the price mechanism in these 'factor' markets behaves like in 'any other market'. Second, the model assumes that there is a spectrum of techniques (for one given technology which is given by the production function) that can be chosen from and that economies can smoothly and easily adjust to, along a continuous production function that relates output to the 'factor inputs'.

Box 11.1: The Solow-Swan growth model: some assumptions

A key assumption of the Solow-Swan growth model is constant returns to scale (CRS), meaning that increases in both capital and labour by the same factor (for instance, doubling the amount of workers and also doubling the number of machines used) result in proportional growth of total output Y (which, in our example, then also doubles). Conceptually, this means that all gains from the division of labour and specialisation have been exhausted in the past, an assumption that was vehemently contested by economists like Young or Kaldor.

The assumption of CRS allows for a simplification by expressing the model in per worker form. Initially, we can also assume technological progress A to be negligible (or $A = 0$):

$$\frac{Y}{L}=F\left(\frac{K}{L},\frac{L}{L}\right) \tag{11.10}$$

which conventionally is denoted in the following way:

$$y = f(k) \quad (11.11)$$

where $y = \frac{Y}{L}$ and $k = \frac{K}{L}$, while $\frac{L}{L}$ becomes 1. This allows us to represent the aggregate production function in a two-dimensional space (see Figure 11.1). It states that output per worker (*y*) is a function of the capital-to-labour ratio ($k = \frac{K}{L}$).

In the model, saving is defined by a Keynesian savings function. What people save in a given period depends on their income and the saving propensity (*s*), i.e. a measure of how much they are inclined to save:

$$S = sY \quad (11.12)$$

Investment is simply measured as the change to the capital stock (*K*) over time. Thus, in period 1 + *t* the capital stock consists of the capital stock of the previous period *t* plus any investment which was undertaken in that period (I_t):

$$K_{t+1} = K_t + I_t \quad (11.13)$$

Since the production process wears machinery down we have to account for depreciation at rate *d*. This reduces our capital stock:

$$K_{t+1} = (1-d)K_t + I_t \quad (11.14)$$

In a closed economy with full employment, saving and investment must be equal (*S* = *I*) and changes in savings are presumed to translate into changes in investment.

Box 11.2: The Humbug production function

The Cambridge Capital Controversies proposed a theoretical critique of the APF, focusing on the implications of extending the APF beyond one sector (see Chapter 4). These critiques raised serious questions about the conclusions drawn from the APF by Neoclassical economics, by showing that they are unlikely to hold when more than one sector is included in the model. While these theoretical critiques have been widely accepted, the use of the APF to analyse (aggregate) economic phenomena is still widespread in Neoclassical economics.

The continued use of the APF has been defended by Neoclassical economists on empirical grounds. Neoclassical economics tends to emphasise the predictive power of models, rather than how well these explain reality. Friedman (1953, pp. 4–5) clearly illustrates this when he argues that '[t]ruly important and significant hypotheses will be found to have "assumptions" that are wildly inaccurate descriptive representations of reality' but 'yield sufficiently accurate predictions'. As Felipe and McCombie (2014, p. 61) point out: 'the reason that the aggregate production function is so widely used, no matter what the theoretical shortcomings are, is that "it works" in the sense that Friedman had in mind. That is to say, it usually gives plausible and statistically significant estimates'.

However, Shaikh (1974) and Felipe and McCombie (2014) have shown that this defence is invalid as the results supporting the APF can be obtained for any data set as long as factor shares are fairly stable. The reason for this is that there exists an underlying national accounting identity within the data that is used to calculate APF:

$$V \equiv wL + \pi K$$

Where, V = total value of output, w = wages, L = labour, π = profits, K = value of capital. That is, the value of output must necessarily be equal to sum of the income going to labour and income going to capital (where only two inputs are considered).

It can be shown that, via mathematical manipulation, a Cobb-Douglas APF, such as Solow's, can be obtained from this identity. This means that estimation of the APF is merely tracing the national income identity, meaning that no matter the nature of the data, they can be used to represent a Cobb-Douglas APF with constant returns to scale (Felipe and McCombie, 2014). This was illustrated by Shaikh (1974, p. 118) who showed that a data set that spells out HUMBUG when output and capital are graphed together 'can be extremely well represented by a Cobb-Douglas production function having constant returns to scale, neutral technical progress, and marginal products equal to factor rewards'. This means that the argument that empirical evidence supports the use of the APF, based on it fitting the data well, is invalid. 'Good fit' results are produced purely because of the national accounting identity regardless of the data, as shown by the HUMBUG production function (for more detail, see Felipe and McCombie [2014]).

The Solow model consists of three components: (1) per capita savings/investment; (2) steady-state per capita investment; (3) aggregate production function. The main elements of the theory are represented in Figure 11.2. The graph shows a per capita production function (see Box 11.1), which links per capita output (y) to the capital–labour ratio (k). The sf(k) curve gives the per capita saving, and as it is assumed that S=I, it gives the actual level of per capita investment. The steady-state investment per person, the investment that is necessary to equip each member of a growing labour force (n) with the same capital per person (allowing for depreciation, d), is shown by the (d+n)k line. The aggregate output (GDP) per capita (y) for a corresponding k, is determined by the aggregate production function given by f(k). SSBG occurs when the savings equals steady-state investment per person, or where sf(k) intersects with (d+n)k. This give us the capital–labour ratio (k∗), and hence the COR, v∗, and per capita output, y∗, for which the economy is on its SSBG path.

Once SSBG has been reached, capital accumulation no longer drives the growth process. While a higher propensity to save increases per capita income, shown by the sf(k) line shifting upwards, it only temporarily increases growth, during the

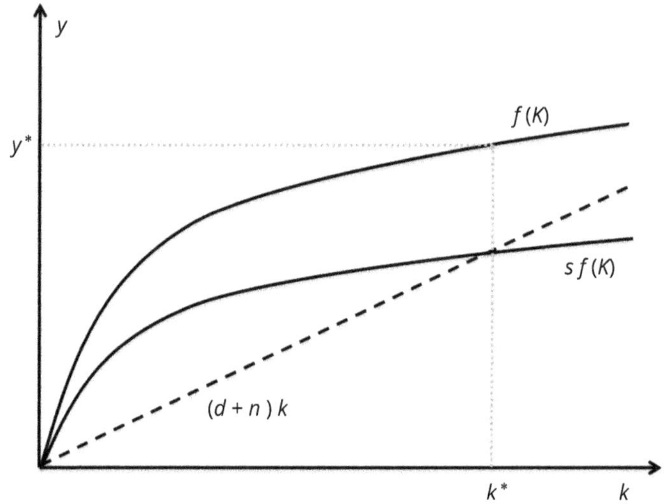

Figure 11.2 The Solow growth model

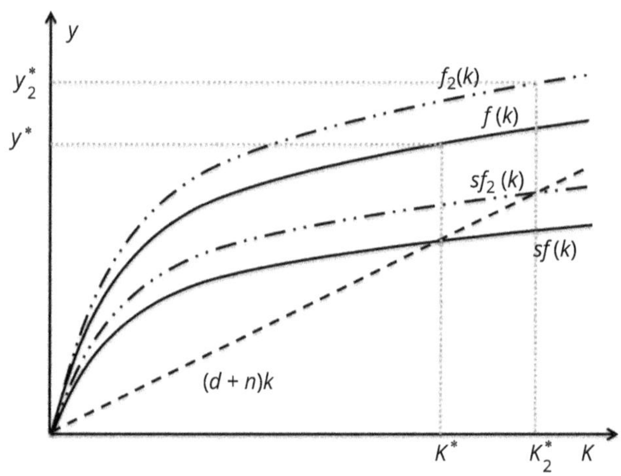

Figure 11.3 Technological progress in the Solow growth model

adjustment from one steady-state per capita income to the other. This is a crucial aspect of the Solow-Swan model, when on the SSBG path, the economy can only grow (in per capita terms) when there is an increase in the productivity of inputs, given by A, resulting from advancement in 'technology'. The effect of technology growth within the Solow model is shown in Figure 11.3. As technology improves the productivity of inputs, the production function simply shifts outwards from $f(k)$ to $f_2(k)$. This means that every worker can now produce more output with the same amount of machinery because technology has improved. As a consequence, there is more saving per head (note that the propensity to save s has not changed, but income has risen). Larger savings translate into more investment and a higher capital–labour ratio. A new equilibrium is found at k_2^* which means that output and income per worker rise to y_2^*. Thus, in the very long-run (once on the SSBG path), only growth in technology is responsible for growth.

This raises a major issue with the Solow model. While technological progress is the ultimate driver of long-run growth in the model, technological progress (A) is assumed to be exogenous. This means that the model does not have anything to say about the reasons for and processes behind technological progress. This issue is further compounded by empirical findings, most notably Solow's (1957) study on the sources of growth in the USA. Solow found that for the period 1909–1949 only 12.5 per cent of US growth could be attributed to increases in factor inputs. This led to him to conclude that 87.5 per cent of growth was driven by technological progress (or changes in A). Since technology is understood as exogenous, it meant that the main driver of growth was not explained by the Solow growth model! This raised the question of how useful a growth model is that has nothing to say about a major – if not the major – reason for growth. Disenchantment with both the assumptions of diminishing returns (and hence smaller and smaller increments to output per capita when savings rates increase) and the exogenous status of technology as the major empirical factor driving growth, led to a new wave of theorising about growth in Neoclassical economics. The main aim of new Neoclassical growth theory was twofold: to provide endogenous accounts of technological change and to produce models that could incorporate increasing returns to scale – which would imply that as capital accumulation proceeds, output per capita expands at an increasing or more than proportionate rate.

New Neoclassical growth theory: growth through technological progress

Solow's growth model struggles to capture one of the main sources of growth, technological progress. In the 1980s, economists like Romer (1986) and Lucas (1988) set out to endogenise technological change, i.e. to explicitly account for technological progress in the growth model rather than to assume it to be exogenously determined. These new models, so-called new growth models, embrace the aggregate production function used by Solow but relax some of its underlying assumptions. For instance, marginal returns to capital and labour are assumed constant (rather than diminishing as suggested by Solow), allowing for increasing returns to scale.

The change in assumptions had some important consequences. In contrast to the Solow growth model, an increased saving rate results in a higher growth rate in new growth models. Empirically, this gives rise to a claim that the new growth model can account for the divergence in growth rates between rich and poor countries which remained unaccounted for by the Solow model (see Box 11.3 below on the convergence hypothesis). New growth models also rehabilitated growth policy. According to these models, growth can be actively influenced by governments especially through policies supporting education and innovation rather than being determined by variables such as the growth in population and depreciation. Additionally, macroeconomic policies were once again given room to influence growth, via their effect on investment and learning.

The simplest new growth model is the so-called AK model. In this model, the two production inputs – capital and labour – are replaced by a broad measure of capital (K_{PH}) which represents both physical capital (i.e. machinery) and human capital (i.e. labour). Human capital is a very broad concept seeking to capture the level of education, experience, talent and other characteristics of the workforce. This new type of capital does not possess a declining marginal product (as is the case in the 'well-behaved' production function), but enjoys constant productivity. This change in assumptions means that there is no steady-state level of capital intensity or growth. An increased saving propensity (*s*) can therefore influence growth rates in a lasting manner and convergence of income levels is no longer a prediction of the model.

The new production function can be written as:

$$Y = F\left(A, K_{PH}\right) \tag{11.15}$$

$$Y = AK_{PH} \tag{11.16}$$

A captures all economy-wide factors affecting technology. In a given country, technology is assumed to be non-exclusive in use, meaning that each worker can access the same knowledge as society at large. But the level of technology can differ across countries, which is generally understood to explain divergence in growth rates. Hence, technology is no longer an international common good.

Abstracting from depreciation (*d*) for simplicity, we arrive at the following equilibrium condition (see Equations 11.9, 11.10, 11.11, and 11.12 for the derivation):

$$\dot{K}_{PH} = sF\left(A, K_{PH}\right) \tag{11.17}$$

$$\dot{K}_{PH} = sAK_{PH} \tag{11.18}$$

This means that the growth rate of the capital stock (remember this is physical and human capital) is given by:

$$\frac{\dot{\mathrm{K}}_{\mathrm{PH}}}{\mathrm{K}_{\mathrm{PH}}} = \mathrm{sA} \tag{11.19}$$

Hence, the saving propensity (*s*) and the level of economy-wide knowledge (*A*) determine the growth rate. Increases in saving rates result in permanent rises in the growth rate rather than a one-off increase in income per head as in the Solow growth model. Output (*Y*) and the capital stock (K_{PH}), which makes up a constant proportion (*s*) in total output, can be graphically represented as shown below in Figure 11.4.

New growth models have been criticised for bringing back Harrod's knife-edge problem. According to Equation (11.19) the growth rate of the capital stock (K_{PH}) does not depend on the size of the capital stock itself. This is the assumption of constant marginal productivity of our human and physical capital because you can read Equation (11.18) as:

$$\dot{\mathrm{K}}_{\mathrm{PH}} = \mathrm{sAK}_{\mathrm{PH}}^{\alpha} \text{ with } \alpha = 1 \tag{11.20}$$

Solow (1997, p. 654) has criticised new growth models as very fragile and unrobust because they require '*exactly* constant returns to capital'. If α turns out to be even slightly larger than 1, say 1.05 which would represent a weak dose of increasing

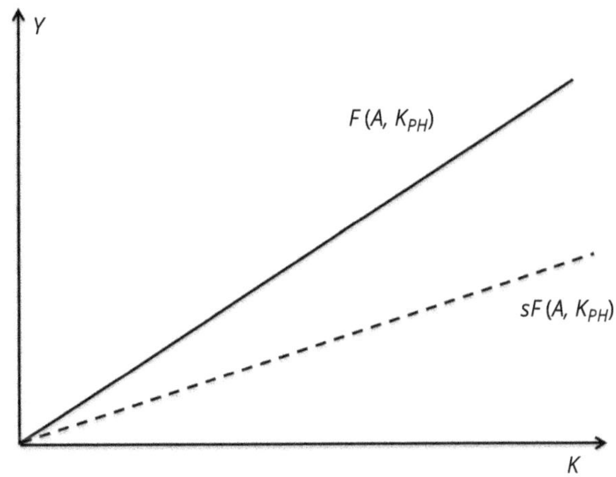

Figure 11.4 The AK model

returns to capital, output in a country would become infinite in finite time. Solow uses the example of a country with a saving propensity of 10 per cent and $\alpha = 1.05$ to show that output would be infinite within 200 years. This is implausible and re-introduces the explosive growth path of the HD model that Solow tried to counter.

Another important shortcoming of new growth models is that they don't deliver what they seem to promise. They don't explain how technological progress happens and what is driving it in the real world. They merely theorise how it may happen without consulting empirical evidence. For instance, Romer (1986), inspired by Arrow's early work on learning-by-doing (Arrow, 1962), developed a model in which firm investment has a positive effect on knowledge and technology through a learning effect (learning-by-investment).

Lucas (1988) argued that human capital accumulated through education is an important driver of technological progress. His model centres on the individual's trade-off either to work (which provides income to consume) or to invest in education. While investing in human capital means that output and consumption is lower in the current period, as labour is diverted from production, it creates knowledge which increases future productivity, and thus allows for higher output (and consumption) in the future. Hence, agents face an intertemporal choice whether to work in the current period or to invest and sacrifice consumption in the current period. Hence, the driver of technological progress is a different one for Romer and Lucas. However, in both cases the central assumption is that there are constant returns to capital (physical capital for Romer, but human capital for Lucas).

Other new growth models stress the importance of investment into research and development (R&D). Romer (1990), for example, put forward a three-sector model of an economy where one sector produces final goods, another one manufactures intermediate goods and finally a research sector discovers new ideas. Other authors (Grossman and Helpman, 1991) have developed similar models, characterised by so-called horizontal innovation. Here, technological progress is understood as widening the variety of goods while improving their quality. But new products do not render existing goods obsolete. This rather benevolent view of technical progress is contested in economics. The Austrian economist Schumpeter most famously put forward the idea that technological change puts some firms out of business as other companies successfully bring in new products (he called this process 'creative destruction') (see below).

Thus, there are different possibilities regarding how to model what drives technological change. Is it education or innovation through investment? If it's investment, does expenditure on new machinery suffice or is R&D spending crucial? Would innovation only result in an increase in producers and products supplied, or would some existing firms and products be pushed out of the market, becoming obsolete? In order to answer questions about how the innovation process actually works Solow (1997, p. 657) suggested consulting 'the variegated mass of case studies, business histories, interviews, expert testimony, anything that might throw light on good ways to model the flow of productivity-increasing innovations and improvements'. However, new growth theory has not engaged much with this type of qualitative research so far.

Box 11.3: The convergence hypothesis

The Solow growth model was developed with industrial economies in mind. In the context of developing countries, the Solow growth model gave rise to the convergence hypothesis. The absolute convergence hypothesis claims that all countries' income levels should converge in the long run if capital is free to flow across borders. The logic proceeds as follows. All countries have access to the same production technology. Income per head is determined by saving in the model. In Neoclassical theory, the marginal product of inputs decreases the more abundant the input factor. As consequence, the model's prediction is that capital should flow from rich to poor countries because in poor countries capital can fetch higher marginal returns due to its relative scarcity. Over time capital intensity should equalise across countries, resulting in converging levels of per capita income across the world and poorer economies experience higher growth rates in their transition towards steady state.

However, what has actually been observed since the early nineteenth century? – 'Divergence, Big Time!' (Pritchett, 1997) (see Figure 11.5). The absolute convergence hypothesis is implausible: few poor countries across the globe have managed to catch up with rich countries. Empirically, the large flows of capital from rich to poor countries have not materialised (Lucas, 1990), which undermines the assumption of decreasing marginal productivity of capital. Economists have struggled to account for income differentials between rich and poor countries through differences in capital intensity as predicted by the model (Mankiw, 1995).

Alternative claims have been put forward. Conditional rather than absolute convergence might exist. Here, '[e]ach economy converges towards its own steady state, which in turn is determined by its own saving and population growth rate' (Mankiw, 1995). The conditional convergence hypothesis acknowledges that the assumption of equal and free access to technology among countries is incorrect. Thus, 'convergence clubs' might emerge: i.e. a tendency towards equalisation of income levels among countries that are in some way similar. Such convergence can be observed among US federal states or European regions and among OECD countries after the Second World War. But what are these similarities?

This question gave rise to a research agenda on the link between socio-economic institutions and growth. New Institutionalist economists like North (1989) or Acemoglu and Robinson (2003) have argued that democracy and strong property rights are necessary preconditions for growth, explaining the convergence in growth paths among some regions but the absence of absolute convergence across the globe. Critics of this view have pointed out that today's rich countries did not have stable property rights or working democratic systems in place at earlier stages of development (Chang, 2002). Hence, it is difficult to claim that these 'good' institutions are preconditions for growth. Indeed, causality might run the other way around. Once countries become rich, they have also more capacity to develop and sustain 'good'institutions. Chapter 12 discusses these issues in more detail.

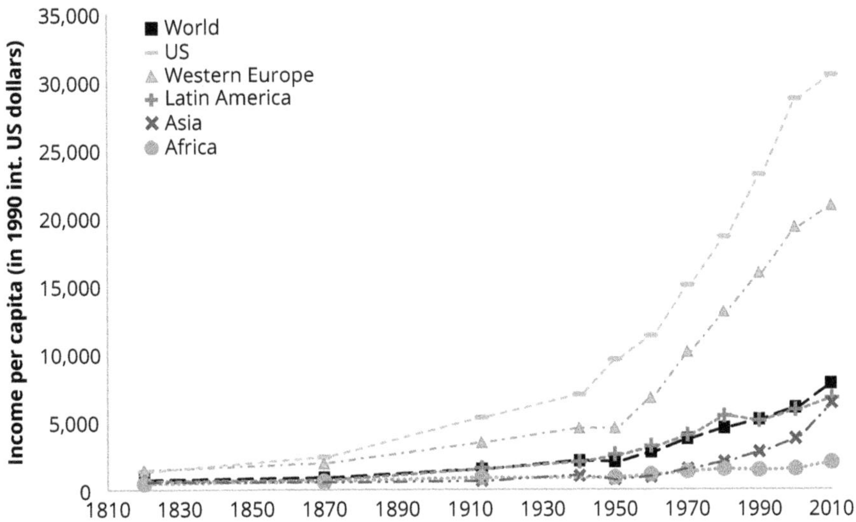

Figure 11.5 The Great Divergence: developments in income per since 1820

Source: Maddison dataset, Groningen Growth and Development Centre

Maddison Project Database, version 2018. For the references to the original research on individual countries, see Appendix A of Bolt et al. (2018)

Alternative theories of economic growth

Growth in classical political economy

Based on the Industrial Revolution during the eighteenth and nineteenth centuries, growth became a central preoccupation in the Classics' study of the capitalist economy. For Smith, growth played a central role in *The Wealth of Nations*. It derives, in essence, from the accumulation of capital driving the division of labour which was the primary source of growth in output, Smith (1976, p. 277):

> As the accumulation of stock must, in the nature of things, be previous to the division of labour, so labour can be more and more subdivided in proportion only as stock is previously more and more accumulated.

Savings play a central role in this account as the view prevailed that savings would be transformed into investments via the capital market. Capital is mobile between sectors, seeking out profitable investment opportunities and this tends to equalise the profit rate across the economy (see Chapter 7). The expansion of markets, domestically and internationally, determines (and constrains) growth and limits to such an expansion can induce a stationary state of the economy when growth comes to a halt. However, Brewer (2010, p. 12) emphasises that while for Classical political economists: '[g]rowth might eventually come to a halt, as a stationary state was reached … [they] treated that as such a distant prospect that it is not easy to tell whether they thought of the stationary state as a real future possibility or a mere analytical device'.

Ricardo further develops Smith's original account of growth driven by capital accumulation, by combining it with his insights into the distribution of income and in particular what happens when a growing population's food needs drive agriculture onto increasingly marginal land with implications for food prices, wages, profits and hence accumulation (see Chapter 7): increasing costs of producing food fuel rising wages, rents and falling profits. This, in turn, slows down accumulation (and growth) until the economy reaches a stationary state (where no accumulation takes place). In the Ricardian analysis, the available land (and its landholding structure) ultimately imposes a limit on growth. It has already been pointed out in Chapter 7 that Ricardo vigorously campaigned for the repeal of the Corn Laws in England, which protected large landowners from the competition of cheap imports of food, as a way to avert (or delay) the stationary state of the economy where accumulation (and growth) would come to a halt.

Marx, along similar lines to Smith and Ricardo, also accounted for economic growth as an outcome of the process of accumulation, though, as noted in Chapter 5, for Marx accumulation (in the capitalist sense as distinct from primitive accumulation) derives from the appropriation of surplus value created by workers in the production process. Revisiting the circuit of capital covered in Chapter 6, once surplus value has been realised in the form of a new quantity of money (M') which is larger than the original quantity of capital forwarded by the capitalist (M), the capitalist then has to make a decision regarding the next round of investment in the means of production and labour power. The capitalist has a number of options regarding what to do with this new quantity of money, such as how much to spend on consumption, how much to save/hoard, and how much to reinvest. If the capitalist forwards the same quantity of money as in the first cycle of production, then the same amount of surplus value will be created. In this situation, referred to as Simple Reproduction, the system (re)produces the same value of commodities that have been used up in the production process in the previous cycle of production, and so there is no growth. However, if the capitalist purchases more means of production and labour power than in the previous cycle, more surplus value is thus created, leading to Extended Reproduction, in which the amount of surplus value produced in each production cycle is higher than the previous one. Therefore, increases in the quantity of capital accumulated provide the resources for capitalists to constantly increase the scale of production (i.e. economic growth). Competitive forces compel the capitalist to invest in Extended Reproduction rather than Simple Reproduction, placing the need for infinite economic growth as the key driving factor of the capitalist economy.

Post-Keynesian theories of growth

Post-Keynesian economists across generations, including Kaldor, Kalecki, Harrod, Passinetti, Robinson, Arestis, Blecker, Cornwall, Lavoie, Palley, Sawyer and Setterfield, have made important contributions to the theories of growth (and development). Post-Keynesian theories of growth emphasise the importance of aggregate demand in the growth process. At the heart of their analysis is the belief that even in the long run there is no guarantee that aggregate demand will converge to the full employment output level. Thus, Post-Keynesian analysis seeks to analyse long-run aggregate demand determination and how it relates to the growth of full employment output. This is in sharp contrast to Neoclassical growth theory which, as seen above, focuses solely on the supply side and attaches little to no importance to demand in the long run. Within Post-Keynesian growth analysis emphasis is often placed on the role that income distribution has in the growth process through its impact on aggregate demand. This section will focus on reviewing this literature. First a brief outline of the historical development of Post-Keynesian growth theories will be provided. This is followed by current Post-Keynesian debates on the growth process in the form of wage- versus profit-led growth and a brief outline of models which endogenise the SSBG path to the actual growth level.

To understand the development of Post-Keynesian growth theory, it is necessary to go back to the Harrod-Domar model and early Post-Keynesian extensions upon it. While the works of Harrod are regarded to be Post-Keynesian, there was dissatisfaction with the restrictive nature of the Harrod-Domar model and the knife-edge issue. Early Post-Keynesian economists extended the Harrod-Domar model by incorporating a mechanism that would allow the economy to converge to the SSBG path. While some attempts focused upon the relationship between the actual and the warranted rates of interest (see Harrod, 1939), the most influential models focused on the warranted and natural rates.

Returning to the Harrod-Domar model, the condition for the SSBG, for which the warranted and natural rate of growth need to equalise, is given by $s/v = m + n$. As highlighted above, this occurrence was unlikely given the exogeneity of s, v, m and n. While Neoclassical economists 'solved' the issue via changes in the capital–output ratio (v), there are other possible mechanisms which allow the SSBG path to emerge. These include changes in the savings rate, technological growth, or population growth.

Some Post-Keynesians, notably Kaldor (1955, 1957) and Pasinetti (1962), focused on the savings rate (s) as the mechanism to restore equilibrium between the warranted and natural growth rates. This was achieved by understandings as a function of the distribution of income. The economy is understood to be divided into two groups, capitalists and workers. These have different marginal propensities to save (MPS), with the MPS for capitalists (s_c) assumed to be greater than that of workers (s_w). Changes in the distribution of income then allows for s to adjust so that $G_W = G_N$.

So, total savings (S) depends upon the distribution of income as follows:

$$S = s_c \pi + s_w W \qquad where\, s_c > s_w \tag{11.21}$$

Where π is total profits, which are assumed to only go to capitalists (for simplicity) and are obtained from capital. W is the total amount of wages, assumed only to go to workers. The average saving rate (s) can be obtained by dividing by Y (total income or GDP).

$$s = \frac{S}{Y} = \frac{s_c \pi}{Y} + \frac{s_w W}{Y} \tag{11.22}$$

$$Where\ Y = \pi + W \tag{11.23}$$

As income comes from either wages (W) or profits (π); π/Y gives the share of income that goes to profits (and thus capitalists), while W/Y gives the income share of wages. When the share of wages in income increases/decreases, the average savings rate will decrease/increase, as $s_w < s_c$. Note also that, from Equation (11.23), as the wage share increase/decreases, the profit share decreases/increases.

However, why would income distribution change in a way that restores equilibrium, satisfying the condition for SSBG? Kaldor (1957) suggested that the pricing mechanism lies behind this process. If the average saving rate (s) is too high so that $G_w > G_n$, capital will grow faster than labour. This will result in a shortage of labour, putting pressure for wages to increase, shifting distribution towards workers, in turn leading to a fall in s, thereby restoring equilibrium. On the other hand, if *s* is too low, labour will grow faster than capital, resulting in a shortage of capital leading to increase in profit share, causing s to rise.

While such a mechanism can exist in theory, Post-Keynesians hold that full convergence to the SSBG is unlikely to occur in the real world. Kalecki (1938) emphasised that the real world is dominated by oligopolistic competition, this results in output and wages being depressed below their SSBG values (even in the long run) preventing the economy from converging to the SSBG due to depressed levels of demand. This means that, unlike in Neoclassical theory where only the growth of the supply side matters in the long run, growth is viewed as demand-determined with the level of demand acting as a constraint on the ability of the economy to converge to the SSBG. This emphasises the need for the distribution of income to produce a sufficient level of aggregate demand in the long run. Literature focusing on income distribution and long-run aggregate demand has led to the emergence of the profit- versus wage-led growth debate which dominates most modern Post-Keynesian discourse on growth.[4] The debate places distribution of income at the centre of the analysis and asks how changes in distribution affect growth through changes in aggregate demand and (sometimes) supply (see below). The literature asks whether redistribution of income towards labour has a positive impact on long-run aggregate demand. Does a higher wage share result in higher consumption which may also spur investment to meet the higher demand (wage-led)? Or conversely, does it have a negative impact, as a higher wage share squeezes profit margins which may in turn discourage investment (profit-led). The answer to the question depends on behavioural aspects of the economy, including the propensities to consume out of wage and profit incomes, the sensitivity of investment to changes in sales or profit margins and changes in costs, and the sensitivity of imports and exports to changes in costs (Lavoie and Stockhammer, 2013). These behavioural aspects determine the impact of an increase in the wage rate on the demand and supply side of the economy, and hence its overall macroeconomic effect. Where there are small/large differences between the marginal propensities to consume, and where investment isn't/is sensitive to sales but is/isn't sensitive to income share, and where exports and imports are/aren't sensitive to changes in costs, increases in wages are likely to have a negative/positive effect on aggregate demand, and thus the economy has a profit-/wage-led demand regime.

So far it has been assumed that the growth of the SSBG is exogenous to the path of aggregate demand and income distribution. Some Post-Keynesian literature has, however, attempted to articulate models where both the path of the actual growth towards the SSBG and the distribution of income have long-run implications. These works follow on from the original contributions by Kaldor (1954, 1957) who argued that, when an economy constantly pushes against the SSBG path, incentives are created to overcome the limitations imposed by it (Kaldor, 1954, p. 67). In such an economy, one would expect more resources to be dedicated to technological innovation. Elsewhere, Kaldor (1957) suggested what is now known as Verdoorn's Law, that increased output levels spur increased productivity growth through learning effects. Additionally, it has also been suggested that the distribution of income itself can influence innovation. For example, a higher wage share by increasing labour costs incentivises activities to increase the productivity of labour, so that labour input can be diminished, thus having a beneficial effect on full employment aggregate supply (Lavoie and Stockhammer, 2013). These contributions add a form of path dependency to the wage- versus profit-led growth debate. For example, if an economy experiences long periods of demand deficiency due to a long period of low wage share, its technology will be at a lower level than an economy that did not suffer from deficient demand.

Schumpeter to evolutionary economics

Inspired by and building on the works of the Classics, especially that of Marx, Schumpeter argues that economic development occurs through a qualitative progression in production techniques and outputs (and market interactions) that are caused by firm level 'innovations'. Innovations are defined as the use of a new idea or method, or of an old idea in a new setting. Thus, Schumpeter focuses on the process of innovation and the agents responsible for innovating, 'entrepreneurs'. Schumpeter argued that development occurs through a process of 'creative destruction', as innovations cause the decline and destruction of old techniques, technology, outputs and structures which are incompatible or uncompetitive compared to the new innovations. More specifically, Schumpeter (1983/1934, p. 66) argues that economic development can occur through five types of firm and industry level innovation. First there is product innovation, which captures 'The introduction of a new good … or of a new quality of a good'; second, production innovation, referring to the 'introduction of a new method of production'; third, market innovation, which is the 'opening of a new market, that is a market into which the particular branch of manufacture of the country in question has not previously entered'; fourth, input innovation as 'a new source of supply of raw materials or half-manufactured goods'; and, finally, fifth, organisation innovation or the 'carrying out of the new organisation of any industry, like the creation of a monopoly position ... or the breaking up of a monopoly position'. Schumpeter argues that there are interdependencies between innovations, and that one innovation can open up opportunities for other innovations to occur. To take a modern example, globalisation and outsourcing (as a type of process innovation) would have been impossible without the development of information and communication technologies (ICT). Interdependencies between innovations suggests that innovations are path dependent in Schumpeter's theory, as decisions to undertake certain innovation projects will mean that not only will different innovations occur but the resulting chain of innovations may be different.

At the centre of Schumpeter's analysis are entrepreneurs and financial markets. Schumpeter uses the label 'entrepreneur' for anyone who carries out innovative activity. The chance of gaining 'entrepreneurial profits', which are temporary monopoly profits only gained through successful innovation, is what motivates entrepreneurs. As these profits are linked to innovation (and are thus called 'innovation rents'), in a competitive economy they are only temporary, as imitation and new innovations destroy them. The opportunity to gain such profits, and the links of success to innovation, are a large part of the reason for the dynamism of capitalism. Schumpeter argues that once the process of development has started, in a capitalist economy, where the fortunes of families and businesses depend on their ability to adapt, the presence of both opportunities to gain wealth from innovating and the threats of liquidation posed by new innovation mean that there will be continual innovation (Schumpeter, 1994/1976, pp. 73–74). As a result, the economy will be in a continual state of restructuring and reallocating resources from old (now obsolete) methods and outputs to new ones. As entrepreneurial profits are only achievable when there is a degree of monopoly (see Chapter 4), Schumpeter argues that in a dynamic economy, markets where there is a degree of monopoly (i.e. monopolistic and oligopolistic competition or a monopoly) are more efficient than perfect competition, as in the latter case there is no incentive to innovate. However, monopolistic competition is not beneficial *per se*, as the benefits only stem from its importance to innovation.

In Schumpeter's analysis, a major issue facing entrepreneurs is accessing the necessary inputs of production that enable them to innovate. Schumpeter argues that financial markets are pivotal in enabling innovation by allowing entrepreneurs to finance innovative activity. Thus, within his analysis, Schumpeter draws attention to both the societal system and the structure and operation of markets.

While Schumpeter emphasises the importance of innovation for the development process, he had little to say on how innovations actually arise and the question of where the knowledge for these innovations comes from remained unanswered. Evolutionary economics seeks to answer this question and focuses on learning dynamics, feedbacks from production and interaction, highlighting how what is learned is shaped by experiences, past knowledge and circumstances.[5] Being based on the competence-based approach to the firm (also known as the capabilities approach), which explicitly recognises that production of different goods requires fundamentally different production processes and different sets of knowledge and abilities, Evolutionary economics emphasises that innovations occur through changes in the competences of firms. As the competence of firms shape how products are produced, existing competences (along with the organisational structure of the firm) shape opportunities to learn and thus what is learnt. Evolutionary economists emphasise that the knowledge of how to produce something new does not just come out of the blue but builds upon existing knowledge that a firm possess: new competences build on old competences (see Andreoni [2014]; and the various contributions in Dosi et al. [2009]). Therefore, growth and development within Evolutionary economics are fundamentally a path-dependent process (see Wernerfelt [1984] for the path dependent nature of competence development).

Evolutionary economics draws on Structural and Institutional economics (see also Chapter 12) to emphasise the importance of structural, social, and institutional aspects of the economy for growth and development. Within Structural and Evolutionary economics, economic development is understood as moving to increasingly high-tech industries (and manufacturing). These industries command higher value added as the competences necessary to produce in such industries are scarce, due to the advancement of the knowledge required, meaning that high-tech firms have significant market power when selling their products. The importance of industry and manufacturing to the development process is emphasised (except for extremely low levels of development), because of learning dynamics and feedbacks – even at very high levels of economic development which rely on innovation. For instance, in the USA, manufacturing remains vital as it provides knowledge feedbacks enabling innovation to occur (see Andreoni and Chang, 2016; Andreoni and Gregory, 2013). Within industries, building on the works of Hirschman, the importance of interdependencies (termed as 'linkages') for learning dynamics is emphasised (see Chapter 12). As a result, policy recommendations not only emphasise the promotion of manufacturing in general, but focus on promoting industries that have linkages with the current firms in the economy and knowledge exchange across interdependent firms and industries (see Pitelis et al., 2006; Hirschman et al., 2015).

Conclusion

This chapter provided an introduction to economic growth theory across the history of economic thought. The key conceptual issue of time was explored before outlining the contributions of Neoclassical, Classical, Post-Keynesian and Evolutionary schools to growth theory. The chapter traced the development of Neoclassical growth theory, which can be divided into two distinct phases. Old exogenous growth theory (the Harrod-Domar model and the Solow-Swan model) focused on capital accumulation as the source of growth. New endogenous growth theory focuses on productivity growth as the main source of growth. Whilst there are substantial differences between the two vintages of Neoclassical growth theory, central features of old growth theory have been maintained, most notably the focus of growth along a single (unique) SSBG path which the economy automatically converges to. This has meant that Neoclassical growth theories, new and old, have failed to recognise how the growth process is accompanied by changes in the structure of the economy and the role of demand within the growth process. In addition, it is often assumed, that any short-run changes have no lasting effects, so that in the long run growth is 'path independent'.

Alternative growth theories, namely Classical, Post-Keynesian and Evolutionary, have also been reviewed and contrasted to Neoclassical growth theory. As seen above, these theories are substantially different from Neoclassical growth theory. Four key differences (although more exist) can be highlighted: first the way in which time is conceptualised within the models, logical or historical time, and in turn whether the economy is seen as path independent or path dependent; second, the role of and the view taken of equilibrium, and the role of the SSBG path in the analysis; third, the role of demand in the growth process; and fourth, how the process of growth is envisioned–a process of gradual stable change along a SSBG path or a process of change that disrupts the current working of the economy.

Discussion questions and seminar activities

- Which theoretical approach do you find most convincing in helping to explain economic growth in the real world?
- How important is 'time'?
- What role does the distribution of income play in different theoretical perspectives on growth?
- What are the main determinants of growth that appear in most theoretical approaches?

Further reading

On the subject of time: Sanfilippo (2011) and Arestis and Sawyer (2009a, b).
On Classical Growth theory: Brewer (2010).
On An overview of Alternative growth theories: Setterfield (2010).
On Post-Keynesian growth theory: Lavoie and Stockhammer (2013), Lavoie (2015), and Setterfield (2002).
On Evolutionary growth theory: Hirschman et al. (2015), Nelson and Winter (2004), Dutrénit et al. (2013), and Pitelis et al. (2006).

References

Acemoglu, D., & Robinson, J. A. (2003). *Economic backwardness in political perspectives.* NBER working paper no. 8831.

Andreoni, A. (2014). Structural learning: Embedding discoveries and the dynamics of production. *Structural Change and Economic Dynamics, 29*, 58–74.

Andreoni, A., & Chang, H.-J. (2016). Bringing production and employment back into development: Alice Amsden's legacy for a new developmentalist agenda. *Cambridge Journal of Regions, Economy and Society, 10*, 173–187.

Andreoni, A., & Gregory, M. (2013). Why and how does manufacturing still matter: Old rationales, new realities. *Revue d'économie industrielle, 144*(4), 17–54.

Arestis, P., & Sawyer, M. C. (2009a). Path dependency and demand-supply interactions in macroeconomic analysis. In P. Arestis & P. Arestis (Eds.), *Path dependency and macroeconomics* (International papers in political economy series) (pp. 1–37). New York: Palgrave Macmillan.

Arestis, P., & Sawyer, M. C. (Eds.). (2009b). *Path dependency and macroeconomics* (International papers in political economy series). New York: Palgrave Macmillan.
Arrow, K. J. (1962). The economic implications of learning by doing. *The Review of Economic Studies, 29*, 155–173.
Bhaduri, A. (1993). *Unconventional economic essays*. New Delhi: Oxford University Press.
Bolt, J., Inklaar, R., de Jong, H., & van Zanden, J. L. (2018). *Rebasing 'Maddison': New income comparisons and the shape of long-run economic development*. Maddison project working paper 10.
Brewer, A. (2010). *The making of the classical theory of economic growth*. London: Routledge.
Chang, H. J. (2002). *Kicking away the ladder*. London: Anthem Press.
Domar, E. D. (1947). Expansion and employment. *The American Economic Review, 37*, 34–55.
Dosi, G., Nelson, R. R., & Winter, S. G. (Eds.). (2009). *The nature and dynamics of organizational capabilities* (Reprint ed.). Oxford: Oxford University Press.
Dutrénit, G., Lee, K., Nelson, R. R., Soete, L., & Vera-Cruz, A. O. (Eds.). (2013). *Learning, capability building and innovation for development* (EADI global development series). Houndmills/Basingstoke/Hampshire/New York: Palgrave Macmillan.
Felipe, J., & McCombie, J. S. L. (2014). The aggregate production function: 'Not even wrong'. *Review of Political Economy, 26*, 60–84.
Fine, B., & Dimakou, O. (2016). *Macroeconomics: A critical companion, political economy and development*. London: Pluto Press.
Grossman, G. M., & Helpman, E. (1991). Quality ladders in the theory of growth. *The Review of Economic Studies, 58*, 43–61.
Harrod, R. F. (1939). An essay in dynamic theory. *The Economic Journal, 49*, 14.
Harrod, R. F. (1948). *Towards a dynamic economics* (1st ed.). London: Macmillan.
Hirschman, A. O., Adelman, J., Rothschild, E., & Sen, A. (2015). *The essential Hirschman*. Princeton: Princeton University Press.
Kaldor, N. (1954). The relation of economic growth and cyclical fluctuations. *The Economic Journal, 64*, 53–71.
Kaldor, N. (1955). Alternative theories of distribution. *The Review of Economic Studies, 23*, 83–100.
Kaldor, N. (1957). A model of economic growth. *The Economic Journal, 67*, 591–624.
Kalecki, M. (1938, April). The determinants of distribution of income. *Econometrica*.
Keynes, J. M. (1936). *The general theory of employment interest and money*. London: Macmillan.
Lavoie, M. (2015). *Post-Keynesian economics: New foundations* (Paperback ed. reprinted with amendments). Cheltenham: Edward Elgar.
Lavoie, M., & Stockhammer, E. (2013). Wage-led growth: Concept, theories and policies. In M. Lavoie & E. Stockhammer (Eds.), *Wage-led growth* (pp. 13–39). London: Palgrave Macmillan.
Lucas, R. E. (1988). On the mechanics of economic development. *Journal of Monetary Economics, 22*, 3–42.
Lucas, R. E. (1990, May). Why doesn't capital flow from rich to poor countries? *American Economic Review*.
Mankiw, N. G. (1995). *The growth of nations*. Brookings papers on economic activity.
Nelson, R. R., & Winter, S. G. (2004). *An evolutionary theory of economic change, digitally* (Reprinted. ed.). Cambridge, MA: The Belknap Press of Harvard University Press.
North, D. C. (1989, September). Institutions and economic growth: An historical approach. *World Development*.

Pasinetti, L. L. (1962). Rate of profit and income distribution in relation to the rate of economic growth. *The Review of Economic Studies, 29*, 267–279.

Pitelis, C., Sugden, R., & Wilson, J. R. (Eds.). (2006). *Clusters and globalisation: The development of urban and regional economies*. Cheltenham/Northampton: Edward Elgar.

Pritchett, L. (1997). Divergence, big time. *The Journal of Economic Perspectives, 11*, 3–17.

Romer, P. M. (1986). Increasing returns and long-run growth. *Journal of Political Economy, 94*, 1002–1037.

Romer, P. M. (1990). Endogenous technological change. *Journal of Political Economy, 98*, 32.

Sanfilippo, E. (2011). The short period and the long period in macroeconomics: An awkward distinction. *Review of Political Economy, 23*, 371–388.

Sawyer, M. (1989). *The challenge of radical political economy*. Chester: Harvester Wheatsheaf.

Schumpeter, J. A. (1983). *The theory of economic development: An inquiry into profits, capital, credit, interest, and the business cycle* (Social science classics series). New Brunswick: Transaction Books.

Schumpeter, J. A. (1994). *Capitalism, socialism and democracy*. London: Routledge.

Sen, A. (1970). *Growth economics: Selected readings, penguin modern economics readings*. Harmondsworth: Penguin.

Setterfield, M. (Ed.). (2002). *The economics of demand-led growth: Challenging the supply-side vision of the long run*. Cheltenham/Northampton, MA: Edward Elgar.

Setterfield, M. (Ed.). (2010). *Handbook of alternative theories of economic growth*. Cheltenham/Northampton: Edward Elgar.

Shaikh, A. (1974). Laws of production and laws of algebra: The humbug production function. *The Review of Economics and Statistics, 56*, 115–120.

Solow, R. M. (1956). A contribution to the theory of economic growth. *The Quarterly Journal of Economics, 70*, 65–94.

Solow, R. M. (1957). Technical change and the aggregate production function. *The Review of Economics and Statistics, 39*, 312–320.

Solow, R. M. (1988). Growth theory and after. *The American Economic Review, 78*, 307–317.

Solow, R. M. (1997, May). Is there a core usable macroeconomics that we should all believe in? *American Economic Review*.

Swan, T. W. (1956). Economic growth and capital accumulation. *Economic Record, 32*, 334–361.

Wernerfelt, B. (1984). A resource-based view of the firm. *Strategic Management Journal, 5*, 171–180.

12 HOW DO COUNTRIES DEVELOP?

Ewa Karwowski and Elisa Van Waeyenberge

Introduction

The growth theories discussed in Chapter 11 were often presented explicitly for developed countries and were not intended initially to capture the realities facing the developing world. Since the 1940s, however, economists have sought to theorise the specificities of developing countries. This has given rise to 'development economics', with initial contributions to development economics, or what often is referred to as 'old' development economics, strongly inspired by Classical ideas around structural transformation. Development economics then emerged as a heterodox tradition in economics, with explicit links to Classical political economy. Contributions to this heterodox tradition within economics tended to draw on historical patterns of development and favoured inductive methods of reasoning. They drew attention to the broader economic and social transformations implied by development, with a strong role for the state.

By the early 1980s, however, the economic study of development came to be marked by a dramatic narrowing of topic and method, as Neoclassical economics increasingly encroached upon this terrain with the promotion of a 'new' development economics. This was characterised by the indiscriminate adoption of Neoclassical ideas in the study of development. In this Neoclassical tradition, development economics, as any other branch of economics, is to proceed on the basis of economic rationality and the theory of choice, and so the reasons for its separateness as a sub-discipline disappear. This set off a new path in development economics, which became anchored in deductive principles with little interest in the broader historical trajectories of structural transformation and socio-political and economic change. As mainstream economics itself evolved, the new development economics sought to incorporate its discoveries, including those related to market failures and increasing returns to scale. This gave rise to a 'newer' development economics, seeking to bring back some of the core features of developing country contexts that had been ignored in the new development economics of the 1980s. This also includes subsequent attempts to reformulate some of the structuralist ideas of the old development economics within the straitjacket imposed by Neoclassical economics. These attempts at bringing back in core features of developing country realities were, however, circumscribed by the initial principles upon which theorising proceeds when based on Neoclassical premises. These include the persistent commitment to rational choice and rationality principles, impeding a comprehensive understanding of the complex issues of socio-economic and political change implied by development.

Before discussion Neoclassical development economics and its alternatives across the History of Economic Thought, we want to make an important preliminary remark. Contributions to the economic analysis of development have often been characterised by a perceived need to provide 'solutions' rather than mainly 'explanations'. A famous development economist, Hirschman (1981, p. 13) indeed highlighted that '[d]evelopment economics ... was born from the marriage between the new insights about the sui generis economic problems of the underdeveloped countries and the overwhelming desire to achieve rapid progress with the instruments at hand, or thought to be within reach, such as large scale foreign aid'. This proximity has been marked by the rise to prominence of a particular international development institution, the World Bank, which has taken on a leadership role in the international development community, mainly since the 1980s. As such, within development, you are likely to hear reference, for instance, to the Washington and post-Washington Consensus. These capture specific ideas regarding how policy in developing countries should proceed that have been strongly promoted by the World Bank. We are then interested to understand what the specific, if distinct, Neoclassical analytical foundations are to these particular (and very influential) policy paradigms.

The chapter proceeds as follows. The next section discusses the main developments in Neoclassical development economics, as it rose to prominence from the 1980s onwards. This is followed by an overview of alternative theories of economic development, drawing on a broad number of contributions that dominated the discipline as it initially emerged when large parts of the developing world successfully fought for independence and a clear need for a separate sub-discipline focused on its specific problems transpired. These contributions are sometimes lumped together as part of the development economics, and include such divergent approaches like structuralist economics, dependency theory and modernisation theory. These alternatives have strong links to earlier debates of Classical political economy around accumulation and growth, some of which was discussed in Chapter 11.

Neoclassical development economics

As will be discussed at length further below, development economics started off as a heterodox tradition, not governed by Neoclassical principles. It was instead inspired by the debates of the Classical political economists around accumulation and structural transformation. This implied that structural change stood at the heart of how development was understood. Much of this emphasis, however, disappeared with the rise of the new development economics during the 1980s that was heavily promoted by the World Bank. The new development economics provided analytical underpinnings to a policy agenda that had been taking form in the early 1980s and that sought to emphasise the role of markets and price incentives in developing countries. This agenda was promoted via the so-called Washington Consensus.[1] It displaced a development policy paradigm that had sought to emphasise the central role of the state in development (see below and in Chapter 15).

With the new development economics, the idea came to prevail that 'economic rationality' characterised agents in the less- and more-developed countries. The postulates of Neoclassical economics including the principles of rationality and optimisation were understood to have universal applicability. As a result, development economics ceased to exist as a sub-discipline with the rise of 'monoeconomics', applicable across time and space and hence to developed and developing countries alike (Hirschman, 1981). These ideas were clearly articulated by Krueger (1986, p. 62), who became the Chief Economist of the World Bank in the early 1980s, when she wrote: "Once it is recognised that individuals respond to incentives, and that "market failure" is the result of the inappropriate incentives rather than of non-responsiveness, the separateness of development economics as a filed largely disappears.'

What came to be known as the Washington Consensus aimed at economic policy reform with the purpose of eliminating all obstacles to a 'perfect market' as the presumed optimal path to growth. It proposed to stabilise an economy through control of the money supply and enhance growth through a set of supply-side measures aimed at boosting private sector activity. This development policy paradigm built on Walrasian General Equilibrium theory, according to which competitive markets yield welfare-maximising (or Pareto-efficient) outcomes (in the absence of externalities, public goods, natural monopolies and when there is a complete set of market [first welfare theorem]) (see Chapters 5 and 6). Every Pareto-efficient allocation can be attained through the market (the second welfare theorem), implying a distributionally neutral market mechanism. Equilibrium here implies full employment as long as there is no interference with the workings of the market. The amount of money circulating in the economy does not affect this (real) outcome (see also Chapter 8). Inflation is then understood to be caused by excessive monetary growth and needs to be tackled by decreasing the money supply. The role of government is to provide well-defined property rights and allow price signals to be 'right' (reflecting scarcities and preferences) and for individual economic agents to allocate resources efficiently in response to these price signals (see also Chapter 15).

These arguments of static allocative efficiency gains through liberalised markets combined with particular ideas on constraints on growth emerged from a modified version of the Harrod-Domar model, namely the Revised Minimum Standard Model which was used by the World Bank to assist in its allocation of concessional development finance (see Tarp, 1993). As discussed in Chapter 11, in this model, capital appears as the main constraint on growth, the growth process is modelled as a steady-state balanced process, there is an underlying presumption that available investible resources are automatically invested (there are no deficiencies in aggregate demand) and the economy is modelled in aggregate single sector terms (see Chapter 11 for a critique of these various points). In the context of development, the following limitations of the model stand out: a lack of acknowledgment of structural transformation as core to the development process (ruled out by the steady state balanced growth path); the focus on capital scarcity draws attention away from fragmented domestic resource mobilisation and the importance of factors complementary to capital that are likely to be in short supply (such as, for instance, skilled labour); and demand constraints (including as a result of low average incomes) have implications for capacity utilisation (and hence investment levels). These combine with a limited understanding regarding technological change and the difficulties in extrapolating insights from a one-sector model to a multi-sector economy (this is known as the Cambridge Capital Critique, see Chapter 11).

Unsurprisingly perhaps, the Washington Consensus-style policy conditionalities of programmes financed by the World Bank and the International Monetary Fund failed to deliver their projected results. Growth and development in large parts of the developing world failed to register significant improvements, with particularly negative effects on investment levels, debt overhang and social realities (for example, real wages in the developing world fell dramatically together with formal sector employment and the provision of public services was severely cut back). By the early 1990s, these failings were widely acknowledged and strong calls were made to move beyond the Washington Consensus. This included pressures from the second-largest shareholder of the World Bank, Japan, to recognise that the historical experience of the East Asian economies, which had grown very rapidly since the 1960s, was not adequately captured in the Neoclassical prescriptions that were promoted by the World Bank.

The World Bank initially sought to respond to these demands with the publication of a report specifically focused on the experience of East Asian development (World Bank, 1993). The East Asia Miracle Report, however, remained anchored in the limitations of Neoclassical economics and failed to accommodate core dynamic realities of development, including those related to technological progress and general productivity increases that necessitate various forms of 'market-distorting policies' often lumped together as 'industrial policy' interventions. The challenge then became to find a way to move on from Neoclassical principles in the study of development, which, in the words of a Japanese aid official, was a question 'at the frontier of development economics' (Goto, 1997, p. 8).

Stiglitz (1998), who had become Chief Economist of the World Bank in 1997, took up this challenge when he called for a post-Washington Consensus. For Stiglitz (1998), the Washington Consensus had been misguided and incomplete. It was anchored on an erroneous set of analytical principles that promoted a 'perfect market' paradigm. Instead, he argued, developing country markets are characterised by multiple failures and the Washington Consensus prescriptions of blanket liberalisation, deregulation and privatisation failed to take these into account. The post-Washington Consensus sought to promote an 'imperfect market' paradigm and drew on a set of innovations that had become increasingly popular in mainstream economics. These included the rejection of Walrasian General Equilibrium theory, via new Keynesian or New Institutionalist Economics, as well as innovations in growth theory, via endogenous growth theory. Once it was recognised that developing countries tended to be characterised by violations of Walrasian assumptions, because of imperfect competition, imperfect information, bounded rationality, missing markets, or increasing returns to scale, the traditional conclusions of the allocative efficiency of perfect working markets no longer applied. Furthermore, as documented in Chapter 11, growth theory had moved on from exogenous accounts to attempts to endogenise technological change and incorporate increasing returns to scale. The post-Washington Consensus sought to incorporate these insights into the study of economic development. One commentator observed how 'as economic theory has turned more toward the study of information-based market failures, coordination failures, multiple roles of prices and the general idea of the potential complexity of market interactions, it has inevitably turned to questions that have long exercised development economics' (Bardhan, 1993, p. 139).

After the temporary retreat during the reign of the Washington Consensus, a resurgence of development economics then seemed to take place, with the framework of the newer development economics (Fine, 2006) seeking to incorporate issues whose neglect had rendered the analysis of the 'monoeconomics' incomplete. The post-Washington Consensus also claimed to anchor the economic analysis of development in its broader realities. It offered, in the words of its proponents, a comprehensive development framework beyond a macro-bias towards stabilisation (of inflation) and a micro-bias towards markets and prices that had characterised the Washington Consensus. However, the question remained whether the post-Washington Consensus could live up to these claims. Upon closer examination, the newer development economics as proposed by Stiglitz and others essentially proceeds on the same principles of optimisation and choice as its predecessor. Its main difference resides in the changes it makes regarding the attributes of economic agents and the environments within which these optimise (by allowing for imperfect information, bounded rationality, increasing returns, missing markets or imperfect competition). A 'softening' of the assumptions then strengthens social theory (or economics) on the basis of methodological individualism. The latter, however, has well-known limitations to address the 'economic' (or social) as it first takes the social out, only to re-introduce it afterwards as the result of optimisation exercises of independent economic agents.

The analysis of the post-Washington Consensus, then, remained fundamentally hampered by its ahistorical, asocial and reductionist method. Individual choice and optimisation continue to provide the ultimate explanation for economic and social phenomena. Crucially, despite incorporation of increasing returns, production remained ill-understood, the post-Washington Consensus remained ill-equipped to deal with such issues as technological progress and general productivity growth. The economy remains predominantly understood through the prism of exchange (with the production function still at the heart of the analysis of production and hence a black box) with little insight into the institutional arrangements that affect value creation. In essence, successful industrialisation is understood as the result of the removal of market failures and a movement towards well-functioning markets. This ignores that market failures are intrinsic to the process of production and that successful industrialisation frequently involves the creation of market failures and distortions in resource allocations (not their correction). Deliberate attempts to 'get prices wrong' are often part and parcel of successful trajectories of industrialisation (see Amsden, 2004).

These issues were emphasised by a thriving (heterodox) debate around the *developmental state,* which drew attention to the central role of the state in the historical experience of development. This highlighted the use of a host of different policy instruments, including trade tariffs, import substitution, export promotion, performance requirements on investment, etc. (Amsden, 1989; Wade, 1990) (see also Chapter 15).

While the post-Washington Consensus lingers on in development economics, there has been another attempt from within the World Bank to reorient the discipline – Lin's (2012) New Structural Economics. Lin was appointed Chief Economist of the World Bank in 2008, where he served until his term drew to a close in 2012.

He was the first Chief Economist of the Bank to be a national from the Global South. With his New Structural Economics, Lin has sought to draw attention to the need for industrial policy, particularly in low-income countries. However, while Lin clearly insists on the need for an interventionist role for the state to foster development, his commitment to such a positive role for the state remains narrowly defined, mainly in terms of how the state can support the private sector in its pursuit of comparative advantage. Indeed, his theoretical framework is centrally organised around the concepts of factor endowments and comparative advantage. In a nutshell, all countries have given endowments of labour, capital and natural resources. These are given rather than understood as the result of historical trajectories or situated within the broader context of international and domestic political, financial, economic and commercial relations. For Lin, factor endowments give rise to a particular comparative advantage in production. Industry should be developed in line with this comparative advantage as this provides the most competitive or optimal path to growth, which would produce the largest economic surplus and the fastest capital accumulation. The role of the state is then to support the private sector in structuring productive capacity according to this comparative advantage. As capital accumulates, factor endowments change and a new comparative advantage emerges. In essence, governments should follow comparative advantage rather than defy it. While providing a welcome shift of attention towards the core role of production in development, his analysis remains clouded by Neoclassical premises, which do not accommodate the complexities of traditional arguments around, for instance, infant industries (see further below) nor does his analysis overcome the flaws of comparative advantage theory (which only strictly holds in a world of two goods, two countries, given technology, no factor mobility, etc.).[2]

A final strand of mainstream development economics, and one that is becoming increasingly influential, is the 'poor economics' championed by Banerjee and Duflo (2011). This approach seeks to unpack the decision-making processes of the poor in developing countries, and to map out the incentive structures they face and consequently how these incentive structures can be modified to enable improved (and 'better') decisions to be made. This approach, drawing on insights from behavioural economics (see Chapter 3) and using experimental methods and Randomised Control Trials (RCTs, see Box 12.1), emphasises the behaviour of individuals in contrast to discussions about industrialisation and/or macroeconomic development. Interventions forwarded include microfinance schemes designed to promote entrepreneurial activity, cash transfers and social protection schemes, and insurance and saving schemes targeted at those previous excluded from formal financial institutions. These interventions are viewed as key mechanisms through which a range of secondary developmental issues are addressed (for example, microfinance improving intra-household gender relations), with impacts on a range of outcomes quantified through RCTs.

These final comments bring us to the next section, which discusses how the old development economics sought to deal with core features of development, without limiting itself by adopting Neoclassical principles of analysis.

Box 12.1: Randomised controlled trials – the new gold standard in development economics?

The dominance of the 'monoeconomics' view on development came with a stronger focus on so-called rigorous method. This meant that quantitative techniques were increasingly favoured as development economics turned away from other social sciences that might hold useful insights into socio-economic phenomena – such as anthropology or sociology – instead looking inwards or to STEM (science, technology, engineering and mathematics) disciplines. Today, a notable share of policy-oriented development research within the World Bank and the IMF is carried out using RCTs. Proponents of this research design claim it is the new 'gold standard' in development economics, implying that only RCTs allow 'evidence-based' policy making (Ravallion, 2018).

RCTs were developed and are prominently used to assess the effectiveness of new pharmaceuticals. The idea is to provide a treatment to one group of people while using a control group from whom this intervention is withheld to assess the impact of this treatment. For instance, certain schools might receive funding to pay additional teaching with the aim of assessing whether the presence of a second teacher in the classroom improves pupils' exam scores. If the RCT is well-designed the two groups should represent random samples from one join population and the difference in average outcome between the two groups gives us an estimate of the intervention's, that is the policy intervention's, impact. Proponents of RCTs claim that this is the best method available to assure unbiased impact evaluation of policies. While RCTs have become increasingly popular since 2000 there has also been a rise in criticism yielded towards this type of research design voice by economists within the mainstream (Deaton and Cartwright, 2018; Ravallion, 2018) as well as from outside (Reddy, 2012).

There are three broad types of criticisms of RCTS: those focusing on their statistical characteristics, those flagging ethical concerns and those stressing their broader societal significance. Leading econometricians have pointed out that claims that RCT are necessarily unbiased are misleading. The randomness of two samples drawn from the same population only provides an estimate (not the true value) of a treatment impact. Furthermore, RCT might be underpowered given the high cost of implementing these types of studies, meaning too few people might be included and surveyed yielding statistically unreliable results (Deaton and Cartwright, 2018). Ethically, randomisation is highly questionable as it amounts to withholding resources from individuals who need them while offering them to others who do not require them. This in fact means resources are deliberately misallocated (Reddy, 2012). Finally, RCTs tend to be used for well-defined 'small-fix' interventions, but many policies crucial for development are macroeconomic. Hence, it seems difficult if not impossible to design RCTs assessing approaches to climate change or exchange rate regimes. Thus, a focus on RCTs avoids asking questions about what (and how) economic institutions work for development and structural transformation (Reddy, 2012).

Alternatives in development economics

The predominant approaches to development economics today, which were discussed above and which are dominated by Neoclassical principles, look very different from the initial contributions when a separate sub-discipline emerged in the 1940s–1950s. These contributions, which are often grouped together under the moniker of the old development economics, can broadly be distinguished as representing two dominant perspectives. On the one hand are scholarly contributions that originated mainly in Europe and North America, including by Hirschman, Lewis,[3] Nurkse, Rostow and Rosenstein-Rodan, sometimes referred to as 'modernisation theory'. On the other are contributions that came largely from Latin America, including by Prebisch and colleagues at the United Nations Economic Commission for Latin America (UNECLA, or CEPAL following the Spanish and Portuguese acronym). These are often referred to as 'structuralism'. Furthermore, in the late 1960s and early 1970s, another distinct school emerged emphasising themes of underdevelopment and unequal exchange in a 'dependency' framework.

While offering distinct analyses, these earlier development economists often drew inspiration from Classical Political Economists and economic history. They shared a rejection of Neoclassical principles as a way to offer a viable economic analysis of less developed countries and highlighted that industrialisation and structural transformation were key to economic development. These ideas combined with an awareness that successful economic development would necessitate substantial degrees of state intervention (see Hunt, 1989). The old development economics had a particular interest in historical trajectories and highlighted how specific structural features, like for instance those deriving from land ownership or the nature of the integration of a country in the world economy, had important repercussions for development. We discuss each strand in turn.

Modernisation theory

While rooted in Classical political economy, modernisation theorists drew on a twentieth-century formalisation of some of the ideas originally put forward by Smith (1776). Young (1928) revisited Smith's emphasis on the size of the (domestic and international) market for the division of labour to yield its productivity gains. However, he added that markets grew not only because of geographical expansion or population growth but also as a result of rises in income per head. These in turn were driven by productivity increases linked to the mechanisation of the production process. Therefore, returns to scale would not be constant, as claimed by Neoclassical theory, but increase with production volumes, because productivity would rise as more goods were manufactured. Hence, Young highlighted two important aspects which became prominent features of modernisation theory. First, there was the awareness that growth creates markets. Secondly, Young drew attention to the manufacturing sector as engine of development. Poor countries have typically very limited manufacturing capacity with much of their labour force employed in and output generated through agriculture and mining. Thus, Young's argument stressed the need for economic transformation towards industrial production.

One of the first economists to address the challenge of development in poor countries was the Polish-born Rosenstein-Rodan. In 1943, he discussed the question of how to jump-start development in Eastern and South-Eastern Europe, envisaging the economic challenges to come with the end of the Second World War. Rosenstein-Rodan believed that a *Big Push* was necessary in the form of large-scale investment planning to shift large numbers of rural poor, who were actually or effectively unemployed, into industrial employment. Planning was crucial because private investment would not be forthcoming according to Rosenstein-Rodan due to three major impediments – or as he dubbed them three indivisibilities. First, domestic markets tended to be weak in poor economies due to low income levels. Only simultaneous growth across a large number of sectors could generate enough demand to make private investment viable, i.e. the indivisibility of demand. Rosenstein-Rodan (1943, p. 206) illustrated this point, using the example of a shoe factory:

> If a hundred workers who were previously in disguised unemployment ... in an underdeveloped country are put into a shoe factory, their wages will constitute additional income. If the newly employed workers spend all of their additional income on the shoes they produce, the shoe factory will find a market and will succeed. In fact, however, they will not spend all of their additional income on shoes.

Since the shoe manufacturer cannot pay his employees in shoes, he is likely not to start up a business. However, if a hundred factories producing all the different goods that are needed for everyday life – say food, clothing, shoes, kitchenware, etc. – were to start up at the same time there would be enough workers to buy the produced shoes, clothes and other goods. Yet, for these hundred companies to start operating, infrastructure is required. This brings us to the second indivisibility, i.e. the indivisibility of production.

Production requires infrastructure, including energy generation, water supply, functioning roads, railways and other transport connections as well as telecommunication networks. Infrastructure is unlikely to be built by private investors because it is costly and benefits cannot be completely internalised by them. Thus, it is a classic case of an investment generating a positive externality, i.e. someone else who did not pay anything towards the construction of a road, for instance, will benefit from its existence. But Rosenstein-Rodan went beyond externalities pointing towards the 'indivisibilities' which in turn characterise infrastructure. These refer to timing, durability, construction period and a minimum mix across types of utilities. Typically, infrastructure needs to be provided first before any factory can start operating. A road, for instance, is built to last, meaning it could well outlive a company, making it little likely that the company owner will build the road connecting the factory to the nearest city. Infrastructure often takes a long time in construction, which a private investor might not be able to afford. And finally, there is an irreducible industry mix for the infrastructure that has to be provided. Hence, it is not enough to build a road, water supply and a sewage system as electricity supply will also need to be provided.

Finally, accelerated investment, as prescribed by modernisation theorists, depends on a high saving rate well beyond saving capacities in poor countries, pointing to the indivisibility of saving. Since savings are made out of income, total savings are small in poor countries and private investment will be impeded.

Nurkse (1952) put forward a similar argument to Rosenstein-Rodan, calling for *Balanced Growth* in poor countries. Both drew on Young's idea that rising income will expand markets which will only then stimulate private sector investment and productivity growth. Rosenstein-Rodan and Nurkse were both pessimistic about export markets as drivers of industrialisation in developing countries.

Both Rosenstein-Rodan and Nurkse argued against the view that the market will allocate resources – i.e. labour and capital – best, which would result in spontaneous growth and development in poor countries. Their Neoclassical contemporaries – such as Viner (1953) – argued that a *Big Push* was not necessary since international markets would offer poor countries sufficient demand and economies of scale regardless of domestic investment. Neoclassical development economists followed the mantra of 'getting prices right' because the price mechanism would allocate scare resources best. Simply opening up to global trade – by removing tariffs and other trade barriers – would enable poor countries to produce and export those goods that they could produce best (according to comparative advantage). This should then over time help countries to increase their income levels. Neoclassical economists, therefore, objected to large investment programmes rolled out by governments that aimed at industrialisation because such programmes would distort prices favouring industrial investment through subsidised credit for manufacturing firms, for instance (see above).

Rosenstein-Rodan and Nurkse alongside the Latin American structuralists (see below) were sceptical with regard to the Neoclassical recommendation that free trade would bring development to poor countries. They rightly diagnosed that poor economies tended to sell primary goods in international markets such as agricultural produce and mined resources. But for modernisation theorists, development was not possible without industrialisation. After all, this was the route that rich countries had taken as well. For Nurkse, a vigorous increase in world demand for primary commodities would have been needed to help these economies set up domestic industry. In the absence of such a development, diversification of production for the domestic market was necessary. This could be best achieved through investment in the manufacturing sector.

Nevertheless, not all proponents of industrialisation agreed with the *Big Push* approach. Rosenstein-Rodan and Nurkse were criticised by their contemporaries, in particular Hirschman (1958), who, in turn, advocated *Unbalanced Growth*. Hirschman was sceptical about the ability of poor countries to plan and roll out large investment programmes. He agreed that domestic demand and saving were scarce in developing countries, but stressed that management skills of the sort required to devise and run such large investment programmes would be equally scarce. Thus, he viewed the creation of imbalances or bottlenecks as important signals of investment opportunities for potential entrepreneurs. He, however, agreed on the importance of promoting manufacturing production. For Hirschman, manufacturing was a key driver of structural transformation because setting up manufacturing factories would stimulate the emergence of further manufacturing activity due to forward and backward linkages. For instance, the establishment of a cement plant encourages the setting up of a nearby factory for industrial packaging producing multi-wall bags. This is a backward linkage since it stimulates production of goods that can be used as inputs in the cement business. A forward linkage stimulates the emergence of manufacturers that further process existing goods. In our example, a factory producing cement breeze blocks, i.e. concrete building blocks, could set up next to the cement manufacturer. Hirschman's ideas remain important today in the industrial policy debate, which addresses the question of how developing countries should design policies aiming at industrialisation and growth.

Kaldor, a Post-Keynesian economist, also made important contributions to development economics as he advocated export-led industrialisation to achieve development.

This policy recommendation was based on Kaldor's (1966, 1981) three growth laws which he formulated in the 1960s and 1970s. Studying leading industrialised economies, Kaldor observed that, firstly, increases in per capita income were closely correlated with expanding manufacturing production. He argued that industrialisation drove growth (rather than the other way around) because the positive link between manufacturing output and GDP empirically held for countries with small, but growing manufacturing sectors, rather than rich countries that had large established manufacturing output. According to Kaldor, manufacturing is central to development because it is the only sector that enjoys increasing returns to scale. Therefore, secondly, productivity increases in manufacturing are closely linked to rising manufacturing output (this is also called Verdoorn's Law). This is the case because companies improve their technology and workers learn while producing and with growing cumulative manufacturing output. Thirdly, growth in the manufacturing sector is positively correlated with improving productivity in agricultural production and services. If there are diminishing returns or disguised unemployment of agriculture and services, rising employment in manufacturing will increase the productivity of these sectors as well.

Kaldor believed that developing countries should target global demand as engine of growth and structural transformation rather than the domestic market. After all, global demand is much vaster. In this sense, Kaldor agreed with the Neoclassical critics of the *Big Push*. What he did not agree with was the Neoclassical proposition that markets and 'correct' prices would guide structural transformation. While for Neoclassical economists this implies limiting government intervention, economists like Kaldor favoured active industrial policy entailing subsidies and other state support.

Finally, perhaps the single most influential modernisation theorist was the St Lucian Nobel Prize-winning economist Lewis (Kirkpatrick and Barrientos, 2004). His major contribution 'Economic Development with Unlimited Supply of Labour' (Lewis, 1954) reflected his keen interest in unemployment in poor countries. Lewis (1954) coined the term 'surplus labour', arguing that in developing countries a large share of the population is unemployed, sometimes in a disguised way. Following his argument, many people in developing countries, while not formally unemployed, tend to carry out jobs which neither require their entire time nor strength or skills during a working day. His dual sector model illustrated the meaning of development as structural transformation most powerfully (see Box 12.1). He introduced duality and convention as important factors in the development process and set the tone in development economics to the present day by highlighting the need for larger volumes of savings:

> [T]he central problem in the theory of economic development is to understand the process by which a community which was previously saving and investing 4 or 5 per cent of its national income or less, converts itself into an economy where voluntary saving is running at about 12 to 15 per cent of national income or more. (Lewis, 1954, p. 155)

As typical for modernisation theory, Lewis believed that once some internal barriers to growth – e.g. a shortfall in saving – were overcome, virtuous growth dynamics would manifest themselves in a country almost automatically. In his model, persistently low wages benefit a small group of domestic capitalists who are consequently able to accumulate savings which they re-invest entirely. Low wages are a result of a dual labour market. A traditional sector where labour is abundant in supply coexists with employment in a modern sector where workers are paid their marginal product as assumed by Neoclassical theory (see Chapter 7). The accumulation process carries on until all surplus labour is employed, at which point the development process is completed. Despite its lasting influence, the Lewis model has been criticised severely. It crucially depends on wage stagnation and assumes growing income inequality as not only inevitable but also a necessary by-product of development.

The model also caricatures duality. In reality, traditional and modern sectors are not entirely separate, but typically feed off and nurture each other. Lewis's simplistic portrayal of duality invites interpretations of the model identifying the modern sector with manufacturing and the traditional sector with agriculture. This is, however, not necessarily what Lewis had in mind since he stressed the need to mechanise agricultural production to ensure sufficient (and cheap) food supply for workers in the modern sector to keep food prices (and consequently wages) from rising prematurely (Box 12.2).

Box 12.2: Lewis's dual sector model

Lewis (1954) put forward his dual sector model in the attempt to account for the structural differences that distinguish poor economies from rich ones. He explicitly rejected both, Neoclassical economics and Keynes's analysis – the two dominant approaches in economics during the 1950s – for the context of developing countries. While the former assumed full employment, the latter took savings as abundant. However, in poor countries 'surplus labour' would prevail while there was a lack of savings according to Lewis. The concept of 'surplus labour' was controversially discussed in the 1950s (see Viner, 1953). Today it is generally accepted that formal sector employment is missing in poor economies, while people in the informal sector are often underemployed, taking on survivalist and other low-productivity jobs for lack of alternatives.

Lewis modelled poor countries as consisting of two sectors: a traditional sector with surplus labour and basic production techniques. Here, labour's marginal product (MPL) is close to zero, which means that some of the labour force can be shifted out of the sector without a decline in its output. This is because the remaining workers would pick up the slack, working longer. 'Pay' in the traditional sector is determined by convention and equals the subsistence wage (S). In later interpretations of the model, the traditional sector is often taken to be subsistence agriculture, which, according to Lewis, is only part of the traditional sector. In contrast, in the modern sector, which is characterised by more advanced technology, workers are paid their marginal product.

The model attempts to capture the complex interactions between these two sectors, stating that the wage in the modern sector (W) is determined by subsistence wage (S) topped up by a certain amount to attract workers into the more inconvenient employment in the modern sector. Therefore, the labour supply curve in the figure below is flat. This means that, as long as there is surplus labour, labour supply is perfectly elastic at wage W. In period 1, capitalists in the modern sector will demand Q_1 workers. This will leave capitalist with a profit equal to the piece of pie above the labour supply curve (i.e N_1Q_1W). Lewis assumed that capitalists reinvest their entire profit in period 2, resulting in growing employment (now at Q_2). Profits increase to N_2Q_2W as wage W remains unchanged. This process of accumulation will go on until all surplus labour is absorbed when the (labour market for the) two sectors will be fully integrated. This is the Lewisian turning point. Here wages start to rise and modern technology has presumably been disseminated across the economy. The two sectors integrate and the process of development through structural transformation is complete.

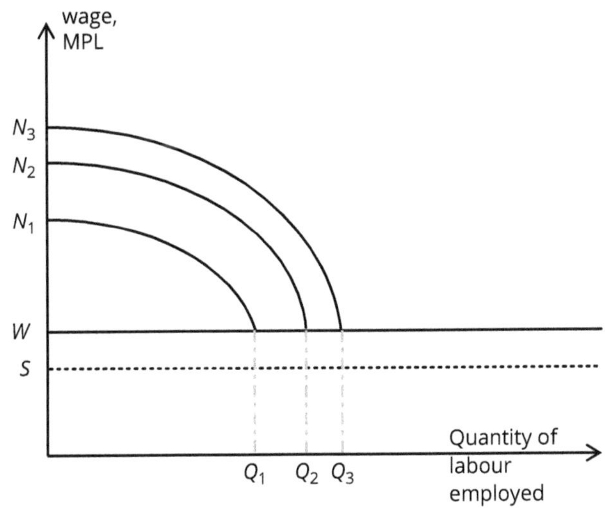

A main shortcoming of the model is its assumption that re-investment of capitalists' savings is automatic, resulting in the persistent absorption of surplus labour. Take the example of the oil industry. Many developing economies are rich in resources and possess a modern sector that focuses on primary extraction. Oil and mining industries are notoriously capital-intensive and produce few jobs. Even worse, in many countries those industries are owned by multinational companies that might re-invest, but abroad rather than locally. Alternatively, companies might not re-invest their profits at all, at least not in job-creating production. They have the alternative to invest in financial assets, that is in stocks, bonds or other lucrative financial paper. Very few, if any, jobs will be gained if, for instance, an Italian oil company re-invests the profits it accumulated through oil extraction in Ghana on the London Stock Exchange. Much of modernisation theory is blind to the global context in which developing countries operate, focusing on domestic barriers to growth and development.

Structuralism

Structuralism put forward an alternative understanding of development, also stressing the need for economic transformation. However, while modernisation theorists focused on domestic barriers to this transformation, the structuralist school that emerged in Latin America in the late 1940s explicitly stressed external constraints to development. The Argentine economist Prebisch is regarded as the founding father of this development tradition. In 1950, he was appointed as general secretary to the newly-created UN Economic Commission for Latin America (ECLA, or CEPAL). Prebisch was preoccupied with the economic challenges of Argentina, and Latin American countries more generally, which despite their integration into global trade struggled to improve the economic situation of their citizens. He observed that every time there was economic turmoil in Europe (e.g. during the world wars), Latin America would be negatively affected due to falling European demand for its export goods. Simultaneously, subdued trade links with Europe seemed to stimulate the development of domestic industries, replacing European imports of consumer and investment goods with local products. In response, the structuralist school formulated the core–periphery paradigm.

The core–periphery paradigm captures stylised facts about the trade relationship between poor and rich countries. The rich countries of the Global North, i.e. Europe and the USA, make up the core. Here technology is advanced, trade unions strong and employment and wages relatively high. In the periphery, i.e. the Global South including Latin America, in contrast, technology tends to be more basic, possibly with the exception of a few industrial islands that produce for export, and the periphery mostly exports raw materials. However, these export industries are often owned by foreign companies headquartered in rich countries. Most consumption and investment goods are imported from the core to the periphery because production capacity is lacking in the Global South.

The situation is further tilted against development in poor countries because labour is abundant in the periphery and trade unions are either weak or non-existent, resulting in low wages and high unemployment. In this setting, development requires structural transformation in the form of industrialisation, as argued by modernisation theorists. However, structuralists add that links with the core or 'centre' impedes development in the periphery. Free trade between core and periphery prevents the development of a domestic manufacturing in poor countries, as the latter are unable to compete with more advanced and competitive producers from the Global North. Therefore, import-substituting industrialisation (ISI) policies are required to foster local manufacturing. The protection of local markets against foreign competition was a priority in this policy agenda. Since local manufacturers were in their infancy in comparison to globally operating companies from the Global North, they needed government support such as import tariffs, enabling them to produce and compete with foreign firms despite their higher production costs. The aim was to bring domestic producers gradually up to speed with international technology and competition. This idea was that they would learn while being protected, increase their competitiveness and lower cost of production. Eventually, they would be able to compete in the global market without government support and trade barriers or subsidies and other support policies could be phased out. Hence, goods that were produced abroad and imported could be replaced by domestically manufactured products. Hirschman advised that light consumer goods (clothing and foodstuffs, for instance) should be produced first, followed by white goods (fridges and washing machines) and finally investment goods (industrial machinery and equipment).

While ISI initiated industrialisation in Latin America, the policies were not necessarily successful in reducing inequality and industry concentration as hoped for by

Table 12.1 Comparison of selected Latin American countries with South Korea

	GDP growth (%)			Investment (% of GDP)			Trade deficit (% of GDP)		
	1960s	1970s	1980s	1960s	1970s	1980s	1960s	1970s	1980s
Argentina	4.0	3.0	−1.4	22.3	26.0	19.9	0.3	1.2	2.4
Brazil	6.2	8.5	1.8	19.7	22.9	21.0	0.2	−1.2	2.4
Mexico	6.8	6.7	1.9	18.9	22.6	22.3	−2.0	−1.2	3.4
South Korea	8.7	9.1	9.7	18.9	26.7	28.3	−10.3	−5.9	0.4

Source: World Bank World Development Indicators

CEPAL. The idea was that as employment increases, the wage level would rise and consequently income inequality would be reduced. Simultaneously, the emergence of new manufacturers would reduce industry concentration, making Latin American economies more dynamic and less oligopolistic. While growth accelerated in many Latin American economies with ISI (see Table 12.1), income inequality and industrial concentration were exacerbated rather than reduced (Hira, 2007). The need to import more machinery from rich countries in order to intensify manufacturing production also implied rising trade deficits in some countries, such as for instance Brazil (see Table 12.1). This was very disappointing for the Latin American structuralists and led some of the CEPAL members to adopt a much more pessimistic outlook for Latin America, to which we turn next.

Dependency theory

The dependency school (the so-called *dependentistas*) emerged, arguing that any attempt by countries to industrialise under capitalism would necessarily lead to more dependency on the core rather than to economic emancipation from it. Rising trade deficits and increasing foreign indebtedness among Latin American economies were interpreted as signs of this dependency. The only escape, according to the *dependentistas*, was to break with capitalism all together and either adopt socialism or (less realistically) autarky.

Two main currents can be identified within dependency theory. On the one hand, a strong dependency movement emerged within the core, and especially in the US, around the German-American economist Frank. On the other hand, disillusioned Latin American structuralists, like Dos Santos, developed dependency thought in the periphery. Both approaches were strongly influenced by Marxist thought and are also sometimes referred to as neo-Marxist theories of development. Frank (1978) built on the concept of monopoly capitalism put forward by the Marxist economist Baran. According to Baran (1957), mature capitalism in rich countries will reach a point when profits cannot be lucratively reinvested into domestic production any more. In the search for a profit 'fix' capitalists turn to other investment opportunities including foreign investment in poor countries. Because the power relationship between poor and rich countries is skewed in favour of the latter, the drive to invest abroad becomes very quickly imperialist. Profits made in the periphery – for instance, in mining – are extracted and repatriated to the core by large companies based in rich countries. Therefore, the main mechanism for this surplus extraction from the periphery to the core, according to Frank, is trade. The periphery finds itself confronted with monopolistic traders from the core – i.e. more powerful entities which can dictate prices, buy cheap and sell dear. Hence, the development of the core brings about the underdevelopment of the periphery. *Dependentistas* argued that poor countries are not merely at an earlier stage of development than rich countries, a claim popular among modernisation theories. Instead, the development process is neither linear nor even, while prosperity in rich societies is directly linked to destitution in poor ones.

A second important strand of dependency theory developed in Latin America, i.e. from within the periphery. Dos Santos strived to develop dependency theory while accounting for the domestic characteristics of countries in the periphery. For him, Frank and others did not sufficiently engage with class dynamics in dependent societies, portraying dependency as a purely external phenomenon. Instead, peripheral elites actively helped surplus extraction towards the core, hindering domestic development. For Dos Santos, there were three chief constraints to economic transformation in the periphery. First, peripheral economies are dependent on their export sectors for generation of foreign exchange in turn necessary to import key inputs for industrial production. This makes capitalists controlling those industries economically powerful and politically influential. Often these are foreign capitalists, repatriating profits abroad rather than investing them domestically. Second, periphery countries are prone to trade deficits due to the import requirements of industrial production, but more so because international exchange relations are tilted in favour of rich countries. Indeed, raw materials exported by poor economies tend to be cheap and can be replaced with synthetics, while manufactured products from the core are expensive and not easily replicable. Trade deficits generate a financial dependency of the periphery on the core since capital inflows are necessary to balance external accounts in the periphery. Finally, industrial production relies on imported inputs because of the technological dependency of the periphery on the core. Machinery and equipment have to be purchased abroad, straining the trade balance while importing technology which is not suitable for a labour-abundant economy.

The different strands of dependency theory were heavily criticised in particular by the Marxist community, questioning the interpretations of some Marxist concepts adopted by dependency theory. Empirical developments, however, provided the most damning criticism of the theory. According to the *dependentistas*, structural constraints make development in the periphery impossible. Therefore, the school struggles to explain the East Asian Miracle, an important development success of the twentieth century. Table 12.1 above indicates how South Korea, a successful industrialiser, experienced persistently high trade deficits during the 1960s and 1970s, before it could successfully balance its trade account.

In hindsight, many economists regard Latin American efforts to industrialise and pursue ISI strategies as a failure. This assessment does not seem to be entirely justified since many Latin American countries managed to accelerate growth and structural transformation substantially during the ISI years. The most obvious example is Brazil which was recently named one of thirteen international growth success stories by the World Bank (World Bank, 2008). The negative assessment of ISI appears to be mainly based on a comparison with the successful East Asian economies (nine East Asian countries were among the thirteen success stories). ISI in Latin America is often contrasted with the so-called East Asian Miracle that is attributed to an export-led growth strategy followed first by Japan and then South Korea, Taiwan and the two city states Singapore and Hong Kong. The simplistic interpretation of these two regional growth stories is that Latin American ISI failed because it was protectionist and inward-oriented, whereas the East Asian Miracle was a success due to trade openness. A more sophisticated reading of the two experiences stresses the ISI-type interventions that East Asian economies used to support their export-led strategies (see Zhu, 2006, for more details).

Conclusion

This chapter sought to give an overview of the way in which development economics has evolved over the last century. While the old development economics explicitly draws on Classical political, it is a relatively new sub-discipline, which itself was rapidly displaced in the early 1980s by an unholy alliance of neo-Marxists, via dependency theory, and a revival of Neoclassical economics in the study of the development. Since then, the World Bank has played a core role in influencing how development is understood and what policies should be promoted to accelerate increases in living standards in the developing world.

While the beginning of the twenty-first century has seen increased heterogeneity across various countries in the Global South, stark realities of underdevelopment persist across broad swathes of the Global South. Yet, the narrow analytical frame deployed by Neoclassical economics gives rise to a narrowly conceived policy space, where those instruments that have been highlighted as core to the historical experience of development and which reflect core analytical insights regarding the role of manufacturing in development remain persistently ill-appreciated and often explicitly out of reach as a result of manifold restrictions on developing countries' policy space, including as a result of conditionalities of official loans, bilateral investment treaties or accession to the World Trade Organization.

Discussion questions and seminar activities

- What do you think are essential elements of a successful development trajectory? Can you discuss these with reference to a country that has successfully developed in the latter part of the twentieth century?
- Do you think that Neoclassical economics can easily account for such a successful development experience?
- What is the role of the World Bank in development? Can you discuss what the implications have been of its role for both the analysis of and policies for development?
- Can you identify essential elements that are shared across the alternative (non-Neoclassical) schools of development economics discussed in this chapter?
- In what way can you identify a strong legacy of Classical political economy in the contributions of the old development economics?

References

Amsden, A. (1989). *Asia's next giant: South Korea and late industrialisation*. New York: Oxford University Press.

Amsden, A. (2004). *The rise of 'the rest'. Challenges to the west from late-industrialising countries*. New York: Oxford University Press.

Banerjee, A., & Duflo, E. (2011). *Poor economics*. London: Penguin.

Baran, P. (1957). *The political economy of growth*. New York: Monthly Review Press.

Bardhan, P. (1993). Economics of development and the development of economics. *Journal of Economic Perspectives, 7*(2), 129–142.

Bayliss, K., Fine, B., & Van Waeyenberge, E. (Eds.). (2011). *The political economy of development. The World Bank, Neoliberalism and development research*. London: Pluto Press.

Chang, H. J. (2002). *Kicking away the ladder*. London: Anthem Press.

Chang, H. J. (Ed.). (2003). *Rethinking development economics*. London: Anthem Press.

Deaton, A., & Cartwright, N. (2018). Understanding and misunderstanding randomized controlled trials. *Social Science and Medicine, 210*, 2–21.

Fine, B. (2006). Introduction. In K. S. Jomo & B. Fine (Eds.), *The new development economics. After the Washington Consensus. London*. New York: Zed Books.

Fine, B., & Van Waeyenberge, E. (2013). A paradigm shift that never was. *Competition and Change, 17*(4), 355–371.

Frank, A. G. (1978). *Dependent accumulation and underdevelopment*. Basingstoke: Macmillan.

Goto, K. (1997). Some thoughts on development and aid: Japan's strategic response. *OECF Journal of Development Assistance, 3*(1), 1–18.

Hira, A. (2007). Should economists rule the world? Trends and implications of leadership patterns in the developing world, 1960-2005. *International Political Science Review/Revue internationale de science politique, 28*(3), 325–360.

Hirschman, A. (1958). *The strategy of economic development*. New Haven: Yale University Press.

Hirschman, A. (1981). The rise and decline of development economics. In *Essays in trespassing*. Cambridge: Cambridge University Press.

Hunt, D. (1989). *Economic theories of development*. Lanham: Barnes and Noble.

Jomo, K. S., & Fine, B. (Eds.). (2006). *The new development economics. After the Washington consensus*. London/New York: Zed Books.

Kaldor, N. (1966). *Causes of the slow rate of growth of the United Kingdom*. Cambridge: Cambridge University Press.

Kaldor, N. (1981). The role of increasing returns, technical progress and cumulative causation in the theory of international trade and economic growth. *Economie Appliquée, 34*(4), 593–615.

Kirkpatrick, C., & Barrientos, A. (2004). The Lewis model after 50 years. *The Manchester School, 72*(6), 679–690.

Kitching, G. (1989). *Development and underdevelopment in historical perspective*. Milton Keynes: The Open University.

Krueger, A. (1986). Aid in the development process. *World Bank Research Observer, 1*(1), 57–78.

Lewis, W. A. (1954). Economic development with unlimited supplies of labour. *The Manchester School, 22*(2), 139–191.

Lin, J. (2012). *New structural economics. A framework for rethinking development and policy*. Washington, DC: The World Bank.

Nurske, R. (1952). Some international aspects of the problem of economic development. *American Economic Review, 42*(2), 571–583.

Orqubay, A. (2015). *Made in Africa: Industrial policy in Ethiopia*. Oxford: Oxford University Press.

Ravallion, M. (2018). *Should the randomistas (continue to) rule?* Working paper 492, Center for Global Development.

Reddy, S. (2012). Randomise this! On poor economics. *Review of Agrarian Studies, 2*(2), 60–73.

Rosenstein-Rodan, P. (1943). Problems of industrialization of Eastern and South-Eastern Europe. *The Economic Journal, 53*(210/211), 202–211.

Smith, A. (1776). *An inquiry into the nature and the causes of the wealth of nations* (5th ed.). London: Methuen &Co Ltd./Library of Economics and Liberty.

Stiglitz, J. (1998, January 7). *More instruments and broader goals: Moving toward the post-Washington consensus*. Wider Annual Lecture, Helsinki.

Tarp, F. (1993). *Stabilisation and structural adjustment: Macroeconomic frameworks for analysing the crisis in SSA*. London: Routledge.

Van Waeyenberge, E. (2006). From Washington to post-Washington consensus: Illusions of development. In K. S. Jomo & B. Fine (Eds.), *The new development economics. After the Washington consensus*. London/New York: Zed Books.

Viner, J. (1953). *International trade and economic development*. Oxford: Clarendon Press.

Wade, R. (1990). *Governing the market: Economic theory and the role of government in East Asian industrialization*. Princeton: Princeton University Press.

Williamson, J. (1990). What Washington means by policy reform. In J. Williamson (Ed.), *Latin American adjustment: How much has happened?* Washington, DC: Institute for International Economics.

World Bank. (2008). *The growth report. Strategies for sustained growth and inclusive development*. Washington DC: The World Bank on behalf of the Commission on Growth and Development.

World Bank. (1993). *The east miracle: Economic growth and public policy*. New York: Oxford University Press.

Young, A. A. (1928). Increasing returns and economic progress. *History of Economic Thought, 38*, 527–542.

Zhu, T. (2006). *Rethinking import-substituting industrialization. Development strategies and institutions in Taiwan and China*. UNU-WIDER working paper 76/2006.

13 HOW DOES ECONOMICS ADDRESS GENDER?

Hannah Bargawi

Introduction

In some ways a chapter concerning the incorporation of gender into economics, both within mainstream economics and throughout the history of the subject, could be very short. Indeed, despite attempts at bringing gender into economic analysis, economics remains a long way from being a fully gendered discipline. Given the piecemeal nature of attempts at incorporating gender into economic analysis both historically and today, this chapter will focus on one particular area in which the issue of gender has repeatedly arisen. This is in relation to work: the chapter attempts to map how gender differences across the world of work and their consequences are understood across the history of economic thought and what particular solutions these different approaches give rise to. By focusing on the issue of gender and work, we are able to gain a rich comparative understanding of how different schools of thought have addressed the topic of gender and work, including regarding what methods and models have been applied and what gaps in understanding remain and why.

This chapter is organised as follows. The first section defines what we mean by gender and explores the importance of such a definition for the way in which economics might incorporate gender. Subsequent sections draw on this definitional discussion, highlighting how particularly truncated understandings of gender have, in turn, influenced methods, approaches to problems and subsequently the solutions that arise.

The next section discusses the ways in which gender has been addressed and incorporated into mainstream economics, focusing in particular on the topic of work. We trace the shift from Neoclassical economics to the New Home Economics and from there to New Institutional approaches to gender in the labour market.

While Neoclassical economics before the 1950s largely ignored gender, the New Home Economics heralded the application of Neoclassical methods and models to understanding behaviour and decision-making within households, thereby ostensibly addressing the gender gap in economics. As will be shown, however, a set of paradoxical developments, especially in relation to labour market developments in industrialised countries, led to a shift towards the application of New Institutional concepts to issues of gender and work, as a way of gaining greater insight. While some of these attempts have proved useful in filling the obvious gaps of the New Home Economics, questions and concerns remain. Subsequent sections of this chapter therefore invite the reader to unpick the mainstream approach to gender further, by exploring alternative approaches to gender in the labour market, originating in other schools of economic thought.

Section 3 explores the alternative approach offered by Old Institutional economics to questions of gender and work, contrasting this with the New Institutional approaches integrated within mainstream economics today.

Section 4 refers back to Classical political economy to contemplate the inclusion of gender and discusses whether the androcentric bias of mainstream economics might be overcome by a return to Classical political economy topics, methods and approaches. An important contribution made by Classical political economists, and in particular Marx, to the treatment of gender and economics, relates to methodology, through their emphasis on social relationships and power dynamics.

Section 5 concludes the chapter by exploring the ways in which Feminist economists have made use of non-mainstream economics approaches, methods and ideas to demonstrate that a *better* economics is possible. The chapter highlights the importance of the history of economic thought to the development of the relatively new field of Feminist economics. Feminist economists share a common dissatisfaction with mainstream, orthodox economics in that the latter fails sufficiently to incorporate questions of gender into the analysis. Feminist economists have frequently drawn on alternative theories to criticise mainstream economics. This critique has spanned the spectrum of topics explored by mainstream economics as well as the methods and models it employs to explore these. For Feminist economists, the use of alternative methods and models, borrowed and extended from the history of economic thought, serves, on the one hand, to gain a richer understanding of existing issues and, on the other hand, to pose new questions as compared to orthodox economics.

How to bring gender into economics?

To establish what is problematic about the current orthodoxy's attempts to tackle gender, and to understand where the limits of previous attempts to incorporate gender lie, an important distinction needs to be made – that between sex and gender. This distinction goes to the heart of why gendering economics matters. It matters not just because there is a need to apply existing accepted methods and models within mainstream economics to topics that bear on women's lives, but also because we need to scrutinise and question the way in which economics is based on a number of gendered assumptions, biases and values, resulting in a truncated understanding of society.

For most Feminist economists, the distinction between sex and gender is therefore a crucial starting point when assessing economics' gender credentials. Engaging with the sex–gender distinction highlights how current Neoclassical economics is masculine in the way it reflects gendered, societal beliefs about masculinity (Nelson, 1995). For economics as a subject to change, we must therefore first acknowledge that such gendered assumptions enter the subject via the questions we ask and the methods and models that we employ to answer those questions. Rather than assuming that economics as a subject is value-free, objective and impartial in the questions it asks and the methods it adopts, the masculine gender norms that have influenced the subject need to be revealed (Box 13.1).

Box 13.1: Sex versus gender in economics

An important distinction that needs to be made is that between 'sex' and 'gender', and how these categories are understood and deployed in economics. While sex concerns biological characteristics associated with being female or male, gender is constructed by society itself on the basis of sex differences. World Health Organisation definitions highlight these definitional differences between sex and gender.

> Sex refers to the biological characteristics that define humans as female or male. While these sets of biological characteristics are not mutually exclusive, as there are individuals who possess both, they tend to differentiate humans as males and females. (World Health Organisation, 2006, p. 5)

However, '(g)ender refers to the economic, social and cultural attributes and opportunities associated with being male or female at a particular point in time' (World Health Organisation, 2001).

But why should these differences matter to economists? This crucial question can be answered by considering an example from the nineteenth century, when it was discovered that women's brains weighed, on average, less than men's brains. This sex difference remains undisputed. However, based on this finding a number of gendered conclusions were drawn. Women were perceived to be less rational, more likely to suffer from hysteria and more driven by emotion than reason, as a result of their smaller brain size (Nelson, 1995; Barker, 2001; Barker and Feiner, 2004).

While we have come a long way towards dispelling such sex-based conclusions, this essentialist view of sex differences underpinning economic realities still inhabits a vast swathe of the economics profession. As this chapter highlights, across questions of gender and work, whether in current or past economic thinking, sex differences have been relied upon both to understand and rationalise phenomena such as the gender pay gap, occupational segregation and the division of labour between men and women within the home.

By acknowledging how gender is embedded within economics, two important steps forward can be made. First, questions of gender can be brought to the forefront of the analysis, rather than lie embedded but poorly understood as they currently are. Second, we might move away from associating judgments about value (what we consider to be worthwhile and valued in economics) from perceptions of gender (Nelson, 1995, 2008). By doing so, economic theorising may come to illuminate economic realities rather than overly abstract from them.

Box 13.2: Gross domestic product: a Feminist critique

Waring's (1988) Feminist critique of our main measures of economic activity and progress, summarised in the measure of a country's Gross Domestic Product (GDP), has shone a light on how such aggregate accounting measures are underpinned by patriarchal values and a reality that has been constructed to reflect a certain, and quite limited, human experience. Waring's work begs us to ask: What does and does not count towards GDP? Who is doing the counting? And, what are the data used for?

Posing such questions immediately clarifies the ways in which work traditionally done by women has been left out of our measures of economic progress. Traditionally, work has been defined as paid economic activity linked to the market. Therefore, on the one hand, work that may be harmful to society, the environment or our health, such as the production of tobacco and pollution from factories, does count in our main measure of economic progress. On the other hand, unpaid care-giving work, traditionally carried out by women, is not deemed to have monetary value and is excluded from GDP accounting. As well as unpaid care-giving, subsistence production, informal employment and voluntary work are also excluded from internationally comparable GDP measures. Each of these activities is notably imbued with gender considerations (Beneria, 2003).

Since Waring's criticisms of national accounting practices and measures, progress has been made to at least measure the contributions made by women to the economy via satellite accounts derived from time-use surveys. However, such surveys are far from universal and work remains to be done to fundamentally shift our definitions of what it is to do productive work and what therefore should count at the aggregate level.

From Homo Economicus to New Institutional economics: mainstream approaches to gender and work

Let us begin by investigating the gender credentials of mainstream economics today. The Marginal revolution of the late nineteenth century brought with it the advent of economics as a scientific study of the optimisation of rational agents' choices under constraints (see Chapter 2). The unit of analysis was the individual or the firm. The behaviour of such entities could be predicated on the basis that they made decisions at the margin, to maximise their utility or profit, given constrained resources. The new economics limited its interest to marketed activities, or as Pigou (1920) put it: economics is concerned with 'that part of social welfare which can be brought directly or indirectly into relation with the measuring rod of money' (Pigou, 1920, p. 11).

As such, Neoclassical economists very quickly drew a distinction between time spent in 'productive' activities in the market sphere and time spent on any other activities outside the market sphere which could be counted as 'unproductive' or 'leisure' activities. Importantly this leaves out activities that cannot be accounted for using the measuring rod of money, including unpaid domestic work, subsistence production and the labour involved in reproducing individuals doing market work, both daily and generationally (see Box 13.2). Such activities instead are classed an unproductive or fall outside of the market sphere and are therefore classed as 'leisure' activities within the Neoclassical framing. The rational individual that lies at the heart of Neoclassical economics as it emerged in the late nineteenth century was most certainly male, making choices between work and leisure in an isolated social vacuum. As Nelson (1995, p. 135) succinctly summarises, 'economic man interacts in society without being influenced by society; his mode of interaction is through an ideal market in which prices form the only, and only necessary, form of communication' (Nelson, 1995, p. 135). To some degree, such assumptions about economic man were influenced by the economic reality of the nineteenth and early twentieth century (or at least that observed by a certain class of men). For example, in 1900, less than 20 per cent of American women worked for pay, with the traditional male breadwinner household being the norm. Such norms, however, mask a contrasting story based on colour, race and class, particularly in the United States, where the rate of labour force participation for women of colour was more than double that of their white counterparts in the late 1800s and early 1900s (Costa, 2000). However, economic reality began to shift over the course of the twentieth century, driven in a large part by the two world wars, and women in the United States, as well as Europe, increasingly participated in the formal labour market (Mincer, 1962). By the end of the century, female labour force participation in the United States had risen to 60 per cent (Costa, 2000). Within this changing reality, it is widely argued that Becker (1965, 1981), Schultz (1974, 1975) and Mincer (1962) were the first to challenge the prevailing orthodoxy in economics, pointing out the problems with treating the household and synonymous with the individual.

Becker and Schultz, among others, advocated the application of existing Neoclassical methods and tools to understanding decision-making and behaviour *within* the household or family unit. This allowed them to analyse subjects such as marriage, divorce and motherhood by extending rational choice economics to the realm of the family and to explain certain gendered phenomenon and gendered roles. In order to derive such explanations, they based their analysis on a number of simplifying assumptions that derived from standard Neoclassical economics (see Box 13.3) (see also Chapter 5). As will be shown, however, the development of the New Home Economics did not sufficiently tackle the economic realities relating to gender and the labour market that begun to emerge over the second half of the twentieth century. Only once New Institutional economic approaches were incorporated by the mainstream economics profession were issues such as persistent gender pay gaps and labour market discrimination analysed. We will return to these.

Box 13.3: Assumptions about the family in New Home Economics

- Households consume but also produce: each household or family is like a small firm, producing market and non-market outputs or services of value to the economy and to family members.
- Primary inputs into the family are the time of each family member.
- Household/family outputs include market goods and services (paid work outside the home) and non-market goods and services (unpaid work inside the home such as childcare, cleaning, cooking).
- Family members are rational utility-maximisers, maximising a joint household utility function.
- Resources (time and money) are scarce and choices are made under these resource constraints.
- Preferences are stable, interdependent and exogenous to the household.

Based on the assumptions in Box 13.3, the New Home Economists sought to answer questions such as why do couples marry and why do they divorce? Importantly, they also began to tackle questions in relation to work and labour markets. In particular, they sought to explain why women earned less than men in paid work and why women were more inclined to specialise in household work than men and why men specialised in higher-paying paid work? Their reasoning relied heavily on the human capital approach, which was then linked to an application of Smith's division of labour to the household. The reasoning proceeded as follows (see Mincer, 1962; Schultz, 1974).

To begin with, men and women's earnings and productivity are a reflection of their individual investment in human capital. Over their lifetime, on average women choose not to invest in the same amount or type of human capital as men, and further interrupt such investments by leaving the labour market to raise children, which is in turn reflected in their lower productivity and therefore lower relative pay. Such a human capital analysis can therefore explain why women are paid less than men and why they choose to work in specific 'lower-skilled' sectors, where their human capital is less likely to be depleted during their time out of the labour market, raising children.

The human capital approach is also used to explain the division of labour between paid and unpaid work within families (Becker, 1965). Based on the assumptions in Box 13.3, particularly that households are producers as well as consumers, individual household members should be allocated to activities according to their comparative or relative efficiencies so that ultimately joint household utility is maximised. This means that members of the household that are more efficient at market activities should specialise in these and household members more efficient at home production activities should specialise here. They can then pool the resources produced to maximise their joint household utility. How do we know which household member is more efficient at home or market production activities? The gender differences attributed to human capital investment discussed above and the outcomes of these in terms of differences in remuneration in market activities helps to explain why men end up specialising in market activities and women in home production activities.

The causes of the gap in earnings between men and women in market production activities were, until recently, left unexplored among mainstream economists. What matters to the division of labour within the household is the reality that such a gap in earnings exists and is exploited to determine who should specialise in home and market activities. The differences between men and women's earnings might be quite small and crucially either one may be more efficient at both market and home production, but once their comparative advantages are taken into account, a gendered division of labour still prevails. As Becker (1981, p. 39) summarises:

> biological differences in comparative advantage between the sexes explain not only why households typically have both sexes, but also why women have usually spent their time bearing and rearing children and engaging in other household activities, whereas men have spent their time in market activities. This sexual division of labor has been found in virtually all human societies, and in most other biological species that fertilize eggs within the body of the female.

Within mainstream economics, New Institutional approaches have been increasingly incorporated over the second half of the twentieth century. Issues relating to gender and work have not been left untouched by such developments within economics. In particular, the unanswered concerns over gender pay gaps and the shifting tide over women's increased labour market participation begged researchers to look beyond the New Home Economics for answers. North's (1991) and Williamson's (1993) foundations of the New Institutional Economic (NIE) have heralded a new era of attention on the role of institutions in shaping the context in which individual- or firm-level decisions are made. NIE still relies on a Neoclassical framework, considering how and why institutions matter to efficiency or competitive outcomes.

Applying such a framework to gender concerns has resulted in works that seek primarily to answer two open questions. These are, first, to explain rising female labour force participation rates; and, second, to explain occupational segregation and related gendered pay gaps in paid work.

Turning to the first of these, the rising female labour force participation rate in the United States and Europe, it has become clear that the Neoclassical explanation arising from the human capital approach falls dramatically short. Goldin's (2014) research has repeatedly shown that we must look beyond increases in educational attainment and the training of women to understand why women have entered the labour market as never before over the second half of the twentieth century. Filling this void, Oppenheimer (1970) turns to institutional factors to explain such gendered labour market changes. Oppenheimer's research, rather than relying solely on supply-side factors relating to education and training, also considers how changes on the demand side among firms and employers led to an increase in jobs specifically for women. She accepts the gendered segregation of jobs in the economy, seeing this as a result of societal institutions or norms that require a long time to change. Instead, her argument rests on the assumption that there has been a growing demand for female-specific jobs. One can see this as part of the wider shift towards the service-dominated economy in the United States and Europe and the movement away from manual work towards jobs requiring brain rather than brawn.

NEI-related work exploring the second question on labour market outcomes in relation to pay and occupation segregation is heavily influenced by the economics literature on discrimination in the context of asymmetric information (Goldin, 2014a, b). Bergmann's (1974) pioneering work in this area demonstrates that the underlying reason for the lower pay of women as compared to men does not result from rational choices to consume less human capital than men, but rather from discrimination among employers. Bergmann's overcrowding thesis takes the existence of discrimination between men and women (or for that matter discrimination based on race or ethnicity) as given and focuses on the consequences of such discrimination. Her work borrows concepts from Neoclassical economics, assuming that workers, whether male or female, are paid their marginal product of labour and that they are equally productive. Crucially, however, Bergmann drops the assumption of perfectly clearing, competitive labour markets, proposing instead that labour markets are segmented into female-dominated and male-dominated sectors.

Bergmann argues that, due to the existence of gender-based discrimination, women are restricted to a smaller pool of available jobs than men. As a result, women compete with each other over the small number of jobs available to them, pushing up the labour supply in these jobs and therefore causing the wage in these sectors to decrease. Men, unhampered by such discrimination, can 'freely choose the job they want' and face less competition from women in male-dominated sectors. This results in reducing labour supply in male-dominated sectors, in turn pushing up wages in these sectors. Bergmann's work, by doing away with the assumption that labour markets are perfectly competitive as in the original Neoclassical model, but instead understanding labour markets as segmented, provides a link between occupational segregation and the gender pay gap.

Questioning the mainstream approach to gender and work

Scrutinising the mainstream approach to incorporating gender into labour markets analysis brings out a number of concerns. Such concerns have been the starting point for Feminist economists to explore alternative explanations, including by delving into the history of economic thought (see below).

What clearly emerges from the discussion of the mainstream economics approach to gender and work is that the outcomes we observe in the real world, including the gender divisions of labour between domestic and paid work, the gender earnings gap, and occupational segregation along gender lines, are all explained by choices of rational agents. The approach implies that these outcomes can be sufficiently understood on the basis of individual, household or firm decision-making processes without the need to consider other factors that might bear on these outcomes. Yet there are a number of factors, including society's social and gender norms, that affect gendered decisions within the household and society at large (Folbre, 1997).

One persistent problem for the New Home Economics has been its inability to explain various paradoxical trends in relation to gender and the labour market. For example, the rise in female labour market participation over time is accounted for in the New Home Economics by assuming that there has been a redistribution of domestic work to other household members, most notably men, as well as technological advances within the home which have permitted women to take on additional paid work outside the home. However, Feminist economists have time and again shown that this has not occurred to the extent the theory would suggest. Instead we see rising double burdens of paid and unpaid work for women (England, 2005; Antonopoulos, 2009).

It is now apparent that the restrictive assumptions outlined in Box 13.2 concerning the way in which rational individuals and households make decisions are so abstracted from reality that ultimately they cannot explain very much at all (Kabeer, 1998). Indeed, the New Home Economics and its treatment of gender highlights how economics as a discipline has been open to the incorporation of gender in a very limited way. Precisely because of the weaknesses of the mainstream approach to understanding intra-household dynamics and broader structural features of the economy, a wide array of alternative household models have emerged within applied economics and Feminist economics. Those interested in reading further about such models should consult Agarwal's (1997) review as well as the overview by Himmelweit et al. (2013).

Despite such criticisms and the emergence of alternative household models, the New Home Economics remains a centrepiece of microeconomics, particularly in relation to the way in which it is taught at undergraduate level. Pollak (2003, p. 137) observes how:

> Gary Becker's influence on the economics of the family has been pervasive. His ideas have dominated research in the economics of the family, shaping the tools we use, the questions we ask, and the answers we give.

Given the issues raised with the New Home Economics and its failure to grapple with deeper issues around gender and work, it is worth assessing the merits of NEI-influenced approaches to gender and work. Waller and Jennings (1990) highlight that despite the availability of tools to incorporate gender into contemporary institutional analyses, Institutional economics (or rather the New Institutional Economics) remains hampered by the tools of mainstream economics, instead of pursuing the broader perspective of its institutional forefathers, which will be discussed below.

One major shortcoming of the NEI approach has been its lack of a dynamic analysis, i.e. of changes over time, as well as its neglect of the role of power in accounting for how gendered outcomes, determined by institutional norms, in turn influence the development of the economy or society more broadly. This is exemplified in the influential contributions of Bergmann (1974) and Oppenheimer (1970), which are unable to explain where segmented labour markets originate from and take the existence of discrimination within the labour market as given, rather than attempting to unpick this. Nonetheless, both Bergmann and Oppenheimer's research opened the door for other Feminist economists to question the concept of discrimination more deeply, arguing that 'labor market discrimination is a multi-dimensional interaction of economic, social, political, and cultural forces in both the workplace and the family, resulting in differential outcomes involving pay, employment, and status' (Figart, 1997, p. 7). As such, the NEI contributions did highlight the need for alternative policy prescriptions on the question of women and work. Instead of prescribing what women themselves could do to raise their human capital investment, the focus shifted to what companies and the state might need to do to address discrimination and gender biases in the workplace.

A further issue with both the New Home Economics and NEI approach has been their limited ability to see the bigger picture. For example, understanding gender outcomes in the labour market also requires an understanding of the nature and role of the state. Similarly, viewing the labour market as segmented along gender lines misses some other important segmentations (and their intersections), including those of class and race. Some of the concerns raised above pertaining to the bigger societal questions have been central to the analysis of the Classical political economists of the eighteenth and nineteenth centuries. Let us now revisit what they had to say in relation to gender, by first considering the Old Institutional thinkers, and, subsequently, the Classical political economists.

An Old Institutional economics contribution to our understanding of gender

Despite their name, the NIE perspective differs dramatically from the Old Institutional view of gender and work. In fact, the latter has more in common with sociology and anthropology than with the economists discussed above and proposes an understanding of gender that is much richer than that of their mainstream colleagues.

Veblen, the father of the Old Institutional Economics, addresses questions of gender implicitly, by considering economic realities as firmly rooted within social institutions and, not abstracting from these, as is the case with Neoclassical economics (both New Home Economics and the NEI). Decisions, behaviours and outcomes in relation to consumption, work and leisure do not emerge from individual rational choices, but are understood to be socially constructed (see Chapter 5). In Veblen's *Theory of the Leisure Class* (1899), patriarchy and societal gender norms are central in explaining how and what we consume (Gilman, 1999). Such gendered norms, for example, help to explain why 'conspicuous consumption' is often gendered, with women acting as proxies for their husbands in consuming conspicuously so that women, and particularly middle-class women,

> must appear to be idle in order to be respectable ... They have to supply not only the means of living, but also the means of advertising the fiction that they live without any gainful occupation; and they have to do all this while encumbered with garments specially designed to hamper their movements and decrease their industrial efficiency. (Veblen, 1894, p. 204)

While Veblen's ideas regarding consumption were insightful (see Chapter 5), his analysis of women in the workplace was given less attention. However, it has since been picked up by a number of Feminist economists who have deployed elements of his more dynamic institutional approach to understanding gendered labour market outcomes. They specifically root their discussion in a deeper understanding of power, in relation to both capitalism and patriarchy, and apply this to an understanding of gendered societal norms and how these relate to the labour market. This is exemplified by approaches that view the labour market itself as a gendered institution (Elson, 1999), which continuously embodies and transmits gender inequalities in a multitude of ways. Such approaches argue that such an understanding of economic interactions must be the starting point for any analysis of gendered labour market outcomes and policy decisions (Odebode and van Staveren, 2014).

Classical political economy, gender and work

It will come as no surprise to readers that the Classical political economists, by which we mean the likes of Smith, Marx and Ricardo, did not consider gender a central object of their analysis. However, to discard their contribution to our understanding of gender within economics is perhaps premature.

The Classical political economists were concerned with distribution as much as they were with production. Unlike their Neoclassical descendants, these *political* economists were concerned with very different questions than the optimisation of utility under constraints, including the nature and causes of the wealth of nations, its accumulation and distribution (Smith, 1776).

However, Smith had little to say about the role of women in fostering such wealth of nations. Indeed, his writings contributed to the division of spheres of interest among subsequent economists. As Pujol (1992, pp. 22–23) highlights: 'As the divisions between the public and private sphere, between the market and the home, between production and reproduction, are perfected, economic writings come to focus exclusively upon the first elements of these dichotomies.' The result has been that very little can be found in the writings of Classical political economists and their Neoclassical descendants that focuses on women, the domestic sphere or the relationship between reproductive and productive activities.

Notwithstanding these general remarks, economic historians (Pujol, 1992; Dimand et al., 2004) now concede that Smith's ideas on the 'women's question' was further developed than his official publications would suggest. A closer reading of his *Lectures on Jurisprudence* (Smith, 1762–64 [1978]) reveals the beginnings of a distinction between sex and gender, highlighting that there are innate differences between men and women but that 'the social significance of these forms of human diversity depends on the material and cultural character of society' (Dimand et al., 2004, p. 231). The overall argument for Smith was that the development of commerce and industry would improve the lot of women by increasing the importance of brains over brawn. The outcome of this would be that the innate differences between men and women would become less significant in a society built on commerce than in a predominantly peasant society.

Smith's ideas in relation to gender equality were not developed elsewhere in his economic writings and were halted by his death in 1790. It was therefore left to his students, such as Millar (1771 [2006]) and Mill (1869), to take these ideas forward. On the one hand, social conservatives such as Millar (1771 [2006]) were concerned with the potential implications of Smith's emancipatory view of economic development for women, arguing that if women gained economic freedom they would begin to demand the sexual freedoms enjoyed by men and that this could potentially undermine paternity and destroy the Victorian family unit (Dimand et al., 2004). On the other hand, libertarians such as Mill (1869) took a different stance. Together with his wife, Harriet Taylor, they were deeply concerned by the subjugation of women in Victorian society (Mill, 1869). Harriet Taylor's influence on her husband's writing (even to the point of some questioning the sole authorship of some of Mill's work [Pujol, 1992]) has been a subject of interest to a number of economic historians (Pujol, 1992; Bodkin, 1999). Mill and Taylor shared the view that the oppression of women was one of the few remaining relics from a previous period that severely impeded the progress of humanity:

> the principle which regulates the existing social relations between the two sexes – the legal subordination of one sex to the other- is wrong in itself, and now one of the chief hindrances to human improvement; ... it ought to be replaced by a principle of perfect equality, admitting no power or privilege on the one side, nor disability on the other. (Mill, 1869)

For Mill, three major aspects of women's lives prevented them from attaining full economic autonomy, namely the construction of society and its beliefs about gender; the level of education among women; and the institution of marriage. Mill and Taylor, in opposition to their Neoclassical offspring, for the first time expose the relationship between men and women for what it is – a power relationship in which women depend on men and are treated like children rather than autonomous beings. Such a treatment of women is seen within the home as much as within the labour force where women do not receive equal pay and where women's jobs are often overcrowded, leading to a further deterioration of pay (Mill, 1848, 1869).

Such an assessment of the situation of women in Victorian England was incredibly avant-garde for the nineteenth century. Despite these forthright views, when it came to recommendations for action, Mill and Taylor's ideas parted ways, with Mill's conclusions remaining embedded in his liberal Victorian and class bias. For Mill, marriage and employment remained incompatible for a woman. Instead he supported men receiving a family wage that in turn could support women to remain at home to take care of domestic duties. Taylor, however, argued that women should be permitted to enter the labour force with the same rights and responsibilities as men (for more on their differing views, see Pujol, 1992).

Mill's assessment falls short because it is littered with contradictions on his ideas about women and the family unit. As Pujol (1992, p. 36) succinctly concludes:

> The main weaknesses of Mill's liberalism in his parallel belief in the perfectability of the basic institutions of patriarchy (marriage and the family) and capitalism (private property) as evidenced by his declaration that none of these institutions have 'had a fair trial'. He fails to see that both systems rely on power relations, between classes and between the sexes, and are incompatible with equality.

Mill and Taylor's liberation stance on the question of women within society also met the disapproval of a number of political economists following in the footsteps of Marx, most notably Luxemburg, who saw the fight for women's suffrage, to which Mill and Taylor contributed, as a fight for bourgeois society women in opposition to working-class men. Luxemburg (1973) therefore viewed the bourgeois woman of her time as a 'parasite of a parasite' without considering her commonality with the proletarian woman who is the slave of a slave (MacKinnon, 1982, pp. 521–522).

Turning now to Marx himself, it is evident that he had little to say on the question of gender and women. However, his schema for understanding the capitalist mode of production and his labour theory of value were subsequently developed further from a gender perspective, particularly by Engels (1902), Luxemburg (1973) and Bebel (1910). Nonetheless, their treatment of questions relating to gender has been critiqued for its class-reductionism, assuming that, like race, ethnicity and other arenas of power relations, gender can be viewed as derivative of class relations (Albelda, 2001).

Engels (1902) argued that women's subordinate economic position derived from the social organisation of production rather than biology. In other words, the capitalist system was organised in such a way that it also fostered the subordination and exploitation of working-class women via their domestic work within the home. Engels and Bebel's solution to women's super-exploitation was the overthrowing of capitalism. This would result in women becoming full members of social reproduction, equal to men and 'women's equality would follow automatically when capitalist exploitation was removed' (Himmelweit, 1984, p. 169). For Bebel, the arrival of socialism had benefits for men and women equally: 'The "golden age" of which men have been dreaming, and for which they have been yearning for thousands of years, will come at last. Class rule will forever be at an end, and with it the rule of man over woman' (Bebel, 1910).

It is unfortunate that the mechanisms through which such an end to female exploitation within the home would occur were not fully developed by Engels or Bebel. As a result, they came under heavy criticism by feminists such as Hartmann (1979) who argued that such Marxist-rooted analysis is sex-blind by ignoring the importance of patriarchy and the dynamics that drive the 'rule of man over woman' that operate separately from the capitalist mode of production. Hence, the conclusion that the end of capitalism would also mark the liberation of women was one many feminists struggled to accept (Jefferson and King, 2001).

Feminist economists re-visit Marx

While Marx himself and those that directly followed his approach in the early twentieth century offered only a limited analysis of gender within the economic system and as a result failed to suggest fruitful solutions to persistent gender inequalities, Marx's approach was revisited by so-called Socialist feminists or Marxist feminists in the 1970s and 1980s and continues to be discussed today (Fraser, 2014). These feminists sought to revive and extend Marx's methodological approach, that of historical materialism, to shed light on women's oppression through their lived experiences.

Marxist feminists highlight that Marx's analysis of the exploitation of workers' labour power by capitalists, as the driving force of the capitalist mode of production, does not explain where such workers arise from and how they reproduce themselves. In other words, how are such workers able to survive daily? Who cleans their homes and clothes while they are working? Who purchases food and cooks their meals? Where does the next generation of workers emerge from? Clearly, the wage labour that the capitalist system relies on 'could not exist in the absence or housework, child-raising, schooling, affective care and a host of other activities which help to produce new generations of workers and replenish existing ones, as well as to maintain social bonds and shared understandings' (Fraser, 2014, p. 61).

A number of notable debates arise from these observations of Marxist feminists. The first of these relates to how domestic labour is incorporated in to a Marxist schema. For Delphy (1980), domestic labour can be viewed as a distinct mode of production in its own right rather than such labour contributing and coexisting with other forms of production under capitalism (or other modes of production) (Hartmann, 1979). Delphy (1980) continues by highlighting that, while it is possible for almost all of a housewife's services to be marketised and therefore theoretically abolished, domestic labour continues to persist precisely because it is unpaid and because it is provided by women. Given women's exploitation by men via the unpaid domestic work they conduct, Delphy is able to treat women as a distinct 'class' of their own, sharing in common their sex-based exploitation.

However, for many Marxist feminists such an analysis left more questions than answers, taking male power over women within the family unit as given, rather than questioning its origin and existence under different modes of production and social structures. The notion that housework could be viewed as a distinct mode of production with men and women as separate classes was also quickly dismissed, given the inability of such a mode of production to recreate itself independently. In other words, such 'housework' must coexist or be linked to some other mode of production, such as capitalism (Himmelweit, 1984).

A further important aspect of the debate originating from a Marxist tradition has centred on whether or not domestic labour can be viewed as being productive or whether it creates value and surplus value in the Marxist sense (Dalla Costa and James, 1975). Such questions led to debates beyond the academic realm including through campaigns such as the 'Wages for Housework' protests of the 1970s. The campaign argued that housework and domestic labour, by being unpaid, had reinforced the common assumption that it was not real work, thus not permitting women to struggle against it (Federici, 1975). By giving women a wage for their domestic labour contribution, the productive nature of this work would become recognised and, in turn, those involved in such work would increase their bargaining power as a collective in a similar vein to waged workers.

However, the campaign had to confront a number of concerns. On the one hand, the nature of domestic work as creating surplus value in the Marxist sense remains disputed. On the other hand, concerns were voiced over the payment of wages for housework as entrenching the gender-based division of labour rather than helping to overcome it (Himmelweit and Mohun, 1977).

More generally, the debate on domestic labour of the 1970s and 1980s, in attempting to build on Marx's framework, gave rise to further debate (Molyneux, 1979). For some, there was a disproportionate focus on women as housewives rather than acknowledging the increasing role of women as both waged labour and domestic workers (Coulson et al., 1975). For others, the role of the state was not sufficiently clarified, while the catch-all term of 'domestic labour' was too general to allow for a thorough understanding of what aspects of care-giving and domestic work bear on women's lives (Fine, 1992).

Despite some concerns over specific debates stemming from Marx's writing, the contribution of Marxist broader thinking to Feminist economics needs to be emphasised. In particular, Marx's historical materialist approach that emphasises real, socially and historically conditioned contexts and focuses on issues of the production and reproduction of everyday life, is a particular approach shared by Feminist political economists. While the focus for Marx was on class relations, such an approach also lends itself to an analysis of other power relations in society, including gendered social relationships. In the context of rapidly changing global and local conditions, understanding how such changes shape gender relations and women's lived experiences remains strongly relevant and important. As such, Feminist political economists increasingly analyse other categories alongside gender and do not consider gender the sole purpose or lens for their analysis.

The policy conclusions drawn from Feminist political economists, following Marx's political economy approach, in relation to gender and work, tend to be context-specific, focusing not only on gender dimensions but also on how these intersect with a number of other social categories, including class, race and ethnicity. They tend to demonstrate the importance of the state and public policies in playing a part in outcomes in relation to gender and work and bring unpaid caring work to the forefront of analysis, emphasising that these are currently left ignored or poorly understood by mainstream economic theories (Elson, 2008; De Henau et al., 2010; Bargawi et al., 2017).

Marx's understanding of knowledge as historically and socially determined has been of particular importance to Feminist economists, who have shone a light on economics as an academic subject and raised concerns over the continued gender-blindness of mainstream economics. These methodological influences are perhaps the most important contribution of Classical political economy, and specifically Marx's analysis, to Feminist economics.

Conclusions

This chapter has concerned itself with the question of gender in the history of economic thought by focusing, in particular, on issues in relation to women and work, given the rich debates and discussion this subject has evoked among economists old and new.

The chapter begun with establishing a clear distinction between sex and gender and demonstrated the need for economics to address gender. The chapter proceeded to outline the orthodox or mainstream incorporation of gender. It did so by tracing the shift from Neoclassical economics to the New Home Economics and from there to New Institutional approaches to gender in the labour market.

The subsequent section discussed some of the concerns with these standard approaches and invited us to consider whether alternative approaches from the history of economic thought would help address these shortcomings. The chapter therefore went on to discuss two broad strands of alternative approaches. The first was the Old Institutionalist perspective on issues of gender. Second, we turned to Classical political economy and strands of Marxist feminist scholarship that it gave rise to. In both cases we offered a critical discussion, demonstrating the importance these alternative methods play in fostering new ways of answering questions and proposing alternative policy solutions in relation to gender and work.

Discussion questions and seminar activities

- 'The Gender Pay gap only exists because women 'choose' professions that are less well paid.' Evaluate this statement using the different theoretical approaches discussed in the chapter.
- To what extent do you think that 'Wages for Housework' would address contemporary gender issues?
- Compare and contrast the Marxian and Neoclassical approaches to gender and the care economy.

References

Agarwal, B. (1997). 'Bargaining' and gender relations: Within and beyond the household. *Feminist Economics, 3*(1), 1–51.

Albelda, R. (2001). Marxist political economics. In J. Peterson & M. Lewis (Eds.), *The Elgar companion to feminist economics* (pp. 536–544). Cheltenham/Northampton: Edward Elgar.

Antonopoulos, R. (2009). *The unpaid care work – Paid work connection*. ILO Working Paper, 86.

Bargawi, H., Cozzi, G., & Himmelweit, S. (2017). *Economics and austerity in Europe: Gendered impacts and sustainable alternatives*. Oxford: Routledge.

Barker, D. K. (2001). Gender. In J. Peterson & M. Lewis (Eds.), *The Elgar companion to feminist economics* (pp. 390–396). Cheltenham/Northampton: Edward Elgar.

Barker, D. K., & Feiner, S. (2004). *Liberating economics: Feminist perspectives on families, work and globalization*. Ann Arbor: University of Michigan Press.

Bebel, A. (1910). *Women and socialism*. New York: Socialist Literature Company.

Becker, G. (1965). A theory of the allocation of time. *Economic Journal, LXXX(200)*, 493–517.

Becker, G. (1981). *A treatise on the family*. Cambridge, MA: Harvard University Press.

Beneria, L. (2003). *Gender, development and globalization: Economics as if all people mattered*. New York/Abingdon: Routledge.

Bergmann, B. (1974). Occupational segregation, wages and profits when employers discriminate by race or sex. *Eastern Economic Journal, 1*(2), 103–110.

Bodkin, R. G. (1999). Women's agency in classical economic thought: Adam Smith, Harriet Taylor Mill, and J. S. Mill. *Feminist Economics, 5*(1), 45–60.

Costa, D. L. (2000). From mill town to board room: The rise of women's paid labor. *Journal of Economic Perspectives, 14*(4), 101–122.

Coulson, M., Magas, B., et al. (1975). The housewife and her labour under capitalism – A critique. *New Left Review, 90*, 59–71.

Dalla Costa, M., & James, S. (1975). *The power of women and the subversion of the community*. Bristol: Falling Wall Press.

De Henau, J., Meulders, D., et al. (2010). Maybe baby: Comparing partnered women's employment and child policies in the EU-15. *Feminist Economics, 16*(1), 43–77.

Delphy, C. (1980, Summer). The main enemy. *Feminist Issues*, pp. 23–40.

Dimand, R. W., Forget, E. L., et al. (2004). Gender in classical economics. *Journal of Economic Perspectives, 18*(1), 229–240.

Elson, D. (1999). Labour markets as gendered institutions: Equality, efficiency and empowerment issues. *World Development, 27*(3), 611–627.

Elson, D. (2008). *The three R's of unpaid work: Recognition, reduction and redistribution*. Expert group meeting on unpaid work, economic development and human well-being. New York: United Nations Development Programme.

Engels, F. (1902). *Origins of the family, private property and the state*. Chicago: Charles H. Kerr & Co..

England, P. (2005). Gender inequality in labor markets: The role of motherhood and segregation. *Social Politics: International Studies in Gender, State & Society, 12*(2), 264–288.

Federici, S. (1975). *Wages against housework*. New York: Power of Women Collective and Falling Wall Press.

Figart, D. M. (1997). Gender as more than a dummy variable: Feminist approaches to discrimination. *Review of Social Economy, 55*(1), 1–32.

Fine, B. (1992). *Women's employment and the capitalist family*. Oxford: Routledge.
Folbre, N. (1997). Gender coalitions: Extra family influences on intrafamily inequality. In H. Alderman, L. Haddad, & J. Hoddinot (Eds.), *Intrahousehold allocation in developing countries* (pp. 263–274). Baltimore: Johns Hopkins University Press.
Fraser, N. (2014). Behind Marx's hidden abode: For an expanded conception of capitalism. *New Left Review, 86*, 55–72.
Gilman, N. (1999). Thorstein Veblen's neglected feminism. *Journal of Economic Issues, 33*(3), 689–711.
Goldin, C. (2014a). A grand gender convergence: Its last chapter. *American Economic Review, 104*(4), 1091–1119.
Goldin, C. (2014b). A pollution theory of discrimination: Male and female differences in occupations and earnings. In L. P. Boustan, C. Frydman, & R. A. Margo (Eds.), *Human capital in history: The American record* (pp. 313–348). Chicago: University of Chicago Press.
Hartmann, H. (1979). The unhappy marriage of Marxism and feminism: Towards a more progressive union. *Capital & Class, 3*(2), 1–33.
Himmelweit, S. (1984). The real dualism of sex and class. *Review of Radical Political Economics, 16*(1), 167–183.
Himmelweit, S., & Mohun, S. (1977). Domestic labour and capital. *Cambridge Journal of Economics, 1*, 15–31.
Himmelweit, S., Santos, C., et al. (2013). Sharing of resources within the family and the economics of household decision-making. *Journal of Marriage and Family, 75*(3), 625–639.
Jefferson, T., & King, J. E. (2001). Never intended to be a theory of everything: Domestic labor in Neoclassical and Marxian economics. *Feminist Economics, 7*(3), 71–101.
Kabeer, N. (1998). Jumping to conclusions. In C. Jackson & R. Pearson (Eds.), *Feminist visions of development: Gender analysis and policy* (pp. 91–107). London/New York: Routledge.
Luxemburg, R. (1973). *Gesammelte Werke*. Berlin: Dietz.
MacKinnon, C. A. (1982). Feminism, Marxism, method, and the state: An agenda for theory. *Signs, 7*(3), 515–544.
Mill, J. S. (1848). Principles of political economy. In W. J. Ashley (Ed.), *Principles of political economy with some of their applications to social philosophy*. London: Longmans, Green and Co.
Mill, J. S. (1869). *Subjection of women*. London: Longmans, Green, Reader and Dyer.
Millar, J. (1771 [2006]). The origin of the distinction of ranks. In A. Garrett (Ed.), *The works and correspondence of John Millar*. Indianapolis: Liberty Fund.
Mincer, J. (1962). *Labor force participation of married women: A study of labor supply*. Aspects of labor economics. National Bureau Committee for Economic Research. Princeton: Princeton University Press.
Molyneux, M. (1979). Beyond the domestic labour debate. *New Left Review, 116*, 3–27.
Nelson, J. (1995). Feminism and economics. *The Journal of Economic Perspectives, 9*(2), 131–148.
Nelson, J. (2008). Feminist economics. In S. N. Durlauf & L. E. Blume (Eds.), *The new Palgrave dictionary of economics*. London: Palgrave Macmillan.
North, D. C. (1991). Institutions. *Journal of Economic Perspectives, 5*(1), 97–112.
Odebode, O., & van Staveren, I. (2014). Feminist development economics: An institutional approach to household analysis. In C. Verschuur, I. Guérin, & H. Guétat-Bernard (Eds.), *Under development: Gender* (pp. 103–126). London: Palgrave Macmillan UK.

Oppenheimer, V. (1970). *The female labor Force in the United States: Demographic and economic factors governing its growth and changing composition*. Berkeley: University of California.

Pigou, A. (1920). *The economics of welfare*. London: Macmillan.

Pollak, R. (2003). Gary Becker's contributions to Family and household economics. *Review of Economics of the Household, 1*(1), 111–141.

Pujol, M. A. (1992). *Feminism and anti-feminism in early economic thought*. Brookfield: Edward Elgar.

Schultz, T. (1974). *The economics of the family*. Chicago: University of Chicago Press.

Schultz, T. (1975). The value of the ability to deal with disequilibria. *Journal of Economic Literature, 13*(3), 827–846.

Smith, A. (1762–64 [1978]). Lectures on jurisprudence. In R. L. Meek, D. D. Raphael, & P. G. Stein (Eds.), Glasgow edition of the works and correspondence of Adam Smith. Oxford: Clarendon Press.

Smith, A. (1776). *An inquiry into the nature of causes of the wealth of nations*. Oxford: Clarendon Press.

Veblen, T. (1894). The economic theory of woman's dress. *Popular Science Monthly, 46*(November), 198–205.

Veblen, T. (1899). *The theory of the leisure class*. London: Macmillan.

Waller, W., & Jennings, A. (1990). On the possibility of a feminist economics: The convergence of institutional and feminist methodology. *Journal of Economic Issues, 24*(2), 613–622.

Waring, M. (1988). *If women counted: A new feminist economics*. San Francisco: Harper Collins.

Williamson, O. E. (1993). *The economic analysis of institutions and organisations – In general and with respect to country studies*. Economics Department Working Papers No. 133, pp. 1–75. Paris: OECD.

World Health Organisation. (2001). *Transforming health systems: Gender and rights in reproductive health: A training manual for health managers*. Geneva: WHO.

World Health Organisation. (2006). *Defining sexual health: Report of a technical consultation on sexual health, 28–31 January 2002, Geneva*. Geneva: WHO.

14 HOW DOES ECONOMICS ADDRESS THE ENVIRONMENT?

Ben Groom and Marta Talevi

Introduction to environmental and resource economics

The study of Environmental and Resource Economics (ERE) is often seen as a new and emerging discipline in social science. However, looking back at some of the seminal writings from the Classical political economists of the eighteenth and nineteenth centuries, and at related works in sociology, political science and philosophy, it becomes clear that the scarcity and exploitation of natural and environmental resources has long been a central theme of discourses on well-being, development and the wealth of nations. Indeed, many of the names discussed in what follows, who have historically been regarded as among the leading thinkers of environmental and natural resource economics, will already be familiar from other chapters in this volume. As Heal (2007) points out, ERE is interdisciplinary by its very nature, and has always been highly permeable to the other branches of economics, borrowing and lending ideas, theoretical models, methodologies and empirical contributions, so that the boundaries of the disciplines are often blurred.

ERE is composed of two methodologically distinct sub-disciplines, environmental economics and natural resource economics, which analyse natural resources, nature and the environment from different starting points and through different methodological lenses. Another important distinction in the economic study of the environment and resources is between environmental and resource economics, on the one hand, and *ecological* economics, on the other. The former takes Neoclassical economic theory as its departure point, and characterises environmental and resource issues within this framework. It largely sees the environment as an input to economic activity. Ecological economics, on the other hand, has its methodological departure more firmly rooted in ecology, seeing the economic system as part of a larger environment–economy–society nexus. Broadly speaking, ERE sees the environment as part of the economic system and emphasises market failures as the cause of environmental degradation and overexploitation. Ecological economics, by contrast, sees the economy as part of an overarching ecological system and emphasises ecological and physical limits to growth as the key concerns. The former argue for regulation to correct of market (and government) failures within the current economic system. The latter argue for a realignment of the economy to match ecological and physical boundaries of ecosystems and, more broadly, the planet. Table 14.1 attempts to draw some broad comparisons between these different approaches. In practice, these different perspectives generate a certain amount of disagreement on matters of methods and, ultimately,

Table 14.1 The sub-disciplines of the study of environment and economics

	Natural resource economics	**Environmental economics**	**Ecological economics**
Methodological departure point	Neoclassical growth economics	Welfare economics and the analysis of market failures	Integrates elements of natural sciences, social sciences and humanities.
Lens	Population ecology (resource management), i.e. interested in the dynamics (i.e. behaviour over time) of interacting population, while rest of the ecosystem is given, exogenous	Ecosystem ecology, i.e. 'biotic and abiotic processes which underlie various ecosystem functions' (Dasgupta, 1996), the ecosystem is not given but is the main object of study	Ecology of the economy–society–environment nexus Systemic interactions
Topics of concern	Bioeconomic models, e.g. dynamic models to study the interaction of predator-prey (or, in this case, population-natural resource) systems; Dynamic harvesting rules, e.g. Hotelling rule for the optimal extraction of non-renewable resources; forestry, fishery and aquifer management	Environmental pollution and externalities, valuation of environment, (use, non-use values) for CBA and policy. E.g. Health and amenity value of nature, water and air quality, landscape amenities, noise and economic effects of climate change	Tipping points and ecological thresholds, i.e. non-linear ecological processes, scarcity and irreplaceability of certain goods and services
Aims	Determine optimal harvest/extraction rate of a resource given different institutional settings, such as open/closed access to the resource, property-rights regime (e.g. Gordon, 1954), harvest costs, harvesters' time preferences (i.e. discount), etc.	Determine the effects of economic activities (i.e. technology and productivity, costs and revenues, time preferences) on ecosystems (e.g. Stern, 2007 for climate change). Inform instruments to correct market failures	Consider the energy and materials inflows and outflows and the biophysical limits that socio-economic systems must respect as key components of the analysis
Focus of analysis, i.e. state (or stock) variables	Quantities, such as biomass for forests, population size, sub-soil mineral and oil stock, stock pollutants such as CO_2 Divisible resources, which can be allocated at the margin (barrels of oil, tons of fish, cubic m of water, etc.)	Quality indices, such as air, soil, water quality measures, or other indices referring to the provision of ecosystem services Indivisible ecosystem services, which can be examined at the margin in terms of quality but not quantity: life support, climate regulation, aesthetic benefits	Bi-products and irreversibility of production processes, distinction between strong and weak sustainability. Zero growth dynamics

Source: Based on Dasgupta (1996) and Perman (2003)

policy. One key area of disagreement concerns the ability of technological change to relax ecological constraints and de-couple growth and environment. Nevertheless, there is also a great deal of overlap between environmental, natural resource and ecological economists, who often share similar objectives in emphasising the importance of environment, ecology and resources as determinants of long-term well-being. This chapter focuses on ERE and discusses ecological economics as an *alternative* approach.

The origins of ERE and its framing as a separate discipline are moot. Some argue that ERE became a discipline on its own after the Second World War, driven by the emergence of the ideologies of environmentalism and the ecological movement. Indeed, it was in the post-war period that economists started in earnest to formalise environmental and resource problems using what would become the mainstream marginalist methodologies of general equilibrium theory and dynamic optimisation techniques and optimal control. In many ways this reflects the interaction of tools and problems that tends to be a characteristic of Neoclassical economics, as pointed out by Sandmo (2015) through the words of Koopmans (1957, 170): 'The solution of important problems may be delayed because the requisite tools are not perceived. Or the availability of certain tools may lead to an awareness of problems, important or not, that can be solved with their help.' The rise of ERE in the post-war period was also driven by emerging issues of scarcity and degradation. Difficulties in sourcing materials such as food, fuels and metals during the Second World War made clear that they are both essential and scarce. Later on in the twentieth century, key events such as the energy crises of the 1970s and 1980s triggered a further interest in growth in a context of exhaustible resources. Similarly in the 1990s, the damage litigation which followed the *Exxon Valdez* oil spill in Alaska re-orientated the academic and policy focus towards valuing non-use values (see Chapter 9) for the environment for the purposes of estimating liability and informing Cost–Benefit Analysis (CBA) more generally.

Yet many point to the early 1950s, the foundation of Resources For the Future (RFF) in Washington DC, and the US President's Materials Policy Commission – also known as the 'Paley Commission' – as the starting point for ERE. This commission directed its interest towards the dynamics of agricultural resources, mineral reserves and energy supply whose importance for the economy and potential scarcity had emerged during the Second World War. During this period the traditional view of natural resources as a 'free gift', a view taken inter alia by Marx (1894, Vol. III, Part VI, ch. 44), was replaced by a narrative of scarcity. Natural resources therefore started to be considered as scarce economic goods to be managed carefully, in order to maximise human welfare. On the environmental side, the growing environmentalist movement, and important publications such as Carson's *Silent Spring* (1962), typified the growing realisation of the impact of industrial practices, particularly in agriculture, on the environmental quality. Economists framed these pervasive impacts as environmental *externalities,* which had hitherto been thought of as minor aberrations to the economic system. The term 'environmental economics' begins to be used at this time, and the theoretical consolidation of the subject followed in the 1970s, when environmental and natural resource economics finally came of age (Pearce, 2002; Heal, 2007).

Compared to this timeline, Heal (2007) moves the starting date a few decades backwards and points to Hotelling's seminal article on 'The Economics of Exhaustible

Resources' as the first analytical article in the field (Hotelling, 1931). Sandmo (2015) argues instead that even if the subject reached its maturity only in the twentieth century, the 'true beginnings' of the subject can be traced as far back as the eighteenth century and the Classics.

In this chapter we delve further into these historical matters and paint a picture of the historical roots of ERE and the frontiers that this sub-discipline is currently pushing. The following section summarises the early works on environment and resource issues. Subsequent sections explain how the Neoclassical paradigm mainly ignored nature in its early models, but nonetheless provided a basis for the formalisation of both environmental and natural resource economics in the 1970s, drawing from growth theory and welfare/public economics. Alternative perspectives and critiques are then discussed before we illustrate the impact that ERE has had on policy in recent years (Box 14.2), most notably in relation to pollution regulation, sustainable development and climate change.

Classical approaches to the environment

In the early history of economic thought, natural resources and the environment in general were a more prominent part of the discourse than would be the case in later years. During the Industrial Revolution agriculture and mining still made up the lion's share of the economy, and natural resources were consequently an important focal point for economics. Yet because natural resources such as land and minerals were very much seen as a 'free gift of nature to capital' (see e.g. Marx, 1894, Vol. III, Part VI, ch. 44), the methodological approach was very different. Analysis was mostly limited to agriculture and to the theory of price formation, while the concepts of externalities, market failures and resource management, which form the basis for ERE today, were absent. Contrary to the early Neoclassical theories, in which natural inputs were mainly ignored, the Classics did consider natural resources as an integral part of the wealth and growth of countries. Notions of scarcity at this point revolved around the idea that resources were finite and, particularly with regard to land, subject to diminishing returns to scale. Hence many Classical discourses tended to advance the idea that growth could not continue forever, and would eventually converge towards a (subsistence) stationary state. However, the way in which resources were discussed in this early period of economic thought varied considerably among the chief thinkers of the time.

An important exception to Smith's invisible hand theorem was his acknowledgement of market failures for certain goods and services, and the role of government to correct these failures. In relation to what economists now know as public goods, Smith (1776, Vol. I, Book V, Ch. 1, Part 3) wrote:

> the duty of the sovereign or commonwealth is that of erecting and maintaining those public institutions and those public works, which, though they may be in the highest degree advantageous to a great society, are, however, of such a nature that the profit could never repay the expense to any individual or small number of individuals.

These principles are at the core of ERE today. Twenty years later, Malthus' "Essay on the Principle of Population" (Malthus, 1798) focused on the dynamic interaction of population and resource scarcity in the context of agricultural production. The nexus between environment, natural resources and population growth, and its emphasis on ecological ideas of carrying capacity and limits to growth, remain key perspectives in ERE and in ecological economics today. Indeed, it is the distinction between the ideas attributed to Malthus and those of Ricardo that better reflect the differences between the latter day ERE and ecological economics disciplines. Ricardo's *Principles of Political Economy and Taxation* (1817) shifts the focus from the limits of the physical environment towards how to best use it by introducing technological change, and thereby developing a theory of growth. Ricardo formalised the concept of a 'steady state' in which environmental quality and well-being were maintained. The ideas of Malthus and Ricardo resurfaced in the 1970s when population growth and limits to growth became a renewed concern. Ricardo's notion of resource rents remains a crucial concept in the study of scarcity in natural resource economics.

In the work of **Mill**, one of the founding fathers of Utilitarianism, are found the philosophical underpinnings of mainstream economics and welfare economics. In the context of ERE, Mill's *Principles of Political Economy* (1848) discusses public and common-pool resources, and the importance of well-specified rights and institutions to regulate their use. Of natural resources in general, Mill (1848, Book V, ch. 1) wrote:

> These are the inheritance of the human race, and there must be regulations for the common enjoyment of it. What rights, and under what conditions, a person shall be allowed to exercise over any portion of this common inheritance cannot be left undecided. No function of government is less optional than the regulation of these things, or more completely involved in the idea of civilized society.

So Mill's work is echoed in one of the essential themes of ERE: intergenerational justice and sustainable economic development, which are still debated at length today. Also noteworthy is Mill's focus on the use and allocation of resources rather than on the limits emphasised by previous thinkers. This position was influenced no doubt by the rapid technical innovation and scientific progress, e.g. in the use of fossil fuels and in agricultural production, as well as more intense exploitation of the colonies, which appeared to make the issue of the limits to growth less urgent. At the same time, Mill makes some of the first references to environment as a source of recreation and amenity, values which should be balanced against their use as inputs in industrial production in the pursuit of long-term happiness (Mill, 1848, book IV, ch. 6, section 2):

> Nor is there much satisfaction in contemplating the world with ... scarcely a place left where a wild shrub or flower could grow without being eradicated as a weed in the name of improved agriculture. If the earth must lose that great portion of its pleasantness ... for the mere purpose of enabling it to support a larger, but not a better or a happier population, I sincerely hope, for the sake of posterity, that they will be content to be stationary, long before necessity compels them to it.

Interpretations of Marx's relationship with the environment range from his being anti-ecological to being considered one of the precursors of the discussion on sustainability and ecological economics (Foster, 1997, 1999). Marx's theory on the environment revolves around the idea that capitalist production creates an 'irreparable rift in the interdependent process of social metabolism' (Marx, *Capital*, Vol. III). The growing divide between town and country, and between colonies and the centre of the empires, means that, on one side, nature is exploited and robbed of its minerals, trees, and soil nutrients, and on the other, cities are polluted by the waste resulting from a production process centred on unrestrained consumerism. Marx therefore stresses the physical limits of the environment and encourages a reduction in consumption alongside re-use and recycling ('Utilization of the Refuse of Production' in Vol. III of *Capital*). The radical roots of the green movement and some aspects of ecological economics have been influenced by these ideas. Marx's contributions on environment reflect the industrial and demographic issues of the time, referring to agriculture, mining, pollution and deforestation, culminating in a discussion of the physical limits of the environment due to demographic pressure. Marx was also more specific than other classical thinkers in relation to the role of technological change, noting that it can be at the same time both beneficial to the environment – mentioning the growth of the fertiliser industry and the revolution in organic chemistry – and harmful – as in the case of the accelerating depletion of the soil, pollution and deforestation. Marx is unsurprisingly in opposition to Mill on the role of property rights in sustaining resource use in the long run, stating: 'private land-ownership, appears as a barrier to production itself ... exploitation and squandering of the vitality of the soil ... takes the place of conscious rational cultivation of the soil as eternal communal property, an inalienable condition for the existence and reproduction of a chain of successive generations of the human race' (Marx, 1894, *Capital*, Vol. III, Part VI, ch. 47). As for other problems of society, this unsustainability, according to Marx, would not be addressed by the blind forces of the market, but rather needs central planning and State intervention. According to other interpretations, Marx's conception of nature was instead generally anti-ecological, and *de facto* still permeated with the same idea of his predecessors of natural resources as a 'free gift of nature' (Marx, 1894, *Capital*, Vol. III, Part VI, ch. 44), whose value is merely instrumental to human welfare (e.g. Clark, 1989). Sometimes the environmental exploitation of the Soviet Union in the twentieth century is used as evidence for this position, albeit unfairly.

Towards the end of the nineteenth century, important changes occurred in the economics discipline. The labour theory of value, typical of Classical economics, now had to compete with a theory of value formation based on relative scarcity and the forces of demand and supply (see Chapter 9). The analysis of the demand side of economics began to flourish in this period, and the theory of utility maximisation, rooted in the utilitarianism philosophical framework, laid the foundational pillar for the development of welfare economics. Marginal analysis and mathematical formalisation became the dominant methodology (see Chapter 3), and the Marginalist revolution was under way.

With regard to the environment and natural resources, rapid economic growth in the West eclipsed the narratives on scarce resources and fixed land that had characterised previous periods. As a result, land and natural resources disappeared altogether from the analysis of production. Marshall's 'Principles of Economics' (Marshall, 1890) marks the shift from political economy toward the formalisation of economics, a defining feature of the Neoclassical period. Importantly, Marshall formulated the concept of 'external economies and diseconomies' – or externalities. Yet, Marshall's interest was mainly in positive externalities of industrial agglomeration, rather than the negative externalities associated with pollution, but the same important conclusion was reached: 'in the presence of externalities, the competitive equilibrium will no longer be socially efficient, … no longer maximise social surplus' (Marshall, 1890). In other words, markets fail to reflect social value, leading to under-supply of goods, and over-supply of bads. This is the language of modern ERE.

Neoclassical approaches to environmental and natural resource economics

Neoclassical environmental economics: welfare economics, externalities and missing markets

Building on the consequentialist Utilitarian objectives of Bentham and Mill, and using mathematical tools introduced by the Marginalists, Neoclassical economists led by Pareto started exploring how resources should be allocated in order to maximise social welfare: the aggregation of individual utilities in society.

In particular, Pigou – Marshall's successor at Cambridge – further developed the theory of externalities, analysing many issues typical of environmental economics, such as pollution and forests' carbon storage services (Pigou, 1920, Part II, ch. IX, paragraph 11):

> Uncompensated services are rendered when resources are invested in private parks in cities; for these, even though the public is not admitted to them, improve the air of the neighbourhood … It is true, in like manner, of resources devoted to afforestation, since the beneficial effect on climate often extends beyond the borders of the estates owned by the person responsible for the forest … It is true of resources devoted to the prevention of smoke from factory chimneys: for this smoke in large towns inflicts a heavy uncharged loss on the community, in injury to buildings … and in many other ways.

Importantly, Pigou advanced the possibilities of using fiscal instruments, such as taxes and subsidies, to correct the resulting inefficiency in the allocation of resources. The 'Pigouvian' tax remains a key instrument in the ERE toolkit today despite, as recognised by Pigou himself, the application of this theoretical prescription into the real world may be less straightforward than it sounds due to government/institutional failures, or pure political economy arguments (e.g. lobbying, transactions costs).[1]

Pigou's arguments were made in a partial equilibrium framework, as were Marshall's before him. Years later, the landmark paper entitled 'Existence of an Equilibrium for a Competitive Economy' by Arrow and Debreu (1954) heralded the era of general equilibrium analysis and the pinnacle of Neoclassical formal analysis. In the subsequent years, welfare economics mainly focused on the conditions that need to hold to make sure that the exchanges that occur in a competitive market economy would result in a socially optimal allocation of the available resources (first and second theorems of the welfare economics). Yet of more concern for ERE were the failures of the first and second welfare theorems in the presence of externalities, public goods and non-convexities. In this sense, Arrow's work ultimately exposes the limitations of the welfare theorems, and arguably lead to ERE becoming established as a separate subdiscipline in later years.[2] ERE, however, draws substantially from the utilitarian and welfarist theoretical background, including welfare-maximising policies to correct market failures, and willingness to pay measures based on utility theory to value non-marketed environmental resources. Environmental issues have been translated into problems of missing markets and externalities, with a perfectly functioning market held up as the ideal benchmark. Indeed, the existence of Pigouvian taxes in the current toolkit of ERE relies in part on Baumol (1972; see also Baumol and Oates, 1988), who showed their corrective, welfare-enhancing properties in the context of general equilibrium. The Neoclassical paradigm has also shaped early environmental economics by framing the way of thinking about environmental issues in an anthropocentric way, as a matter of maximisation of human welfare.

The formal nature of Neoclassical economics tended to conceal the ethical and moral legacy stemming from the consequentialist Utilitarian ethical framework. Within environmental economics, however, as opposed to say trade or labour economics, ethical issues have often been central to the debate, and the limitations of consequentialist arguments, the ethical underpinnings of willingness to pay, and the longer-term ethics associated with climate change, sustainability and other long-term issues that raise issues of inter-generational equity, are typically not too far from the surface.

The Coase theorem

The field of law and economics developed alongside Neoclassical economics and became concerned with the legal and institutional issues associated with externalities. In his 1960 publication, 'The Problem of Social Cost', Coase recognised that the reciprocal nature of externalities implies that market-based mechanisms could be leveraged to address the problem (Coase, 1960). In the case of pollution, for example, it is possible to find a polluter willing to pay something in order to continue production or to accept something in order to forego production and therefore emissions, and a victim of pollution willing to pay to stop the emissions and willing to accept compensation for bearing with them. The resulting 'Coase Theorem'[3] thus says that provided property rights are well-specified, and there are no transaction costs, market exchanges will converge towards the efficient outcome, i.e. the right to pollute will end up with the party who values it the most, regardless of whether the rights were initially endowed with the polluters or with the victims of pollution. That is to say, external effects would be fully internalised with no need for government's intervention, at least as far as efficiency is at stake – distributional concerns are a different matter, not explicitly addressed.

The key assumptions of the theorem are the presence of well-specified property rights and the absence of transaction costs that may therefore prevent bargaining. Indeed, Coase cautions about considering State intervention as a panacea for every market failure, as in the real world government's actions are hardly ever costless or flawless: governments may fail as well as markets. On top of the costs required for the functioning of the bureaucratic machine, the government may have less information than affected parties, may suffer from principal–agent problems, lobbying, corruption and vested interests. The strategic considerations of the election cycle, or a lack of authority and legitimacy may also hinder policy. Even costless intervention may prompt negative and unintended second-order effects (defined as 'legalized nuisances' by Coase) which could result in a situation worse than the initial status quo. So for precisely the political economy reasons mentioned by Pigou, Coase argued that defining property rights and allowing them to be exchanged between polluter and pollutee could well be the most effective way to internalise environmental externalities.

Cost–benefit analysis and non-market valuation

But what should we do when transaction costs are non-negligible and both market and institutional failures are likely? Using the framework established in welfare economics, Cost–Benefit Analysis has become one of the main tools to compare different policies and projects in terms of individual preferences. Already used in an intuitive form in the past,[4] a full-fledged theory was later formalised by Kaldor and Hicks in 1939 (Hicks, 1939; Kaldor, 1939). Although developed independently from environmental considerations, early applications were indeed in the field of environmental conservation and natural resource management. Krutilla and Eckstein's *Multipurpose River Development* and Eckstein's *Water resource development – the economics of project evaluation*, both from 1958 (Eckstein, 1958; Krutilla and Eckstein, 1958), are just two notable examples. Similarly, today's pollution control policies are determined by comparing the costs of emission abatement and the damages from pollution.

One of the main difficulties in environmental Cost–Benefit Analysis is to put a monetary value on goods and services for which a market, and therefore a price tag, does not exist (see also Chapter 9). In this direction, non-market valuation is probably one of the main contributions of environmental economics to the broader economic science (Box 14.1). Non-market valuation currently relies on two main approaches: *revealed* and *stated preferences*. In the first case, preferences for non-marketed goods are inferred from the behaviour of individuals in related markets. As an example, consider Hotelling's valuation of national parks (Hotelling, 1947), one of the first cases in which this approach was used. Commissioned by the US National Parks Service, Hotelling used the cost incurred by people travelling from different places in order to visit a park as a lower bound for what they are willing to pay to enjoy the public recreation service provided by the park itself. From that, a demand schedule and an estimate of the consumer surplus can be derived. This method is now known as the travel cost method. Hedonic pricing might instead be used when environmental attributes, such as distance to green spaces or air quality, directly affect the market price of goods they are embedded into, such as houses. The disadvantage of revealed preferences is that it cannot capture other components of the 'total economic value' of a good beyond its immediate use value, in particular the 'option' value (the value attached to the possibility of being able to use the good in the future, identified by Weisbrod, 1964) and the 'non-use' value (the value attached to the existence of the good per se, first theorised by Krutilla, 1967). The difficulty in the valuation of these components is that they do not trigger any behaviour, and are therefore difficult to capture unless asked directly. Stated preferences were used for the first time during the litigation related to the Exxon Valdez's oil spill in Alaska to estimate the damages caused to the environment, beyond the mere economic profits foregone (Carson et al., 1994).

Box 14.1: The importance of environmental valuation in policy

- Cost–Benefit Analysis: need to measure benefits and costs in monetary terms.
- Taxation: measuring the externality in monetary terms in order to set the Pigouvian tax.
- Damage litigation: valuation can be used in the US to set e.g. compensation for oil spills, land contamination, etc.
- 'Natural wealth' and 'green' national accounting: natural capital should be included when measuring the 'wealth of a nation'.
- Creation of missing markets: payment for ecosystem services require knowledge of the value of the service to set the right price.

Neoclassical natural resource economics: growth, sustainability and the optimal extraction of resources

The idea that natural resources are not a 'free gift' but rather scarce economic inputs, coupled with the utility-maximising framework and the mathematical formalisation of Neoclassical economics, led to an interest in natural resource modelling in a general equilibrium framework. The aim was to use dynamic optimisation tools to determine the optimal rate of extraction and therefore the optimal pattern of use of renewable and non-renewable natural resources. While natural resource analysis defined optimal paths of extraction over time, optimal growth theory formed the basis for the analysis of sustainable growth and intergenerational equity in the presence of natural resources. The Ramsey model was an important departure point for such questions (Ramsey, 1928; Dasgupta and Heal, 1979).

Around the same time, in 'The Economics of Exhaustible Resources' (Hotelling, 1931), Hotelling employed the calculus of variation, devised at the end of 1800s, to analyse the optimal extraction of non-renewable resources. This led to the so-called Hotelling rule, a pricing condition for exhaustible resources, stating that in equilibrium the return on physical capital and the return on any other forms of capital – including natural resources – should be the same, otherwise arbitrages are possible in the market and further profits can be made. According to Heal (2007), this paper is the foundation point of analytical environmental and natural resource economics. The pioneering use of dynamic optimisation methods[5] by Hotelling meant that economics was then particularly receptive to the new mathematical tools being developed in the 1950s, which opened up a new array of possibilities for economic analyses dealing with the temporal dimension.[6] This, together with contextual historical events, triggered investigations in whether aggregate consumption and economic growth could be sustained in a world with finite resources. After the Second World War and the Paley Commission in the US, further concerns were raised about the sustainability of economies that were dependent on finite stocks of natural resources by the Club of Rome in 1972 (Meadows et al., 1972). The final report, often known as the 'Limits to Growth' report, estimated the time until depletion for several non-renewable resources such as copper, tin, oil, and discussed how this would be cut shorter by population growth.[7] This Malthusian scarcity narrative was consolidated by the Yom Kippur War and the subsequent oil crisis in 1973, and by the 1979 energy crisis following the Iranian Revolution. These events triggered academic interest on growth in non-renewable resources and long-term sustainability, using the Neoclassical toolkit of analysis. The main contributions on this topic at the time were collected in the 'Symposium on the Economics of Exhaustible Resources' in the *Review of Economics and Statistics* in 1974. In particular, Solow (1974) investigated whether sustainable consumption is possible in an economy with non-renewable finite resources, and concluded that it can be, under certain assumptions on production and substitutability of the inputs. Dasgupta and Heal (1974) formalised a utilitarian present value utility maximisation problem with non-renewable resource, while Stiglitz (1974a, b) extended the previous models to account for technological change and population growth. A key insight of these contributions was the acknowledgement that sustainability is not necessarily compatible nor coincident with *optimality* as typically defined in the utilitarian Neoclassical framework. The objective of a constant consumption path, for example, was later interpreted by Hartwick (1977) as an optimal solution when the social welfare function is maximin/Rawlsian, rather than Utilitarian. These findings make clear how the definition of sustainability intimately depends on the ethical position on inter-generational equity.

Economic definitions of sustainability, such as constant or non-declining consumption or utility, have been commonly used within economics to pin down the concept of sustainability first announced by the Brundtland Commission in 1978:

> Sustainable development is development that meets the needs of the present without compromising the ability of future generations to meet their own needs. It contains within it two key concepts: the concept of 'needs', in particular the essential needs of the world's poor, ... and the idea of limitations imposed by the state of technology and social organization on the environment's ability to meet present and future needs. (World Commission on Environment and Development, 1987)

The operational definitions of sustainability offered by these approaches also lead to operational policies that could be put in place to measure the sustainability of an economy, and attempt to attain sustainable economic development. The Hartwick-Solow Rule states that if the resource rents from a non-renewable resource are re-invested, then the overall comprehensive measure of the capital stock, which includes man-made and environmental capital, will be constant, and hence consumption will also be constant (under certain technical conditions). Since then a variety of theoretical results have generalised this basic result, and several countries have started using this policy rule to ensure that Genuine Savings, that is savings minus resource depletion, is positive (Hamilton and Hartwick, 2014; Hamilton and Hepburn, 2017).

Climate change

Human-induced climate change started to feature highly in environmental economics in the 1990s and 2000s. *The Stern Review* (Stern, 2007; Weitzman, 2007) defined climate change as 'the greatest market failure the world has ever seen' – clearly framing the problem in the context of market failures in the form of public goods and externalities. The Neoclassical approach to study the economics of climate change relies on Integrated Assessment Models (IAMs). These models link simple models of the economy to simplified models of climate developed in the natural sciences. One of the first examples of an IAM is the Dynamic Integrated Climate and Economy (DICE), developed by Nordhaus in the 1990s (Nordhaus, 1994; Nordhaus and Boyer, 1999). The economic models contained within IAMs fall squarely within the Neoclassical growth paradigm (see Chapter 11), with aggregate production functions representing the economy, and Utilitarian inter-temporal social welfare functions as the societal objective.

Yet some of the main criticisms of these models have come from within economics itself and has been aimed at the arbitrary nature of many key components of the model, such as the sensitivity of the climate to emissions of CO_2, and the economic damages caused by climate change (see e.g. Pindyck, 2013). There is a great deal of uncertainty about these factors, and the time horizons over which the analyses take place tends to amplify these uncertainties. Estimates of the damages per ton of CO_2, known as the Social Cost of Carbon (SCC), take this uncertainty into account using expected utility approaches, Monte Carlo (simulations) approaches, and by presenting ranges of the estimates across different models (NAS, 2017; Nordhaus, 2017; Stern, 2007). Estimates of the SCC across models and across simulations range from the low values \$1/tCO_2 used by the US government in 2018, to higher values of around \$40–\$100/tCO_2 in which global damages and intergenerational equity issues are emphasised (NAS, 2017). The main critique of these estimates is that, while they might be fine for illustrative purposes, their use in policy is not very satisfactory at all. Pindyck (2017, 2019) proposes that garnering expert opinions would provide a more transparent estimate of the SCC than the black boxes of IAMs. This transparent approach does nothing to narrow down the range of estimates unfortunately, in fact the opposite is true with SCC value ranging from \$10 to \$250t/CO_2. The procedural point about transparency is also open to debate.

Part of the variability of these IAM estimates of the SCC stems from the choice of the discount rate for long-term climate change damages. While Stern (2007) proposed immediate action against climate change and an effective SCC of more than \$200/tCO_2, Nordhaus (1994, 2007, 2017) has always proposed a more gradual response, and a commensurately lower SCC of around \$20 to £40/tCO_2. The main difference between these two proposals lies in their different perspectives on the discount rate and inter-generational equity. It is well documented that Stern (2007) argued from a normative perspective that the pure rate of time preference (the discount rate on utility) should be approximately 0 per cent. This follows a long tradition in welfare economics of impartial consequentialism, and the ethical views held by Ramsey, Pigou, Harrod and Sidgwick among others.[8] Nordhaus, on the other hand, argued that this rate ought to be determined by positive principles and calibration to the market place and should rather be in the order of 2–3 per cent based on observations of the '"real" real interest rate' used in the markets. These different perspectives on discounting explain the lion's share of the difference in recommendations and serve to illustrate the importance of the discount rate in public policies with long horizons. Beyond climate change, such policies include biodiversity loss, nuclear power, and public health. Once again, the analysis of long-term environmental problems requires the analyst to choose an ethical position on inter-generational equity in order to make a welfare judgement on the extent of intervention.

These are difficult decisions, and a preference for a zero utility discount rate is not the ethically obvious choice. Some argue that a zero utility discount rate would justify drastic reductions in current consumption and impoverishment of the present generation in order to save the benefits for the very distant future. Arrow (1999), therefore, argues in favour of a shift to 'agent-relative ethics' and non-zero discounting, to avoid impoverishing the current generation. So there is disagreement on the social discount rate and matters of intergenerational equity. Yet a recent survey of experts on the discount rate revealed that 90 per cent of experts would agree with a discount rate between 1 per cent and 3 per cent for a 100-year time horizon (Drupp et al., 2018).

The key issue determining the SCC and the value of mitigating climate change turns out to be the damage function and the prospect of catastrophic damages from climate change (Weitzman, 2010). Weitzman (2009) shows that Stern was 'right for the wrong reasons' in his call for rapid action on climate change. The correct reason being that if the probability distribution of climate damages has 'fat tails' (i.e. is not vanishing to zero as quickly as, e.g. a normal distribution) then the expected value today of avoiding catastrophes in the future is extremely high, almost irrespective of the discounting assumptions. So, the welfare treatment of uncertainty and a more precise calibration of the damage function remain the major challenges in the economic analysis of climate change. Indeed, both of these areas remain important areas of research in economics at present, with simplified expressions for the SCC being proposed (e.g. van den Bijgaart et al., 2016), and empirical estimations of the damage costs of climate change becoming ever more detailed in the 'new climate-economy' literature (see e.g. Dell et al., 2014).[9]

Alternative approaches

Deviations from and augmentations of the Neoclassical ERE

Several schools of thought have developed from, or in antithesis to, the Neoclassical approach to ERE, and economics in general. While ERE considers any violations of the assumptions of its model as imperfections that bias the correct functioning of the markets and that therefore need to be removed, these alternative schools of thought attribute the gap between the real world and the predictions of the Neoclassical models to the inadequacy of the models themselves. From this starting point, some lines of research – such as Behavioural economics (see Chapter 2) – continue to use the general framework of welfare maximisation, but question its starting assumptions. Among the main environmental applications, it is worth citing the use of preferences and incentive mechanisms to influence environmental behaviour ('nudging') and to design policy for conservation, and public good and common-pool resource management (Goldstein et al., 2008; Venkatachalam, 2008). More recently, subjective well-being valuation has developed to substitute monetary measures with life-satisfaction or happiness indices, and the concept of experienced utility – or stated happiness – has emerged as an alternative over decision utility, although both approaches are still in their infancy.

Other approaches have distanced themselves from the overly-general and over-mathematised Neoclassical models of the market, and have moved the focus of their analysis towards the institutions, both social and legal, that underlie the economic structure. The methodology for the New Institutional Economics opened up to include case studies and local and context-specific models. Williamson used Coase's ideas as a starting point to study the role of institutions, but framing them into a co-evolutionary and multidimensional perspective, rather than using a market-centred approach. In particular, he argued that institutions are endogenous to the economic system, and evolve with human preferences, power relationships and other contextual elements. The importance of property rights and institutions became even more apparent in the literature on public goods and common-pool resources. The dominant narrative in the 1960s–1990s followed Hardin's 'tragedy of the commons' idea in which, in line with the prediction of game theory for the Prisoner's Dilemma, the dominant strategy of rational agents with access to an open-access resource is to free-ride on the efforts of the others and overharvest from the stock of common natural resources (Hardin, 1968). The only solution to the 'commons dilemma' seemed therefore to lie in either privatisation or in strict centralised government management. This framework started to be questioned in the 1990s, when political economist Ostrom showed in a series of case studies of natural resource management that resources could be effectively managed as de facto or de jure common-property resources without privatisation or central control. The success of common property management regimes, either in harvesting or provision of local public goods, relied on the existence of well-defined monitoring and enforcement at the local level, and collective rules and norms on harvesting and provision that were tailored to the resource in question and the characteristics of the communities (see Ostrom, 1990; Schlager and Ostrom, 1992). The real 'tragedy' lies in the (mis)specification of the property rights – i.e. the fact that the good is open access – rather than the shared nature of the resource.[10] Cooperation and collective action were shown to be efficient and often durable management approaches for natural resources.[11] As a result of Ostrom's work, common property regimes emerged as an alternative – or better, as a continuum of alternatives – between private and State property.

Ecological economics

More radically, some scholars have questioned the neglect of economic analysis for planetary boundaries and the wider biophysical system of which economic dynamics are just one component. Ecological economics therefore advocates for an ecological perspective around the broader economy–society–environment nexus, taking into consideration the possibility of irreversible processes and complexity of systems, and employing a more interdisciplinary approach, encompassing social and natural sciences, and humanities.

The 'Planetary Boundaries' framework and the idea of biophysical limits that socio-economic systems must respect (see Rockström et al., 2009 and the update in 2015 by Steffen) was not an entirely new idea in economics, as it can be traced back to Malthus's notion of 'absolute limits'. Its popularity was then revived in the 1960s–70s, with Boulding's powerful metaphor of Earth as a 'spaceship' with limited resources (Boulding, 1966). At the same time environmental activism and social movements for environmental justice were blooming. In this context, the Neoclassical production theory came under attack for ignoring the exhaustion of natural resources and energy inputs, and the waste and pollution generated as a by-product of the desired output. In 1971, Georgescu-Roegen integrated these concerns in 'The Entropy Law in the Economic Process', where he extended the concept of entropy and the law of thermodynamics into economics. According to the second law of thermodynamics, in particular, the entropy of a closed system always tends to increase, meaning that production processes are nothing else that a transformation of usable energy – natural resources – into unusable waste – such as heat and other waste – and, even more importantly, are irreversible (Georgescu-Roegen, 1971, 1975). Daly then went on to consider the consequences that the irreversibility of production processes has on the debate on substitutability of forms of capital and measures of sustainable welfare, and later became an advocate for a 'steady-state economy'. Given these premises, some ecological economists go even further and advocate for 'degrowth' (see Chapter 16), claiming that infinite economic growth is not compatible with planetary physical limits, although this school is still divided on the topic. Following these landmark contributors, ecological economists argue that economic processes should not be thought of as taking place in a vacuum, as they are in reality embedded in a wider environment that includes energy and materials inflows and outflows, and are subject to bio-physical limits such as the carrying capacity of the Earth and the laws of thermodynamics on energy conservation and entropy. The Neoclassical production functions including only man-made capital, and neglecting energy, raw materials, waste, heat and entropy, and all the supporting ecosystem services make no sense:

> We might say that Solow's recipe calls for making a cake with only the cook and his kitchen. We do not need flour, eggs, sugar, etc., nor electricity or natural gas, nor even firewood. (Daly, 1997)

An important tenet of ecological economics that follows is the distinction between strong and weak sustainability. Neoclassical production functions as well as marginal valuation, assume substitutability between different forms of assets and different natural resources, a strong assumption that is not always backed by evidence and not everyone is willing to make. When the assumption of substitutability is rejected, the concept of sustainability is affected too, as it is no longer enough to maintain the overall sum of the assets as prescribed by the 'Hartwick rule', but a minimum amount of each non-substitutable – or 'critical' – asset should also be ensured (strong sustainability). While the weak sustainability approach relies on the assumption that it could be feasible – and possibly even optimal – to consume the entire stock of natural assets, the strong sustainability approach of ecological economics argue that natural capital is not substitutable with man-made capital, and its life-supporting functions – such as atmospheric and climate regulation, sink and absorption functions, water cycle – are irreplaceable. Ecological economists therefore reject the assumptions of smoothness and continuity used in Neoclassical models as mathematical artifices that fail to account for the ecological thresholds, tipping points and discontinuities typical of the natural environment, where even small changes to one element may trigger the collapse of an entire ecological system. Given this radical shift in perspectives, ecological economics may be considered as a discipline of its own, rather than a branch of ERE, despite some overlap. From a methodological perspective, ecological economists advocate for a more holistic and systemic framework. Although interdisciplinarity is undoubtedly a strength of ecological economics, the discipline has not yet succeeded in presenting an organic and consistent methodology, resulting in a variety of approaches that distance themselves more or less radically from traditional ERE. Those closer to the field of ecological political philosophy, for example, go as far as to question the anthropocentrism of economics, arguing that the environment should not only be considered as a means towards human well-being, but as an end to itself, stressing its intrinsic value (Kortenkamp and Moore, 2001).

Box 14.2: Policy

Despite the young age of this field and its abstraction and stylisation, its findings have inspired a wide array of policy instruments. ERE has had the merit of stripping complex problems down to simple solutions, that, far from perfect, are nonetheless important first steps to tackle many urgent problems of the 'Anthropocene'. The list that follows is by no means complete, but it is meant to present the most important instruments that stemmed from the theories covered in this chapter. Although adapted to the specific contexts of use, the mechanisms underlying these instruments are at the basis of most of the environmental policies currently implemented in the world.

Pigouvian tax/subsidy: Originally proposed by Pigou, a Pigouvian tax is a fee levied on market activities that generate negative externalities, in an attempt to close the gap between the marginal social cost and the marginal private cost of production and achieve the optimal output. This becomes a subsidy in the case of positive externalities.

Tradeable permits: A tradeable permit system lets a purposely created market set the price of the externalities, and is therefore closer in spirit to the 'Coase theorem'. Several of these schemes exist. Emission Reduction Credits allow countries or single activities to receive credits when they reduce emissions above a set standard, with these credits then sold to those countries or activities which have higher costs of abatement and therefore struggle to keep below the set standard. An example of this are the Certified Emission Reduction (CERs) units within the Clean Development Mechanism (CDM) defined in the Kyoto Protocol. Cap-and-trade mechanisms are instead a mix of political and economic mechanisms.

A political body sets the total quantity of emissions to be allowed, a corresponding number of permits is then allocated between facilities and traded in a market, as in the US Acid Rain Program and the EU Emission Trading Scheme (ETS) for GHG emissions. In the case of pollution, this result in a so-called carbon price, that – under optimal conditions – should reflect the social cost of emissions (or any other pollutant). Cap-and-trade schemes have also been applied in the fishery sector, where a maximum total allowable catch (TAC) is divided into individual transferable quotas (ITQs) that are then traded between fishermen.

Other property rights-based mechanisms: In some cases, such as fishery, forestry, and international emission agreements, we are more interested in regulating a system of interdependent elements rather than focusing on just one pollutant or one species. In this case territorial use rights can be set over the geographical space of interest to solve the issue of open access, in the spirit of New Institutional Economics. Successful examples of these are Territorial Use Rights Fisheries (TURFs), such as the centuries-old nearshore TURF system in Japan and the more recent management and exploitation areas (MEAs) in Chile.

Resource rents and payment for ecosystem services (PES): Applying the 'Coase theorem' to positive externalities, some countries and 'donor' groups have started to pay landowners, communities, and countries to conserve specific ecosystems, especially forests or watershed, creating a sort of market for ecosystem services. Examples are the national-level Pagos Por Servicios Ambientales in Costa Rica, and the REDD (Reducing Emissions from Deforestation and forest Degradation) international scheme.

Hartwick rule: The Hartwick rule is a simple and intuitive rule-of-thumb for sustainable[12] resource management, prompting agents to 'invest all profits or rents from exhaustible resources in reproducible capital such as machines' (Hartwick, 1977). In this way, the value of the overall stock of assets is preserved for future generations. Norway's oil fund and its strict policy on how much of the oil revenues can be spent and how, as well as Botswana's programmes for investing the revenues of its diamonds in health and education, draw inspiration from the rule.

Natural capital committees, Green National Accounts, and alternatives to GDP: Finally, the concept of 'natural capital' used in growth and sustainability theories has succeeded in framing the natural environment and ecosystem services as forms of capital assets and an integral component of wealth, rather than a constraint to societal welfare. As a result, many countries, including the UK, are appointing Natural Capital Committees to oversee the management of the country's natural assets in a similar way to what is done for other forms of financial and physical assets. Thanks to progresses in valuation techniques, Green National Accounts are being set up to keep track of the amount of natural assets pertaining to the countries in a similar way to what gross national products (GNP) does for man-made capital. Measures of wealth that include the accumulation of other forms of assets, such as human and natural capital – or liability, such as the pollution stock – have also been proposed as alternative to GDP and GNP, such as 'Green GDP', World Bank's 'net adjusted savings' (also known as 'genuine savings') and 'inclusive wealth'.

Conclusion

While the history of economic thought shows that environmental and resource issues have always been central to the discussion about well-being and development, Environmental and Resource Economics (ERE) has its methodological roots clearly embedded in the methods and formality of Neoclassical economics, with its framing around externalities, public goods and other market failures. While in recent years there have been departures into e.g. Behavioural economics and the modelling of the economic–climate interface, and while ethical issues are more predominant in ERE than in many other areas of economics, the essential apparatus remains largely the same. Whatever one thinks of this apparatus, the policy impact of ERE has been noticeable, and ERE has led to a number of important policy instruments being put into practice, often successfully in terms of environmental and economic outcomes (Box 14.2).

The challenges for ERE remain plentiful, and revolve around the analysis of some of the most important problems facing humanity: climate change, sustainability and the conservation of ecosystem services. While the empirical tools of mainstream economic analysis have proven useful in elaborating on the damages of climate change, and in establishing which policy works and when, in relation to the global environmental issues that currently present themselves, ERE may well have something to learn from its more radical sister discipline of ecological economics, which emphasises more the constraints that environmental resources present to sustainability, and emphasises less the objective of perpetual growth in consumption. The evident overlap between these two disciplines may well increase in the future as the planetary boundaries of resource use are approached.

Seminar questions and activities

- **Scarcity narrative, prices and the theory of value formation**: how did the narrative on resource scarcity evolve throughout the history of ERE? How can it be reconciled with the theory of value formation? In your discussion, make sure to include the marginalist approach of the Neoclassicals and their idea of value at the margin; the idea of natural capital and how to measure it;
- **Natural Capital and sustainability**: (1) What are the pros and cons of conceptualising natural resources and eco-system services as elements of 'Natural Capital'? (2) How useful is a definition of sustainability that relies on non-declining utility?
- **Intergenerational equity and justice**: What are the pros and cons of the Utilitarian approach to social discounting and intergenerational equity? Explain the principle behind the normative approach to social discounting, and the positive approach. Which one would you choose for the economic analysis of climate change and why?
- **Hotelling's rule**: the theory of rent and who should appropriate it (labour, physical capital owners, natural capital owners, ...). How does this link to modern valuation techniques?

- **Policy applications**: think of real-world environmental and natural resource policies that have been implemented or are under discussion around the world. Can you trace them back to the theories and thinkers presented in this chapter?
- **Ecological economics and ERE**: what are the main differences? What are the overlapping points? Think in terms of their epistemology, methodology, objectives, ...
- **Neoclassical economics**: how did neoclassical economics contribute to the development of modern ERE? How did it hinder it?
- **The environment in the Classics and in modern ERE**: what are the main differences? What are the overlapping points? Think in terms of their epistemology, methodology, objectives.

References

Arrow, K. (1999). Discounting, morality, and gaming. In P. R. Portney & J. P. Weyant (Eds.), *Discounting and intergenerational equity* (pp. 13–21). Washington, DC: Resources for the Future.

Arrow, K., & Debreu, G. (1954). Existence of an equilibrium for a competitive economy. *Econometrica: Journal of the Econometric Society, 22*(3), 265–290.

Arrow, K., Cropper, M., Gollier, C., Groom, B., Heal, G., Newell, R., Nordhaus, W. D., Pindyck, R. S., Pizer, W. A., Portney, P. R., Sterner, T., Tol, R. S. J., & Weitzman, M. L. (2013). Determining benefits and costs for future generations. *Science, 341*(6144), 349–350.

Atkinson, G., Groom, B., Hanley, N., & Mourato, S. (2018a). Environmental valuation and benefit-cost analysis in UK policy. *Journal of Benefit-Cost Analysis, 9*(1), 97–119.

Atkinson, G., Groom, B., & Mourato, S. (2018b). *Cost benefit analysis for the environment 2018*. Paris: OECD.

Baumol, W. J. (1972). On taxation and the control of externalities. *The American Economic Review, 62*(3), 307–322.

Baumol, W. J., & Oates, W. E. (1988). *The theory of environmental policy*. Cambridge: Cambridge University Press.

Boulding, K. (1966). The economics of the coming spaceship earth. In H. Jarett (Ed.), *Environmental quality in a growing economy* (pp. 3–14). Baltimore: Johns Hopkins University Press.

Carson, R. T. (1962). *Silent spring*. Greenwich: Fawcett Publications.

Carson, R. T., Mitchell, R. C., Hanemann, W. M., Kopp, R. J., Presser, S., & Ruud, P. (1994). *Contingent valuation and lost passive use: Damages from the Exxon Valdez* (Discuss. Paper 94-18). Washington, DC: Resources for the Future.

Clark, J. P. (1989). Marx's inorganic body. *Environmental Ethics, 11*(3), 243–258.

Coase, R. H. (1960). The problem of social cost. In *Classic papers in natural resource economics* (pp. 87–137). London: Palgrave Macmillan.

Daly, H. E. (1997). Georgescu-Roegen versus Solow/Stiglitz. *Ecological Economics, 22*(3), 261–266.

Dasgupta, P. (1996). The economics of the environment. *Environment and Development Economics, 1*(4), 387–428.

Dasgupta, P., & Heal, G. (1974). The optimal depletion of exhaustible resources. *Review of Economic Studies, 41*(5), 3–28.

Dasgupta, P. S., & Heal, G. M. (1979). *Economic theory and exhaustible resources*. Cambridge: Cambridge University Press.

Dell, M., Jones, B. F., & Olken, B. A. (2014). What do we learn from the weather? The new climate–economy literature. *Journal of Economic Literature, 52*(3), 740–798.

Drupp, M., Freeman, M. C., Groom, B., & Nesje, F. (2018). Discounting disentangled. *American Economic Journal: Economic Policy, 10*(4), 109–134.

Eckstein, O. (1958). *Water resource development–The economics of project evaluation*. Cambridge, MA: Harvard University Press.

Foster, J. B. (1997). The crisis of the earth: Marx's theory of ecological sustainability as a nature-imposed necessity for human production. *Organization & Environment, 10*(3), 278–295.

Foster, J. B. (1999). Marx's theory of metabolic rift: Classical foundations for environmental sociology. *American Journal of Sociology, 105*(2), 366–405.

Georgescu-Roegen, N. (1971). *The entropy law in the economic process*. Cambridge, MA: Harvard University Press.

Georgescu-Roegen, N. (1975). Energy and economic myths. *Southern Economic Journal, 41*(3), 347–381.

Goldstein, N. J., Cialdini, R. B., & Griskevicius, V. (2008). A room with a viewpoint: Using social norms to motivate environmental conservation in hotels. *Journal of Consumer Research, 35*(3), 472–482.

Gollier, C. (2013). *Pricing the planet's future: The economics of discounting in an uncertain world*. Princeton: Princeton University Press.

Gordon, H. S. (1954). The economic theory of a common-property resource: The fishery. *Journal of Political Economy, 62*, 124–162.

Hamilton, K., & Hartwick, J. (2014). Wealth and sustainability. *Oxford Review of Economic Policy, 30*(1), 170–187.

Hamilton, K., & Hepburn, C. (Eds.). (2017). *National wealth: What is missing, why it matters*. Oxford: Oxford University Press.

Hardin, G. (1968). The tragedy of the commons. *Science, 162*, 1243–1248.

Harrod, R. (1948). *Towards a dynamic economics, some recent developments of economic theory and their application to policy*. London: Macmillan.

Hartwick, J. M. (1977). Intergenerational equity and the investing of rents from exhaustible resources. *The American Economic Review, 67*(5), 972–974.

Heal, G. (2007). A celebration of environmental and resource economics. *Review of Environmental Economics and Policy, 1*(1), 7–25.

Hicks, J. R. (1939). The foundations of welfare economics. *The Economic Journal, 49*(196), 696–712.

Hotelling, H. (1931). The economics of exhaustible resources. *Journal of Political Economy, 39*, 137–175.

Hotelling, H. (1947). The economics of public recreation. In *The Prewitt report*. Washington, DC: National Parks Service.

Kaldor, N. (1939). Welfare propositions of economics and interpersonal comparisons of utility. *The Economic Journal, 49*, 549–552.

Koopmans, T. C. (1957). *Three essays on the state of economic science*. New York: McGraw-Hill.

Kortenkamp, K. V., & Moore, C. F. (2001). Ecocentrism and anthropocentrism: Moral reasoning about ecological commons dilemmas. *Journal of Environmental Psychology, 21*(3), 261–272.

Krutilla, J. V. (1967). Conservation reconsidered. *American Economic Review, 57*(4), 777–786.

Krutilla, J. V., & Eckstein, O. (1958). *Multipurpose river development: Studies in applied economic analysis*. Baltimore: Johns Hopkins.

Malthus, T. R. (1798). *An essay on the principle of population* (2nd ed., 1803). Edited with an Introduction by Donald Winch. Cambridge: Cambridge University Press, 1992.

Marshall, A. (1890). *Principles of economics*. London: Macmillan (8th ed, 1920).

Marx, K. (1894). *Capital, Vol. III*. New York: Vintage, 1981.

Meadows, D. H., Meadows, D. H., Randers, J., & Behrens, W. W., III. (1972). *The limits to growth: A report for the Club of Rome's Project on the Predicament of Mankind*. New York: Universal Books.

Mill, J. S. (1848). *Principles of political economy*. In Collected works of John Stuart Mill. Toronto: University of Toronto Press, 1965.

National Academies of Sciences, Engineering, and Medicine (NAS). (2017). *Valuing climate damages: Updating estimation of the social cost of carbon dioxide*. Washington, DC: National Academies Press.

Nordhaus, W. D. (1994). *Managing the global commons: The economics of climate change* (Vol. 31). Cambridge, MA: MIT Press.

Nordhaus, W. D. (2007). A review of the Stern review on the economics of climate change. *Journal of Economic Literature, 45*(3), 686–702. https://doi.org/10.1257/jel.45.3.686.

Nordhaus, W. D. (2017). Revisiting the social cost of carbon. *Proceedings of the National Academy of Sciences, 114*(7), 1518–1523.

Nordhaus, W. D., & Boyer, J. G. (1999). Requiem for Kyoto: An economic analysis of the Kyoto Protocol. *The Energy Journal, 20*, 93–130.

Ostrom, E. (1990). *Governing the commons: The evolution of institutions for collective action*. Cambridge: Cambridge University Press.

Pearce, D. (2002). An intellectual history of environmental economics. *Annual Review of Energy and the Environment, 27*(1), 57–81.

Perman, R. (2003). *Natural resource and environmental economics*. Harlow: Pearson Education.

Pigou, A. (1920). *The economics of welfare*. London: Macmillan.

Pindyck, R. S. (2013). Climate change policy: What do the models tell us? *Journal of Economic Literature, 51*(3), 860–872.

Pindyck, R. S. (2017). Taxes, targets and the social cost of carbon. *Economica, 84*, 345–364.

Pindyck, R. S. (2019). The social cost of carbon revisited. *Journal of Environmental Economics and Management, 94*, 140–160.

Ramsey, F. (1928). A mathematical theory of savings. *Economic Journal, 38*, 543–559.

Ricardo, D. (1817). *The principles of political economy and taxation* (P. Straffa, Ed.). Cambridge: Cambridge University Press, 1951.

Rockström, J., Steffen, W., Noone, K., Persson, Å., Stuart Chapin, F., Lambin, E. F., Lenton, T. M., et al. (2009). A safe operating space for humanity. *Nature, 461*(7263), 472–475.

Sandmo, A. (2015). The early history of environmental economics. *Review of Environmental Economics and Policy, 9*(1), 43–63.

Schlager, E., & Ostrom, E. (1992). Property-rights regimes and natural resources: A conceptual analysis. *Land Economics, 68*(3), 249–262.

Smith, A. (1776). *An inquiry into the nature and causes of the wealth of nations*. London: Printed for W. Strahan and T. Cadell ....

Solow, R. M. (1974). Intergenerational equity and exhaustible resources. *The Review of Economic Studies, 41*, 29–45.

Steffen, W., Richardson, K., Rockström, J., Cornell, S. E., Fetzer, I., Bennett, E. M., Biggs, R., et al. (2015). Planetary boundaries: Guiding human development on a changing planet. *Science, 347*(6223), 1259855.

Stern, N. H. (2007). *The Stern review: The economics of climate change*. Cambridge: Cambridge University Press.

Stigler, G. J. (1966). *The theory of price* (3rd ed.). New York: Macmillan.

Stiglitz, J. (1974a). Growth with exhaustible natural resources: Efficient and optimal growth paths. *Reviews of Economic Studies, 41*, 123–138.

Stiglitz, J. (1974b). Growth with exhaustible natural resources: The competitive economy. *Reviews of Economic Studies, 41*, 139–152.

van den Bijgaart, I., Gerlagh, R., & Liski, M. (2016). A simple formula for the social cost of carbon. *Journal of Environmental Economics and Management, 77*, 75–94. https://doi.org/10.1016/j.jeem.2016.01.005.

Venkatachalam, L. (2008). Behavioral economics for environmental policy. *Ecological Economics, 67*(4), 640–645.

Weisbrod, B. (1964). Collective consumption services of individual consumption goods. *The Quarterly Journal of Economics, 78*, 471–477.

Weitzman, M. L. (2007). A review of 'The Stern review on the economics of climate change'. *Journal of Economic Literature, XLV*, 703–724. https://doi.org/10.1257/jel.45.3.703.

Weitzman, M. L. (2009). On modeling and interpreting the economics of catastrophic climate change. *Review of Economics and Statistics, 91*(1), 1–19. https://doi.org/10.1016/10.1162/rest.91.1.1.

Weitzman, M. L. (2010). What is the 'damages function' for global warming and what difference might it make? *Climate Change Economics, 1*, 57. https://doi.org/10.1142/S2010007810000042.

World Commission on Environment and Development (WCED). (1987). *Our Common Future*. Oxford: Oxford University Press.

15 WHAT IS THE ROLE OF THE STATE IN ECONOMICS?

Shawky Arif

Introduction

Economists' views on the role of the state have ranged from advocating the doctrine of laissez-faire (i.e. non-interference) to favouring an active role for the state in the economy. While Classical economists recognise what is known today's mainstream terminology as market failure, they strongly defended the doctrine of laissez-faire, believing that the free market system is the guarantor of economic freedom as well as liberty. State intervention, for Mill (1848, p. 314), if not 'required by some great good', reduces individuals' welfare and liberty. This view has dominated economic thought since the publication of *The Wealth of Nations* in 1776 but was challenged by the crisis of the 1930s. The severity of the crisis led economists to rethink the fundamental assumptions and views of the dominant doctrine, especially those related to the role of the state in the economy.

Writing during the crisis of the 1930s, Keynes (1936) took issues issue with the dominant economic doctrine of his time, and advocated increasing government spending to stimulate the economy. With declining levels of private investment and high levels of unemployment, Keynes (1936/2013, p. 164) 'expect[s] the State ... taking an ever greater responsibility for directly organising investment.' A particular interpretation of Keynes as offered by Hicks (1937), Modigliani (1944) and Samuelson (1955), also known as the Neoclassical Synthesis dominated economics departments and policymaking circles and served as the ideology in support of the macroeconomic management of the post-war period.[1] The new social contract, also known as the welfare state, sought to minimise output and employment fluctuations. However, by the 1970s, the welfare state was abandoned in favour of an ideology that claims to be a revival of the Classical creed of laissez-faire.

Uncompromising in its critique of the welfare state, Neoliberalism maintains that state intervention stifles private initiative and produces inefficient outcomes. However, Neoliberals do not advocate the abolition of the state. Rather, they are in favour of reshaping its functions to create an institutional framework conducive to private enterprise and protective of economic rights such as private property. The financial crisis of 2007/2008, however, challenged the Neoliberal consensus and put into question the assumption of the rationality of the market, and revived the discussion about the role of the state in the economy. According to the Institutionalists, in particular those in line with Old Institutionalism, ascribe the crisis to the lack of regulations. Moreover, they take issue with the market primacy assumption and argue that the market is as important as other institutions such as the state, and that well-functioning markets require a well-functioning state (Chang, 2002). For Marxists, however, the state is an instrument of oppression in the hands of the dominant class – the bourgeoisie. The task of the working class is to seize power and nationalise the economy ushering in a workers' state that would over time give way to a classless society based on the principle of the common ownership of the means of production.

This chapter provides an overview of the major historic and influential schools and traditions of economic thought on the role of the state in the economy. It starts by outlining, briefly, the main aspects of the Neoclassical theory of state intervention which proceeds entirely on the basis of market failure. We then turn to the Classics who viewed state intervention as an exception to the rule of laissez-faire. Subsequently we discuss Keynes who, writing in the middle of the crisis of the 1930s, supported state intervention in the form of an increase of government spending in order to stimulate the economy. The chapter then considers the views of authors like Hayek (of the Austrian School of Economics) and Friedman (of the Monetarist School) who were instrumental in the advent of Neoliberalism. Drawing upon the work of North and Chang, the Institutionalist approach with regard to the role of the state is reviewed, before finally reviewing the Marxist position.

Market failure and the Neoclassical theory of the state

Notwithstanding the diversity of views on the role of the state in economic thought, the standard economics textbook promotes a stylised version of the economy where the state is typically absent or mentioned to draw attention to the allegedly deleterious effect of its intervention. George (1990, p. 863) notes that the mainstream textbook presents the government as an 'Intrusive Alien … emerging only after the private sector had established itself.' In the absence of the state, mainstream economics models society as a perfectly competitive market with utility-maximising, self-interested and rational consumers acting independently, buying goods and service from competing profit-maximising firms (see Chapters 4 and 5). In this economy the firm hires labour which is paid its marginal product in order to sell goods and services at the ongoing price (see Chapter 7). The individual firm does not influence the price, it is said to be a price taker. The worker, however, who according to Neoclassical economics dislikes work, trades off work (hence consumption) and leisure. The consumer, on the other hand, modelled as a sophisticated calculating machine is constantly processing complex algorithms involving the ranking of bundles of goods and services based on the level of utility they generate. The Neoclassical consumer is always interested in the bundle that generates the highest level of utility given a budget constraint and other relevant information (see Chapter 5).

Assuming an initial distribution of resources, symmetry of information, the rationality of economic agents, as well as a free market setting (that is no state interference), the mainstream economic textbook posits that interaction between economic agents produces the most efficient outcome. In this scenario, the market plays a central role in ensuring the efficient allocation of resources. State interference is, however, undesirable because it disturbs the finely tuned logic of the market, hence leading to a loss in welfare. Subsidies, price ceilings and price floors, for example, are generally opposed by mainstream economists because they are seen as distortions leading to an inefficient allocation of resources, except in a well-defined set of exceptions of market failure.

While Neoclassical economics strongly advocates laissez-faire as a rule, it argues that state intervention is needed to address market failure. Market failure refers to a situation whereby the market fails to allocate resources efficiently. Cases of market failure include provision of public goods, lack of property rights, abuse of market power, asymmetry of information, and externalities. State intervention via taxes, regulations, and subsidies is required to tackle those failures and to ensure an efficient allocation of resources. One typical example used in the standard mainstream textbook to illustrate market failure is national defence system as a public good. Once provided all residents benefit from it whether or not they are willing to pay for it (Mankiw and Taylor, 2014; Greenlaw and Taylor, 2017). Another example is market failure arising from the abuse of market power where a monopoly (single seller) or a monopsony (single buyer) can influence prices or output. This type of market failure is typically addressed by antitrust law (also known as competition law) which aims to penalise anti-competitive behaviour. Asymmetric information is another instance that gives rise to market failure and occurs when one party to a contract has more information than the other party, providing an advantage to the former. A well-known example of this type of market failure is the case of car selling (see Akerlof, 1970). Unlike the salesperson, the buyer is likely to have limited knowledge about the vehicle (e.g. service history, past accidents, reliability). In this scenario, market failure occurs when the buyer pays more than the car is worth. A fourth example of market failure is negative externalities, that is the negative effect of a particular economic activity such as pollution, on a third party (see Chapter 14). In the presence of such externalities, the social cost is not covered by the private cost, and in order to correct for that a tax should be imposed on the activity in question. The tax (known as a Pigouvian tax) should be equal to the social cost of the negative externality to offset its impact (Pigou, 1932).

The Classics: state intervention as an exception to the rule of laissez-faire

The economic thought that dominated for one and a half centuries following the publication of *The Wealth of Nations* advocates the superiority of the free market as an economic system conducive to prosperity as well as liberty. Classical political economists like Smith, Ricardo, Say and Mill shared the view that self-interested economic agents interacting in a free-market setting and unfettered by state intervention will reach the maximum level of satisfaction. In a well-known passage in *The Wealth of Nations*, Smith (1776/2012, p. 19) argues that:

> [i]t is not from the benevolence of the butcher, the brewer, or the baker, that we can expect our dinner, but from their regard to their own interest. We address ourselves, not to their humanity but to their self-love, and never talk to them of our own necessities but of their advantages.

In pursuing their own interest in the selfish manner suggested by Smith, economic agents would inadvertently maximise the welfare of the community as a whole. Smith (1776/2012, p. 445) argues that:

> [e]very individual ... neither intends to promote the public interest, nor knows how much he is promoting it ... he intends only his own security; and by directing that industry in such a manner as its produce may be of the greatest value, he intends only his own gain; and he is in this, as in many other cases, led by an invisible hand to promote an end which was no part of his intention ... By pursuing his own interest he frequently promotes that of the society more effectually than when he really intends to promote it.

It follows that the maximum level of welfare is attained when individuals are free in deciding how to spend their time or in what manner to employ the resources available to them, because for '[e]very individual, it is evident, can in his local situation judge much better than any statesman or lawgiver can do for him' (Smith, 1776/2012, pp. 445–446).

Taking the example of France in the late eighteenth century, Say (1803/1971, p. 144) argues that state interference went to such lengths as to 'persecute and even [bring] to the scaffold' those people who saw an opportunity of making more profit in converting corn land into pasturage. Say (1803/1971, p. 144) concludes that '[w]hen authority throws itself in the way of [the] natural course of things ... it evidently directs a portion of the productive energies of the nation towards an object of less desire, at the expense of another of more urgent desire', leading to an inefficient use of resources and a loss in the nation's welfare.

Agreeing with Smith, Mill (1859/2005, p. 93) posits that the maximum level of happiness for the greatest number derives from a policy of non-interference with individuals' actions, because 'neither one person, nor any number of persons, is warranted in saying to another human creature of ripe years, that he shall not do with his life for his own benefit what he chooses to do with it. He is the person most interested in his own well' For Mill (1848/1985, p. 314) 'laissez-faire, in short, should be the general practice: every departure from it, unless required by some great good, is a certain evil'. Individuals are better off without interference, be it from a government, from a group of individuals, or from any other kind of authority (p. 307).

Like the domestic economy, international trade should be conducted according to the doctrine of non-interference. In 1815, the British parliament, dominated by the landed interests, enacted the Corn Law. The legislation was designed to protect the domestic market by imposing tariffs on the importation of wheat and other grains, referred to collectively as corn, into Britain. In a pamphlet published later that year, Ricardo argued that the Corn Law would hurt the profit of the capitalist class by increasing the price of the means of subsistence of the working class (see Chapter 7). Ricardo maintained that as the profit rate declines at home, domestic capital would leave England in pursuit of higher remuneration abroad. He concludes that 'this consideration ought therefore to be a powerful reason to prevent us from restricting [the] importation [of corn]' (Ricardo 1815, fn p. 13). Two years after his polemical pamphlet, Ricardo reiterated his commitment to the principle of laissez-faire in his major work *Principles of Political Economy and Taxation*. He argues that '[u]nder a system of perfectly free commerce, each country naturally devotes its capital and labour to such employments as are most beneficial to each' (Ricardo (1817/1996, p. 93). He goes on to advising that 'wine shall be made in France and Portugal, that corn shall be grown in America and Poland, and that hardware and other goods shall be manufactured in England' (p. 93). And just as Smith's invisible hand that promotes the general interest inadvertently by individuals pursuing their own interests, Ricardo notes that specialisation and the efficient use of resources while it increases 'the general mass of productions, it diffuses general benefit, and binds together by one common tie of interest and intercourse, the universal society of nations throughout the civilized world' (p. 93).

Despite their strong commitment to the doctrine of non-interference, the Classics recognise exceptions to the rule and attribute some roles to the state. For Smith (1776/2012, p. 686):

> According to the system of natural liberty, the sovereign [i.e. the state] has only three duties to attend to ... first, the duty of protecting the society from violence and invasion of other independent societies; secondly, the duty of protecting, as far as possible, every member of the society from the injustice or oppression of every other member of it, or the duty of establishing an exact administration of justice; and, thirdly, the duty of erecting and maintaining certain public works and certain public institutions which it can never be for the interest of any individual, or small number of individuals, to erect and maintain.

Mill adds education to Smith's list of the duties assigned to the state. He argues that education should be provided by the state and mandatory for children regardless of their parents' consent. Moreover, while he believes that individuals are the best judges of their own interest, Mill argues that there is no reason to assume the interests of a third party are better managed by the private sphere compared to the state. Mill (1848/1985, p. 326) maintains that if a business is managed by an agent on behalf of a principal, then there is no reason to suppose that private management is better than public management. He writes that:

> [g]overnment management is, indeed, proverbially jobbing, careless, and ineffective, but so likewise has generally been joint-stock management. The directors of a joint-stock company, it is true, are always shareholders; but also the members of a government are invariably taxpayers; and in the case of directors, no more than in that of governments, is their proportional share of the benefits of good management equal to the interest they may possibly have in mismanagement, even without reckoning the interest of their case.

Mill (1848/1985) further identifies a number of exceptions to the general rule in which state intervention is required. These include situations in which individuals are incapable of judging or acting for themselves; an individual attempting to decide irrevocably now what will be best for his interest at some future and distant time;

actions that are done for the self-interest of others (e.g. charities); acts that are done by individuals that involve consequences extending beyond them; public services need to be performed but in which there is no specifically interested person. Some of these exceptions are precursors to the market failures highlighted by the neoclassical school discussed above.

Writing on what some refer to in modern jargon as 'good governance', Say (1803/1971, pp. 131–132) argues that:

> public authority [when] is not itself a spoliator, it procures to the nation the greatest of all blessings, protection from spoliation by others. Without this protection of each individual by the united force of the whole community it is impossible to conceive any considerable development of the productive powers of man, of land, and of capital; or even to conceive the existence of capital at all.

The French economist concludes that:

> [t]his is the reason why no nation has ever arrived at any degree of opulence, that has not been subject to a regular government. Civilised nations are indebted to political organisation for the innumerable and infinitely various productions, that satisfy their infinite wants, as well as for the fine arts and the opportunities of leisure that accumulation affords, without which the faculties of the mind could never be cultivated, or man by their means attain the full dignity, whereof his nature is susceptible.

The views of the Classics about the role of the state echo the liberal consensus over limiting the powers of the state in an era of absolute monarchies and lack of freedoms. One of the fundamental principles of Classical Liberalism is that the law should be designed for the good of the people. Applied to the economic sphere, Classical Political economists advocated laissez-faire (or non-interference) as a fundamental principle governing economic life. No one 'is warranted in saying to another human creature of ripe years, that he shall not do with his life for his own benefit what he chooses to do with it' (Mill, 1859/2005, p. 93) since 'every individual … in his local situation judge much better than any statesman or lawgiver can do for him' (Smith, 1776/2012, pp. 445–446).

However, and in contrast with the mainstream interpretation which promotes the Classics as unconditionally pro-free-market, Smith and his fellow political economists had a somewhat nuanced view of the roles of both institutions, i.e. the market and the state. While advocating laissez-faire as a principle, the Classics assigned some roles to the state. Smith, for example, expects the state to erect and maintain public institutions, uphold the law and run the judicial system, and to protect the nation from foreign threats and invasions. The role of the state is not only limited to what mainstream economics calls market failure, it extends to managing businesses. Writing on the management of a business by an agent on behalf of a principle, Mill (1848/1985) argues that there is no reason to suppose that the private sector is effective than the public sector.

The pragmatism of Keynes

On 15 October 1929, Fisher (cited in Keen 2011, p. 270) observed in the *New York Times* that the '[s]tock prices have reached what looks like a permanently high plateau. I do not feel that there will soon, if ever, be a fifty or sixty point break below present levels … I expect to see the stock market a good deal higher than it is today within a few months.' Two weeks later, the same newspaper reported that '[s]tock prices virtually collapsed yesterday … Billions of dollars in open market values were wiped out as prices crumbled under the pressure of liquidation of securities which had to be sold at any price.'[2] The collapse of the US stock market had far-reaching consequences and the global economy plunged into a depression.

Up until the crisis, economic orthodoxy assumed that markets are efficient, rational, and self-regulating. While occasional mismatches between supply and demand occur causing oscillations around equilibrium (see Chapter 6), nothing like the 1929 financial crash was expected. The economic crisis that followed put into question a number of assumptions. For example, according to the dominant economic orthodoxy at the time, unemployment is voluntary or frictional. In other words, if there is unemployment in the economy it is because some workers choose not to work at the ongoing wage rate, or because workers are moving from one job to another (frictional unemployment). The economic crisis, however, highlighted that unemployment could be involuntary. There were workers willing to work at the ongoing wage rate who could not find employment. Moreover, the severity and the scale of the crisis showed that markets were not as efficient or self-regulating as had been presumed.

In the third chapter of his General Theory, Keynes explains effective demand – a central concept in his theory. Assuming that both aggregate supply (Z) and aggregate demand (D) are functions of the number of employed workers (N), Keynes (1936/2013, p. 25) argues that:

> if for a given value of N … *D* is greater than *Z*, there will be an incentive to entrepreneurs to increase employment beyond *N* and, if necessary, to raise costs by competing with one another for the factors of production, up to the value of *N* for which *Z* has become equal to *D*. Thus the volume of employment is given by the point of intersection between the aggregate demand function and the aggregate supply function; for it is at this point that the entrepreneurs' expectation of profits will be maximised. The value of *D* at the point of the aggregate demand function, where it is intersected by the aggregate supply function, will be called *the effective demand*.

Note that the above analysis assumes a free-market economy where competing capitalists employ labour to produce goods and services without state interference. However, the socioeconomic and political context of the 1930s (i.e. the economic crisis and the rise of Fascism) led Keynes to take issue with the laissez-faire dogmatism and advised that the government should increase spending to stimulate the economy when in a downturn. For Keynes (1936/2013, p. 380), his theory sought to avoid 'the destruction of existing economic forms [i.e. capitalism] in their entirety'. As one commentator observed, for Keynes, 'the choice between a controlled and a 'free' economy no longer existed; there was only the choice between different sets of controllers'

(Mattick 1974, p. 113). However, persuading the dogmatic proponents of laissez-faire, who saw Keynes's views as a threat to the free-market system, would not be an easy task. Keynes (1936/2013, p. 380) was aware that although 'the enlargement of the functions of government … would seem to a nineteenth-century publicist or to a contemporary American financier to be a terrific encroachment on individualism, [he] defend[s] it'.

Noting that a rise in unemployment and a fall in income 'once started, might proceed to extreme lengths', Keynes (1936/2013, p. 98) argues:

> that employment can only increase pari passu [i.e. at the same rate] with an increase in investment; unless, indeed, there is a change in the propensity to consume. For since consumers will spend less than the increase in aggregate supply price when employment is increased, the increased employment will prove unprofitable unless there is an increase in investment to fill the gap.

Who is going to fill the investment gap? The state, answers Keynes. Sceptical of the efficacy of the monetary policy in stimulating investment, Keynes (1936/2013, p. 164) 'expect[s] to see the State … taking an ever greater responsibility for directly organising investment'. At the extreme, Keynes (1936/2013, p. 129) reasons as follows to drive home his point:

> [i]f the Treasury were to fill old bottles with banknotes, bury them at suitable depths in disused coal mines which are then filled up to the surface with town rubbish, and leave it to private enterprise on well-tried principles of laissez-faire to dig the notes up again ... there need be no more unemployment and, with the help of the repercussions, the real income of the community, and its capital wealth also, would probably become a good deal greater than it actually is. It would, indeed, be more sensible to build houses and the like; but if there are political and practical difficulties in the way of this, the above would be better than nothing.

The views of Keynes and his policy recommendations revolve around stimulating effective demand during economic downturns. Taking issues with the economic orthodoxy of his time, the British economist argued that during economic crises, the capitalist has no incentive to invest. Investment, notes Keynes, is determined by two factors; the marginal efficiency of capital, and the state of confidence. Moreover, investors 'base their expectations on the assumption that the most recently realised results will continue, except in so far as there are definite reasons for expecting a change' (Keynes, 1936/2013, p. 51). This clearly shows that Keynes, unlike mainstream economists, did not believe that markets self-regulate, and that in times of crises with low levels of confidence, capitalists expect the current state of things to continue in the foreseeable future leading to inaction on their part, which would worsen the problem of unemployment. With the political developments in neighbouring countries in his mind, Keynes (1936/2013, p. 381) writes that '[t]he authoritarian state systems of to-day seem to solve the problem of unemployment at the expense of efficiency and of freedom. [However,] it may be possible by a right analysis of the problem to cure the disease whilst preserving efficiency and freedom.' According to Keynes, the right analysis requires a rethinking of the role the state which he expects to take 'an ever greater responsibility for directly organising investment' (Keynes, 1936/2013, p. 164).

Box 15.1: Was Keynes the economist who figured out a solution to the crisis of the 1930s?

[In a BBC show on Keynes (part of the Masters of Money series), Mervyn King, the former governor of the Bank of England, stated that 'the intellectual climate [of the post-war period] was driven by the idea that Keynes had solved the economic problem' of his time. The evidence, however, suggests otherwise. Politicians were already contemplating the option of increasing government spending as a way of stimulating the economy, but they probably were reluctant for political reasons.[3] In 1933, President Hoover attempted to stimulate the economy with government-funded projects. The programme was, however, limited and the downward economic spiral continued; investment continued falling and unemployment rising. In March 1933, Roosevelt was installed president and expanded the programme under the banner of the New Deal. In 1934, two years before the publication of The General Theory and one year after the introduction of the New Deal in the US, Keynes, during a visit to the US and upon noticing how government spending could stimulate the economy recommended expanding the programme. Nonetheless, US data show that Keynes's advice was practically ignored, and the impact of the New Deal was limited.[4] What enabled the US economy to recover from the crisis was the massive government spending during the years of the war (1939–1945). This 'conclusion appears in the works of numerous economists and historians. The consensus has been that federal fiscal policies associated with the War brought the economy to potential output (that is, full-employment output), with monetary policies aiding the process by accommodating the fiscal stimulus' (Vernon 1994, p. 850).]

The Neoliberal state or market fundamentalism

Between 1945 and the 1970s, a period of three decades dubbed *Les Trente Glorieuses* (the Golden Age of Capitalism), the advanced capitalist economies registered high levels of economic growth. Chang (2011b, p. 484) documents that during that period characterised by a heavy involvement of the state in the economy, the advanced capitalist economies 'grew three to four times faster than during the period of classical liberalism (1820–1950) and twice faster than during the subsequent neoliberal period (1980–2009)'.

By the late 1960s, however, what was known as the Golden Age of capitalism started to unravel. Western economies started to show signs of growth slowdown, rising inflation and rising unemployment. By the mid-1970s, various OECD economies were experiencing a full-blown economic recession and the Keynesian consensus that had provided the ideological foundation for state intervention during the post-war boom started to unravel. Hayek (2011, p. 238), of the Austrian School and a key architect of the ideology of Neoliberalism, argued that inflation was caused by organised labour's collective bargaining, and that the state should intervene to reverse that trend and save the existing social order. 'Once government undertakes to determine the whole wage structure and is thereby forced to control employment and production, there will be a far greater destruction of the present powers of the unions.' For Friedman (cited in Backhouse, 2009, p. 21), an influential Monetarist and Neoliberal theorist, 'if governments increased aggregate demand and pushed unemployment below its "natural" rate, the result would be an unsustainable wage–price spiral and accelerating inflation'. The recommendation was for strict monetary policy to be combined with supply-side policies instead of the expansionary fiscal policy that dominated the post-war period. Governments were recommended to impose strict cash limits on their spending, to raise interest rates to slow down the growth of the money supply and to undertake a raft of reforms allegedly aimed at increasing the efficiency of the private sector. These included labour market deregulation, privatisation, financial deregulation, etc.

With the election of Margaret Thatcher as prime minister in Britain in 1979, and Ronald Reagan as president in the United States in 1980, the debate over inflation was settled in favour of the monetarists and their politically conservative allies. Since then a new set of economic policies and priorities replaced those of the post-war period. The shift to the right in the countries of the North had far-reaching consequences. It also had an impact on international institutions, and via them on the economies of the Global South through the policies of stabilisation and structural adjustment imposed by the World Bank and the International Monetary Fund (see Chapter 12).

Central to the ideology of Neoliberalism is the view that the welfare state had become so generous that it made individuals dependent on it and that it created a culture of entitlement that hobbled private initiative. In opposing state intervention, some Neoliberals go to the extent of advocating the abolition of state institutions. Rothbard (2006, p. 276), for example, argues that 'the government and its central bank act precisely as would a Grand Counterfeiter, with very similar social and economic effects'. What needs to be done 'is not term limits for elected politicians, but the abolition of the civil service … and, above all, [the] elimination of the despotic judiciary' (Rothbard, 2006, p. 486).

Unfettered markets, we are told, are prerequisites for the price system to function properly. State interference in the form of subsidies, minimum wage or price floors and ceilings, or in the form of planning are opposed because it creates distortions and lead to inefficient outcomes. Hayek argues that '[w]e must look at the price system as such a mechanism for communication of information if we want to understand its real function'. Only a system of 'decentralised planning by many separate persons [would allow for a] fuller use … of the existing knowledge' (Hayek, 1945, pp. 526, 526, 521), and achieve more efficient outcomes. In this statement Hayek reiterates what Mises wrote in 1920 on what he described as the problem of calculation in a planned economy. Mises (1920/2012, p. 25) states that '[w]here there is no free market, there is no pricing mechanism; without a pricing mechanism, there is no economic calculation'. Accordingly, no matter how sophisticated the state is, it will always miss out bits of knowledge and make ill-informed decisions leading to inefficient outcomes. The problem the state faces in using aggregate statistics for economic planning is that the data 'which such a central authority would have to use would have to be arrived at precisely by abstracting from minor differences'. And it is those differences involving the 'location, quality, and other particulars' (Hayek, 1945, p. 524) of the exchanged goods and services unknown to the central planner but known to individual economic agents that make the free market more efficient.

In advocating free-market and opposing state intervention, Neoliberalism presents itself as the heir of Classical liberalism. Critics maintain, however, that there are significant differences between Neoliberalism and Classical liberalism. For example, Mirowski (2009, p. 433) argues that, unlike Classical liberalism which had a concern for:

> individual liberty, political equality and human rights [Neoliberalism is] a purely economic ideology whose concerns lie with the establishment of free markets and in keeping state intervention in such markets at bay. Neoliberalism thus understood is primarily a theory of how the economy ought to be organized, and not a political ideology in the same sense as political liberalism.

The Institutionalists: 'there is no such thing as a free market'

According to Institutional political economist Chang (2011a, p. 1) the 'free market doesn't exist. Every market has some rules and boundaries that restrict freedom of choice'. Taking the example of child labour, Chang argues that in today's advanced capitalist societies 'even the most ardent free-market proponents ... would not think of bringing child labour back as part of the market liberalisation package that they so want'. If one perceives a given market as free it is because they 'totally accept the regulations that are propping them up that they become invisible' (Chang 2011a, pp. 1, 2, 3).

The state and other institutions 'are the humanly devised constraints that structure political, economic and social interaction. They consist of both informal constraints (sanctions, taboos, customs, traditions, and codes of conduct), and formal rules (constitutions, laws, property rights)' (North, 1991, p. 97). The mere existence of rules and regulations and even a general acceptance of them, however, does not by itself guarantee their enforcement. There need to be some agency that oversees the rule of law and intervenes when the law is broken. In modern societies, that agency is the state. The state via its different bodies and institutions (e.g. the executive, the parliament, the judiciary, the police) enacts laws and regulations and enforces them.

According to the New Institutionalist approach, institutions function as parameters or boundaries that reduce uncertainty and enable economic agents to make informed decisions and to formulate clear expectations upon which they can act. For North (1991, p. 97), institutions 'define the choice set and therefore determine transaction and production costs and hence the profitability and feasibility of engaging in economic activity'.

'While firmly believing that markets and private property are essential institutions for economic prosperity', Chang (2011b, p. 3) takes issue with what he describes as the 'market primacy assumption' that characterises North's approach. According to this assumption, non-market institutions are 'man-made substitutes for the "natural" institution called the market' (Chang, 2002, p. 547). The notion that the market is *the* natural order of things is simplistic and overlooks the relationship between the institution of the market and other institutions such as the state. Chang (2002, p. 547, italics in original) notes that 'the market was *not* an important, and even less the dominant, part of human economic life until the rise of capitalism'. Moreover, the view that the market evolved and developed naturally is not supported by historical evidence. In line with Polanyi's (1944/2001) earlier contributions, Chang (2002, p. 547) emphasises that 'the emergence of markets was almost always deliberately engineered by the state, especially in the early stage of capitalist development'. Even in contemporary capitalism, the state plays a central role in shaping and designing markets. A well-functioning market requires a well-functioning state (Chang, 2002).

The Marxist view: the state as an instrument of oppression

In the mainstream economic literature, the concepts of state and government are used interchangeably. This is a common mistake. The government, the military, the police, the judiciary, the parliament, local authorities acting on behalf and representatives of the central government are all institutions 'which make up "the state", and whose interrelationship shapes the form of the state system' (Miliband, 1970, p. 54).

Unlike the liberal tradition, which regards the state as an institution embodying collective norms and values voluntarily agreed to (Barry, 1982), Marxism regards the state as an instrument of oppression in the hand of the dominant class, and if it appears to be agreed to by the majority, it is because various institutions like the educational system, the judiciary, media and religion reproduce the conditions whereby people are led to accept the state as a natural and neutral institution. The state in capitalist society serves as an instrument to advance and preserve the interests of the bourgeoisie. Marx and Engels write in the *Manifesto of the Communist Party* that the bourgeoisie has, 'since the establishment of Modern Industry and of the world market, conquered for itself, in the modern representative State, exclusive political sway'. The authors of the *Manifesto* add that '[t]he executive of the modern State is nothing but a committee for managing the common affairs of the whole bourgeoisie'. The workers, on the other hand, are the 'slaves of the bourgeois class, and of the bourgeois State' (Marx and Engels, 1848/2002, pp. 221, 227). Agreeing with Marx and Engels, Lenin (1919/1967, p. 286) argues that '[t]he state is a machine for the oppression of one class by another, a machine for holding in obedience to one class other, subordinated classes'.

In subjugating the working class, the state resorts to various forms of oppression, including violence and legal tricks. For example, for centuries the working class was denied the right to organise. Furthermore, its press was subject to continuous campaigns of censorship and prosecution (Goldstein, 1983). By the time a voting system was introduced, the right to vote was tied to wealth. Even when some form of democratic government was established, the ruling classes introduced a panoply of provisions into the law to limit political freedoms. Studying the new regime in Germany following the 1848–9 revolutions in Europe, Engels writes that while the 'people had been victorious [in the sense of winning] freedoms of a decisively democratic nature ... the immediate ruling power passed not into their hands but into the big bourgeoisie's' (Engels, 1848). The control of the working class went to the extent of imposing restrictions on free movement. In France, for example, the government introduced a system of internal passports to regulate labour movement within the country. Denouncing the system as despotic, Marx (1851) comments that '[n]o serfdom of the feudal ages – no pariahdom of India has its parallel'. In today's world, while the ruling classes in most developing countries still resort to violence against the working classes to preserve their interests, the ruling classes in the advanced capitalist countries resort to soft means including the promotion of consumerism, exploitation of racial tensions, and democracy – reduced to elections and a multi-party system.

From a Marxist standpoint, the aim of controlling the working class is to create the conditions favourable for capital accumulation and to preserve the interests of the bourgeoisie. This conflict of interests between social classes is referred to as class struggle and the state plays an important role in managing the conflict. On this role Engels (1884/1981, p. 229) writes that in order that the social 'classes with conflicting economic interests, shall not consume themselves and society in fruitless struggle, a power, apparently standing above society, has become necessary to moderate the conflict and keep it within the bounds of "order"; and this power, arisen out of society but placing itself above it, and increasingly alienating itself from it, is the state'.

Critics, however, argue that the relationship between the workers and the capitalists is based on mutual benefits. This is the view of Butler (2013, p. 89), for example, who writes that 'capitalism has always brought [the masses] material improvements'. Butler's point has, however, been addressed by Luxemburg (1900/2008) over a hundred years ago when she argued that while the state in the capitalist society is representative of the interests of the bourgeoisie, it could assume functions favouring social developments that might be beneficial to the working class but only to the extent that those developments do not conflict with the interests of the bourgeoisie. The economic arrangements of the post-war period in the advanced capitalist economies illustrate this point. While the welfare state had benefited the working class (employment, health care, social welfare, education), it enabled the ruling class to rebuild the productive capacities of the economy and to restore the conditions of the accumulation of capital. However, with the collapse of the rates of economic growth in the 1970s and the decline of profit rates, the ruling classes attacked the welfare state by launching a campaign of privatisation and deregulation that has had a negative effect on labour.

During Marx's time, capitalism was by and large a national system and the accumulation of capital was conducted within the national borders. However, the high level of development the capitalist countries had reached towards the end of the nineteenth century and the need to capitalise their surplus values put them in fierce competition in expanding beyond their national borders. Those developments marked a qualitative shift in capitalism; it has become a global imperialist system.

Drawing upon the work of Hobson (1902) and Hilferding (1910/1985), Lenin (1917/1967) describes imperialism as the highest stage of capitalism and observes that it is a stage characterised by the dominance of monopolies and finance capital. For Luxemburg (1913/2016, p. 325), imperialism is 'the political expression of the accumulation of capital in its competitive struggle for what remains still open of the non-capitalist environment'. Moreover, this process, notes Luxemburg (1913/2016, p. 325), has increased the levels of 'lawlessness and violence, both in aggression against the non-capitalist world and in ever more serious conflicts among the competing capitalist countries'.

In the imperialist stage of capitalism and besides the oppression and exploitation of the working class within its national borders, the state competes with other states over dominating and controlling other territories for the benefit of its national bourgeoisie. European statemen understood that the colonialism was a question of survival. For Cecil Rhodes, a British statesman and an ardent supporter of colonialism, imperialism was inevitable if the British ruling class 'want[s] to avoid [a bloody] civil war' (Rhodes cited in Lenin, 1917/1967, p. 76). On the other side of the channel, Jules Ferry (1890, pp. 40, 42, 43), a French statesman, stated that the '[c]olonial policy is the offspring of the policy of industrialisation ... Social peace is, in the industrial age of humanity, a question of markets... we must cause fresh categories of consumers to appear in other parts of the world, for, if we fail to do so, modern society will go bankrupt.'[5]

Despite the end of the colonial enterprise in the sense of the direct application of military and political force, the state stills play a crucial role in preserving and advancing the interests of their capitalist classes around the world. This is particularly true for imperialist states like the US and Western Europe which dominate international institutions and interfere with them, and occasionally intervene militarily to preserve the interests of their corporations. Take, for example, the international financial institutions which deals mostly with developing countries. Rather than one country one vote, the voting system in those institutions is modelled in a way that gives the imperialist states more power than poor countries. By the end of 2018, the US alone has about 16 percent of total votes in the IMF and the World Bank's International Bank for Reconstruction and Development (IMF, 2018; World Bank, 2018). Moreover, in his work on international trade and in contrast with the simplistic account of mainstream economics, Tandon (2015) documents how the US and European countries interfere with the WTO rules and pressurise African leaders to accept trade agreements that have an adverse impact on the lives of their populations but that are beneficial to US and European corporations.

Conclusion

The mainstream economics textbook promotes the view that the state is an alien intruder interfering with the finely tuned logic of the market. This view is presented to students as the consensus, while other views are conveniently ignored. However, the diversity of views of the various schools and traditions of economic thought on the role of the state shows that what is presented as a consensus is actually one view among others. The Classics, for example, while advocating laissez-faire as a rule, assign some roles to the state. Those roles include upholding the law, national defence and the provision of education. The doctrine of laissez-faire which dominated economic thought since the publication of *The Wealth of Nations* was challenged by the crisis of the 1930s. Writing during the years of the Great Depression, Keynes supported increasing government spending to stimulate the economy. A particular interpretation of the views of Keynes, known as the Neoclassical Synthesis, formed the consensus that provided the ideological foundation of the economic model of the post-war period. However, by the late 1960s the advanced capitalist economies started to show signs of growth slowdown. By the late 1970s, Neoliberalism, an ideology that claims to be the revival of the Classical creed of laissez-faire, replaced the Keynesian consensus of the post-war period. Uncompromising in its opposition of state intervention, Neoliberalism claims that the policies of the welfare state had led to inefficient outcomes and stifled private initiative. Accordingly, the role of the state is to create an institutional framework conducive to private enterprise and, above all, to protect economic rights such as private property. However, the economic crisis that followed the financial crash of the late 2000s put into question the Neoliberal consensus over the rationality of the market and revived the debate about the role of the state. For the Institutionalists, the crisis was caused by the deregulations that have been implemented since the early 1980s, especially, of the financial sector. Unlike Neoliberals who view the market as the natural order of things, Institutionalists argue that the market institution is as important as other institutions such as the state, and that well-functioning markets require a well-functioning state. In their analyses of its nature and role, Marxists view the state as an instrument of oppression in the hand of the bourgeoisie – the dominant class under capitalism. The workers, however, are the slaves of that class and its state. In order to end exploitation, the proletariat need to organise, seize the state apparatus and nationalise the economy ushering in a classless society based on the common ownership and management of the means of production.

Seminar questions and activities

Discuss the following statements:

- The Classics had a nuanced view about the role of the state.
- To what extent is the ideology of Neoliberalism a revival of Classical liberalism?
- The welfare state of the post war period (1945–1970s) was a concession made by capital to labour in order to save the capitalist order.
- Is the state an expression of the economically and politically dominant social class.

Should the State engage in the following activities? How would economists from different perspectives answer?

- Ban smoking
- Tax sugar
- Invest in the army

References

Akerlof, G. (1970). The market for 'lemons': Quality uncertainty and the market mechanism. *The Quarterly Journal of Economics, 84*(3), 488–500.

Backhouse, R. E. (2009). Economists and the rise of neo-liberalism. *Renewal, 17*(4), 17–25.

Barry, N. (1982). *An introduction to modern political theory*. Reprint. Surrey: The Macmillan Press.

Blanchard, O. J. (1991). Neoclassical synthesis. In J. Eatwell, M. Milgate, & P. Newman (Eds.), *The world of economics* (pp. 504–510). London: The Macmillan Press.

Butler, E. (2013). *Ludwig von Mises – A primer*. London: The Institute of Economic Affairs.

Chang, H.-J. (2002). Breaking the mould: An institutionalist political economy alternative to the neoliberal theory of the market and the state. *Cambridge Journal of Economics, 26*(5), 539–559.

Chang, H.-J. (2011a). *23 things they don't tell you about capitalism*. London: Penguin Books.

Chang, H.-J. (2011b). Institutions and economic development: Theory, policy and history. *Journal of Institutional Economics, 7*(4), 473–498.

Cole, H. L., & Ohanian, L. E. (1999). The Great Depression in the United States from a Neoclassical perspective. *Minneapolis Federal Reserve Quarterly Review, 23*(1), 2–24.

Engels, F. (1848, June 14). The Berlin debate on the revolution. *Neue Rheinische Zeitung*, No. 14. https://www.marxists.org/archive/marx/works/1848/06/14a.htm

Engels, F. (1884/1981). *The origin of the family, private property, and the State*. London: Lawrence & Wishart.

Ferry, J. (1890). *Le Tonkin et la Mère-Patrie: Temoignages et Documents* (V. Havard, Ed.). Paris: Soc. d'Imp. Paul Dupont.

George, D. (1990). The rhetoric of economics texts. *Journal of Economic Issues, 24*(3), 861–878.

Goldstein, R. J. (1983). *Political repression in nineteenth century Europe*. Totowa: Barnes & Noble.

Greenlaw, S., & Taylor, T. (2017). *Principles of Microeconomics*. Scotts Valley: CreateSpace Independent Publishing Platform.

Hayek, F. A. (1945). The use of knowledge in society. *The American Economic Review, 35*(4), 519–530.

Hayek, F. A. (2011). *The constitution of liberty: The definitive edition* (The collected works of F. A. von Hayek) (R. Hamowy, Ed.). Chicago: University of Chicago Press.

Hicks, J. R. (1937). Mr. Keynes and the 'classics': A suggested interpretation. *Econometrica, 5*(2), 147–159.

Hilferding, R. (1910/1985). *Finance capital: A study of the latest phase of capitalist development*. London: Routledge.

Hobson, J. A. (1902). *Imperialism: A study*. New York: James Pott & Company.

IMF. (2018). *IMF members' quotas and voting power, and IMF Board of Governors*. https://www.imf.org/external/np/sec/memdir/members.aspx

Kalecki, M. (1943). Political aspects of full employment. *The Political Quarterly, 4*(14), 322–330.

Keen, S. (2011). *Debunking economics: The naked emperor dethroned?* London: Zed Books.

Keynes, J. M. (1936/2013). The general theory of employment, interest and money. In E. Johnson & D. Moggridge (Eds.), *The collected writings of John Maynard Keynes Vol. VII*. London: Cambridge University Press for the Royal Economic Society.

Lenin, V. (1917/1967). Imperialism the highest stage of capitalism. In *Selected works Vol. I* (pp. 673–777). Moscow: Progress Publishers.

Lenin, V. (1919/1967). The state: A lecture delivered at the Sverdlov University. In *Selected works Vol. III* (pp. 277–293). Moscow: Progress Publishers.

Luxemburg, R. (1900/2008). Reform or revolution. In H. Scott (Ed.), *The essential Rosa Luxemburg: Reform or revolution & the mass strike* (pp. 41–104). Chicago: Haymarket Books.

Luxemburg, R. (1913/2016). The accumulation of capital. In P. Hudis & P. le Blanc (Eds.), *The complete works of Rosa Luxemburg, Volume II: Economic writings 2* (pp. 6–342). Verso: London.

Mankiw, G. N., & Taylor, M. P. (2014). *Microeconomics* (3rd ed.). Hampshire: Cengage Learning EMEA.

Marx, K. (1851, June 14). *The Constitution of the French Republic Adopted November 4, 1848*. Notes to the People No. 7. https://marxists.catbull.com/archive/marx/works/1851/06/14.htm

Marx, K., & Engels, F. (1848/2002). In G. Jones (Ed.), *The communist manifesto (Penguin classics)*. London: Penguin.

Mattick, P. (1974). *Marx and Keynes: The limits of the mixed economy*. London: Merlin Press.

Miliband, R. (1970). *The state in capitalist society*. London: Weidenfeld & Nicolson.

Mill, J. S. (1848/1985). *Principles of political economy with some of their applications to social philosophy, books IV and V* (D. Winch, Ed.). London: Penguin Books.

Mill, J. S. (1859/2005). *On liberty*. New York: Cosimo Inc.

Mirowski, P. (2009). Postface: Defining Neoliberalism. In P. Mirowski & D. Plehwe (Eds.), *The road from Mont Pèlerin: The making of the Neoliberal thought collective* (pp. 417–455). Cambridge, MA: Harvard University Press.

Mises, L. (1920/2012). *Economic calculation in the socialist commonwealth*. Alabama: Ludwig von Mises Institute.

Modigliani, F. (1944). Liquidity preference and the theory of interest and money. *Econometrica, 12*, 45–88.

North, D. C. (1991). Institutions. *The Journal of Economic Perspectives, 5*(1), 97–112.

Pigou, A. C. (1932). *The economics of welfare* (4th ed.). London: Macmillan and Co.

Polanyi, K. (1944/2001). *The great transformation: The political and economic origins of our time*. Boston: Beacon Press.

Ricardo, D. (1815). *An essay on the influence of a low price of corn on the profits of stock; showing the inexpediency of restrictions on importation* (2nd ed.). London: Printed for John Murray.

Ricardo, D. (1817/1996). *Principles of political economy and taxation*. New York: Prometheus Books.

Rothbard, M. (2006). *Making economic sense*. Auburn: The Ludwig von Mises Institute.

Samuelson, P. A. (1955). *Economics* (3rd ed.). New York: McGraw-Hill.

Say, J.-B. (1803/1971). *A treatise of political economy or the production, distribution, and consumption of wealth*. New York: Augustus M. Kelley Publishers.

Smith, A. (1776/2012). *An inquiry into the nature and causes of the wealth of nations*. Hertfordshire: Wordsworth Editions Limited.

Tandon, Y. (2015). *Trade is war: The west's war against the world*. London: OR Books.

Vernon, J. R. (1994). World War II fiscal policies and the end of the Great Depression. *The Journal of Economic History, 54*(04), 850–868.

World Bank. (2018). *International bank for reconstruction and development: Subscriptions and voting power of member countries*. http://pubdocs.worldbank.org/en/795101541106471736/IBRDCountryVotingTable.pdf

16 CAN ECONOMICS EXPLAIN EVERYTHING AND SOLVE ALL OUR PROBLEMS?

Kevin Deane

Introduction

Economics, in its mainstream guise, has begun to permeate popular culture in the form of an expanding range of books that seek to provide explanations of human behaviour and society through the application of standard neoclassical economic tools and principles. Current well-known books, generally targeted at the general public and positioned as an attempt to demystify and promote economics, are titles such as *Freakonomics* (Dubner and Levitt, 2006), *The Undercover Economist* (Harford, 2007), and *The Economic Naturalist* (Frank, 2008). The topics of these books are not necessarily the economy, but rather take an economic approach to a wide range of issues such as whether sumo wrestlers cheat (Dubner and Levitt, 2006), why American teenagers are having more oral sex (Harford, 2007) and why your fridge has a light but your freezer does not (Frank, 2008). Whilst the need for these issues to be explained or not can be debated, the manner in which they are approached is illustrative of the way that economic tools are applied to topics that are not traditionally considered to be within the scope of the field of economics. These books are very clear about the sort of economic principles that are being applied. For example, Frank (2008) discusses the opportunity cost and the cost–benefit principle (essentially the marginal principle) in which the additional benefits are weighed against the additional costs (of a given action), and Harford (2007) places central importance on the rational behaviour of individuals (see Chapter 2) as a vital tool in helping us peel back the layers and understand the complexity of the world around us (Harford 2007). These principles have been discussed at length in this book, and should be recognisable as central to the standard textbook economics that most students are exposed to. The importance of this application of the core neoclassical concepts also rests on the degree of explanatory power ascribed to this framework, with Harford noting that 'if you do not understand the rational choices that underlie much of our behaviour, you cannot understand the world in which we live' (Harford 2007), and Frank (2008) claiming that 'economics explains almost everything' (Frank 2008).

The final chapter of this book discusses the question of whether economics can explain everything and solve all our problems. As previous chapters have shown, economics as a discipline addresses many important issues that are related to our daily lives and the society that we live in, from shedding light on questions concerning why and how we consume products (Chapter 5), how we produce these goods in the first place (Chapter 6), to broader issues concerning global economic crises (Chapter 10), the environment (Chapter 14) and gender relations (Chapter 13). This has hopefully convinced the reader that economics, in its many and varied guises, has something important and unique to say about the real world. Further, the motivation for this question arises not just from the books discussed above which lay claim to the explanatory power of the mainstream Neoclassical framework, but a general recognition that economists working from different perspectives throughout the recent history of economic thought have exerted great influence. As Heilbroner (2000) notes:

> [The great economists] commanded no armies, sent no men to their deaths, ruled no empires, took little part in history-making decisions. A few of them achieved renown, but none was ever a national hero; a few were roundly abused, but none was ever quite a national villain. Yet what they did was more decisive for history than many acts of statesmen who basked in brighter glory, often more profoundly disturbing than the shuttling of armies back and forth across frontiers, more powerful for good and bad than the edicts of kings and legislatures. It was this: they shaped and swayed men's minds.

This chapter will compare and contrast a range of approaches that put forward claims of the overarching explanatory power of economics and the ability of economics to solve all our problems. The chapter commences with a comparison of the Neoclassical and Marxist frameworks, which both lay claims to an expanded explanatory power, though in very different ways. This is followed by a discussion of Keynes's views on the power of economics to solve the central human problem, and his speculation that this could lead to a downgrading of the importance of economics. However, alternative approaches view economics as the problem, including calls for a new direction that focuses on human well-being and sustainability above economic growth.

Economics imperialism

The extension of the standard Neoclassical economic tools and concepts discussed above are examples of a broader phenomenon that has been labelled 'Economic Imperialism' (Lazear, 2000):

> Economics is not only a social science, it is a genuine science. Like the physical sciences, economics uses a methodology that produces refutable implications and tests these implications using solid statistical techniques. In particular, economics stresses three factors that distinguish it from other social sciences. Economists use the construct of rational individuals who engage in maximizing behaviour. Economic models adhere strictly to the importance of equilibrium as part of any theory. Finally, a focus on efficiency leads economists to ask questions that other social sciences ignore. These ingredients have allowed economics to invade intellectual territory that was previously deemed to be outside the discipline's realm. (Lazear, 2000)

This succinct passage contains a number of the themes and issues that have been touched upon and discussed in previous chapters (Chapters 2, 3, 5 and 6). For the purposes of this chapter, it illustrates the application of core economic concepts, such as the notion that individuals behave in a rational and optimising way, the centrality of equilibrium, and the concerns around efficiency and problems of allocation to issues that usually would be associated with other disciplines, such as sociology, politics, and the social sciences more generally. Whether this is a new invasion of intellectual territory previously considered outside of economics, or whether this is an application of the now dominant Neoclassical framework to subject matter that had been explicitly purged from economics following the Marginalist revolution and the turn to a more mathematical economics approach (Fine, 2002), is an ongoing debate. However, what is clear is that in Lazear's view, the economic approach has something unique to offer in terms not only of method, but the additional insights that follow. Whilst this is not a new phenomenon, the timing of Lazear's statement is reflective of the dominance that Neoclassical economics had gained within the economics discipline by the end of the 1990s. Further, the language used (imperialism) is also indicative of a political project, a discipline that is actively seeking to invade and colonise other disciplines, and to remake them in its own image. This project reflects the view that (Neoclassical) economics has a greater degree of superiority in comparison to other social sciences, in part due to the seemingly rigorous and relatively unified technical framework in which these core principles are, broadly speaking, agreed upon by most economists (Fourcade et al., 2015).

An early, and perhaps one of the most well-known, proponents of this approach was Gary Becker, an economist associated with the Chicago School, who investigated a range of issues through the prism of Neoclassical economic tools, including (but not limited to) crime and punishment, marriage instability, discrimination and the inner workings of the household (Becker, 1968, 1971, 1981; Becker et al., 1977). Whilst Becker himself had not coined the term economic imperialism, it is clear that Becker (1973) viewed his engagement with these issues on a similar basis, emphasising the application of the economic framework, and the potential for almost universal explanatory power:

> In recent years, economists have used economic theory more boldly to explain behaviour outside the monetary market sector, and increasing numbers of noneconomists have been following their examples ... Indeed, economic theory may well be on its way to providing a unified framework for all behaviour involving scare resources, nonmarket as well as market, nonmonetary as well as monetary, small group as well as competitive. (Becker, 1973)

Becker's work on the division of labour within the household is a good example of the application of economic principles to a topic that is not necessarily associated with economics, and is useful to explore to illustrate how and in what form the Neoclassical economic framework is applied. In his *Treatise on the Family*, Becker seeks to investigate the reasons behind the division of labour within the household, and specifically differences between what men and women do. The starting point for this analysis is the case of a single person household, in which the individual chooses to allocate their time between 'domestic' and 'market' activities to maximise household consumption of commodities. This optimising framework is set up in the following way:

$$Z = Z(x, t_h') = Z\left[\frac{a\hat{H}^1 t_w}{p_x}, t_h \psi \hat{H}^2\right].$$

In this utility function, aggregate household consumption (Z) is comprised of wage related goods where $\hat{H}^1$ is the optimal capital stock for wages, $a\hat{H}^1$ the wage rate, p_x the price of market goods and t_w the time allocated to wage goods, and household goods, where $\hat{H}^2$ is the optimal capital stock for household goods, t_h is the amount of time allocated to households goods, and Ψ is the productivity of household time. The solution to this optimisation, subject to a time constraint in which the available time can be allocated to either household or market sectors (once time invested in maintaining the optimal level of human capital is deducted), is one in which the marginal productivity of the household sector equals the marginal productivity of the market sector.

This framework is then applied to the situation in which the household contains multiple individuals. In this case, aggregate household consumption for a household of *n* members is simply the sum of wage and households goods consumed by each household member in both sectors, where optimal capital stocks and time spent in each sector for the *t h* individual.

$$Z = Z\left(\sum_{i=1}^{n} x_i, \sum_{i=1}^{n} t'_{h_i}\right) = Z\left(\sum_{i=1}^{n} \frac{a\hat{H}_i^1 t_{w_i}}{p_x}, \sum_{i=1}^{n} \psi\left(\hat{H}_i^2\right) t_{h_i}\right).$$

Whilst Becker discusses a range of implications of this framework, one important implication is that the allocation of time between sectors for each individual will depend on each individual's human capital stock in each sector (and hence how effective their time will be in each sector). Where individual's time is perfectly substitutable, then aggregate consumption will depend on the aggregate number of hours allocated to each sector. However, if individual household members accumulate different levels of market and household capital, then aggregate consumption will depend on how time for each sector is distributed across household members. It is this second scenario that is most important. If human capital differs between individuals, this creates a comparative advantage in either the market or household sector. Following, the optimal solution to the maximisation of aggregate household consumption will be where the marginal productivity of the household sector equals the marginal productivity of the market sector, in which household members supply time to each sector based on their comparative advantage, and indeed importantly this implies an increasing degree of specialisation in investment in different sector capitals and time allocated to each sector. Becker demonstrates that in an efficient household, members would specialise completely in either household or market sectors. This optimisation problem is used to explain the sexual division of labour, as women accumulate domestic human capital (looking after children and other domestic activities) and men 'market' human capital (employment, etc.) due to differences in biology and their life experiences. Therefore, women have a comparative advantage in the household sector, and men a comparative advantage in the market sector, and so it is optimal for women to dedicate all their time (and investment in human capital) to the domestic sector, and men to the market sector following the logic presented above.

A second example from the author's areas of expertise relates to sexual behaviour change in sub-Saharan Africa in light of the HIV/AIDS epidemic, in which Oster (2012) sets up a behavioural model to describe the factors that relate to how individuals chose the number of sexual partners they have, given that there is a degree of risk of HIV infection. In the model, individuals maximise their lifetime utility over two 'life-periods' in a world with HIV (Oster, 2012):

$$U_{tot} = u(\sigma_1) + p(1 - \sigma_1 \gamma \beta h) u(\sigma_2)$$

Individuals gain utility only through the number of sexual partners they choose in period one ($\sigma 1$) and two ($\sigma 2$), and make an optimal choice over the number of partners to have sex with in period one, taking into account information about how the number of partners they choose to have might impact their probability of surviving into period two: the general rate of HIV (h), the HIV transmission rate (β), and also their perceptions about the HIV rate (Υ). In period two, the choice of partner is independent of the HIV rate, in which case, if an individual manages to survive beyond period one, in theory they can choose to have as many sexual partners as they want until the marginal utility of each additional partner is non-positive. On this basis, Oster (2012) anticipates that someone who is more likely to live longer has more of an incentive to reduce the number of partners they have in period one. This is tested for by estimating the relationship between levels of sexual behaviour and child mortality, malaria and maternal mortality, variables used to represent non-HIV adult mortality. Sexual behaviour is thus reduced to a trade-off between the lost utility of having less sex in period one, and the lost utility of dying prematurely and losing the opportunity of gaining utility through having sex in period two. The lesson from this model is that individuals in sub-Saharan Africa will respond rationally to external incentives, and that the key to stimulating health-enhancing investment (as having fewer partners is characterised as) is in improving non-HIV related life expectancy.

These examples illustrate the application of the Neoclassical framework, and specifically how optimisation models applied to non-economic issues are constructed based on a set of assumptions about how things work, the types of constraints involved, what outcomes are to be optimised, the decisions that need to be made within the model, and the efficient (in the economic sense) solutions that follow. This approach has been applied in many forms across a wide range of topics, issues and disciplines. In this way, Neoclassical economics not only invades the territory of other disciplines to answer commonly asked questions, but also determines how these questions are answered.

An alternative view – Marx's base and superstructure

Having looked at one framework that purports to explain almost everything, we now turn to an alternative theoretical approach that also views the 'economic' as central, if not of utmost importance, when trying to understand both the economic and society more generally. In contrast to the application of a specific technical framework, the Marxian approach attempts to explain society at a different level of abstraction and in a markedly different way.

As discussed in Chapter 4, Marx gave primacy in his analysis to the sphere of production, rather than the sphere of exchange, and viewed the dynamics of economic and social change through the lens of Historical Materialism. One of the reasons that he did so is the philosophical underpinnings of the way that Marx viewed humans as a species. He recognised that for all species, the most important problem that confronts them in both the long term and the short term was how to reproduce themselves on a daily basis, and how to reproduce themselves as a species (sexual reproduction). This is, as Eagleton notes, 'what men and women, most of the time, have had to concern themselves with' (Eagleton, 2000). One important distinguishing characteristic that sets humans (as a species) apart from the rest of the natural world is that the way humans reproduce themselves has changed over time, whereas for most (if not all) other species, this has remained fairly static. Further, these changes are brought about by conscious thought. This is discussed in a famous passage when Marx (1976) compares the actions of spiders and bees, who from some inbuilt instinct build complex webs and hives every year, to the practice of man:

> A spider conducts operations that resemble those of a weaver, and a bee puts to shame many an architect in the construction of her cells. But what distinguishes the worst architect from the best of bees is this, that the architect raises his structure in imagination before he erects it in reality. (Marx, 1976)

In this way, bees construct complex hives, and have done so for many thousands of years with little change and will likely continue to do so in the future as they are not consciously involved in the process of designing them. This is not the case for man as a species, as the way that man has reproduced him/herself over time has changed significantly, from epochs in which humans were largely hunter gatherers living in caves, to later periods when humans began to settle on the land and engage in agriculture and animal husbandry, to recent times when our daily needs and wants are produced on an industrial scale. This defining characteristic diverts attention within Marx and Engels' work to the ways that productive and reproductive activities have been organised across time, leading to the identification of a number of modes of production that are denoted by the differences in the way that production was socially organised (and thus leading to the development of a historical materialist understanding of history). As Engels notes, 'according to the materialist conception of history, the *ultimately* determining element in history is the production and reproduction of real life' (Engels, 1890).

The production and reproduction of real life is shaped by two different elements of these processes; the forces of production (technology, raw materials, labour power etc.) and the relations of production (how production is socially organised) (see Chapter 4). Marx conceptualises the forces and relations of production as the economic structure of society, which are referred to as the 'base', and which determine and conditions all other aspects of society:

> In the social production of their life, men enter into definite relations that are independent of their will, relations of production which correspond to

> a definite stage of development of their material productive forces. The sum total of these relations of production constitutes the economic structure of society, the real basis on which rises a legal and political superstructure and to which correspond definite form of social consciousness. The mode of production of material life conditions the social, political and intellectual life process in general. It is not the consciousness of men that determines their being, but, on the contrary, their social being that determines their consciousness. (Marx, 1993)

Simply put, Marx is forwarding the notion that the world around us, the institutions, habits and customs, reflect the way that we, as a society, produce and reproduce ourselves. At this point in time, then, all aspects of society are influenced and shaped by capitalism, the current mode of production. Within the Marxist literature, there has been much debate (and disagreement) about this schema in terms of the way that the different layers of the base and superstructure are ordered, the extent to which they determine the other layers, and the degree to which the layers associated with the superstructure influence and condition the base. Further, the base–superstructure analogy has been accused of being overly deterministic and mechanistic, removing any notion of agency that is associated with other elements of Marx's work in which political struggle and action is viewed as necessary. Whilst this debate will not be resolved here, one version of this framework is presented by Plekhanov. The productive forces are viewed to be the starting point which condition the relations of production, and thus from which the socio-political system and mentality of man arise:

1. The state of the productive forces
2. The economic relations these forces condition
3. The socio-political system that has developed on the given economic basis
4. The mentality of social man, which is determined in part directly by the economic conditions obtaining, and in part by the entire socio-political system that has arisen on that foundation
5. The various ideologies that reflect the properties of that mentality (Plekhanov, Selected Philosophical Works, vol. III, pp. 167–168 in (Collier, 2008)

This schema is not viewed to be deterministic, as all levels will influence and condition each other. However, the economic structure is viewed to be the determining factor in the last instance (Smith, 1984). The superstructure also has an important role to play in terms of managing the contradictions that arise from the mode of production (contradictions which Marx views as inevitable) in line with ruling class interests (Eagleton, 2000).

So what does Marx mean in practice when he views the 'superstructure' being determined by the base? One good example of the base-superstructure relation is education and the role of the schooling system in the capitalist economy. In the Marxist schema, education is viewed as a means of supporting the smooth functioning of a capitalist society, and this is its primary function, as opposed to other conceptions of education as a means of self-transformation and empowerment. Firstly, the school system is primarily designed to serve the needs of the capitalist class by producing the next generation of workers, who are obedient and accepting of their place in society (and capitalism). They do this by ensuring that school mirrors the structure and power relations of the workplace (Bowles and Gintis, 2002) in which the school is a setting where pupils are subordinate to teachers, have little control over what they do, and engage in a number of specific but seemingly unrelated tasks, with rewards for good performance. Secondly, the education system reproduces the inequities that are associated with the economic superstructure whilst giving the illusion of fairness and a meritocratic system, in which students are rewarded for hard work. This papers over the wealth of evidence that suggests educational outcomes are highly correlated with socio-economic indicators such as class, race and parents income (Au, 2006). Finally, the schooling system promotes and entrenches core capitalist values, and thus plays an important ideological role, encouraging pupils to accept the economic system. In this way, the education system reflects the needs of the capitalist system, and the ideology of the ruling classes. More recently, as current students will know, the logic of the market is increasingly being applied to higher education. Following the financial crisis and debates about levels of government debt, universities are increasingly expected to serve the interests of business, with government demanding that universities produce graduates with the skills and capabilities demand by employers, and students are being recast as consumers who borrow large sums of money to pay for their studies as an investment in future income. Whilst historically higher education institutions have enjoyed a larger degree of autonomy from the state, this is being eroded, with higher education now reflecting more closely the demands and logic of the private sector (Naidoo, 2008). Other issues that the base–superstructure analogy can be applied to include legal institutions (which are designed to primarily protect individual private property rights as opposed to collective property rights) (Pashukanis, 1924/2003), culture (such as art, music) (Williams, 1980), language and religion, to name but a few.

A second example serves to highlight why Marx (and others, such as Althusser) view the forces of production as the determining factor in the last instance, but also the interconnectedness of the base and superstructure. The forces of production, and in particular technological change, are viewed to be the starting point for a reorganisation of the relations of production, and other institutional changes at higher levels. This was the case during the emergence of the Industrial Revolution, a process in which Marx was particularly interested in due to the period in which he was writing. The invention of the steam engine enabled a number of different developments, including the rapid extension of a railway network that could be used to transport goods in greater quantities and more quickly than ever before, this opening up new markets, and the range of goods that could now be transported for sale in new markets (and especially perishable goods). Further, steam power was also utilised within the workplace, rapidly enhancing productivity as tasks that previously could only be carried out on a small scale by physical human labour could now be conducted by machine to an ever-expanding degree of scale and efficiency. These new capabilities lead to an expansion of larger-scale industrial plants, with smaller petty capitalists put out of business and forced to enter formal waged employment, leading to a concentration of production in a limited number of larger scale enterprises. This illustrates how one important technological advancement in the forces of production thus had an impact on how production was organised (the relations of production). However, further technological developments would themselves be influenced by newly established relations of production, such as technology designed to extract labour from workers and to control and monitor workers' productivity as employment in large scale industrial enterprises became more common. In this way (without reverting to a chicken-and-egg-style debate), different layers of the base and superstructure influence each other, emphasising that this is not intended to be a hierarchical, deterministic framework.

In this way, Marx's ideas can provide a theoretical framework (Historical Materialism) through which we can understand the world around us in a dynamic sense, a meta-narrative that helps us explain how societies evolve and change, and the central importance of the economic sphere in this process. Whilst this framework can be applied to many things, it won't necessarily give us the answer to why fridges have lights and freezers do not. However, it emphasises the importance of the economic system in shaping the world around us, and thus an explanatory power that is distinct from the application of the Neoclassical framework through a focus on the totality of society as the unit of analysis, rather than the individual, and a focus on the workings of the social system rather than individual choices (as discussed in previous chapters).

Solving the economic problem – what next?

Keynes, writing in the 1930s during the Great Depression, speculated on the potential for the economic problem to be permanently solved. The economic problem as defined by Keynes takes a similar line to Marx, in which the economic problem is 'the struggle for subsistence [which] has always been hitherto the primary, most pressing problem of the human race – not only of the human race, but of the whole of the biological kingdom from the beginning of life in its most primitive forms' (Keynes, 1931). Whilst Marx formulates a materialist conception of history from this ongoing struggle, Keynes argues that man (as a species) may, in a hundred years, have solved this problem entirely. For Keynes, despite the fact that the great depression that was in full swing at the time of his essay on 'Economics Possibilities for our Grandchildren', the recent decades had seen huge increases in the productive capacity and efficiency of the industrial nations and living standards despite the large accompanying growth in the size of the population. These gains were contrasted against thousands of years of relative stagnation, with the source of this rapid change located in technological advancement and the accumulation of capital, itself in part based on the profits accumulated as a result of colonial expansion, and the reinvestment of these profits.

These forces lead to sustained and remarkable increases in output. For example, Keynes notes that factory output in the US increased by 40 per cent between 1919 and 1925. Even at what may seem to be relatively low levels of expansion, a 2 per cent per year increase in capital accumulation would lead to a situation in which the capital stock will have increased by 5 to 7 times in a hundred years, a power he ascribes to the laws of compound interest (Keynes, 1931). Keynes's emphasis on technological change also led him to believe that 'we may be able to perform all of the operations of agriculture, mining and manufacture with a quarter of the human effort to which we have been accustomed' (ibid.). Therefore, due to this degree of progress, Keynes speculated that with the standard of living between four to eight times higher in a hundred years (2030), that the economic problem, the struggle for subsistence, would have been solved. In this respect, Keynes differentiates the needs of human beings into those that are satiable (needs connected to the struggle for subsistence), and those that may still be insatiable (needs which are relative and primarily serve to make us feel superior to others). Amongst the many implications of solving the economic problem, Keynes goes on to speculate that the working week could be reduced to 15 hours (3 hour shifts) to ensure that the required employment is spread around (but more thinly) to compensate for the reduced demand for employment. Having solved the economic problem, man would then be faced with 'his real, his permanent problem – how to use his freedom from pressing economic cares, how to occupy the leisure, which science and compound interest will have won for him, to live wisely and agreeably and well' (ibid.). Of course, Keynes recognised that this would come with challenges of adjustment, as man has been conditioned to 'strive and not enjoy' and has become used to the routine of the struggle for subsistence.

Although it is clear that some of these predictions have failed to materialise for a range of reasons, such as the failure of these gains to be distributed equally, the rise of new and expanding consumption needs, and the issue of labour being replaced by machinery (Carabelli and Cedrini, 2011), there are some good reasons for revisiting this more obscure essay that has been written off by some Keynesian economists (Skidelsky, 1992 in Carabelli and Cedrini, 2011). In particular, Keynes raises some important general questions about the role of economics in society and the potential for a different sort of human existence, along with a critical reflection on the way that the current economic system works:

> When the accumulation of wealth is no longer of high social importance, there will be great changes in the code of morals. We shall be able to rid ourselves of many of the pseudo-moral principles which have hag-ridden us for two hundred years, by which we have exalted some of the most distasteful of human qualities into the position of the highest virtues. We shall be able to afford to dare to assess the money-motive at its true value. The love of money as a possession – as distinguished from the love of money as a means to the enjoyments and realities of life – will be recognised for what it is, a somewhat disgusting morbidity, one of those semi-criminal, semi-pathological propensities which one hands over with a shudder to the specialists in mental disease. All kinds of social customs and economic practices, affecting the distribution of wealth and of economic rewards and penalties, which we now maintain at all costs, however distasteful and unjust they may be in themselves, because they are tremendously useful in promoting the accumulation of capital, we shall then be free, at last, to discard. (ibid.)

This passage captures some of Keynes's unease at the way that capitalism as a system operates, as well as emphasising that changes in the economic system are inevitable and also desirable. The inequities in terms of access to resources and wealth that are inherent to the capitalist system and indeed necessary to support the accumulation of capital are viewed as temporary and perhaps necessary evils, until a time when accumulation of wealth is not of central importance. Keynes's views also force a rethink about broader, more philosophical questions related to the purpose of life as well as a reflection on socio-economic morals and values that are inherent in the current system, such as the pursuit and love of money. Indeed, this short essay sheds a critical light on central tenets of Neoclassical theory such as the infinite potential for consumption to provide utility, and the equating of high levels of consumption with happiness and the accumulation of material possessions (Carabelli and Cedrini, 2011).

To some extent, the themes reflected in this short essay bear some similarity, entirely unintended, to Marx's ideas. Marx, like Keynes, certainly viewed technological change as being vitally important as a driver of change. Further, Marx also shared the view that the solving of the economic problem would precede the transition to socialism, that only when the productive forces of capitalism have matured and man as a species is able to provide for himself on a material basis can questions around a more equitable distribution and perhaps a reorientation of social life away from the drudgery of material production to more humanly self-fulfilling activities. Finally, Marx also understood that inequalities in the distribution of wealth and access to resources underpinned processes of accumulation which are central in enabling investment in productive expansion. Indeed, to some extent Marx acknowledged (and perhaps even admired) the changes in productive capacity that the capitalist system had brought about:

> The bourgeoisie cannot exist without constantly revolutionising the instruments of production, and thereby the relations of production, and with them the whole relations of society. Conservation of the old modes of production in unaltered form, was, on the contrary, the first condition of existence for all earlier industrial classes. Constant revolutionising of production, uninterrupted disturbance of all social conditions, everlasting uncertainty and agitation distinguish the bourgeois epoch from all earlier ones. (Marx and Engels, 2002)

Therefore, and in contrast to claims about the explanatory power of economics, Keynes and to some extent Marx understood the potential for economics to solve the most pervasive and central problem that is faced by man, which would set the platform for the development of a different kind of world, free from the pressures of the struggle for subsistence. For Keynes, the achievement of this goal and the ushering of the era of the 'good life' would entail a downgrading of the importance of economics and economists, a 'matter for specialists – like dentistry' (Keynes, 1931), and thus the success of economists to solve this problem at the same time makes them redundant!

Economics is the problem

In contrast to the views of Keynes in which growth in capital accumulation and technological change could solve the economic problem, the focus on growth within capitalist economies has been subjected to criticism from the school of ecological economics (see Chapter 14). This critique discusses the relationship between economic growth within capitalist economies and environmental change, and proposes a radical re-orientation of the economy away from an economy that is primarily structured to deliver (or attempt to deliver) continuous economic growth, towards an economy that does not have growth as the sole end and is more focused on improving well-being in the broader sense, and perhaps even an economy that not only stops growing but also shrinks to a lower steady state. Of course, as discussed in Chapter 14, concerns about the environment and the physical limits of production are not new, having been a concern as far back as Malthus. The literature on 'degrowth' dates back to the early 1970s, though as with a number of alternative economic perspectives, has experienced a revival following the financial crisis in 2008 (Kallis et al., 2012). Whilst a range of views exist within the degrowth literature (see (van den Bergh, 2011), there are a number of core issues that are addressed and discussed. The underlying logic of this approach is that the current economic system is reliant on infinite economic growth, but that economic growth itself is unsustainable and will ultimately lead to dangerous and potentially catastrophic levels of climatic and environmental changes, as well as eroding the resource base upon which human life depends. Therefore, the economic system needs re-orientating towards a new paradigm in which degrowth (as in the economy not growing or contracting to a more manageable steady state) or a-growth (in which economic growth is no longer a central concern within the economy, but with economic growth itself not always viewed as a bad thing).

The starting point for most analyses is the fact the capitalist economies are structured to focus on delivering economic growth, and that this leads to a number of problems, as well as to some perverse outcomes. The economy is viewed to have three primary levels: the financial level, the real economy, and the ecological level (Alier, 2009; Kallis et al., 2012). Whilst the financial level has gained prominence in recent years, the expansion of this level through the creation of loans and thus future debt obligations relies on the continuing expansion of the real economy to provide the means to pay back these debts. The real economy itself relies on the availability of natural resources and energy, and thus is conditioned by the ecological level. Offering an alternative explanation for the financial crisis, and perhaps the inevitability of crises in a system that is set up in such a way, as being caused by the fact that the real economy could no longer support the level of debt that had built up in the economy, and that the level of growth of GDP required to service these debts is ecologically unsustainable (Alier, 2009). The interdependencies of the levels of this system also mean that other strategies for dealing with debt, such as cutting back on consumption, create even more problems through slowdowns in investment, increasing unemployment and consequent reductions in demand, so that the only way that debt obligations can be met is through growth. Conversely, whilst the system is dependent on infinite economic growth, above certain levels of income, increasing income and thus the potential for expanded consumption does not lead to increased levels of happiness within the population (Easterlin et al., 2010). Therefore, whilst ever more attention is focused on supporting economic growth, economic growth itself is having little impact on the more general well-being. A second key theme highlighted in the degrowth literature which is related to the doctrine of economic growth and that requires addressing is the culture of consumerism, and the notion that, in contrast to Neoclassical conceptions of economic man, that material desires are insatiable. Indeed, the degrowth literature (as would other views) sees this notion as one that is socially constructed, and an important element that is required in an economic system that is reliant on continuous expansion.

Even on its own terms, the Easterlin paradox provokes questions concerning the desirability or even the purpose of economic growth. However, within the degrowth literature, economic growth is not benign or welfare-enhancing, it has a large negative impact on the environment, and is one of the main contributing factors to the rapid pace of environmental destruction and the lack of progress towards achieving global environmental targets (such as the amount of carbon in the atmosphere). This is because economic growth requires an ever-increasing supply of natural resources, which are finite, and increasing amounts of by-products of industrial production, such as carbon dioxide, that require dealing with (and that are not finite). As Latouche notes, 'human beings are turning resources into waste faster than nature can transform waste into new resources' (Latouche, 2009). Further, and drawing on the above, the focus on economic growth in the light of the limited impact this has on human well-being, coupled with natural resource depletion and environmental destruction is thus characterised as a system that is out of control, that has been decoupled from human needs, and a system in which 'we are heading for a crash. We are in a performance car that has no driver, no reverse gear and no brakes and it is going to slam into the limitations of the planet' whilst being 'well aware of what is happening' (Latouche, 2009). This to some extent mirrors other views in terms of the dominance of the market, and how this human institution has taken on a life of its own.

Modelling in a range of scenarios suggests that the pace of technological change required to cope with current levels of economic growth to ensure that environmental targets can be achieved are up to 10 times faster than the current rate of technological progress (Jackson, 2009). This leads to the conclusion that economic growth is environmentally unsustainable in the long run. A further concern is that stocks of finite natural resources are not accounted for in standard measures of GDP, constituting inputs to the production process but without any consideration of the reduction in natural stocks as resources are utilised, which skews and overinflates growth figures.

The solution(s) posed to this issue relate to the re-orientation and restructuring the economy to cope with either a slower or negative growth rate to reach a lower level steady state, in which growth is no longer a requirement. Whilst this realignment process may have potentially damaging effects such as unemployment, lack of demand and a negative impact on state finances, these can, by and large, be addressed in the short term by focusing new investment on green technologies (and thus maintaining employment), the reduction of hours worked, reduced material consumption, and investments in low-productivity and profitability but high labour intensity and satisfaction (Kallis et al., 2012). In the long term, more radical changes to the economy may involve new forms of property and ownership and communal forms of living (Kallis et al., 2012) that do not prioritise the needs of the economic system above the needs of the people and the planet (Muraca, 2013). Latouche proposes a virtuous circle of contraction, as opposed to a virtuous circle of growth, achieved through a programme based on the eight R's: re-evaluate, reconceptualise, restructure, redistribute, relocalise, reduce, re-use and recycle (Latouche, 2009).

This view of economic growth as something that is damaging and unsustainable is in contrast to other views of economic growth, such as the Keynesian view discussed above. As Whitehead (2013) notes, in Classical and perhaps even Neoclassical economics, economic growth is seen as a sign that the economy is in a healthy state (Whitehead, 2013). This emphasises that it is important to interrogate even the most taken-for-granted phenomenon in economics. There are also some similarities between the degrowth literature and views relating to the role of consumption as a source of welfare (see Chapter 5), and the need to think about well-being in a broader sense. In the case of the degrowth literature, a change in economic and social values relating to consumption are vital if the system is to be re-orientated, echoing some of the comments made by Keynes about the present economic system. Further, and importantly, these ideas force us to think about more philosophical questions related to the sort of society we want to live in, the nature of human beings and the fact the economic values such as consumerism are not necessarily universal, rather temporary states of being that can (and perhaps should) be transcended. These questions are not unfamiliar to economics, as from the time of the Classical economists, economics has always been influenced by philosophical ideas. As discussed above, Smith and Marx both drew on philosophy to underpin their work.

Conclusion

This chapter, through a discussion of a number of different economists, has illustrated that alternative economic perspectives make competing claims relating to the explanatory power of economics, the ability (or not) of economics and capitalism specifically to solve the basic economic problem, as well as posing questions concerning the role of economics and the possibility of a time in which economics does not have the prominent position that it currently enjoys, and thus raises possibilities for a different kind of future. As with the previous chapters, this chapter has emphasised how different approaches come to different conclusions about the role of economics. It also enables a reflection on broader philosophical questions about social life and what it means to be a human being and the sort of future(s) that humans can imagine for themselves. These deeper questions also speak to economists such as Smith and many others since who are interested in fundamental concerns about human nature, illustrating that these questions have been at the centre of debates concerning economics for several centuries. Whilst these debates will continue in the coming years, we hope that this book has been convincing in promoting the view that many different perspectives have something to say about these questions, and that there is value in understanding, many, and not just one, way of thinking about economics.

Discussion questions and seminar activities

- Do you agree with the claim that 'economics explains almost everything'?
- Should the aim of economists be to make themselves redundant?
- Is there too much emphasis on economic issues and ways of thinking, and not enough thinking about what non-economic things help humans to live 'the good life'?

- Should increases in productivity be used to help us work less instead of consuming more?
- Is economic growth always beneficial?

Watch the film (or a section) of *Freakonomics*. Discuss the extent to which the approach taken influences:

- the sort of issues addressed,
- how they are addressed and
- limitations of the approach.

How would Marx have approached the same issues?

Further reading

For students interested in degrowth and ecological economics, see Tim Jackson (2009) *Prosperity without growth*. London: Earthscan.

The transition from a broader political economy to a narrower version of economics is discussed in more detail in Dimitris Milonakis and Ben Fine and (2009) *From Political Economy to Economics*, London: Routledge.

References

Alier, J. M. (2009). Socially sustainable economic de-growth. *Development and Change, 40*(6), 1099–1119.

Au, W. (2006). Against economic determinism: Revisiting the roots of neo-Marxism in critical educational theory. *Journal for Critical Education Policy Studies, 4*(2), 28–55.

Becker, G. S. (1968). Crime and punishment: An economic approach. *Journal of Political Economy, 76*(2), 169–217.

Becker, G. S. (1971). *The economics of discrimination*. Chicago/London: University of Chicago Press.

Becker, G. S. (1973). A theory of marriage: Part I. *Journal of Political Economy, 81*(4), 813–846.

Becker, G. S. (1981). *A treatise on the family*. Cambridge, MA: Harvard University Press.

Becker, G. S., Landes, E. M., & Michael, R. T. (1977). An economic analysis of marital instability. *Journal of Political Economy, 85*(6), 1141–1187.

Bowles, S., & Gintis, H. (2002). Schooling in capitalist America revisited. *Sociology of Education, 75*(1), 1–18.

Carabelli, A., & Cedrini, M. (2011). The economic problem of happiness: Keynes on happiness and economics. *Forum for Social Economics, 40*(3), 335–359.

Collier, A. (2008). *Marx: A beginner's guide*. Oxford: Oneworld Publications.

Dubner, S., & Levitt, S. (2006). *Freakonomics: A rogue economist explores the hidden side of everything*. New York: William Morrow.

Eagleton, T. (2000). Base and superstructure revisited. *New Literary History, 31*(2), 231–240.

Easterlin, R. A., McVey, L. A., Switek, M., Sawangfa, O., & Zweig, J. S. (2010). The happiness–income paradox revisited. *Proceedings of the National Academy of Sciences, 107*(52), 22463–22468.

Engels, F. (1890). *Engels to J. Bloch in Königsberg*. Marx–Engels Correspondence. www.marxists.org

Fine, B. (2002). 'Economic imperialism': A view from the periphery. *Review of Radical Political Economics, 34*(2), 187–201.

Fourcade, M., Ollion, E., & Algan, Y. (2015). The superiority of economists. *Journal of Economic Perspectives, 29*(1), 89–114.

Frank, R. H. (2008). *The economic naturalist: Why economics explains almost everything*. London: Virgin Books.

Harford, T. (2007). *The undercover economist*. London: Little, Brown Book Group.

Heilbroner, R. L. (2000). *The wordly philosphers: The lives, times, and ideas of the great economic thinkers*. London: Penguin.

Jackson, T. (2009). *Prosperity without growth: Economics for a finite planet*. London: Earthscan.

Kallis, G., Kerschner, C., & Martinez-Alier, J. (2012). The economics of degrowth. *Ecological Economics, 84*, 172–180.

Keynes, J. M. (1931). *Economic possibilities for our grandchildren. Essays of persuasion. J. M. Keynes*. London: Macmillan.

Latouche, S. (2009). *Farewell to growth*. Cambridge: Polity Press.

Lazear, E. P. (2000). Economic imperialism. *The Quarterly Journal of Economics, 115*(1), 99–146.

Marx, K. (1976). *Capital, Volume I*. London: Penguin Books.

Marx, K. (1993). *A contribution to the critique of political economy*. www.marxists.org

Marx, K., & Engels, F. (2002). *The communist manifesto*. London: Penguin.

Milonakis, D., & Fine, B. (2009). *From political economy to economics*. London: Routledge.

Muraca, B. (2013). Decroissance: A project for a radical transformation of society. *Environmental Values, 22*(2), 147–169.

Naidoo, R. (2008). The competitive state and the mobilised market: Higher education policy reform in the United Kingdom (1980–2007). *Critique Internationale, 39*(2), 47–65.

Oster, E. (2012, January). HIV and sexual behaviour change: Why not Africa? *Journal of Health Economics, 31*, 35–49.

Pashukanis, E. (1924/2003). *The general theory of law and Marxism,* London: Transaction Publishers.

Smith, S. B. (1984). Considerations on Marx's base and superstructure. *Social Science Quarterly (University of Texas Press), 65*(4), 940–954.

van den Bergh, J. C. J. M. (2011). Environment versus growth—A criticism of 'degrowth' and a plea for 'a-growth'. *Ecological Economics, 70*(5), 881–890.

Whitehead, M. (2013). Editorial: Degrowth or regrowth? *Environmental Values, 22*(2), 141–145.

Williams, R. (1980). *Base and superstructure in Marxist cultural theory. Problems in materialism and culture: Selected essays. R. Williams*. London: Verso.

NOTES

Chapter 1

1. See Dow (2002) for an overview of different research strategies in economics.
2. See Lawson (2004) for an introduction to the ontological assumptions of Neoclassical economics.
3. See Fischer et al. (2018) for an overview of some heterodox schools in economics.

Chapter 2

1. Kreps defines microeconomic theory as concerning 'the behaviour of individual economic actors and the aggregation of their action in different institutional frameworks'. He further explains that '[i]n the standard approach, behaviour always takes the form of constrained maximization. The actor chooses from some specified set of options, selecting the option that maximizes some objective function' (Kreps, 1990, pp. 3–5).
2. It is worth noting that the use of psychology to explain economic behaviours is not new – see e.g. Smith's moral philosophy, as well as Keynes's appeal to the psychology of herd behaviour, both in this chapter.

Chapter 3

1. Besides his work on different market structures, Cournot has been credited for the first diagram appearing in economics to depict how supply and demand explain price in a competitive market (Backhouse, 2002, ch. 7).
2. The *Methodenstreit*, which commenced in the 1880s and persisted over the next couple of decades, was an intellectual fight between predominantly C. Menger (Austrian School) and G. Schmoller (German Historical School). The main argument was methodological: whether economic theory should be built obstructively, deductively and hypothetically or inductively, with detailed descriptions of historical and social conditions and data (historical empiricism).
3. Originally funded by the US Air Force and later by the Ford Foundation.
4. It is worth noting that aside from his contribution to the surge of mathematics into Economics, von Neumann was a critic of the axiomatisation of mathematics (à la Hillbert) and was concerned with the 'degeneration' this may bring: '... at a great distance from its empirical source, or after much "abstract" inbreeding, a mathematical subject is in danger of degeneration ... the only remedy seems to

me to be the rejuvenating return to the source: the reinjection of more or less directly empirical ideas' (von Neumann, 1947, p. 2063).

5. Nicolas Bourbaki was the pseudonym used by a set of French mathematicians, who among other things, sought to establish the axiomatisation of mathematics (following the visage of Hilbert's programme) and produce a complete and universal mathematical system.

6. As a member of the Scottish Historical School, Smith's historical approach was not only illustrative, but also 'philosophical'.

Chapter 4

1. It will become clear on reading Chapter 5 that isoquants are analytically analogous to the indifference curves that are central to Neoclassical consumer choice theory. Similarly, the production function is analogous to the utility function and the process of profit maximisation by the firm is analytically indistinguishable from utility maximisation by individual consumers. Neoclassical theory simply applies the same technical apparatus to the questions of consumption and production. It should also be noted that the notion of 'well-behaved' isoquants and preferences contain no normative content. They are well-behaved simply in relation to making the theory work.

2. Coase referred to this tendency as 'decreasing returns to the entrepreneur function'.

3. It should be noted that competence-based theories of the firm, which include the subset of evolutionary approaches, consist of a diverse set of theories that are not uniform or consistent. We focus here on a set of key propositions. For a more comprehensive approach, see Nelson and Winter (2002).

4. Smith put forward a second theory of value based upon its distribution across wages, rent and profit known as the adding-up theory of value. There was a contradiction between the two that Ricardo subsequently critiqued as he put forward a labour embodied theory of value (see Chapters 7 and 9).

5. Quote from Volume 1, Chapter 26 of *Capital.*

6. There is great diversity in the chain literature. Different approaches draw from different theoretical and analytical positions and therefore stress different aspects of the articulation and operation of supply chains. For a more detailed exposition of different chain analyses, see Bair (2006) and Newman (2011).

Chapter 5

1. For adaptations and developments to this framework, arrived at through relaxing the assumptions necessary for well-defined utility curves, see Varian (2003).

2. See Fine (2012) for applications to food and fashion.

Chapter 6

1. Entertainingly, Robinson referred to the Neoclassical synthesis as 'bastard' Keynesianism.

Chapter 7

1. The word *commodity* is now often used narrowly to mean primary products, for example crude oil or unprocessed food. This wasn't the usage at the time of the Classical writers, when it referred to any item which was bought and sold in the market. The word is used in the latter sense here.
2. Smith believed that wages increased during periods of capital accumulation because growth of the capital stock leads to a rising demand for labour, while labour supply is mostly determined by the growth of the population, which was in turn determined by the level of subsistence wages. As a result, labour supply would respond only slowly to increased demand, meaning wages would rise above subsistence levels during periods of capital accumulation, falling back to subsistence levels when the population increased.
3. Ricardo assumes that tools will be used in a constant ratio to labour, so we can think of the increase in labour terms only.
4. The money wage and the price of corn vary in the model, but since workers must receive enough food to survive, any increase in corn prices is exactly matched by an increase in money wages.
5. Since total output per worker is the average product, *AP*, and the profit share and profit rate are determined by the marginal product *MP*, the share of income going to rent is equal to $(AP - MP)/AP$.
6. Marshall substituted the 'reward for waiting' for the idea associated with earlier thinkers that interest was the reward for *abstinence*: 'Karl Marx and his followers have found much amusement in contemplating the accumulations of wealth which result from the abstinence of Baron Rothschild, which they contrast with the extravagance of a labourer who feeds a family of seven on seven shillings a week; and who, living up to his full income, practises no economic abstinence at all' (Marshall, 1820/2013, p. 193).
7. '[T]his doctrine has sometimes been put forward as a theory of wages. But there is no valid ground for any such pretension. The doctrine that the earnings of a worker tend to be equal to the net product of his work, has by itself no real meaning; since in order to estimate net product, we have to take for granted all the expenses of production of the commodity on which he works, other than his own wages' (Marshall, 1820/2013, pp. 429–430). Likewise, Marshall argues, his description of saving and accumulation, 'cannot be made into a theory of interest, any more than into a theory of wages, without reasoning in a circle' (ibid., p. 430).
8. See, for example, Woodford (2003).

9. A similar result was shown by Robinson (1956).
10. By 1955, Kaldor had added the 'Keynesian' theory of distribution to the Classical, Marxian and Neoclassical theories (Kaldor, 1955).
11. In a Cobb-Douglas production function, factor income shares are fixed by the parameters of the production function.

Chapter 8

1. The price of a bond is inversely related to the interest rate. The higher the price of a bond, the lower the interest rate its issuer needs to pay.
2. Given that money is the asset with the highest liquidity premium it is chosen as the *numeraire*. This means expected appreciation is not relevant for money.
3. Indeed, money's functions are actually quite similar across the different schools of thought. What differs, as we see in this chapter, is the emphasis put on these different functions.

Chapter 9

1. The adjective 'Neoclassical' was coined by Thorstein Veblen to label Marshall's approach. Marshall himself saw his own work in continuity with the ideas of Classical political economists, notably Smith and Ricardo. For Marshall, prices are only determined by marginal utility in the short run, as supply cannot be augmented and market prices depend mainly on demand. By contrast, machines and buildings have to be replaced in the long run, so that prices are determined by replacement expenses and other 'objective costs', as advocated by the Classicals. However, other Marginalist economists, especially Stanley Jevons and Léon Walras, regarded their own approaches as opposed to the Classical one.
2. Notice that Marshall, unlike other Neoclassical economists, takes the price as the dependent variable, while regarding quantity as the independent variable. Incidentally, Marshall was also the economist who popularised the standard demand and supply graph. This is the historical reason economists still put the price (which is usually regarded as the independent variable) on the vertical axis, while measuring quantity along the horizontal axis.
3. Notice that Classical political economists and Marx used to use the term 'commodities' instead of 'goods'. For the sake of uniformity, we keep on referring to 'goods' hereafter.
4. It must be mentioned that Ricardo developed his theory with the aim of questioning the so-called Corn Laws. These were restrictions and tariffs on imported grain, which were enforced in the United Kingdom between 1815 and 1846.
5. The Classicals and the so-called Ricardian socialists understood that the surplus must arise from 'unpaid' labour, but they attributed it to the prevailing conditions in the circulation sphere.

6. Meaning that they are no longer serfs, as in a feudal society, or slaves, as in a slave society.
7. Marx terms the value of this capital component the 'constant capital', while the component that is turned into wages is named the 'variable capital'.
8. The analysis of value and exploitation is provided by Marx in the first volume of *Capital* (1867), whereas the 'transformation' procedure is described in the third volume. The latter was outlined by Marx between 1863 and 1883. However, the manuscript was completed and published in 1894 by Engels, eleven years after the death of Marx.
9. In short, the point is that there is no simple monotonic relationship between the kind of the techniques of production used and the rate of profit. It may well be the case that more capital-intensive techniques are associated with higher profit rates. Remuneration rates of inputs do not mirror inputs' marginal productivities and prices are not indexes of scarcity. The Marginalist-Neoclassical theory of production, value and distribution lacks foundation. See Chapter 7.
10. Notice that the superscript 'T' is a mathematical convention and stands for 'transpose of matrix'. In the equation above it means the transpose of a column vector, which, of course, is a row vector.
11. Each technique of production is therefore defined by $\mathbf{l}^T$ and $\mathbf{a}^{\mathbf{j}} = \left[a_i^j\right]$, where each element a_i^j is the quantity of good i used as an input to produce a unit of good j. Notice that matrix $\mathbf{A}$ is assumed to be viable, meaning that it has a maximum eigenvalue $\lambda_m < 1$. Given the $n \times 1$ column vector of outputs, $\mathbf{q} = \left[q_j\right] \in \mathbb{R}_n^+$, it follows that $\mathbf{q} > \mathbf{Aq}$. Finally, notice that if wages were to be paid '*post factum*, as a share of the annual product', the price system should be redefined as: $\mathbf{p}^T = \mathbf{l}^T w + \mathbf{p}^T\mathbf{A} \bullet (1 + r)$. This is the formulation proposed by Sraffa (1960, p. 11) to highlight the class conflict over the distribution of net product.
12. See Kurz and Salvadori (2001).
13. Indeed, energy-theories of value show an even closer resemblance with pre-Classical theories developed by William Petty and Richard Cantillon in the seventeenth century.
14. The net value of a certain public project, say a wind farm, can be measured by the quantity of energy that can be produced, net of building and maintenance energy costs. Similarly, the net value of a road, a bridge, or a railway, can be calculated as the algebraic difference between energy benefits and energy costs.

Chapter 10

1. These views were challenged by Thomas Malthus and Sismonde de Sismondi, who argued that in fact general 'gluts' could arise, but their attempts were by and large unsuccessful at breaching the consensus around Say's Law.
2. It is interesting to note that the growth of neoclassicism, sometimes referred to as the 'marginal revolution' (Walras, Jevons, Menger, Marshall), which portrays

capitalism as the best of all systems efficiently allocating capital as it moves from one state of equilibrium bliss to the next, took place precisely as capitalism was undergoing its most profound depression to date.

3. Marxian crisis theory – like many other schools of crisis theory – is often unclear about the distinction between fluctuations in real variables associated with the short-term business and long-term industrial cycles the long-term decline of secular stagnation (Sweezy, Steindl); the collapse of output and employment during a financial/economic crisis; and the crises which signal the ultimate breakdown of capitalism (Grossmann).
4. This understanding of the structural constraints on bankers' actions presages the famous comments of former Citibank chief executive Chuck Prince on Citibank's role as a major provider of funds for leveraged buyouts in the run-up to the financial crisis which broke in 2007: 'as long as the music is playing, you've got to get up and dance'.
5. Minsky believed that corporations' incurrence of debt was the critical dynamic for understanding instability. While household and government debt can affect overall stability, he did not view them as 'critical elements' (1982, p. 18). In discussions of whether or not the crisis of 2007 was a 'Minsky moment' this view of Minsky is often invoked to suggest – correctly or not – that it was not.

Chapter 11

1. For example, if an additional three unit of capital is needed to produce one extra unit of output then the capital output ratio is given by 3/1 = 3.
2. Despite solving the issue of the long run instability, they failed to address the main instability of the HD model: the instability between G_A and G_W which was assumed away.
3. See Cohen and Harcourt (2003) for a discussion of the Cambridge Capital Controversies.
4. For a more detailed and understandable introduction to the literature see Lavoie and Stockhammer (2013); also see Bhaduri and Marglin (1990).
5. Among the most prominent Evolutionary economists are: Andreoni, Best, Dosi, Nelson, Di Tommaso, Sugden, Winter.

Chapter 12

1. The Washington Consensus was coined by Williamson (1990) and refers to a set of shared ideas between the World Bank, International Monetary Fund and the US Treasury. It promotes various forms of deregulation, liberalisation and privatisation in development as its sees the market (i.e. the price mechanism) as the most efficient way to allocate resources and stimulate growth (see Van Waeyenberge, 2006).

2. See Fine and Van Waeyenberge (2013) for an elaborate critique.
3. We may want to note that while Lewis was originally from Saint Lucia, he pursued his studies at the LSE in London after which he became a lecturer at the University of Manchester. Subsequently, he spent much of his working life between the USA and the Caribbean.

Chapter 14

1. See for instance, Pigou (1920), Part II, ch. XX, paragraph 4.
2. A similar argument could be used for informational economics which explored informational externalities and related market failures.
3. Despite the name, the author of the 'theorem' is actually George Stigler (see Stigler, 1966).
4. See for example Dupuit, 1853 'On the measurement of the utility of public works'.
5. The objective of dynamic optimisation is to find an optimal path over time, while static optimisation looks at the optimal allocation of resources at one point in time.
6. Pontryagin's Maximum Principle and Optimal Control Theory 1956 & Bellman Dynamic Programming 1957.
7. Note that they did not take into consideration technological change, substitution possibilities, and discoveries of new deposits.
8. Ramsey (1928) argued that 'discount[ing] later enjoyments in comparison with earlier ones [is] a practice which is ethically indefensible and arises merely from the weakness of the imagination'. For Pigou, discounting future utility is only the result of 'defective telescopic faculty' (Pigou, 1920). Harrod, defined discounting as a 'polite expression for rapacity and the conquest of reason by passion' (Harrod, 1948). Other key references on social discounting include Gollier (2013) and Arrow et al. (2013).
9. Details of the approach taken in the US can be found in NAS (2017). Atkinson et al. (2018a, 2018b) document the UK approach, while Atkinson et al. (2018b, ch. 14) reviews the issues associated with the estimation of the SCC.
10. Note that common property, together with private and State property, is a property regime, and as such it is a social construct. The classification in common-pool, public, or club goods depends instead on the physical characteristics of the good itself, and in particular on whether it is excludable and rival.
11. This idea has also been integrated in game theory under the heading of cooperative games, as opposed to non-cooperative games such as the prisoner's dilemma.
12. The Hartwick rule is based on the assumption that natural assets and man-made assets can substitute for one another, and is therefore linked to the concept of 'weak sustainability'.

Chapter 15

1. For a brief overview of the Neoclassical Synthesis from a mainstream perspective, see Blanchard (1991).
2. *New York Times*, 30 October 1929. http://www.nytimes.com/library/financial/103029crash-lede.html.
3. In a lecture given to the Marshall Society in Cambridge in 1942, Kalecki argued that 'under a regime of permanent full employment, "the sack" would cease to play its role as a disciplinary measure. The social position of the boss would be undermined, and the self-assurance and class-consciousness of the working class would grow. Strikes for wage increases and improvements in conditions of work would create political tension. It is true that profits would be higher under a regime of full employment than they are on the average under *laissez-faire* ... But "discipline in the factories" and "political stability" are more appreciated than profits by business leaders' (Kalecki, 1943, p. 326).
4. The data reported in Cole and Ohanian (1999, p. 5) shows that in 1939 real output in the United States was estimated at 27 per cent below its 1929 level. Moreover, government spending remained relatively stable.
5. Jules Ferry (1890, pp. 40, 42, 43) writes that: 'La politique coloniale est fille de la politique industrielle ... La paix sociale est, dans l'âge industriel de l'humanité, une question de débouchés ... La consommation européenne est saturée, il faut faire surgir des autres parties du globe de nouvelles couches de consommateurs, sous peine de mettre la société moderne en faillite et de préparer pour l'aurore du vingtième siècle une liquidation sociale par voie de cataclysme, dont on ne saurait calculer les conséquences.'

INDEX

www.ingramcontent.com/pod-product-compliance
Ingram Content Group UK Ltd.
Pitfield, Milton Keynes, MK11 3LW, UK
UKHW051118290926
15471UKWH00010B/1734